Core Kubernetes

JAY VYAS
CHRIS LOVE

MANNING
SHELTER ISLAND

For online information and ordering of this and other Manning books, please visit
www.manning.com. The publisher offers discounts on this book when ordered in quantity.
For more information, please contact

> Special Sales Department
> Manning Publications Co.
> 20 Baldwin Road
> PO Box 761
> Shelter Island, NY 11964
> Email: orders@manning.com

Manning Publications Co.
20 Baldwin Road
PO Box 761
Shelter Island, NY 11964

Development editor:	Karen Miller
Technical development editors:	Christopher Haupt
Review editor:	Aleksandar Dragosavljević
Production editor:	Keri Hales
Copy editor:	Frances Buran
Proofreader:	Melody Dolab
Technical proofreader:	John Guthrie
Typesetter:	Gordan Salinovic
Cover designer:	Marija Tudor

ISBN 9781617297557

Printed and bound by CPI Group (UK) Ltd, Croydon, CR0 4YY

To Amim Knabben, Ricardo Katz, Matt Fenwick, Antonio Ojea, Rajas Kakodar, and Mikael Cluseau for the countless night and weekend K8s hacking sessions, including the innumerable yelling competitions. To Andrew Stoyocos for taking on the SIG Network policy group. To my wife and family for letting me write this book on Saturdays. To Gary, Rona, Nora, and Gingin for helping my mom.

—Jay

To Kate and all of my loved ones that have supported me on this journey. To the team at LionKube, especially Audrey for keeping me organized and Sharif for his help and support. Also, to my co-author, Jay, who asked me to write this book with him—I thank you for that! Without your hard work, we would not have this book.

—Chris

brief contents

contents

preface

We wrote this book to empower those wanting to take their K8s (Kubernetes) knowledge to the next level by immediately digging into the murky details of various topics related to storage, networking, and tooling.

Although we don't attempt to provide a comprehensive guide to every feature in the K8s API (as that would be impossible), we really believe that, after reading this book, users will have a new-found intuition on how to reason about complex infrastructure-related problems in production clusters and how to think about the overall progression of the Kubernetes landscape in a broader context.

Books exist that allow a user to learn the basics of Kubernetes, but we wanted to make a book that teaches the core technologies that make up Kubernetes. Networking, the control plane, and other topics are covered in low-level detail, which will help you understand how the internals of Kubernetes function. Gaining an understanding of how the system works will make you a better DevOps or software engineer.

We're hoping to inspire new contributors to Kubernetes along the way as well. Please do reach out to us on Twitter (@jayunit100, @chrislovecnm) to get more engaged with the broader Kubernetes community or to help us add more examples where necessary to the GitHub repositories associated with this book.

acknowledgments

We want to acknowledge the community and companies that maintain Kubernetes. Without them and their continual work, this software would not exist. We could mention many people by name, but we know we will miss some.

We'd like to acknowledge our friends and mentors in the SIG Network (Mikael Cluseau, Khaled Hendiak, Tim Hockins, Antonio Ojea, Ricardo Katz, Matt Fenwick, Dan Winship, Dan Williams, Casey Calendero, Casey Davenport, Andrew Sy, and so many others); the tireless open source contributors to the SIG Network and SIG Windows communities (Mark Rosetti, James Sturevant, Claudio Belu, Amim Knabben); the original founders of Kubernetes (Joe Beda, Brendan Burns, Ville Aikas, and Craig McLuckie); and the Google engineers, including Brian Grant and Tim Hockin, who joined them shortly thereafter.

This acknowledgment includes the community shepherds Tim St. Clair, Jordan Liggit, Bridget Kromhaut, and so many others. We'd also like to acknowledge Rajas Kakodar, Anusha Hedge, and Neha Lohia for forging an up-and-coming SIG Network India team, which has inspired so much of the content that we hope to add in the next edition (or potential sequel) of this book as we dive deeper into the network or server proxy, `kube-proxy`.

Jay also would like to acknowledge Clint Kitson and Aarthi Ganesan for empowering him to work on this book as a VMware employee, and his team at VMware (Amim and Zac) for always innovating and being there for us. And, of course, Frances Buran, Karen Miller, and many others at Manning Publications who helped us review this book to get it over the line and into production.

Finally, thank you to all the reviewers: Al Krinker, Alessandro Campeis, Alexandru Herciu, Amanda Debler, Andrea Cosentino, Andres Sacco, Anupam Sengupta, Ben Fenwick, Borko Djurkovic, Daria Vasilenko, Elias Rangel, Eric Hole, Eriks Zelenka, Eugen Cocalea, Gandhi Rajan, Iryna Romanenko, Jared Duncan, Jeff Lim, Jim Amrhein, Juan José Durillo Barrionuevo, Matt Fenwick, Matt Welke, Michał Rutka, Riccardo Marotti, Rob Pacheco, Rob Ruetsch, Roman Levchenko, Ryan Bartlett, Ubaldo Pescatore, and Wesley Rolnick. Your suggestions helped make this a better book.

about this book

Who should read this book

People wanting to learn more about the internals of Kubernetes, how to reason about its failure modes, and how to extend it for custom behavior will get the most out of this book. If you don't know what a Pod is, you may want to buy this book, but get another title that gives you that understanding first.

Additionally, day-to-day operators that want to have a better understanding of the vernacular required for talking with IT departments, CTOs, and other organizational leaders about how to adopt Kubernetes, while retaining core infrastructure principles that existed before the birth of containers, will find that this book really helps to bridge the gap between new and old infrastructure design decisions. Or, at least, that's what we hope!

How this book is organized: A road map

This book contains 15 chapters:

- Chapter 1: Here, we give newcomers a high-level overview of Kubernetes.
- Chapter 2: We look at the concept of a Pod as an atomic building block for applications and introduce the rationale for the later chapters that will dive into low-level Linux details.
- Chapter 3: This is where we dig into the details of how lower-level Linux primitives are used in Kubernetes to build up higher-level concepts, including Pod implementation.

- Chapter 4: We're now rolling full steam ahead into the internal details of Linux processes and isolation, which are some of the lesser-known details of the Kubernetes landscape.
- Chapter 5: After covering Pod details (mostly), we dig into the networking of Pods and look at how they are wired together over different nodes.
- Chapter 6: This is our second networking chapter, where we look at the broader aspects of Pod and network proxy (`kube-proxy`) networking, and how to troubleshoot them.
- Chapter 7: This is our first chapter on storage, which gives a broad introduction to the theoretical basis for Kubernetes storage, the CSI (container storage interface), and how it interplays with the kubelet.
- Chapter 8: In our second chapter on storage, we look at some of the more practical details around storage, including how things like emptyDir, Secrets, and PersistentVolumes/dynamic storage work.
- Chapter 9: We now dig into the kubelet and look at some of the details of how it fires up Pods and manages them, including a look at concepts such as CRI, node life cycle, and ImagePullSecrets.
- Chapter 10: DNS in Kubernetes is a complex topic used in almost all container-based applications to locally access internal Services. We look at CoreDNS, the DNS service implementation for Kubernetes, and how different Pods fulfill DNS requests.
- Chapter 11: The control plane, which we mentioned in early chapters, is now discussed in detail with an overview of how the scheduler, controller manager, and API server work. These form the "brains" of Kubernetes and pull it all together when it comes to the flow of the lower-level concepts discussed in previous chapters.
- Chapter 12: Because we've covered the control plane logic, we now dig into etcd, the rock-solid consensus mechanism for Kubernetes, and how it has evolved to meet the needs of the Kubernetes control plane.
- Chapter 13: We provide an overview of NetworkPolicies, RBAC, and Pod and node-level security, which administrators should know about for production scenarios. This chapter also discusses the overall progression of the Pod security policy APIs.
- Chapter 14: Here, we look at node-level security, cloud security, and other infrastructure-centric aspects of Kubernetes security.
- Chapter 15: We conclude with a generic overview of application tooling, exemplified by the Carvel toolkit for managing YAML files, building Operator-like applications, and managing the life cycle of applications over the long haul.

About the code

We have several examples for this book in the GitHub repository (https://github.com/jayunit100/k8sprototypes/), especially with regard to

- Using kind to install realistic networking on local clusters with Calico, Antrea, or Cillium
- Looking at Prometheus metrics in the real world
- Building applications using the Carvel toolkit
- Various RBAC-related experiments

This book also provides many examples of code. These appear throughout the text and as separate code snippets. Code appears in a fixed-width font like this, so you'll know when you see it.

In many cases, the original source code has been reformatted; we've added line breaks and reworked indentation to accommodate the available page space in the book. In rare cases, even this was not enough, and code snippets include line-continuation markers (➥). Code annotations accompany many of the listings, highlighting important concepts. You can get executable snippets of code from the liveBook (online) version of this book at https://livebook.manning.com/book/core-kubernetes, and from GitHub at https://github.com/jayunit100/k8sprototypes/.

liveBook discussion forum

Purchase of *Core Kubernetes* includes free access to liveBook, Manning's online reading platform. Using liveBook's exclusive discussion features, you can attach comments to the book globally or to specific sections or paragraphs. It's a snap to make notes for yourself, ask and answer technical questions, and receive help from the author and other users. To access the forum, go to https://livebook.manning.com/book/core-kubernetes/discussion. You can also learn more about Manning's forums and the rules of conduct at https://livebook.manning.com/discussion.

Manning's commitment to our readers is to provide a venue where a meaningful dialogue between individual readers and between readers and the author can take place. It is not a commitment to any specific amount of participation on the part of the authors, whose contribution to the forum remains voluntary (and unpaid). We suggest you try asking the authors some challenging questions lest their interest stray! The forum and the archives of previous discussions will be accessible from the publisher's website as long as the book is in print.

about the authors

JAY VYAS, PHD, is currently a staff engineer at VMware and has worked on several commercial and open source Kubernetes distributions and platforms, including OpenShift, VMware Tanzu, Black Duck's internal multipronged Kubernetes installation platforms, and bespoke Kubernetes installations for clients of his consulting company, Rocket Rudolf, LLC. For several years, he acted as a PMC (project management committee) member at the Apache Software Foundation, working across several projects in the BigData space. He's been involved with Kubernetes in various capacities since its inception and currently spends most of his time in the SIG-Windows and SIG-network communities. He got his start in distributed systems while finishing his PhD around bioinformatics data marts (which federated databases into mining platforms for the human and viral proteomes). This led him into the world of BigData and scaling out data processing systems, and, eventually, to Kubernetes.

You can contact Jay at @jayunit100 on Twitter if you're interested in collaborating on . . . anything. His daily workout is a one-mile sprint and pull-ups until failure. He also owns several synthesizers including the Prophet-6, which sounds like a spaceship.

CHRIS LOVE is a Google Cloud Certified Fellow and a co-founder of Lionkube. He has over 25 years of software and IT engineering experience with companies including Google, Oracle, VMware, Cisco, Johnson & Johnson, and others. As a thought leader within Kubernetes and the DevOps community, Chris Love has contributed to many open source projects, including Kubernetes, kops (former

AWS SIG lead), Bazel (contributed to Kubernetes rules), and Terraform (an early contributor to the VMware plugin). His professional interests include IT culture transformation, containerization technologies, automated testing frameworks and practices, Kubernetes, Golang AKA Go, and other programming languages. Love also enjoys speaking around the world about DevOps, Kubernetes, and technology, as well as mentoring people in the IT and software industries.

Outside of work, Love enjoys skiing, volleyball, yoga, and other outdoor activities that come with living in Colorado. He's also been a practicing martial artist for over 20 years.

If you're interested in having virtual coffee or have questions for Chris, you can contact him at @chrislovenm on Twitter or LinkedIn.

about the cover illustration

The figure on the cover of *Core Kubernetes* is "Stern, sailor at the helm of a ship," taken from an engraving of a painting by Alfredo Luxoro, published in *L'Illustrazione Italiana*, No. 19, May 9, 1880.

In those days, it was easy to identify where people lived and what their trade or station in life was just by their dress. Manning celebrates the inventiveness and initiative of today's computer business with book covers based on the rich diversity of regional culture centuries ago, brought back to life by pictures from engravings such as this one.

Why Kubernetes exists

This chapter covers

- Why Kubernetes exists
- Commonly used Kubernetes terms
- Specific use cases for Kubernetes
- High-level Kubernetes features
- When not to run Kubernetes

Kubernetes is an open source platform for hosting containers and defining application-centric APIs for managing cloud semantics around how these containers are provisioned with storage, networking, security, and other resources. Kubernetes enables continuous reconciliation of the entire state space of your application deployments, including how they are accessed from the outside world.

Why implement Kubernetes in your environment as opposed to manually provisioning these sorts of resources using a DevOps-related infrastructure tool? The answer lies in the way we define DevOps to be increasingly integrated into the overall application life cycle over time. DevOps has evolved increasingly to include processes, engineers, and tools that support a more automated administration of applications in a data center. One of the keys to doing this successfully is reproducibility of infrastructure: a change made to fix an incident on one component that's not replicated perfectly across all other identical components means one or more components differ.

In this book, we will take a deep dive into the best practices for using Kubernetes with DevOps, so components are replicated as needed and your system fails less often. We will also explore the under-the-hood processes to better understand Kubernetes and get the most efficient system possible.

1.1 Reviewing a few key terms before we get started

In 2021, Kubernetes was one of the most commonly deployed cloud technologies. Because of this, we don't always fully define new terms before referencing them. In case you're new to Kubernetes or are unsure of a few terms, we provide some key definitions that you can refer back to throughout the first few chapters of this book as you ramp up on this new universe. We will redefine these concepts with more granularity and in greater context as we dig into them later in this book:

- *CNI and CSI*—The container networking and storage interfaces, respectively, that allow for pluggable networking and storage for Pods (containers) that run in Kubernetes.
- *Container*—A Docker or OCI image that typically runs an application.
- *Control plane*—The brains of a Kubernetes cluster, where scheduling of containers and managing all Kubernetes objects takes place (sometimes referred to as Masters).
- *DaemonSet*—Like a deployment, but it runs on every node of a cluster.
- *Deployment*—A collection of Pods that is managed by Kubernetes.
- *kubectl*—The command-line tool for talking to the Kubernetes control plane.
- *kubelet*—The Kubernetes agent that runs on your cluster nodes. It does what the control plane needs it to do.
- *Node*—A machine that runs a kubelet process.
- *OCI*—The common image format for building executable, self-contained applications. Also referred to as *Docker images.*
- *Pod*—The Kubernetes object that encapsulates a running container.

1.2 The infrastructure drift problem and Kubernetes

Managing infrastructure is a reproducible way of managing the "drift" of that infrastructure's configuration as hardware, compliance, and other data-center requirements change over time. This applies to both the *definition* of applications as well as to the *management* of the hosts these apps run on. IT engineers are all too familiar with common toil such as

- Updating the Java version on a fleet of servers
- Making sure certain applications don't run in specific places
- Replacing or scaling old or broken hardware and migrating applications from it

- Manually managing load-balancing routes
- Forgetting to document new infrastructure changes when lacking a common enforced configuration language

As we manage and update servers in a data center, or in the cloud, the odds that their original definitions "drift away" from the intended IT architecture increases. Applications might be running in the wrong places, with the wrong resource allotment, or with access to the wrong storage modules.

Kubernetes gives us a way to centrally manage the entire state space of all applications with one handy tool: kubectl (https://kubernetes.io/docs/tasks/tools/), a command-line client that makes REST API calls to the Kubernetes API server. We can also use Kubernetes API clients to do these tasks programmatically. It's quite easy to install kubectl and to test it on a kind cluster, which we'll do early on in this book.

Previous approaches to managing this complex application state space include technologies such as Puppet, Chef, Mesos, Ansible, and SaltStack. Kubernetes borrows from these different approaches by taking the state management capabilities of tools such as Puppet, while borrowing concepts from some of the application and scheduling primitives provided by software such as Mesos.

Ansible, SaltStack, and Terraform typically have played a major role in infrastructure configuration (paving OS-specific requirements such as firewalls or binary installations). Kubernetes manages this concept as well, but it uses *privileged containers* on a Linux environment (these are known as *HostProcess Pods* on Windows v1.22). For example, a privileged container in a Linux system can manage iptables rules for routing traffic to applications, and in fact, this is exactly what the Kubernetes Service proxy (known as the *kube-proxy*) does.

Google, Microsoft, Amazon, VMware, and many companies have adopted containerization as a core and enabling strategy for their customers to run fleets of hundreds or thousands of applications on different cloud and bare metal environments. Containers are, thus, a fundamental primitive for both running apps *and* managing application infrastructure (such as providing containers with IP addresses) that run the services these apps depend on (such as the provisioning of bespoke storage and firewall requirements), and, most importantly, run the applications themselves.

Kubernetes is (at the time of this writing) essentially undisputed as the modern standard for orchestrating and running containers in any cloud, server, or data center environment.

1.3 *Containers and images*

Apps have dependencies that must be fulfilled by the host on which they run. Developers in the pre-container era accomplished this task in an ad hoc manner (for example, a Java app would require a running JVM along with firewall rules to talk to a database).

At its core, Docker can be thought of as a way to run containers, where a *container* is a running OCI image (https://github.com/opencontainers/image-spec). The *OCI specification* is a standard way to define an image that can be executed by a program such as Docker, and it ultimately is a tarball with various layers. Each of the tarballs inside an image contains such things as Linux binaries and application files. Thus, when you run a container, the container runtime (such as Docker, containerd, or CRI-O) takes the image, unpacks it, and starts a process on the host system that runs the image contents.

Containers add a layer of isolation that obviates the need for managing libraries on a server or preloading infrastructure with other accidental application dependencies (figure 1.1). For instance, if you have two Ruby applications that require different versions of the same library, you can use two containers. Each Ruby application is isolated inside a running container and has the specific version of the library that it requires.

There is a phase that is well known: "Well, it runs on my machine." When installing software, it can often run in one environment or machine but not in another. Using images simplifies running the same software on different servers. We'll talk more about images and containers in chapter 3.

Combine using images with Kubernetes, allowing for running immutable servers, and you have a level of simplicity that is world-class. As containers are quickly becoming an industry standard for the deployment of software applications, a few data points are worth mentioning:

- *Surveying over 88,000 developers, Docker and Kubernetes ranked third among the most loved development technologies of 2020.* This just behind Linux and Docker (http://mng .bz/nY12).
- *Datadog recently found that Docker encompasses 50% or more of the average developer's workflow.* Likewise, company-wide adoption is over 25% of all businesses (https:// www.datadoghq.com/docker-adoption/).

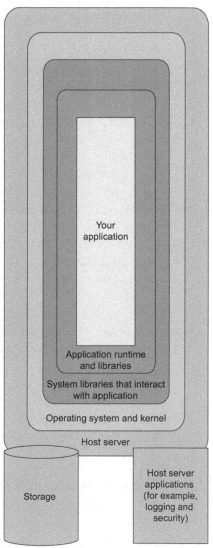

Figure 1.1 Applications running in containers

The bottom line is that we need automation for containers, and this is where Kubernetes fits in. Kubernetes dominates the space much like the Oracle database and the vSphere virtualization platform did during their heydays. Years later, Oracle databases and vSphere installations still exist; we predict the same longevity for Kubernetes.

We'll begin this book with a basic understanding of Kubernetes features. Its purpose is to take you beyond the basic principles to the lower-level core. Let's dive in and look at an extremely over-simplified Kubernetes (also referred to as "K8s") workflow that demonstrates some of the higher-order tenants of building and running microservices.

1.4 *Core foundation of Kubernetes*

At its core, we define everything in Kubernetes as plain text files, defined via YAML or JSON, and it runs your OCI images for you in a declarative way. We can use this same approach (YAML or JSON text files) to configure networking rules, role-based authentication and authorization (RBAC), and so on. By learning one syntax and how it is structured, any Kubernetes system can be configured, managed, and optimized.

Let's look at a quick sample of how one might run Kubernetes for a simple app. Don't worry; we'll have plenty of real-world examples to walk you through the entire life cycle of an application later in the book. Consider this just a visual guide to our hand-waving we've done thus far. To start with a concrete example of a microservice, the following code snippet generates a Dockerfile that builds an image capable of running MySQL:

```
FROM alpine:3.15.4
RUN apk add --no-cache mysql
ENTRYPOINT ["/usr/bin/mysqld"]
```

One would typically build this image (using `docker build`) and push it (using something like `docker push`) to an *OCI registry* (a place where such an image can be stored and retrieved by a container at run time). You can find a common open source registry to host on your own at https://github.com/goharbor/harbor. Another such registry that is also commonly used for millions of applications worldwide resides at https://hub.docker.com/. For this example, let's say we pushed this image, and now we are running it, somewhere. We might also want to build a container to talk to this service (maybe we have a custom Python app that serves as a MySQL client). We might define its Docker image like so:

```
FROM python:3.7
WORKDIR /myapp
COPY src/requirements.txt ./
RUN pip install -r requirements.txt
COPY src /myapp
CMD [ "python", "mysql-custom-client.py" ]
```

Now, if we wanted to run our client and the MySQL server as containers in a Kubernetes environment, we could easily do so by creating two Pods. Each one of these Pods might run one of the respective containers like so:

```
apiVersion: v1
kind: Pod
metadata:
  name: core-k8s
  spec:
  containers:
    - name: my-mysql-server
      image: myregistry.com/mysql-server:v1.0
---
apiVersion: v1
kind: Pod
metadata:
  name: core-k8s-mysql
  spec:
  containers:
    - name: my-sqlclient
      image: myregistry.com/mysql-custom-client:v1.0
      command: ['tail','-f','/dev/null']
```

We would, typically, store the previous YAML snippet in a text file (for example, my-app.yaml) and execute it using the Kubernetes client tool (for example, `kubectl create -f my-app.yaml`). This tool connects to the Kubernetes API server and transfers the YAML definition to be stored. Kubernetes then automatically takes the definitions of the two Pods that we have on the API server and makes sure they are up and running somewhere.

This doesn't happen instantly: it requires the nodes in the cluster to respond to events that are constantly occurring and updates that state in their Node objects via the kubelet communicating to the API server. It also requires that the OCI images are present and accessible to the nodes in our Kubernetes cluster. Things can go wrong at any time, so we refer to Kubernetes as an *eventually consistent system*, wherein reconciliation of the desired state over time is a key design philosophy. This consistency model (compared with a guaranteed consistency model) ensures that we can continually request changes to the overall state space of all applications in our cluster and lets the underlying Kubernetes platform figure out the logistics of *how* these apps are set in motion over time.

This scales into real-world scenarios quite naturally. For example, if you tell Kubernetes, "I want five applications spread across three zones in a cloud," this can be accomplished entirely by defining a few lines of YAML utilizing Kubernetes' scheduling primitives. Of course, you need to make sure that those three zones actually exist and that your scheduler is aware of them, but even if you haven't done this, Kubernetes will at least schedule some of the workloads on the zones that are available.

In short, Kubernetes allows you to define the desired state of all the apps in your cluster, how they are networked, where they run, what storage they use, and so on, while delegating the underlying implementation of these details to Kubernetes itself. Thus, you'll rarely find the need to do a one-off Ansible or a Puppet update in a production Kubernetes scenario (unless you are reinstalling Kubernetes itself, and even then, there are tools such as the Cluster API that allow you to use Kubernetes to manage Kubernetes (now we're getting in way over our heads).

1.4.1 All infrastructure rules in Kubernetes are managed as plain YAML

Kubernetes automates all of the aspects of the technology stack using the Kubernetes API, which can be entirely managed as YAML and JSON resources. This includes traditional IT infrastructure rules (which still apply in some manner or other to microservices) such as

- Server configuration of ports or IP routes
- Persistent storage availability for applications
- Hosting of software on specific or arbitrary servers
- Security provisioning, such as RBAC or networking rules for applications to access one another
- DNS configuration on a per-application and global basis

All of these components are defined within configuration files that are representations of objects within the Kubernetes API. Kubernetes uses these building blocks and containers by applying changes, monitoring those changes, and addressing momentary failures or disruptions until achieving the desired end state. When "things go bump in the night," Kubernetes will handle a lot of scenarios automatically, and we do not have to fix the problems ourselves. Properly configuring more elaborate systems with automation permits the DevOps team to focus on solving complex problems, to plan for the future, and to find the best-in-class solutions for the business. Next, let's review the features that Kubernetes provides and how they support the use of Pods.

1.5 Kubernetes features

Container orchestration platforms allow developers to automate the process of running instances, provisioning hosts, linking containers to optimize orchestration procedures, and extending application life cycles. It's time to dive into the core features within a container orchestration platform because, essentially, containers need Pods and Pods need Kubernetes to

- Expose a cloud-neutral API for all functionality within the API server
- Integrate with all major cloud and hypervisor platforms within the Kubernetes controller manager (also referred to as KCM)
- Provide a fault-tolerant framework for storing and defining the state of all Services, applications, and data center configurations or other Kubernetes-supported infrastructures
- Manage deployments while minimizing user-facing downtime, whether to an individual host, Service, or application
- Automate scaling for hosts and hosted applications with rolling update awareness
- Create internal and external integrations (known as ClusterIP, NodePort, or LoadBalancer Service types) with load balancing
- Provide the ability to schedule applications to run on specific virtualized hardware, based on its metadata, via node labeling and the Kubernetes scheduler

- Deliver a highly available platform via DaemonSets and other technology infrastructures that prioritizes containers that run on all nodes in the cluster
- Allow for service discovery via a domain name service (DNS), implemented previously by KubeDNS and, most recently, by CoreDNS, which integrates with the API server
- Run batch processes (known as Jobs) that use storage and containers in the same way persistent applications run
- Include API extensions and construct native API-driven programs using custom resource definitions, without building any port mappings or plumbing
- Enable inspection of failed cluster-wide processes including remote execution into any container at any time via `kubectl exec` and `kubectl describe`
- Allow the mounting of local and/or remote storage to a container and manage declarative storage volumes for containers with the StorageClass API and PersistentVolumes

Figure 1.2 is a simple diagram of a Kubernetes cluster. What Kubernetes does is by no means trivial. It standardizes the life cycle management of multiple applications running in or on the same cluster. The foundation of Kubernetes is a cluster, consisting of nodes. The complexity of Kubernetes is, admittedly, one of the complaints that engineers have about Kubernetes. The community is working on making it easier, but Kubernetes is solving a complex problem that is hard to solve to begin with.

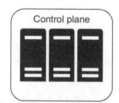

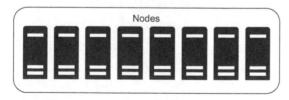

Figure 1.2   An example
Kubernetes cluster

If you don't need high availability, scalability, and orchestration, then maybe you don't need Kubernetes. Let's now consider a typical failure scenario in a cluster:

1. A node stops responding to the control plane.
2. The control plane reschedules the Pods running on the unresponsive node to another node or nodes.
3. When a user makes an API call into the API server via `kubectl`, the API server responds with the correct information about the unresponsive node and the new location of the Pods.

4 All clients that communicate to the Pod's Service are rerouted to its new location.

5 Storage volumes attached to Pods on the failing node are moved to the new Pod location so that its old data is still readable.

The purpose of this book is to give you deeper insight into how this all really works under the hood and how the underlying Linux primitives complement the high-level Kubernetes components to accomplish these tasks. Kubernetes relies heavily on hundreds of technologies in the Linux stack, which are often hard to learn and lack deep documentation. It is our hope that by reading this book, you'll understand a lot of the subtleties of Kubernetes, which are often overlooked in the tutorials first used by engineers to get up and running with containers.

It is natural to run Kubernetes on top of immutable operating systems. You have a base OS that only updates when you update the entire OS (and thus is immutable), and you install your Nodes/Kubernetes using that OS. There are many advantages to running an immutable OS that we will not cover here. You can run Kubernetes in the cloud, on bare metal servers, or even on a Raspberry Pi. In fact, the U.S. Department of Defense is currently researching how to run Kubernetes on some of its fighter jets. IBM even supports running clusters on its next generation mainframes, PowerPCs.

As the cloud native ecosystem around Kubernetes continues to mature, it will continue to permit organizations to identify best practices, proactively make changes to prevent issues, and maintain environment consistency to avoid *drift*, where some machines behave slightly differently from others because patches were missed, not applied, or improperly applied.

1.6 *Kubernetes components and architecture*

Now, let's take a moment to look at the Kubernetes architecture at a high level (figure 1.3). In short, it consists of your hardware and the portion of your hardware that runs the Kubernetes control plane as well as the Kubernetes worker nodes:

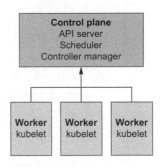

- *Hardware infrastructure*—Includes computers, network infrastructure, storage infrastructure, and a container registry.
- *Kubernetes worker nodes*—The base unit of compute in a Kubernetes cluster.
- *Kubernetes control plane*—The mothership of Kubernetes. This covers the API server, scheduler, controller manager, and other controllers.

Figure 1.3 The control plane and worker nodes

1.6.1 *The Kubernetes API*

If there's one important thing to take away from this chapter that will enable you to go forth on a deep journey through this book, it's that administering microservices and other containerized software applications on a Kubernetes platform is just a matter of declaring Kubernetes API objects. For the most part, everything else is done for you.

This book will dive deeply into the API server and its datastore, etcd. Almost anything that you can ask `kubectl` to do results in reading, or writing, to a defined and versioned object in the API server. (The exceptions to this are things like using `kubectl` to grab logs for a running Pod, wherein this connection is proxied through to a node.) The `kube-apiserver` (Kubernetes API server) allows for CRUD (create, read, update, and delete) operations on all of the objects and provides a RESTful (REpresentational State Transfer) interface. Some `kubectl` commands like `describe` are a composite view of multiple objects. In general, all Kubernetes API objects have

- A named API version (for instance, `v1` or `rbac.authorization.k8s.io/v1`)
- A kind (for example, `kind: Deployment`)
- A metadata section

We can thank Brian Grant, one of the original Kubernetes founders, for the API versioning scheme that has proven to be robust over time. It may seem complicated, and, frankly, a bit of a pain at times, but it allows us to do things such as upgrades and contracts defining API changes. API changes and migration are often nontrivial, and Kubernetes provides a well-defined contract for API changes. Take a look at the API versioning documents on the Kubernetes website (http://mng.bz/voP4), and you can read through the contracts for Alpha, Beta, and GA API versions.

Throughout the chapters in this book, we will focus on Kubernetes but keep returning to the basic theme: virtually everything in Kubernetes exists to support the Pod. In this book, we'll look at several API elements in detail including

- Runtime Pods and deployments
- API implementation details
- Ingress Services and load balancing
- PersistentVolumes and PersistentVolumeClaims storage
- NetworkPolicies and network security

There are around 70 different API types that you can play with, create, edit, and delete in a standard Kubernetes cluster. You can view these by running `kubectl api-resources`. The output should look something like this:

```
$ kubectl api-resources | head
NAME                       SHORTNAMES    NAMESPACED    KIND
bindings                                 true          Binding
componentstatuses          cs            false         ComponentStatus
configmaps                 cm            true          ConfigMap
endpoints                  ep            true          Endpoints
events                     ev            true          Event
limitranges                limits        true          LimitRange
namespaces                 ns            false         Namespace
nodes                      no            false         Node
persistentvolumeclaims     pvc           true          PersistentVolumeClaim
```

We can see that each of the API resources for Kubernetes itself has

- A short name
- A full name
- An indication of whether it is bounded to a namespace

In Kubernetes, *Namespaces* allow certain objects to exist inside of a specific . . . well . . . Namespace. This gives developers a simple form of hierarchical grouping. For example, if you have an application that runs 10 different microservices, you commonly might create all of these Pods, Services, and PersistentVolumeClaims (also referred to as PVCs) inside the same Namespace. That way, when it's time for you to delete the app, you can just delete the Namespace. In chapter 15, we'll look at higher-level ways to analyze the life cycle of applications, which are more advanced than this simplistic approach. But for many cases, the namespace is the most obvious and intuitive solution for separating all the Kubernetes API objects associated with an app.

1.6.2 *Example one: An online retailer*

Imagine a major online retailer that needs to be able to quickly scale with demand seasonally, such as around the holidays. Scaling and predicting how to scale has been one of their biggest challenges—maybe the biggest. Kubernetes solves a multitude of problems that come with running a highly available, scalable distributed system. Imagine the possibilities of having the ability to scale, distribute, and make highly available systems at your fingertips. Not only is it a better way to run a business, but it is also the most efficient and effective platform for managing systems. When combining Kubernetes and cloud providers, you can run on someone else's servers when you need extra resources instead of buying and maintaining extra hardware just in case.

1.6.3 *Example two: An online giving solution*

For a second real-world example of this transition that is worth mentioning, let's consider an online donation website that enables contributions to a broad range of charities per a user's choice. Let's say this particular example started out as a WordPress site, but eventually, business transactions lead to a full-blown dependency on JVM frameworks (like Grails) with a customized UX, middle tier, and database layer. The requirements for this business tsunami included machine learning, ad serving, messaging, Python, Lua, NGINX, PHP, MySQL, Cassandra, Redis, Elastic, ActiveMQ, Spark, lions, tigers, and bears . . . and stop already.

The initial infrastructure was a hand-built cloud virtual machine (VM), using Puppet to set everything up. As the company grew, they designed for scale, but this included more and more VMs that only hosted one or two applications. Then they decided to move to Kubernetes. The VM count was reduced from around 30 to 5 and scaled more easily. They completely eliminated Puppet and the server setup, and thus the need to manually manage machine infrastructure by hand, thanks to their transition to heavy use of Kubernetes.

The transition to Kubernetes for this company resolved the entire class of VM administration problems, the burden of DNS for complex service publishing, and much more. Additionally, the recovery times in cases of catastrophic failures were much more predictable to manage from an infrastructure standpoint. When you experience the benefits of moving to a standardized API-driven methodology that works well and has the power to make massive changes quickly, you begin to appreciate the declarative nature of Kubernetes and its cloud-native approach to container orchestration.

1.7   When not to use Kubernetes

Admittedly, there are always use cases where Kubernetes might not be a good fit. Some of these include

- *High-performance computing (HPC)*—Using containers adds a layer of complexity and, with the new layer, a performance hit. The latency created by using a container is getting much smaller, but if your application is influenced by nano- or microseconds, using Kubernetes might not be the best option.
- *Legacy*—Some applications have hardware, software, and latency requirements that make it difficult to simply containerize. For example, you may have applications that you purchased from a software company that does not officially support running in a container or running their application within a Kubernetes cluster.
- *Migration*—Implementations of legacy systems may be so rigid that migrating them to Kubernetes offers little advantage other than "we are built on Kubernetes." But some of the most significant gains come after migrating, when monolithic applications are parsed up into logical components, which can then scale independently of each other.

The important thing here is this: learn and master the basics. Kubernetes solves many of the problems presented in this chapter in a stable, cost-sensitive manner.

Summary

- Kubernetes makes your life easier!
- The Kubernetes platform can run on any type of infrastructure.
- Kubernetes builds an ecosystem of components that work together. Combining the components empowers companies to prevent, recover, and scale in real time when urgent changes are required.
- Everything you do in Kubernetes can be done with one simple tool: `kubectl`.
- Kubernetes creates a cluster from one or more computers, and that cluster provides a platform to deploy and host containers. It offers container orchestration, storage management, and distributed networking.
- Kubernetes was born from previous configuration-driven, container-driven approaches.

- The Pod is the basic building block of Kubernetes. It supports the myriad of features that Kubernetes allows: scaling, failover, DNS lookup, and RBAC security rules.
- Kubernetes applications are entirely managed by simply making API calls to the Kubernetes API server.

Why the Pod?

This chapter covers

- What is a Pod?
- An example web app and why we need the Pod
- How Kubernetes is built for Pods
- The Kubernetes control plane

In the previous chapter, we provided a high-level overview of Kubernetes and an introduction to its features, core components, and architecture. We also showcased a couple of business use cases and outlined some container definitions. The Kubernetes Pod abstraction for running thousands of containers in a flexible manner has been a fundamental part of the transition to containers in enterprises. In this chapter, we will cover the Pod and how Kubernetes was built to support it as a basic application building block.

As briefly mentioned in chapter 1, a Pod is an object that is defined within the Kubernetes API, as are the majority of things in Kubernetes. The Pod is the smallest atomic unit that can be deployed to a Kubernetes cluster, and Kubernetes is built around the Pod definition. The Pod (figure 2.1) allows us to define an object that can include multiple containers, which allows Kubernetes to create one or more containers hosted on a node.

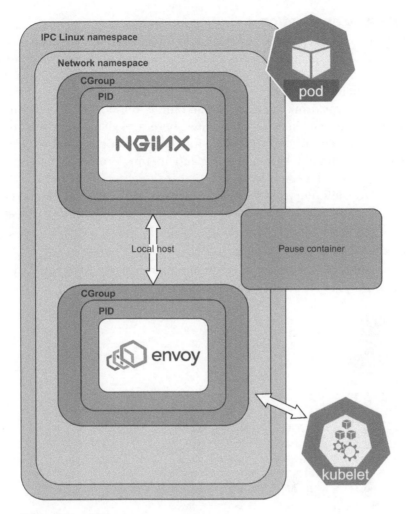

Figure 2.1   A Pod

Many other Kubernetes API objects either use Pods directly or are API objects that support Pods. A Deployment object, for example, uses Pods, as well as StatefulSets and DaemonSets. Several different higher-level Kubernetes controllers create and manage Pod life cycles. Controllers are software components that run on the control plane. Examples of built-in controllers include the controller manager, the cloud manager, and the scheduler. But first, let's digress by laying out a web application and then loop that back to Kubernetes, the Pod, and the control plane.

> **NOTE**   You may notice that we use the control plane to define the group of nodes that run the controller, the controller manager, and the scheduler. They are also referred to as *masters*, but in this book, we will use *control plane* when talking about these components.

2.1   *An example web application*

Let's walk through an example web application to understand why we need a Pod and how Kubernetes is built to support Pods and containerized applications. In order to get a better understanding of why the Pod, we will use the following example throughout much of this chapter.

The Zeus Zap energy drink company has an online website that allows consumers to purchase their different lines of carbonated beverages. This website consists of three different layers: a user interface (UI), a middle tier (various microservices), and a backend database. They also have messaging and queuing protocols. A company like Zeus Zap usually has various web frontends that include consumer-facing as well as administrative ones, different microservices that compose the middle tier, and one or more backend databases. Here is a breakdown of one slice of Zeus Zap's web application (figure 2.2):

- A JavaScript frontend served up by NGINX
- Two web-controller layers that are Python microservices hosted with Django
- A backend CockroachDB on port 6379, backed by storage

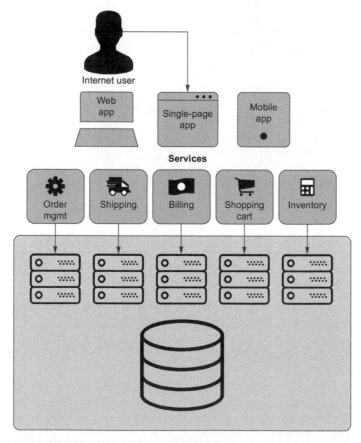

Figure 2.2   The Zeus Zap web architecture

Now, let's imagine that they run these applications in four distinct containers in a production setting. Then they can start the app using these docker run commands:

```
$ docker run -t -i ui -p 80:80
$ docker run -t -i miroservice-a -p 8080:8080
$ docker run -t -i miroservice-b -b 8081:8081
$ docker run -t -i cockroach:cockroach -p 6379:6379
```

Once these services are up and running, the company quickly comes to a few realizations:

- They cannot run multiple copies of the UI container unless they load balance in front of port 80 because there is only one port 80 on the host machine their image is running.
- They cannot migrate the CockroachDB container to a different server unless the IP address is modified and injected into the web app (or they add a DNS server that is dynamically updated when the CockroachDB container moves).
- They need to run each CockroachDB instance on a separate server to result in high availability.
- If a CockroachDB instance dies on one server, they need a way to move its data to a new node and reclaim the unused storage space.

Zeus Zap also realizes that a few requirements for a container orchestration platform exist. These include

- Shared networking between hundreds of processes all binding to the same port
- Migration and decoupling of storage volumes from binaries while avoiding dirtying up local disks
- Optimizing the utilization of available CPU and memory resources to achieve cost savings

NOTE Running more processes on a server often results in the *noisy neighbor* phenomenon: crowding applications leads to over-competition for scarce resources (CPU, memory). A system must mitigate noisy neighbors.

Containerized applications running at large scale (or even small scale) require a higher level of awareness when it comes to scheduling services and managing load balancers. Therefore, the following items are also required:

- *Storage-aware scheduling*—To schedule a process in concert with making its data available
- *Service-aware network load balancing*—To send traffic to different IP addresses as containers move from one machine to another

The revelations just shared in our application resounded equally with the founders of the distributed scheduling and orchestration tools of the 2000s, including Mesos and Borg. Borg is Google's internal container orchestration system, and Mesos is an open source application, both of which provide cluster management and predate Kubernetes.

2.1.1   *Infrastructure for our web application*

Without container orchestration software such as Kubernetes, organizations need many components in their infrastructure. In order to run an application, you need various virtual machines (VMs) on the cloud or physical computers that act as your servers, and as mentioned before, you need stable identifiers to locate services.

Server workloads can vary. For instance, you may need servers with more memory to run the database, or you may need a system with lower memory but more CPUs for the microservices. Also, you might need low-latency storage for a database like MySQL or Postgres, but slower storage for backups and other applications that usually load data into memory and then never touch the disk again. Additionally, your continuous integration servers like Jenkins or CircleCI require full access to your servers, but your monitoring system requires read-only access to some of your applications. Now, add in human authorization and authentication as well. To summarize, you will need

- A VM or physical server as a deployment platform
- Load balancing
- Application discovery
- Storage
- A security system

In order to sustain the system, your DevOps staff would need to maintain the following (in addition to many more subsystems):

- Centralized logging
- Monitoring, alerting, and metrics
- Continuous integration/continuous delivery (CI/CD) system
- Backups
- Secrets management

In contrast to most home-grown application delivery platforms, Kubernetes comes with built-in log rotation, inspection, and management tooling out of the box. Next come the business challenges: the operational requirements.

2.1.2   *Operational requirements*

The Zeus Zap energy drink company does not have a typical seasonal growth period like most online retailers, but they do sponsor various e-sporting events that drive in a lot of traffic. This is because the marketing department and various online gaming streamers run contests that are promoted during these events. These online user traffic patterns give the DevOps team one of the most challenging patterns to manage—

burst traffic. Scaling online applications is a difficult problem to maintain and solve, and now the team has to schedule for burst patterns! Also, due to the online social media campaigns created around the e-sporting events, the business is concerned about outages. The costs for downtimes are ugly and huge.

According to Gartner from a study in 2018 (http://mng.bz/PWNn), the average cost of IT downtime is $5,600 per minute, taking into account the differences between businesses. It is not uncommon for an application to have two hours of downtime, resulting in an average cost of $672,000. Money is one thing, but what about the human cost? DevOps engineers face outages; it is a part of life, but it wears on the staff, as well, and can lead to burn out. Employee burnout in the U.S. costs industries approximately $125 to $190 billion dollars annually (http://mng.bz/4j6j).

Many companies need some level of high availability and rollback in their production systems. These requirements go hand in hand with the need for redundancy of applications and hardware. However, to save on costs, these same companies may want to scale application availability up and down during less demanding time periods. Thus, cost management is often antagonistic to broader business requirements around uptime. To recap, a simple web application needs

- Scaling
- High availability
- Versioning applications to allow rollbacks
- Cost management

2.2 What Is a Pod?

Roughly, a *Pod* is one or more OCI images that run as containers on a Kubernetes cluster node. The Kubernetes *node* is a single piece of computing power (a server) that runs a kubelet. Like everything else in Kubernetes, a Node is also an API object. Deploying a Pod is as simple as issuing the following:

```
$ cat << EOF > pod.yaml        The API version ID that matches
apiVersion: v1        ◁         a version on the API server
kind: Pod       ◁
metadata:                       kind declares the type of API
spec:                           object (in this case, a Pod) for
  container:                    the API server.
    - name: busybox                        Names the image
      image: mycontainerregistry.io/foo  ◁  in the registry
EOF

$ kubectl create -f pod.yaml   ◁──── The kubectl command
```

The previous syntax runs using the Linux Bash shell and the kubectl command. The kubectl command is the binary that provides a command-line interface to work with the Kubernetes API server.

Pods aren't deployed directly in most cases. Instead, they are automatically created for us by other API objects such as Deployments, Jobs, StatefulSets, and DaemonSets that we define:

- *Deployments*—The most commonly used API object in a Kubernetes cluster. They are the typical API object that, say, deploys a microservice.
- *Jobs*—Run a Pod as a batch process.
- *StatefulSets*—Host applications that require specific needs and that are often stateful applications like databases.
- *DaemonSets*—Used when we want to run a single Pod as an "agent" on every node of a cluster (commonly used for system services involving networking, storage, or logging).

The following is a list of StatefulSet features:

- Ordinal Pod naming to get unique network identifiers
- Persistent storage that is always mounted to the same Pod
- Ordered starting, scaling, and updating

> **TIP** Docker image names support using a label called *latest*. Do not use the image name mycontainerregistry.io/foo in production because this pulls the `latest` tag from the registry, which is the latest version of the image. Always use a versioned tag name, not latest, or even better, an SHA to install an image. Image tag names are not immutable but an image SHA is. Many production systems fail because a newer version of a container is inadvertently installed. Friends don't let friends run *latest*!

When the Pod is started, you can view the Pod running in the default Namespace with a simple `kubectl get po` command. Now that we've created a running container, it is a simple matter to deploy the components in the Zeus Zap web application (figure 2.3). Simply use a favorite image tool like Docker or CRI-O to bundle the various binaries and their dependencies into different images, which are just tarballs with some file definitions. In the next chapter, we will cover how to make your own images and Pods manually.

Instead of having the system schedule various `docker run` commands when a server starts, we defined four higher-level API objects that create Pods and that call the Kubernetes API server. As we mentioned, Pods are rarely used to install applications on Kubernetes. Users typically use higher-level abstractions like Deployments and StatefulSets. But we still loop back to the Pod because Deployments and StatefulSets create replica objects, which then create Pods.

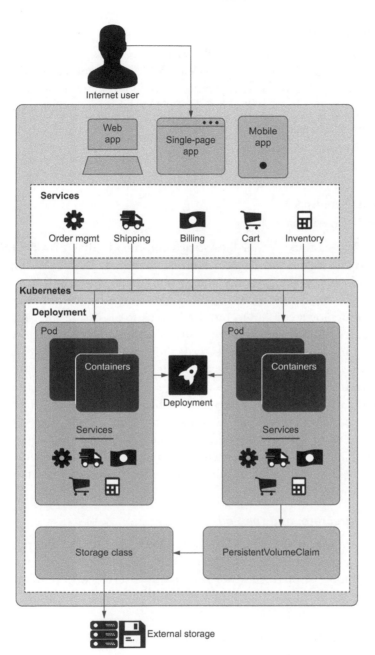

Figure 2.3 The Zeus Zap application running on Kubernetes

2.2.1   *A bunch of Linux namespaces*

Kubernetes Namespaces (the ones you make with `kubectl create ns`) are not the same as Linux namespaces. Linux namespaces are a Linux kernel feature that allows for process separation inside the kernel. Pods, at a base level, are a bunch of namespaces in a specific configuration. A Pod has the following Linux namespaces:

- One or more *PID* namespaces
- A single networking namespace
- `IPC` namespace
- `cgroup` (control group) namespace
- `mnt` (mount) namespace
- `user` (user ID) namespace

Linux namespaces are Linux kernel filesystem components that provide the base functionality to take an image and create a running container. Why is this important? Let's loop back to a couple of the requirements to run the example web app.

What is essential is the capability to scale. The Pod does not just give us and Kubernetes the ability to deploy a container, but it allows us to also scale the capability to handle more traffic. What is required to cut costs and to scale vertically is the ability to adjust resource settings for a container. In order for the Zeus Zap microservices to communicate with the CockroachDB server, a definitive networking and service lookup needs to be deployed.

The Pod and the basis of the Pod, Linux namespaces, provide the support for all of these features. Within the networking namespace, a virtual networking stack exists that is connected into a software-defined networking (SDN) system that spans a Kubernetes cluster. The need to scale is often facilitated via load balancing multiple Pods for the application. The SDN within a Kubernetes cluster is the networking framework that supports load balancing.

2.2.2   *Kubernetes, infrastructure, and the Pod*

Servers are dependent on running Kubernetes and Pods. As a unit of compute, a unit of CPU power is represented by an API object (the Node) within Kubernetes. A node can run on a multitude of platforms, but it is simply a server with defined components. Node requirements include the following:

- A server
- An installed operating system (OS) with a variety of Linux and Windows-supported requirements
- systemd (a Linux system and service manager)
- The kubelet (a node agent)
- The container runtime (such as a Docker engine)
- A network proxy (`kube-proxy`) that handles Kubernetes Services
- A CNI (Container Network Interface) provider

A node can run on a Raspberry Pi, a VM in the cloud, or a multitude of other platforms. Figure 2.4 displays what components form a node running on Linux.

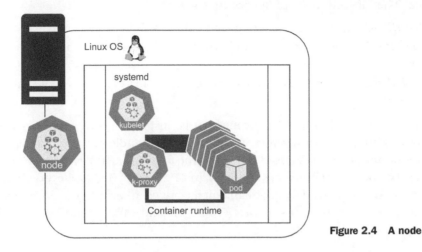

Figure 2.4   A node

The *kubelet* is a binary program that runs as an agent, communicating with the Kubernetes API server via multiple control loops. It runs on every node; without it, a Kubernetes node is not schedulable or considered to be a part of a cluster. Understanding the kubelet helps us to diagnose low-level problems with such things as a node not joining a cluster and a Pod not deploying. The kubelet ensures that

- Any Pod scheduled to a kubelet's host is running via a control loop that watches which Pods are scheduled to which nodes.
- The API server is continually made aware that the kubelet on a node is healthy via a heartbeat in Kubernetes 1.17+. (The heartbeat is maintained by looking at the `kube-node-lease` namespace of a running cluster.)
- Garbage is collected as needed for Pods, which includes ephemeral storage or network devices.

However, the kubelet is incapable of doing any real work without both a CNI provider and a container runtime accessible via a Container Runtime Interface (CRI). CNI ultimately serves the needs of the CRI, which then starts and stops containers. The kubelet utilizes CRI and CNI to reconcile the state of a node with the state of the control plane. For example, when the control plane decides that NGINX will run on nodes two, three, and four of a five-node cluster, it is the kubelet's job to make sure the CRI provider pulls down this container from an image registry and runs with an IP address in the `podCIDR` range. This book will cover how those decisions are made in chapter 9. When mentioning CRI, it is essential to have a container engine to start the containers. Common container engines include Docker engine, CRI-O, and LXC.

Service is an API object defined by Kubernetes. The Kubernetes network proxy binary (`kube-proxy`) handles the creation of the ClusterIP and NodePort Services on every node. The different types of Services include:

- *ClusterIP*—An internal Service that load balances Kubernetes Pods
- *NodePort*—An open port on a Kubernetes node that load balances multiple Pods
- *LoadBalancer*—An external Service that creates a load balancer external to the cluster

The Kubernetes network proxy may or may not be installed as some network providers replace it with their own network component that handles service management. Kubernetes permits multiple Pods of the same type to be proxied by a Service. For this to work, every node in a cluster has to be aware of every Service and every Pod. The Kubernetes network proxy facilitates and manages each service on each node as defined for a specific cluster. It supports TCP, UDP, and STCP network protocols, as well as forwarding and load balancing.

> **NOTE** Kubernetes networking is provided via a software solution called a CNI provider. Some CNI providers are building components that replace the Kubernetes network proxy with their own software infrastructure. That way they can undergo different networking without the use of iptables.

2.2.3   *The Node API object*

As mentioned, nodes support Pods, and the control plane defines the group of nodes that run the controller, the controller manager, and the scheduler. We can view a cluster's node(s) with this simple `kubectl` command:

```
$ kubectl get no   ◄──┐  The full command is kubectl get nodes,      The output from a kind
                       │  which retrieves the Node object(s) for a    cluster. Note that this is
NAME                STATUS      ROLES    AGE    VERSION   Kubernetes cluster.  v1.17.0, which is a little
kind-control-plane  NotReady    master   25s    v1.17.0   ◄──┐               older then what you're
                                                             └─ probably running locally.
```

The full command is kubectl get nodes, which retrieves the Node object(s) for a Kubernetes cluster.

The output from a kind cluster. Note that this is v1.17.0, which is a little older then what you're probably running locally.

Now, let's take a look at the Node API object that describes the node that hosts the Kubernetes control plane:

```
$ kubectl get no kind-control-plane -o yaml
```

The following example provides the entire API Node object value. (In the example, we will break up the YAML into multiple sections because it is long.)

```
apiVersion: v1
kind: Node
metadata:
  annotations:
    kubeadm.alpha.kubernetes.io/cri-socket:
      /run/containerd/containerd.sock   ◄──┐
```

The CRI socket used. With kind (and most clusters), this is the containerd socket.

```
      node.alpha.kubernetes.io/ttl: "0"
      volumes.kubernetes.io/controller-managed-attach-detach: "true"
  creationTimestamp: "2020-09-20T14:51:57Z"
  labels:                              ←──────  Standard labels, including
    beta.kubernetes.io/arch: amd64              the node name
    beta.kubernetes.io/os: linux
    kubernetes.io/arch: amd64
    kubernetes.io/hostname: kind-control-plane
    kubernetes.io/os: linux
    node-role.kubernetes.io/master: ""
  name: kind-control-plane
  resourceVersion: "1297"
  selfLink: /api/v1/nodes/kind-control-plane
  uid: 1636e5e1-584c-4823-9e6b-66ab5f390592
spec:
  podCIDR: 10.244.0.0/24         ←──────  CNI IP address, which is
  podCIDRs:                               CIDR for the Pod network
  - 10.244.0.0/24
# continued in the next section
```

Let's now move on to the status section. It provides information about the node and what the node is composed of.

```
status:                   ←──────  Updates for the API server for
  addresses:                       various status fields of the
  - address: 172.17.0.2            kubelet running on the node
    type: InternalIP
  - address: kind-control-plane
    type: Hostname
  allocatable:
    cpu: "2"
    ephemeral-storage: 61255492Ki
    hugepages-1Gi: "0"
    hugepages-2Mi: "0"
    memory: 2039264Ki
    pods: "110"
  capacity:
    cpu: "2"
    ephemeral-storage: 61255492Ki
    hugepages-1Gi: "0"
    hugepages-2Mi: "0"
    memory: 2039264Ki
    pods: "110"
  conditions:
  - lastHeartbeatTime: "2020-09-20T14:57:28Z"
    lastTransitionTime: "2020-09-20T14:51:51Z"
    message: kubelet has sufficient memory available
    reason: KubeletHasSufficientMemory
    status: "False"
    type: MemoryPressure
  - lastHeartbeatTime: "2020-09-20T14:57:28Z"
    lastTransitionTime: "2020-09-20T14:51:51Z"
    message: kubelet has no disk pressure
    reason: KubeletHasNoDiskPressure
```

```
     status: "False"
     type: DiskPressure
   - lastHeartbeatTime: "2020-09-20T14:57:28Z"
     lastTransitionTime: "2020-09-20T14:51:51Z"
     message: kubelet has sufficient PID available
     reason: KubeletHasSufficientPID
     status: "False"
     type: PIDPressure
   - lastHeartbeatTime: "2020-09-20T14:57:28Z"
     lastTransitionTime: "2020-09-20T14:52:27Z"
     message: kubelet is posting ready status
     reason: KubeletReady
     status: "True"
     type: Ready
 daemonEndpoints:
   kubeletEndpoint:
     Port: 10250
```

Next, let's look at all of the images running on the node:

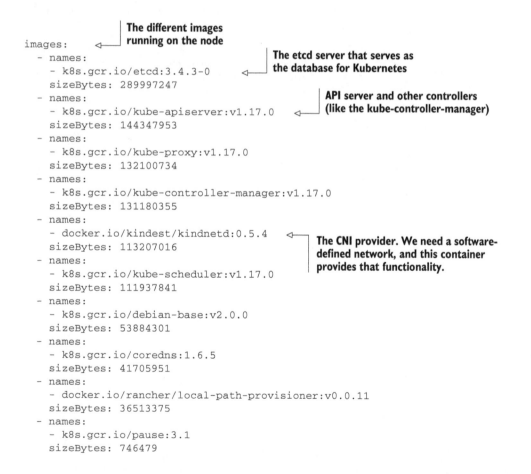

```
images:                    ◄──┐  The different images
  - names:                      running on the node
    - k8s.gcr.io/etcd:3.4.3-0    ◄──┐  The etcd server that serves as
    sizeBytes: 289997247              the database for Kubernetes
  - names:
    - k8s.gcr.io/kube-apiserver:v1.17.0   ◄──┐  API server and other controllers
    sizeBytes: 144347953                        (like the kube-controller-manager)
  - names:
    - k8s.gcr.io/kube-proxy:v1.17.0
    sizeBytes: 132100734
  - names:
    - k8s.gcr.io/kube-controller-manager:v1.17.0
    sizeBytes: 131180355
  - names:
    - docker.io/kindest/kindnetd:0.5.4   ◄──┐  The CNI provider. We need a software-
    sizeBytes: 113207016                       defined network, and this container
  - names:                                     provides that functionality.
    - k8s.gcr.io/kube-scheduler:v1.17.0
    sizeBytes: 111937841
  - names:
    - k8s.gcr.io/debian-base:v2.0.0
    sizeBytes: 53884301
  - names:
    - k8s.gcr.io/coredns:1.6.5
    sizeBytes: 41705951
  - names:
    - docker.io/rancher/local-path-provisioner:v0.0.11
    sizeBytes: 36513375
  - names:
    - k8s.gcr.io/pause:3.1
    sizeBytes: 746479
```

Finally, we'll add the `nodeInfo` block. This includes versioning for the Kubernetes system:

Specifies information about the node including OS, kube-proxy, and kubelet versions

```
nodeInfo:    ⟵
    architecture: amd64
    bootID: 0c700452-c292-4190-942c-55509dc43a55
    containerRuntimeVersion: containerd://1.3.2
    kernelVersion: 4.19.76-linuxkit
    kubeProxyVersion: v1.17.0
    kubeletVersion: v1.17.0
    machineID: 27e279849eb94684ae8c173287862c26
    operatingSystem: linux
    osImage: Ubuntu 19.10
    systemUUID: 9f5682fb-6de0-4f24-b513-2cd7e6204b0a
```

What is needed now is a container engine, the network proxy (`kube-proxy`), and the kubelet to run a node. We'll get to this in a bit.

Controllers and control loops

The word *control* is an overloaded term in the context of Kubernetes; the meanings are related, but it is a bit confusing. There are control loops, controllers, and the control plane. A Kubernetes installation consists of multiple executable binaries called *controllers*. You know them as the kubelet, the Kubernetes network proxy, the scheduler, and more. Controllers are written with computer programming patterns called *control loops*. The control plane houses specific controllers. These nodes and controllers are the mother ship or brain of Kubernetes. More to come on that subject throughout this chapter.

The nodes that comprise the control plane are sometimes referred to as *masters*, but we use control planes throughout the book. At its heart, Kubernetes is a state-reconciliation machine with various control loops, like an air-conditioner. Rather than regulating temperature, however, Kubernetes controls the following (as well as regulating many other aspects of distributed application management):

- Binding storage to processes
- Creating running containers and scaling the number of containers
- Killing and migrating containers when they are unhealthy
- Creating IP routes to ports
- Dynamically updating load-balanced endpoints

Let's loop back to the requirements we have covered thus far: Pods provide an instrument to deploy images. The images are deployed to a node, and their life cycle is managed by the kubelet. Service objects are managed by the Kubernetes network proxy. A DNS system like CoreDNS provides application lookup, allowing microservices in one Pod to look up and communicate with another Pod runnning CockroachDB, for example.

The Kubernetes network proxy also provides the capability of having internal load balancing within a cluster, thus helping with failover, upgrades, availability, and scaling. To address the need for persistent storage, the combination of the `mnt` Linux namespace, the kubelet, and the node allows for mounting a drive to a Pod. When the kubelet creates the Pod, that storage is then mounted to the Pod.

It seems that we are still missing a few parts. What if a node dies—what happens then? How do we even get a Pod on a node? Enter the control plane.

2.2.4   *Our web application and the control plane*

After establishing the Pods and nodes, the next step is to figure out how to get complex requirements, such as high availability. High availability (often referred to as HA) is not just a simple failover, but it meets the requirements of a service-level agreement (SLA). System availability is often measured in the number of 9s of uptime. This is a measurement of how much downtime you can have with an application or set of applications. Four 9s give us 52 minutes and 36 seconds of downtime a year; five 9s (99.999% uptime) give us 5 minutes and 15 seconds of possible downtime. 99.999% uptime gives us 26.25 seconds of downtime a month. Having five 9s means we only have less than half a minute a month where an application hosted on Kubernetes is not available. That is incredibly hard! All of the other requirements we have are not trivial as well. These include

- Scaling
- Cost savings
- Container version control
- User and application security

NOTE Yes, Kubernetes provides all of these capabilities, but applications have to support the way Kubernetes works as well. We will address the caveats about application design in the last chapter of this book.

The first step is the provisioning of Pods. However, beyond that, we have a system that provides us not only with fault tolerance and scalability (and in the same command line) but also the capability to save money and thus control costs. Figure 2.5 shows us the makeup of a typical control plane.

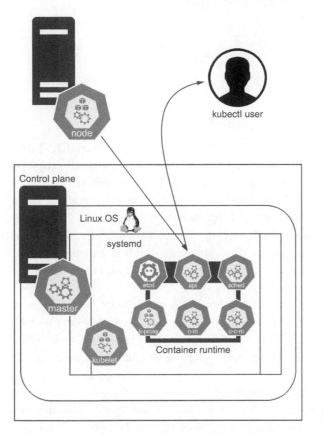

Figure 2.5   The control plane

2.3   *Creating a web application with kubectl*

In order to understand how the control plane facilitates complexity, such as scaling and fault tolerance, let's walk through the simple command: `kubectl apply -f deployment.yaml`. The following is the YAML for the deployment:

```yaml
apiVersion: apps/v1
kind: Deployment
metadata:
  name: nginx
spec:
  replicas: 3
  selector:
    matchLabels:
      app: nginx
  template:
    metadata:
      labels:
        app: nginx
    spec:
      containers:
      - name: nginx
```

```
image: nginx:1.7.9
ports:
- containerPort: 80
```

When you execute `kubectl apply`, kubectl communicates to the first component in the control plane. That is the API server.

2.3.1   *The Kubernetes API server: kube-apiserver*

The Kubernetes API server, `kube-apiserver`, is an HTTP-based REST server that exposes the various API objects for a Kubernetes cluster; these objects range from Pods to nodes to the Horizontal Pod Autoscaler. The API server validates and provides the web frontend to perform CRUD services on the cluster's shared state. Production control planes for Kubernetes typically provide a robust Kubernetes API server, which means running it on every node that comprises the control plane, or running it behind a cloud service that uses some other mechanism for failover and high availability. In practice, this means that access to the API server is done via an HAProxy or cloud load-balancer endpoint.

The components on the control plane communicate with the API server as well. When a node starts, the kubelet ensures that the node registers with the cluster by communicating with the API server. All of the components in the control plane have a control loop that has a watch functionality to monitor the API server for changes in objects.

The API server is the only component on the control plane that communicates with etcd, the database for Kubernetes. In the past, some other components like CNI network providers have communicated with etcd, but currently, most do not. In essence, the API server provides a stateful interface for all operations modifying a Kubernetes cluster. Security for all control plane components is essential, but securing the API server and its HTTPS endpoints is crucial.

When running on a high availability control plane, every Kubernetes API server is active and receives traffic. The API server is primarily stateless and can run on multiple nodes at the same time. An HTTPS load balancer fronts the API servers in a control plane consisting of multiple nodes. But we do not want anyone to have the permissions to communicate with the API server. *Admission controllers* that run as part of the API server provide both authentication and authorization when a client communicates with the API server.

Often, external authentication and authorization systems are integrated into the API server in the form of webhooks. A *webhook* is an HTTP PUSH API that allows for a callback. The `kubectl` call is authenticated, and then the API server persists the new deployment object to etcd. Our next step is to enact the scheduler to get the Pod on the node. New Pods need a new home, so the scheduler assigns Pods to a specific Node.

2.3.2 The Kubernetes scheduler: kube-scheduler

Distributed scheduling is not trivial. The Kubernetes scheduler (`kube-scheduler`) provides a clean, simple implementation of scheduling—perfect for a complex system like Kubernetes. The scheduler considers multiple factors in Pod scheduling. These include hardware components on a node, available CPU and memory resources, policy scheduling constraints, and other weighting factors.

The scheduler also follows Pod affinity and anti-affinity rules that specify Pod scheduling and placement behavior. In essence, Pod affinity rules attract Pods to a Node that match the rules, whereas Pod anti-affinity rules repel Pods from nodes. Taints also allow a node to repel a set of Pods, meaning the scheduler can determine which Pods should not live on which nodes. In the Zeus Zap example (section 2.1.2), three replicas of the Pod are defined. The replicas provide both fault tolerance and the capability to scale, the scheduler determines which node or nodes the replicas can run on, and then the Pods are scheduled for deployment on each of the nodes.

The kubelet controls the Pod life cycle, acting like a mini-scheduler for the node. Once the Kubernetes scheduler updates the Pod with `NodeName`, the kubelet deploys that Pod to its node. The control plane is completely separated from the nodes that do not run the control plane components. Even with a control plane outage, Zeus Zap will not lose any application information if a node goes down. In a control plane outage, nothing new can be deployed, but the website is still up and running.

What if a persistent disk attached to the applications is required? In this case, it's likely that the storage continues to work for these applications, until and unless the nodes running these applications have problems. Even in this event, if the control plane is back online, we can generally expect a safe migration of both data and application to a new home, thanks to the commensurate functionality of the Kubernetes control plane.

2.3.3 Infrastructure controllers

One of the requirements for Zeus Zap's infrastructure is a CockroachDB cluster. CockroachDB is a Postgres-compliant distributed database that runs in a cloud native environment. Applications that are stateful, like databases, often have specific operational requirements. This leads to requiring a controller or an Operator to manage the application. Because the Operator pattern is quickly becoming the standard mechanism to deploy complex applications on Kubernetes, it is our advice to diverge from the use of plain YAML to installing and using an Operator instead. The following example installs an Operator for the CockroachDB:

```
$ kubectl apply -f https://raw.githubusercontent.com/
    cockroachdb/cockroach-operator/master/
    install/crds.yaml              ◁
$ kubectl apply -f https://raw.githubusercontent.com/
    cockroachdb/cockroach-operator/master/
    install/operator.yaml          ◁
```

Installs the custom resource definition utilized by the Operator

Installs the Operator in the default namespace

> ### Custom resource definitions
>
> *Custom resource definitions* (CRDs) are API objects that define new API objects. A user creates a CRD by defining it, which is often in YAML. The CRD is then applied to the existing Kubernetes cluster and actually allows the API to, in fact, create another API object. We can actually use a CRD to define and allow for new custom resource API objects.

After installing the CockroachDB Operator, we can then download the example.yaml. The following shows the `curl` command for this:

```
$ curl -LO https://raw.githubusercontent.com/cockroachdb/
        cockroach-operator/master/examples/example.yaml
```

The YAML snippet looks like this:

```
apiVersion: crdb.cockroachlabs.com/v1alpha1
kind: CrdbCluster
metadata:
  name: cockroachdb
spec:
  dataStore:
    pvc:
      spec:
        accessModes:
          - ReadWriteOnce
        resources:
          requests:
            storage: "60Gi"
        volumeMode: Filesystem
  resources:
    requests:
      cpu: "2"
      memory: "8Gi"
    limits:
      cpu: "2"
      memory: "8Gi"
  tlsEnabled: true
  image:
    name: cockroachdb/cockroach:v21.1.5    ◁──┐ The container that is used
  nodes: 3                                      to start the database
  additionalLabels:
    crdb: is-cool
```

This custom resource uses the Operator pattern to create and manage the following resources (note that these items are easily hundreds of lines of YAML):

- Transport Layer Security (TLS) keys stored in secrets for the database
- A StatefulSet that houses CockroachDB, including PersistentVolume and PersistentVolumeClaim storage

- Services
- A Pod disruption budget (PodDisruptionBudget or PDB)

Considering the example just given, let's dive into the infrastructure controller, called the Kubernetes controller manager (KCM) or the `kube-controller-manager` component, and the cloud controller manager (CCM). With a deployed StatefulSet built on Pods, we now need storage for the StatefulSet.

The API objects PersistentVolume (PV) and PersistentVolumeClaim (PVC) create the storage definitions and are brought to life by the KCM and the CCM. One of the key features for Kubernetes is the capability to run on top of a plethora of platforms: the cloud, bare metal, or a laptop. However, storage and other components are different across platforms: enter KCM and CCM. The KCM is a set of control loops that run various components, called *controllers*, on a node that is on a control plane. It is a single binary, but operates multiple control loops and, thus, controllers.

The birth of the cloud controller manager (CCM)

The Kubernetes development team is comprised of engineers from all around the world, united under the umbrella of the CNCF (Cloud Native Computing Foundation), which includes hundreds of corporate members. Supporting the needs of such a vast array of businesses is impossible without the decomposition of vendor-specific functionality into well-defined, pluggable components.

The KCM has historically been a tightly coupled and difficult-to-maintain codebase, primarily due to the accidental complexity of different vendor technologies. For example, provisioning new IP addresses or storage volumes requires completely different code paths, depending on whether you are in Google Kubernetes Engine (GKE) or Amazon Web Services (AWS). Given that there are also several bespoke, on-premise offerings of Kubernetes (vSphere, Openstack, and so on), a proliferation of cloud provider-specific code has persisted since the first days of Kubernetes.

The KCM codebase is located in the github.com repository kubernetes/kubernetes, which is often referred to as *kk*. There's nothing wrong with having a vast monorepo. Google has just one repo for the company, but the Kubernetes codebase monorepo outgrew GitHub and the use case of one company. At some point, the engineers working on Kubernetes collectively realized that they would need to decompose vendor-specific functionality as previously mentioned. One emerging component in this crusade was the creation of a CCM that generically utilized functionality from any vendor implementing the cloud provider interface (http://mng.bz/QWRv). Moreover, the same pattern is now used with the Kubernetes scheduler and scheduler plugins.

The CCM was designed to allow faster cloud provider development and creation of cloud providers. The CCM creates an interface that allows a cloud provider such as DigitalOcean to be developed and maintained outside of the primary Kubernetes GitHub repository. This restructuring of the repository allows the owners of the cloud provider to manage the code and enables the providers to move at a higher velocity. Each of the cloud providers now lives in their repositories outside of the Kubernetes host.

Since the Kubernetes v1.6 release, work started on moving functionality out of the KCM and into the CCM. CCM promises to make Kubernetes completely cloud-agnostic. This design represents a general trend in how Kubernetes architecture is evolving, being wholly decoupled from the implementations of any vendor-pluggable technologies.

When running Kubernetes on a cloud platform, Kubernetes interacts directly with the public or private cloud APIs, and the CCM executes the majority of those API calls. This component's purpose is to run cloud-specific controller loops and to execute cloud-based API calls. Here's a list of that functionality:

- *Node controller*—Runs the same code as the KCM
- *Route controller*—Sets up routes in the underlying cloud infrastructure
- *Service controller*—Creates, updates, and deletes cloud provider load balancers
- *Volume controller*—Creates, attaches, and mounts volumes and interacts with the cloud provider to orchestrate volumes

These controllers are transitioning to operating against the cloud provider interface, and this trend is pervasive throughout Kubernetes. Other interfaces that are evolving to support a more modular, vendor-neutral future for Kubernetes are

- *Container Networking Interface (CNI)*—Supplies Pods with IP addresses
- *Container Runtime Interface (CRI)*—Defines and plugs in different container execution engines
- *Container Storage Interface (CSI)*—A modular way for vendors to support new storage types without having to modify the Kubernetes codebase

Now, looping back to our example, storage is needed to attach to the CockroachDB Pods. When the Pod is scheduled on a node kubelet, KCM (or CCM) detects that new storage is required and creates the storage depending on what platform it is running on. It then mounts the storage on the node. When a kubelet creates the Pod, it determines which storage to attach, and the storage is attached to the container via the mnt Linux namespace. Now there is storage for our app.

Back to our user case: Zeus Zap also needs a load balancer for their public website. Creating a LoadBalancer Service instead of the ClusterIP Service involves a Kubernetes cloud provider "watching" for a user load-balancer request and then fulfilling it (for example, by making calls to a cloud API to provision an external IP address and binding it to internal Kubernetes service endpoints). From an end-user perspective, however, the request for this is quite simple:

```
apiVersion: v1
kind: Service
metadata:
  name: example-service
spec:
  selector:
    app: example
```

```
ports:
  - port: 8765
    targetPort: 9376
type: LoadBalancer
```

The KCM watch loop detects that a new load balancer is required and makes the API calls needed to create a load balancer in the cloud or calls a hardware load balancer external to the Kubernetes cluster. Within those API calls, the underlying infrastructure understands which nodes are part of the cluster and then routes traffic to the nodes. Once a call reaches a node, the software-defined network that is provided by the CNI provider then routes the traffic to the correct Pod.

2.4 Scaling, highly available applications, and the control plane

The scaling up and down of applications is the underlying mechanism for enabling highly available (HA) applications in the cloud, and especially in Kubernetes. Either you need more Pods to scale, or you need to redeploy Pods because you do not have enough Pods when a Pod or node experiences a failure. Executing kubectl scale can increase and decrease the amount of Pods that are running in a cluster. It operates directly on the ReplicaSets, StatefulSets, or other API objects that use Pods, depending on the input you provide to the command. For example:

```
$ kubectl scale --replicas 300 deployment zeus-front-end-ui
```

This command doesn't apply to DaemonSets. Although DaemonSet objects create Pods, they aren't scalable because, by definition, they run a single Pod on every node of a cluster: their scale is determined by the number of nodes in your cluster. In the Zeus scenario, this command increases or decreases the number of Pods backing the Zeus frontend UI deployment, following the same pattern that the scheduler, KCM, and kubelet followed for the previous example. Figure 2.6 shows the typical sequence for the kubectl scale command.

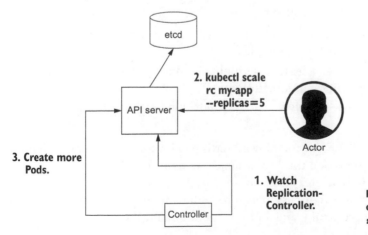

Figure 2.6 The sequence of operations for the kubectl scale command

Now, what happens when things go thud, which they always do? We can break up basic failures or actions into three levels: Pod, node, and software updates.

First, Pod outages. The kubelet is in charge of the Pod's life cycle, which includes starting, stopping, and restarting Pods. When a Pod fails, the kubelet attempts to restart it, and it knows that the Pod has failed either via the defined liveliness probe, or the Pod's process stops. We cover the kubelet in greater detail in chapter 9.

Second, node outages. One of the kubelet's control loops is constantly updating the API server, reporting that a node is healthy (via a heartbeat). In Kubernetes 1.17+, you can see how this heartbeat is maintained by looking at the `kube-node-lease` namespace of a running cluster. If a node does not update its heartbeat often enough, its status is changed to offline by the KCM's controller, and Pods are not scheduled for the node anymore. The Pods that did exist on the node are scheduled for deletion and then rescheduled to other nodes.

You can watch this process by manually running `kubectl cordon node-name` then `kubectl drain node-name`. A node has various conditions that are monitored: network unavailable, no frequent docker restarts, kubelet ready, and more. Any of these heartbeats that fail stop the scheduling of new Pods on the node.

Lastly, with software update outages, many websites and other services have scheduled downtime, but the big players on the web, like Facebook and Google, never have scheduled downtimes. Both of those companies use custom software that predates Kubernetes. Kubernetes is built to roll out both Kubernetes updates and new Pod updates without downtime. There is a huge caveat, however: the software that is running on a Kubernetes platform has to be durable in a manner that supports how Kubernetes restarts applications. If they are not durable enough for outages, data loss can occur.

Applications that are hosted on a Kubernetes platform must support graceful shutdown and then startup. For instance, if you have a transaction running inside an application, it needs to support either redoing the transaction in another replica of the application or restarting the transaction once the application is restarted. Upgrading a deployment is as easy as changing the image version in your YAML definition, which is usually just done in one of three ways:

- `kubectl edit`—Takes a Kubernetes API object as input and opens a local terminal to edit the API object in place
- `kubectl apply`—Takes a file as input and finds the API object corresponding to this file, replacing it automatically
- `kubectl patch`—Applies a small "patch" file that defines the differences for an object

In chapter 15, we'll look at full-blown YAML patching and application life cycle tooling. There, we'll approach this broad subject in a more holistic manner.

Upgrading a Kubernetes cluster is not trivial, but Kubernetes supports various patterns for upgrades. We'll discuss this more in the last chapter of the book, as this chapter is all about the control plane and not operational tasks.

2.4.1 Autoscaling

Manually scaling deployments is great, but what if you suddenly get 10,000 new web requests per minute on a cluster? Autoscaling comes to the rescue. You can allow three different forms of autoscaling:

- Make more Pods (horizontal Pod autoscaling with the HorizontalPodAutoscaler)
- Give Pods more resources (vertical Pod autoscaling with the VerticalPodAutoscaler)
- Create more nodes (with the Custer Autoscaler)

NOTE The autoscalers may or may not be available on some bare metal platforms.

2.4.2 Cost management

When a cluster autoscales, it automatically adds more nodes to the cluster, which means that more nodes equal a higher cloud usage cost. More nodes allow your applications to have more replicas and to handle more load, but then your bosses get the bill and want a solution to save more money. Herein enters Pod density—densely packed nodes.

Pods are the smallest, most basic unit of any Kubernetes application. They are a group of one or more containers sharing the same network. Nodes that host the Pods are either a VM or a physical server. The more Pods assigned to one node, the less spent on additional servers. Kubernetes allows for *higher pod density*, which is the ability to run over-provisioned and densely packed nodes. The Pod density is controlled via the following steps:

1. *Size and profile your applications*—Applications need to be tested and profiled for both memory and CPU usage. Once they are profiled, the resource limits in Kubernetes must be set properly and appropriately for that application.
2. *Pick a node size*—This allows you to pack multiple applications on the same node. Running different VM sizes or bare metal servers with different capacity allows you to save money and deploy more Pods on them. You still need to ensure a high enough node count to allow for high availability, meeting your SLA requirements.
3. *Group certain applications together on certain nodes*—This gives you the best density. If you have a bunch of marbles in a jar, you have a lot of space left in the jar. Adding some sand, or smaller applications, allows you to fill in some of the gaps. Taints and tolerations allow for Operator patterns to group and control Pod deployment.

Another factor you need to consider in all of this is *noisy neighbors*. Depending on your workload, some of this tuning may not be appropriate. Again, you can spread the noisy apps more evenly across your Kubernetes clusters using Pod affinity and anti-affinity definitions. We can explore even further cost savings using autoscaling and cloud-ephemeral VMs. Also, just hitting the off switch helps. Many companies have separate clusters for their development and QA environments. If you do not need your development environment running over the weekend, then why is it up? Simply reduce the number of worker nodes in the control plane to zero, and when you need the cluster back up, increase the worker node count.

Summary

- The Pod is the basic Kubernetes API object that uses Linux namespaces to create an environment to run one or more containers.
- Kubernetes was built to run the Pod in different patterns, which are API objects: Deployments, StatefulSets, and so forth.
- Controllers are software components that create and manage Pod life cycles. These include the kubelet, the cloud controller manager (CCM), and the scheduler.
- The control plane is the brain of Kubernetes. Through it, Kubernetes can bind storage to processes, create running containers, scale the number of containers, kill and migrate containers when they are unhealthy, create IP routes to ports, update load balanced endpoints, and regulate many other aspects of distributed application management.
- The API server (the `kube-apiserver` component) validates and provides the web frontend to perform CRUD operations on the cluster's shared state. Most control planes have the API server running on every node that comprises the control plane, providing the highly available (HA) cluster for the API server.

Let's build a Pod 3

This chapter gives you an introduction to building a Pod via several Linux *primitives* that already exist in your OS. These are the fundamental building blocks in the Linux OS for process management, and we'll soon learn that they can be used to build more sophisticated administrative programs or accomplish basic day-to-day tasks that require access to OS-level functionality in an ad hoc manner. The importance of these primitives is that they both inspire and implement many important aspects of Kubernetes.

We'll also look at the reasons why we need *CNI providers*, which are executable programs that provide Pods with IP addresses. Finally, we'll review the role the kubelet plays in starting a container. Let's begin with a little appetizer to contextualize what you'll learn in the next few sections.

> ### The Guestbook application sandbox
> In chapter 15, we'll go through a realistic Kubernetes application with a frontend, networking, and a backend. Don't hesitate to skip over to that chapter if you want a high-level overview of how Kubernetes Pods work from an application perspective.

Figure 3.1 demonstrates the nature of creating and running a Pod in Kubernetes. It's highly simplified, and we'll evolve some of the details in this figure in further chapters. For now, what's worth noting is that there's a long stretch of time between when a Pod is first created and when it is declared as being in a running state. Assuming you've run a few Pods yourself, you're probably well aware of this latency. What's going on during this time period? A flurry of Linux primitives that you likely don't use in your everyday life are getting summoned to create what is known as a *container*. In short

- The kubelet has to find out that it is supposed to be running a container.
- The kubelet (by talking to a container runtime) then launches a *pause container*, which gives the Linux OS time to create a network for a container. This pause container is the predecessor of the actual application that we'll run. It exists for the purpose of creating an initial home to bootstrap our new container network process and its process ID (PID).
- The state of the various components during startup oscillate as demonstrated in each swimlane in figure 3.1. For example, a CNI provider is mostly idle with the exception of the time it takes to bind the pause container to a network namespace.

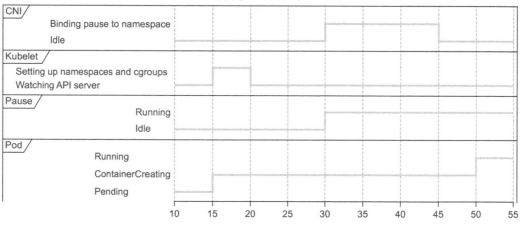

Figure 3.1   Bootstrapping with Linux primitives

In figure 3.1, the x-axis represents the relative timescale of a Pod's startup. Several operations take place over time, which involve the mounting of *subpaths* (the wiring of external storage directories that our container reads or writes). These occur in the same timeframe preceding the 30-second mark where our Pod enters the running state. As mentioned, various Linux commands use basic Linux primitives, triggered by the kubelet, in order to get a Pod into its ultimate running state.

Storage, bind mounts, and subpaths

Storage in Kubernetes Pods typically involves *bind mounting* (attaching a folder from one location to another location). This allows containers to "see" a directory at a specific subpath in their file tree. This is a basic Linux function that is commonly used when mounting an NFS share, for example, outside of the container world.

Bind mounts are used under the hood in all sorts of systems to implement a lot of Kubernetes critical functionality. This includes allowing access to storage for Pods. We can use tools like `nsenter` to investigate which directories are available to an isolated process, without actually relying on the usage of a container runtime (such as Docker or crictl).

Because `nsenter` is a simple Linux executable that operates against the base OS APIs, it's always usable regardless of whether or not you are in a particular Kubernetes distribution. Thus, you can use it even if Docker or crictl aren't available. For Windows clusters, of course, you can't rely on `nsenter`, and you might be more dependent on container runtime tooling when investigating low-level problems.

As an example of the foundational nature of these primitives, we can take a look at the comments for the following code that lives in the pkg/volume/util/subpath/subpath _linux.go file of Kubernetes itself, located here: http://mng.bz/8Ml2. This demonstrates the pervasiveness of these primitives in a Kubernetes implementation:

```
func prepareSubpathTarget(mounter mount.Interface,s Subpath)        Creates the target
(bool, string, error) { ... }                               ◄───── for the bind mount
                                                                    of a subpath
```

After the function `prepareSubpathTarget` creates the target for the subpath's bind mount, the subpath is then accessible inside a container, even though it is created on the kubelet. Previously, an `NsEnterMounter` function provided this functionality in order to accomplish various directory operations inside containers. You may not need to read this code again. However, it's informative to know that there are vestiges of nsenter referenced in Kubernetes itself.

Historically, `nsenter` was utilized at various times in Kubernetes to work around bugs or idiosyncrasies in how container runtimes managed storage. In much the same way, if you ever do run into an issue related to storage or directory mounting, it's nice to know there are Linux tools that can do the same thing as the kubelet and your container runtime, double-checking where a problem exists; nsenter is just one example of a simple Linux command.

3.1 *Looking at Kubernetes primitives with kind*

Let's get started with a simple cluster where we can prove a few of these concepts. There's no easier way to create a reference to the Kubernetes environment than by using kind (https://kind.sigs.k8s.io), a developer tool for Kubernetes. This will be the baseline for many of the experiments we do in this book.

First, we'll need to set up a simple Linux environment so we can explore such concepts. Because we'll use kind, this allows you to run Kubernetes clusters (single or multi-node) inside a container runtime, such as Docker Enginer. kind works on any OS by creating a new container for every node. We can compare a kind cluster to a real-world cluster, as table 3.1 demonstrates.

Table 3.1 Comparing kind to a "real" cluster

Cluster type	Administrator	Kubelet type	Swap-enabled
kind	You (the Docker user)	Docker container	Yes (not for production use)
GKE (Google Kubernetes Engine)	Google	A GCE (Google Compute Engine) node	No
Cluster API	A running master cluster	A VM in whatever provider cloud you've chosen	No

Table 3.1 compares the architecture of a kind cluster with the regular clusters we run in production. There are many aspects of kind that are not production-friendly. For example, because it enables swapping resources, this ultimately means containers might be utilizing disk space for their memory. This has obvious performance and compute costs that might be incurred if many containers suddenly need more memory to operate. The benefit of kind, however, is evident as an exercise where learning is the priority, and

- It costs nothing.
- It can be installed in seconds.
- It can be rebuilt in seconds, if needed.
- It can run basic Kubernetes functionality with no issues.
- It is capable of running almost any networking or storage provider, so it is realistic enough to get started with Kubernetes.

In our case, we'll use a kind Docker container to not only run a few Kubernetes examples, but also to use it as a lightweight Linux VM that we can hack around inside of. We'll conclude the chapter by diving into Kubernetes networking internals, looking at how we can use the iptables command to route traffic inside a Kubernetes cluster.

Setting up your computer

Before we get started, here's a quick note on setting up your computer. We assume you're comfortable using the https://kubernetes.io website and various search engines to find the most up-to-date information on how to install things, and that you have at least some basic Linux experience installing packages for some distribution. In general, we won't give you specific instructions for all of the minute tasks we carry out, but keep in mind that you will need a Linux environment to follow along in this chapter:

- If you are running Windows, you will need to install a VM with Linux on it using VMware Fusion, VirtualBox, or Hyper-V.
- If you are running Linux, you can try many of these examples with or without a `kind` cluster.
- If you are running a Mac, you can simply download the Docker desktop, and you'll be all set.

If you don't have all this set up yet, we encourage you to take the time to do so. If you are a Linux user, you probably are quite used to a DIY setup of different programming tools. For others, simply searching for "Running Linux containers on Windows" or "How to run Docker on OS X" will get you up and running within a few minutes. Almost every modern OS supports running Docker in one way or other.

3.2 What is a Linux primitive?

As mentioned previously, Linux primitives are the fundamental building blocks in the Linux OS. Tools like `iptables`, `ls`, `mount`, and many other basic programs available in most Linux distributions are examples of such primitives. You've almost surely used at least some of these commands before if you've worked on any kind of technology related to software development. For example, the `ls` command is one of the first tools anyone using a Linux terminal learns. It lists all the files in your current directory. If you send it an argument (such as `/tmp`, for example), then it lists all the files in that directory.

Knowing the basics of these tools gives you a powerful leg-up in understanding the myriad of new plugins and add-ons in the Kubernetes ecosystem. That's because they all are largely built on the same set of fundamental building blocks:

- *The network proxy,* `kube-proxy`, *creates iptables rules, and these rules are often inspected to debug container networking issues in large clusters.* Running `iptables -L` in a Kubernetes node illustrates this. Container Network Interface (CNI) providers also use this network proxy as well (for example, for various tasks related to Network-Policies implementation).
- *The Container Storage Interface (CSI) defines a socket for communication between the kubelet and storage technologies.* This includes resources such as Pure, GlusterFS, vSAN, Elastic Block Store (EBS), Network File System (NFS), and so on. For example, running `mount` in a cluster shows you the container and volume mounts managed by Kubernetes without relying on `kubectl` or any other

non-native OS tools, and, thus, is a common debugging technique when troubleshooting low-level storage errors in Kubernetes.

- *Container runtime commands like* unshare *and* mount *are used when creating isolated processes.* These often need to be run by technologies that create the container. The essential ability to run these commands (which often require root privileges) is an important security boundary when it comes to modeling threats in a Kubernetes cluster.

The way we access the ls tool is typically from a shell or by combining many shell commands together into a shell script. Many Linux commands can be run from the shell, and often they return textual output that can be used as input to the next command. The reason we often access ls as part of a broader script is so that we can combine it with other programs (for example, to run a command on all files in a directory). This brings us back to the topic of Kubernetes.

3.2.1 *Linux primitives are resource management tools*

An important part of system administration involves managing resources on a machine. Although ls seems like a simple program, it's also a powerful resource management tool in that regard. Administrators use this program daily to find large files or to check whether a user has the ability to do basic actions in cases of permissions errors reported by users or other programs. It allows us to find

- Whether we can access a certain file
- What files are available in an arbitrary directory
- What capabilities that file has (for example, can it be executed?)

Speaking of files, that brings us to the next aspect of Linux primitives: *everything is a file*. This is a key differentiator between Linux and other OSs such as Windows. In fact, when running Windows nodes in a Kubernetes cluster, the ability to inspect and monitor the status of events can be more complicated because there is no uniform representation of objects. For example, many Windows objects are stored in memory, accessible only through Windows APIs, and are not accessible through the filesystem.

"Everything is a file" is unique to Linux

In Windows, the administration of machines often requires editing the Windows Registry. This requires running custom programs and often using the Windows GUI. There are ways to perform many aspects of system administration using PowerShell and other tools; however, it is not generally possible to administer an entire Windows OS by simply reading and writing files.

In contrast, it is quite common for Linux administrators to perform almost all aspects of system administration by managing plain text files. For example, administrators are well aware of the /proc directory, which has real-time information about running processes. This can be managed as if it were just a directory of files in many ways, even though it is not a "normal" directory in any sense.

3.2.2 Everything is a file (or a file descriptor)

Linux primitives, in some sense, are almost always doing something to manipulate, move, or provide an abstraction over a file of some sort. This is because *everything* you'll need to build with Kubernetes was originally built to work on Linux, and Linux is entirely designed to use the file abstraction as a control primitive.

For example, the `ls` command operates on files. It looks at a file (which is a directory) and reads the filenames inside of that file. It then prints those strings to another file, known as *standard out*. Standard out is not a typical file that we would normally think about; rather, it is a file that, when written to, magically makes stuff show up in our terminals. When we say that in Linux everything is a file, we really mean it!

- *A directory is a file, but it contains the names of other files.*
- *Devices are also represented as files to the Linux kernel.* Because devices are accessible as files, this means that you can use commands like `ls` to confirm whether an Ethernet device, for example, is attached inside a container.
- *Sockets and pipes are also files, which processes can use locally for communications.* Later, we'll see how the CSI heavily utilizes this abstraction for defining a way that the kubelet can talk to volume providers, providing storage for our Pods.

3.2.3 Files are composable

Combining the previous concepts of files and resource management, we now come to the most important point about Linux primitives: they are composable into higher-level actions. Using a pipe (|), we can take the output from one command and process it in another command. One of the most popular incantations of this command is to combine `ls` with the `grep` commands to filter specific files and list them.

A common Kubernetes administration task, for example, might be to confirm that etcd is running and healthy inside a cluster. If running as a container, one can run the following command inside a node that's running the Kubernetes control plane components (which almost always run the critical etcd process):

```
$ ls /var/log/containers/ | grep etcd
etcd-kind-control-plane_kube-system_etcd-44daab302813923f188d864543c....log
```

Likewise, if you were on a Kubernetes cluster of unknown origin, you could find out where etcd-related configuration resources resided. You might run something like this:

```
$ find /etc | grep etcd; find /var | grep etcd
```

That's about as far as we can go with the theory. From here on out, we're going to get our hands dirty and run a lot of Linux commands that allow us to build our own Pod-like behavior from scratch. But before we go down that road, we'll use `kind` to set up a cluster that we can play with.

> **etcd in a container?**
>
> You may be wondering why etcd is running in a container. A brief note so as not to give you the wrong idea: In production clusters, it is common to run etcd in a place separate from the rest of your containers. This can prevent competition over precious disk and CPU resources. Many smaller or developer clusters, however, run all control-plane components in a single place for simplicity. That said, many Kubernetes solutions have demonstrated that etcd can run well in a container as long as the volumes for this container are stored on a local disk so that they are not lost on container restarts.

3.2.4   *Setting up kind*

With Kubernetes and Docker, `kind` is a clever tool maintained by the Kubernetes community. It builds Kubernetes clusters inside Docker containers with no other dependencies. This allows developers to simulate realistic clusters with many nodes locally, without needing to make VMs or use other heavy-weight constructs. It is not a production Kubernetes provider and is only used for development or research purposes. In order to follow along, we'll build some `kind` clusters, and for this chapter, our first cluster can be built by following the instructions at http://mng.bz/voVm.

`kind` installs in just a few seconds on any OS and allows us to run Kubernetes inside Docker. We'll treat each Docker container as a VM and execute into these containers to investigate various properties of Linux in general. The workflow for setting up kind as a basic Kubernetes hacking environment is simple:

1 Install Docker.
2 Install `kubectl` to */usr/local/bin/kubectl*.
3 Install `kind` to */usr/local/bin/kind*.
4 Test the installation by running `kubectl get pods`.

Why are we using `kind`? This book has a lot of examples, so if you want to run them yourself (which we encourage, but it isn't required for reading along), you'll need a Linux environment of some sort. And because we're talking about Kubernetes, we've gone with `kind` for the reasons stated earlier. However, if you are an advanced user, don't feel obligated to use `kind`. If you are familiar with a lot of this stuff and just want to dive in to get to the hard parts, you can also run many of these commands on any Kubernetes cluster. But, of course, we assume you'll be running these on some variant of Linux because cgroups, Linux namespaces, and other fundamental Kubernetes primitives aren't available on commercial OS distros like Windows and Mac OS X out of the box.

> ### Windows users
>
> `kind` is installable as a Windows executable. We encourage you to look at https://kind.sigs.k8s.io/docs/user/quick-start/. It even has Choco `install` commands that you can run. If you are a Windows user, you can run all the commands in this book inside Windows Subsystem for Linux (WSL 2), which is a lightweight Linux VM that can be run readily on any Windows machine.
>
> Note that you can also run `kubectl` as a Windows executable to connect to a remote cluster on any cloud as well. And, although we seem biased toward Linux and OS X in this book, we are fully supportive of you running these commands on a Windows machine!

Once `kind` is installed, you can create a cluster. To do that, use these commands:

```
$ kind delete cluster --name=kind        ◁──┐ Deletes the kind cluster if a
                                             │ previous cluster is running
Deleting cluster "kind" ...

$ kind create cluster        ◁──── Starts your kind cluster
Creating cluster "kind" ...
 ? Ensuring node image (kindest/node:v1.17.0) ?
 ? Preparing nodes ?
 ? Writing configuration ?
?? Starting control-plane ?
```

Now you can see the Pods running in the cluster. To get a list of the Pods, issue the command in the following code snippet, which also shows sample output from the command:

```
$ kubectl get pods   --all-namespaces
NAMESPACE            NAME                        READY   STATUS    AGE
kube-system          coredns-6955-6bb2z          1/1     Running   3m24s
kube-system          coredns-6955-82zzn          1/1     Running   3m24s
kube-system          etcd-kind-control-plane     1/1     Running   3m40s
kube-system          kindnet-njvrs               1/1     Running   3m24s
kube-system          kube-proxy-m9gf8            1/1     Running   3m24s
```

If you're wondering where your Kubernetes node is, you're in luck! It can be listed easily by simply asking Docker:

```
$ docker ps

CONTAINER ID         IMAGE                       COMMAND
776b91720d39         kindest/node:v1.17.0        "/usr/local/bin/entr…"

CREATED              PORTS                       NAMES
4 minutes ago        127.0.0.1:32769->6443/tcp   kind-control-plane
```

Finally, if you are a system administrator and want to be able to ssh into your nodes, you're also in luck. We can get into your Kubernetes node by running

```
$ docker exec -t -i 776b91720d39 /bin/sh
```

along with commands such as those shown earlier in this section. You would run these from inside the node (which is really a container).

By the way, you might be wondering how it is that Kubernetes can run in Docker. Does this mean that Docker containers can spin up other Docker containers? Absolutely. If you look at the Docker image for kind (http://mng.bz/nYg5), you can see exactly how it works. In particular, you can see all the Linux primitives it installs, which include some of the ones we've already discussed. Reading through this code is a great homework assignment to attempt after completing this chapter.

3.3   *Using Linux primitives in Kubernetes*

The way core features in Kubernetes work often links back, either indirectly or directly, to the way that basic Linux primitives work. These primitives form a scaffold for running containers that you will continually come back to after you understand them. Over time, you'll find that many technologies that use buzzwords like "service mesh" or "container native storage" boil down to cleverly assembled menageries of the same basic fundamental OS functionality.

3.3.1   *The prerequisites for running a Pod*

As a reminder, a *Pod* is the fundamental execution unit in a Kubernetes cluster: it is the way that we define containers that will run in our data center. Although there are theoretical scenarios where one might use Kubernetes for tasks other than running containers, we're not concerned with such outliers in this book. After all, we assume you are interested in running and understanding Kubernetes in a traditional context like the rest of us on planet earth.

In order to create a Pod, we rely on the ability to implement isolation, networking, and process management. These constructs can be achieved by using the many utilities already available in the Linux OS. In fact, some of these utilities might be considered *required* functionality, without which a kubelet would not be able to do the necessary tasks to start a Pod. Let's take a quick look at some of the programs (or *primitives*) that we rely on daily in our Kubernetes clusters:

- swapoff—A command that disables memory swapping, which is a known prerequisite for running Kubernetes in a manner that honors CPU and memory settings.
- iptables—A core requirement (usually) of the network proxy, which creates iptables rules to send service traffic to our Pods.

- `mount`—This command (mentioned earlier) projects a resource to a particular location in your path (for example, it allows you to expose a device as a folder in your home directory).
- `systemd`—This command usually starts the kubelet, which is the core process that runs in a cluster to manage all your containers.
- `socat`—This command allows you to establish a bidirectional stream of information between processes; `socat` is an essential part of how the `kubectl port-forward` command works.
- `nsenter`—A tool for entering into various namespaces of a process so you can see what's going on (from a networking, storage, or process perspective). In the same way that a namespace in Python has certain modules with local names, a Linux namespace has certain resources that aren't locally addressable from the outside world. For example, the unique IP address of a Pod in a Kubernetes cluster is not shared by other Pods, even on the same node, because each Pod (usually) runs in a separate namespace.
- `unshare`—A command that allows a process to create child processes running in isolation from a network, mount, or PID perspective. We'll use it thoroughly in this chapter to explore the famous *Pid 1 phenomenon* in containers, where every container in a Kubernetes cluster thinks it's the only program in the entire world.

   `unshare` can also isolate mounts (the / location) and network namespaces (the IP addresses), and thus is the most direct analog to `docker run` that exists in a raw Linux OS.
- `ps`—A program that lists running processes. The kubelet needs to continually monitor processes to find out when they exited and so on. By using `ps` to list processes, you can determine if there are "zombie" processes in your cluster or if a privileged container has gone rogue (creating many new subprocesses) and so on.

3.3.2 Running a simple Pod

Before we see how to utilize these commands, let's take a look at a Pod, using our `kind` cluster to create it. Normally, you wouldn't manually create a Pod but, rather, a Deployment, a DaemonSet, or a Job. For now, it's best to leave those high-level constructs out and create a simple, lonely Pod. We'll create a Pod by running `kubectl create -f pod.yaml` after composing the YAML file in the following code snippet. But before we create it, let's go over two quick notes about this YAML file so as not to confuse you:

- *If you're wondering what the BusyBox image is all about, the BusyBox Pod is just a minimal Linux image that you can run to investigate default container behavior.* Although examples oftentimes use the NGINX Pod as a standard, we choose BusyBox because it comes with the `ip a` command and bundles other basic utilities. Often times, production-grade microservices strip binaries from their containers to reduce potential vulnerability footprints.
- *If you're wondering why we define a* `webapp-port`, *you're on the right track!* It serves no purpose other than to help get you familiar with the syntax of a Pod definition. We're not running any service on port 80, but if you were to replace this image with something like NGINX, that port would then be a load-balanced endpoint that you can use to point to a Kubernetes service.

```
$ cat << EOF > pod.yaml
apiVersion: v1
kind: Pod
metadata:
  name: core-k8s
  labels:            ◄──────┤  The label's metadata lets us select this Pod
                              as a load-balancer target or as a filter in a
                              query to the Kubernetes API server.
    role: just-an-example
    app: my-example-app
    organization: friends-of-manning
    creator: jay
spec:
  containers:                       This docker.io image name has to be real
    - name: any-old-name-will-do    and pullable from the internet or tagged
      image: docker.io/busybox:latest  ◄──  as a local container image.
    command: ['sleep','10000']
      ports:
        - name: webapp-port
          containerPort: 80
          protocol: TCP
EOF
                              ┌─  Creates the Pod in the Kubernetes
$ kubectl create -f pod.yaml  ◄──┘  default namespace
```

Not to be confused with the `kind` tool we used to create this cluster, the `kind` API field in our Pod definition tells the API server when we create this Pod what type of API object it is. If we enter the wrong thing here (for example, `Service`), then the API server tries to create a different object. Thus, the first part of defining our Pod is defining it as a type (or *kind*) of Pod. Later, in this section, we will run a command to see the routing and IP configuration of this Pod, so keep this snippet handy!

After creating the Pod, let's look at the visibility of its processes to our OS when started. It is, indeed, registered in the OS. The following `ps -ax` command is a quick and simple way to list all processes on a system, including those that might not have a terminal. The *x* is particularly important because we are dealing with systems rather than user-level software, and we want a global count of all programs running to illustrate process visibility for pedagogical reasons:

```
$ ps -ax | wc -l          ◁──┐  Counts how many processes
706                            │  were run originally

$ kubectl create -f pod.yml   ◁──┐  Creates a Pod
pod "core-k8s" deleted            │

$ ps -ax | wc -l          ◁──┐  Counts how many processes are
707                            │  running after Pod creation
```

3.3.3 Exploring the Pod's Linux dependencies

We've now run a Pod in a cluster. This Pod runs a program, which needs access to fundamental compute units like CPU, memory, disk, and so on. How does this Pod differ from a regular program? Well, from an end-user perspective, it's no different at all. For example, like any normal program, our Pod

- Uses shared libraries or OS-specific low-level utilities, allowing it to consume keyboard input, list files, and so on.
- Has access to a client that can work with an implementation of the TCP/IP stack so that network calls and receipts can be made. (These are often called *system calls.*)
- Needs some kind of memory address space to guarantee that other programs won't overwrite its memory.

When creating this Pod, the kubelet does many of the same activities that anyone might undertake when attempting to run a computer program on a server. It

- Creates an isolated home for the program to run in (with CPU, memory, and namespace limitations)
- Ensures that its home has a working Ethernet connection
- Gives the program access to some basic files for resolving DNS or for accessing storage
- Tells the program it's safe to move in and start up
- Waits for the program to exit
- Cleans up the program's house and used resources

We'll find that almost everything we do in Kubernetes is a replication of regular, old administrative tasks that we've been doing for decades. In other words, the kubelet is just running the Linux system administrator's playbook for us.

We can visualize this process as a Pod *life cycle*, a cyclical process that reflects the fundamental control loop, which defines what the kubelet itself continually does while it's running (figure 3.2). Because containers in a Pod can die at any time, there is a control loop to bring them back to life in these cases. Such control loops happen in a "fractal" way throughout Kubernetes. In fact, one might say Kubernetes itself is just an intricately organized collection of clever control loops that allow us to run and manage containers at large scale in an automated fashion.

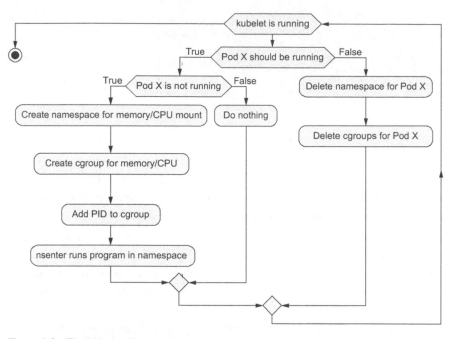

Figure 3.2   The kubelet/Pod life cycle control loop

One of the lowest-level control loops is the kubelet/Pod life cycle itself. In figure 3.2, we represent the termination of the kubelet as a dot. As long as the kubelet runs, there is a continuous reconciliation loop, where we can check for Pods and start them. Although we reference `nsenter` again as one of the downstream actions of the kubelet, note that the use of `nsenter` (which can run and manage containers on Linux), is not going to translate to other container runtimes or OSs.

As we will learn shortly, a Pod can be attained ultimately as the result of running a variety of these commands in the right order at the right time to enable the lovely features we discussed in our previous chapter. The result of our newly created Pod shows several status fields, which are worth inspecting.

Where does Docker fit into all of this?

If you're somewhat new to Kubernetes, you might be wondering when we're going to start talking about Docker. Actually, we won't talk much about Docker at all, as it's increasingly a developer tool that is not relevant to server-side container solutions.

Although Kubernetes shipped with native-Docker support for many years, as of Kubernetes 1.20, the deprecation process for supporting Docker explicitly is well under way, and eventually, Kubernetes itself will have no knowledge whatsoever of any container runtime. Thus, although the kubelet maintains the life cycle of Pods in terms of their resource usage, it defers to an interface known as the CRI (Container Runtime Interface) to start and stop Pods, as well as to pull down images for containers.

The most common implementation of the CRI is *containerd*, and in fact, Docker itself uses containerd under the hood. The CRI represents some (but not all) of containerd's functionality in a minimal interface, making it easy for people to implement their own container runtimes for Kubernetes. The standard containerd executable presents the kubelet with a CRI, and when this CRI is called, containerd (the service) calls programs like runc (for Linux containers) or hcsshim (for Windows containers), again, under the hood.

Once a Pod is running in Kubernetes (or, at least, once Kubernetes knows it's supposed to be running a Pod), you can see that the Pod object in the API server has new status information. On your own, try running the following to see this information:

```
$ kubectl get pods -o yaml
```

You'll see a large YAML file. Because we promised our Pod its own IP address and a healthy place to run its processes, let's now confirm these resources are available. We do this by using jsonpath in our query to find specific details.

INSPECTING A POD USING JSONPATH

Filtering out the attributes from status, let's take a look at a few of these fields. In the meanwhile, we'll also use the JSONPath functionality of Kubernetes to filter the specific information we want. For example:

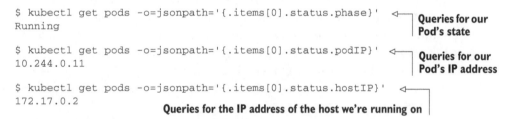

```
$ kubectl get pods -o=jsonpath='{.items[0].status.phase}'
Running
```
Queries for our Pod's state

```
$ kubectl get pods -o=jsonpath='{.items[0].status.podIP}'
10.244.0.11
```
Queries for our Pod's IP address

```
$ kubectl get pods -o=jsonpath='{.items[0].status.hostIP}'
172.17.0.2
```
Queries for the IP address of the host we're running on

> **NOTE** You may notice that, in addition to the new status information on your pod.yaml, you also have some new information in its spec stanza. This is because the API server may need to fix a few elements of your Pod before submitting it. For example, things like terminationMessagePath and dnsPolicy, which often require no changes by a user, can be added for you after you define your Pod. In some organizations, you may also have a customized admission controller in place, which "looks" at incoming objects and modifies them before they are passed to your API server (for example, to add hard CPU or memory limits on containers in large data centers).

In any case, using the previous commands

- We can see our Pod is being monitored by the OS, and it's status is Running.
- We can see that the Pod lives in a separate IP space (called a network namespace) from our host, 10.244.0.11/16.

INSPECTING THE DATA THAT WE MOUNTED INTO OUR POD

One such field that Kubernetes graciously gives to all its Pods is the `default-token`. volume. This gives our Pods a certificate allowing them to communicate to the API server and to "phone home." In addition to Kubernetes volumes, we also give our Pods DNS information. To view this, you can run `mount` inside the Pod by executing `kubectl exec`. For example:

```
$ kubectl exec -t -i core-k8s mount | grep resolv.conf
/dev/sda1 on /etc/resolv.conf type ext4 (rw,relatime)
```

In this example, we can see that the *mount* command, when run inside our container, actually shows that the file /etc/resolv.conf (which tells Linux where DNS servers are located) is mounted from another location. This location (/dev/sda1) is where the volume resides on our host, which has the corresponding resolv.conf file. In fact, in our example, there are other entries in `mount` for other files, many of which are actually symbolically linked back to our /dev/sda1 directory on the host. This directory usually corresponds to a folder in /var/lib/containerd. You can locate this file by running

```
$ find /var/lib/containerd/ -name resolv.conf
```

Don't get too hung up on this detail. It's part of the underlying implementation of the kubelet, but it's nice to know that these files do exist on your system and can be found in a pinch using standard Linux tools (if your cluster is behaving badly, for instance).

In a VM, the *hypervisor* (the thing that makes VMs) has no idea what processes VMs are running. In a containerized environment, however, all processes made by containerd (or Docker or any other container runtime) are actively managed by the OS itself. This allows the kubelet to do a lot of fine-grained cleanup and management tasks, and it also allows the kubelet to expose important information about container status to the API server.

More importantly, this indicates to us that you as an administrator, and indeed the kubelet itself, are capable of managing and querying processes, inspecting volumes for those processes, and even killing those processes when necessary. Although some of this might be obvious to you, we illustrate this because we want to drive home the point that in most Linux environments, the things we call containers are just processes created with a few isolated bells and whistles that enable them to play nicely with hundreds of other processes in a microservices cluster. Pods and processes alike aren't necessarily all that different from regular programs that you might run. In summary, our Pod

- *Has a storage volume with a certificate for accessing our API server.* This gives Pods, in general, a simple way to access the internal Kubernetes API if they want to. It is also the basis for the Operator or Controller patterns, which allow Kubernetes Pods to create other Pods, services, and so on.

- *Has an IP address in the 10 subnet that is specific to it.* This isn't the same as the host IP address in the 172 subnet.
- *Serves traffic on port 80 of its internal namespace on the IP address 10.244.0.11.* Other Pods in our cluster can access this as well.
- *Runs happily in our cluster.* It now has a container with a unique PID that is entirely manageable and visible to our host.

Note that we have yet to do something with iptables for routing traffic to our Pod. When you create a Pod without a service, you don't actually set up networking in the way Kubernetes is usually designed. Although our Pod's IP address is findable within the cluster, there is no way to load balance traffic to our Pod's various other brothers and sisters. For this, we need labels and label selectors associated with services. We will address Kubernetes networking later in chapter 4.

Now that you've explored the basic functionality of a simple Pod in a real cluster, we'll look at how we can build this functionality on our own by using basic Linux primitives. Going through the process of building this functionality *without a cluster* exposes you to many core competencies that will improve your understanding of how a Kubernetes installation works, how to administer large clusters, and how to troubleshoot container runtimes in the wild. Strap in and get ready for an exciting ride!

3.4 *Building a Pod from scratch*

We're about to go back in time as we're going to attempt to build a container management system before the existence of Kubernetes. Where should we start? We've previously gone over four fundamental aspects of our Pod, in particular

- Storage
- IP addressing
- Network isolation
- Process identification

We'll have to use our base Linux OS to implement this functionality. Fortunately, our `kind` cluster already has a basic Linux OS that we can use locally, so we don't need to create a dedicated Linux VM for this exercise.

Will this Pod actually work?

This isn't the type of Pod you'd run in the real world; it will be fraught with manual hacks, and the process we follow to build it won't scale to production workloads. But, at the kernel of what we do here, we will be reflecting the same process that the kubelet goes through when creating containers in any cloud or data center.

Let's get into our `kind` cluster and start hacking! This can easily be done by listing your `kind` container ID by running `docker ps | grep kind | cut -d' ' -f 1` and then by running `docker exec -t -i container_id /bin/sh` to jump into one of these nodes. Because we will edit a text file in our `kind` cluster, let's install the Vim editor or any other editor you might be used to with the following:

```
root@kind-control-plane:/# sudo apt-get update -y
root@kind-control-plane:/#  apt-get install vim
```

In case you're new to Kubernetes and `kind` (and your head is spinning here), yes, you're right; we're doing some meta stuff right now. Essentially, we are simulating a real cluster as well as the SSH debugging that we all know and love. The methodology of running `docker exec` on a `kind` cluster container is (roughly) the equivalent of ssh'ing into a real Kubernetes node in a real cluster.

3.4.1 *Creating an isolated process with chroot*

To begin, we'll create a container in the most distilled sense—a folder that has exactly what it needs to run a Bash shell and absolutely nothing else (as figure 3.3 shows). This is done using the famous `chroot` command. (In its early days, Docker was referred to as "chroot on steroids.")

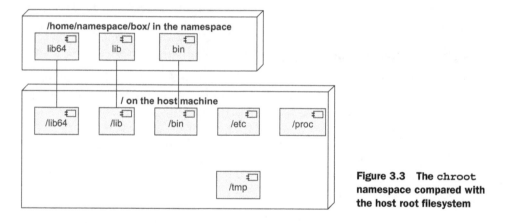

Figure 3.3 The `chroot` namespace compared with the host root filesystem

The purpose of `chroot` is to create an isolated root for a process. There are three steps to this:

1. Decide what program you want to run and where on your filesystem it should run.
2. Create an environment for the process to run. There are many Linux programs that live in the lib64 directory, which are required to run even something like Bash. These need to be loaded into the new root.
3. Copy the program you want to run to the chrooted location.

Finally, you can run your program, and it will be in perfect filesystem isolation. This means that it won't be able to see or touch other information on your filesystem (it won't be able to edit files in /etc/ or /bin/, for example).

Sound familiar? It should! When we run Docker containers, whether in Kubernetes or not, we always have this type of clean, isolated environment to run in. In fact, if you take a gander at issues in Kubernetes itself, you're guaranteed to find many past and present issues and questions around `chroot`-based functionality. Now, let's see how `chroot` works by running a Bash terminal in a chrooted namespace.

The following script creates a box where we can run a Bash script or other Linux program. This has no other visibility into the broader system and no conflicts, meaning that if we want to run `rm -rf /` inside the box, we can do so without destroying all the files in our actual OS. Of course, we don't recommend you try this at home, unless you're on a disposable machine, because one tiny mistake might end up in a lot of data loss. For our purposes, we'll store this script locally as chroot.sh, in case we want to reuse it:

```
#/bin/bash
mkdir /home/namespace/box

mkdir /home/namespace/box/bin
mkdir /home/namespace/box/lib
mkdir /home/namespace/box/lib64

cp -v /usr/bin/kill /home/namespace/box/bin/
cp -v /usr/bin/ps /home/namespace/box/bin
cp -v /bin/bash /home/namespace/box/bin
cp -v /bin/ls /home/namespace/box/bin

cp -r /lib/* /home/namespace/box/lib/
cp -r /lib64/* /home/namespace/box/lib64/

mount -t proc proc /home/namespace/box/proc

chroot /home/namespace/box /bin/bash
```

Makes our box with the bin and lib directories as dependencies for our Bash program

Copies all the programs from our base OS into this box so we can run Bash in our root directory

Copies the library dependencies of these programs into the lib/ directories

Mounts the /proc directory to this location

This is the important part: we start our isolated Bash process in a sandboxed directory.

Remember that our root directory's forward slash (/) will not have any programs that we don't explicitly load. This means that / has no global access to our regular Linux path, where normal programs you run every day live. Thus, in the previous code example, we copied `kill` and `ps` (two essential programs) directly into our /home/namespace/box/bin directory. And because we mounted the /proc directory into our chrooted process, we can see and access the processes in our host. This allows us to use `ps` to explore the security boundaries of our chrooted process. At this point, you should see that

- Some commands like `cat` or `ps` aren't available in our chrooted process, while `ps` and `kill` will be runnable as in any Linux OS.
- Other commands that run (like `ls /`) return quite different results than what you'd normally see in a full-blown OS.
- Unlike what you might see when running a VM on your host, there is no increased performance cost or latency to running or executing things in this chrooted environment, because it's just a regular Linux command. In case you didn't run this on your own, the results look something like this:

```
root@kind-control-plane:/# ./chroot0.sh
'/bin/bash' -> '/home/namespace/box/bin/bash'
'/bin/ls' -> '/home/namespace/box/bin/ls'
'/lib/x86_64-linux-gnu/libtinfo.so.6' ->
    '/home/namespace/box/lib/libtinfo.so.6'
'/lib/x86_64-linux-gnu/libdl.so.2' ->
    '/home/namespace/box/lib/libdl.so.2'
'/lib64/ld-linux-x86-64.so.2' ->
    '/home/namespace/box/lib/ld-linux-x86-64.so.2'

bash-5.0# ls
bin  lib  lib64
```

It is instructive to run `ls` from the root of a Linux OS if you have one around as a comparison. When you're done exploring your barren `chroot` desert, go ahead and type `exit` to return to your regular OS. Whew, that was scary!

Isolated `chroot` environments are on the most foundational building blocks of the container revolution that we live in today, although it was known for quite some time as "the poor man's VM." The chroot command is often used by Linux administrators and Python developers to perform isolated testing and to run specific programs. If you read the earlier section with the "chroot on steroids" reference, maybe this is now beginning to make sense.

3.4.2 *Using mount to give our process data to work with*

Containers typically need access to storage that lives elsewhere: in the cloud or on a host machine. The `mount` command allows you to take a device and expose it to any directory under the / (root) directory in your OS. You typically use `mount` to expose disks as folders. In our running `kind` cluster, for example, issuing `mount` shows us several folders managed by Kubernetes, which are exposed to specific containers in a specific location.

The simplest use of `mount` from an administrative perspective is to create a well-known, constant folder location for a disk point that can live in some other arbitrary place. For example, let's say we want to run the previous program, but we want it to write data to a temporary place that we can scrap later. We could do a simple operation such as `mount --bind /tmp /home/namespace/box/data` to create a /data directory in the previous chrooted program. Then, any user in that namespace would conveniently have a /data directory which they can use to access files in our /tmp directory.

Note that this opens up a security hole! After we mount the contents of /tmp to containers, anybody can now manipulate or read its contents. This is actually why the `hostPath` functionality of Kubernetes volumes is often disabled in production clusters. In any case, let's confirm that we can get some data into our container that we created in the last section using a few basic Linux primitives:

```
root@kind-control-plane:/# touch /tmp/a
root@kind-control-plane:/# touch /tmp/b
root@kind-control-plane:/# touch /tmp/c
```

```
root@kind-control-plane:/# ./chroot0.sh
'/bin/bash' -> '/home/namespace/box/bin/bash'
'/bin/ls' -> '/home/namespace/box/bin/ls'
'/lib/x86_64-linux-gnu/libtinfo.so.6' ->
   '/home/namespace/box/lib/libtinfo.so.6'
'/lib/x86_64-linux-gnu/libdl.so.2' ->
   '/home/namespace/box/lib/libdl.so.2'
'/lib64/ld-linux-x86-64.so.2' ->
   '/home/namespace/box/lib/ld-linux-x86-64.so.2'
bash-5.0# ls data
a   b   c
```

And there you have it! You've now created something that's much like a container and that now has access to storage. We'll look at the more advanced aspects of container-ization later, including namespaces for protecting CPU, memory, and network-related resources. Now, just for fun, let's run ps and see what other processes are floating around in our container. Notice that we'll see ours and a few other processes:

```
bash-5.0# ps
  PID TTY          TIME CMD
 5027 ?        00:00:00 sh
79455 ?        00:00:00 bash
79557 ?        00:00:00 ps
```

3.4.3 *Securing our process with unshare*

Great! So far, we've created a sandbox for our process and a folder that can penetrate the sandbox. Seems pretty close to a Pod, right? Not yet. Although our chrooted pro-gram is isolated from other files (for example, when we run ls inside of it, we only see the files explicitly mounted in the chroot0.sh script), is it secure? It turns out that put-ting blinders on a process isn't quite the same as securing it. As a quick example

1 Run ps -ax inside your kind cluster by having Docker execute into it as we did earlier.
2 Grab the ID of the kubelet (for example, 744). To make this easier, you can run ps -ax | grep kubelet.
3 Run the chroot0.sh namespace script again.
4 Run kill 744 at the bash-5.0# prompt.

You'll immediately see that you just killed the kubelet! Even though our chrooted pro-cess couldn't access other folders (because we moved the location of / to a new root), it can find and kill critical system processes in one fell swoop. Thus, if this was our con-tainer, we would have definitely just found a CVE (Common Vulnerabilities and Expo-sures) liability that could bring down an entire cluster.

   If you want to be really naughty, you can even kill this process by running kill 74994. This results in the bash-5.0#-terminated line being printed in a final gasp by your unsuspecting chroot0.sh process. Thus, not only can other processes see the chroot0 process, but they have the power to kill and control it as well. This is where the unshare command comes into play.

Recall when we "looked around" and saw a few Pods with larger numbers for their PIDs? This tells us that our process is able to access the proc directory to see what's going on. One of the first problems you might need to solve if building a production containerization environment is *isolation*. If you run `ps -ax` from this inside of this process, it will be immediately obvious why isolation is important to solve; if a container has full access to the host, it could damage it permanently, for example, by killing the kubelet process or deleting system-critical files.

Using the `unshare` command, however, we can use `chroot` to run Bash in an isolated terminal with a truly disengaged process space. That is, this time, we won't be able to kill the kubelet. The following example uses the `unshare` command to accomplish this bit of isolation:

```
# Note that this won't work if you've already unmounted this directory.
root@kcp:/# unshare -p -f
            --mount-proc=/home/namespace/box/proc         Creates a new shell running
            chroot /home/namespace/box /bin/bash     ◄——  in a namespace

bash-5.0# ps -ax
PID TTY      STAT    TIME COMMAND      ◄——    Observes all processes visible to the
1   ?        S       0:00 /bin/bash           namespace; seems kind of low, right?
2   ?        R+      0:00 ps -ax
```

Wow! Our previous process thought it was running as 79455, but now it's running in the exact same container. This process started with the `unshare` command actually "thinking" that its PID is 1. Normally, PID 1 is the process ID of the first thing that comes alive in your OS (systemd). Thus, this time around, by using `unshare` to launch `chroot`, we have

- An isolated process
- An isolated filesystem
- The ability to still edit specific files from our filesystem in /tmp

This is now beginning to look a lot like a Kubernetes Pod. In fact, if you exec into any running Kubernetes Pod, you'll see a similar PS (Process Status) table.

3.4.4   *Creating a network namespace*

Although the previous command isolated the process from our other processes, it still uses the same network. If we want to run the same program with a new network, we can again use the `unshare` command:

```
root@kind-control-plane:/# unshare -p -n -f
  --mount-proc=/home/namespace/box/proc chroot /home/namespace/box /bin/bash
bash-5.0# ip a
1: lo: <LOOPBACK> mtu 65536 qdisc noop state DOWN group default...
    link/loopback 00:00:00:00:00:00 brd 00:00:00:00:00:00
2: tunl0@NONE: <NOARP> mtu 1480 qdisc noop state DOWN group default...
    link/ipip 0.0.0.0 brd 0.0.0.0
3: ip6tnl0@NONE: <NOARP> mtu 1452 qdisc noop state DOWN group default...
    link/tunnel6 :: brd ::
```

If we compare this Pod with a real Pod running in a normal Kubernetes cluster, we will see a single, more important distinction: the lack of a functioning `eth0` device. If we were to run our earlier BusyBox Pod with the `ip a` (which we will do in the next section), we would see a much more vibrant network with a usable `eth0` device. This is the difference between a container that has a network (often known as a CNI in the Kubernetes world) and a chrooted process. As mentioned earlier, chrooted processes are the heart of containerization, Docker, and ultimately, Kubernetes itself, but they aren't in and of themselves useful for running containerized applications because of these much needed accoutrements.

3.4.5 *Checking whether a process is healthy*

As an exercise for you, run `exit` and get back into your regular terminal in our `kind` cluster. Do you notice a difference between the output of `ip a`? You certainly should! In fact, if you run in an isolated network, the cURL program (whose command can be copied in just like `kill` and `ls`) will not work to pull down information from outside addresses, whereas it works just fine when running inside the original chrooted namespace. The reason is that when we created a new network namespace, we lost the routing and IP information for our container, which was inherited from the `hostNetwork` namespace. To demonstrate this, run `curl 172.217.12.164` (this is the static IP address of google.com) in these two scenarios:

- Running chroot0.sh
- Running the previous `unshare` command

In both cases, you are running a chrooted process; however, in the latter case, the process has a new network and process namespace. Although the process namespace seems to be OK, the network namespace looks a little empty compared to a typical real-world process (for example, there's no meaningful IP information in the previous example). Let's take a look at what a "real" container networking stack looks like.

Let's recreate our original pod.yaml that ran a BusyBox container. This time, we'll take a look at its networking information and then we can ruthlessly delete it again. Note that there have been cases where CNI providers exhibit bugs when restarting containers fast. In that case, containers are launched without an IP address. This comparison is an important one to keep in mind when debugging container networking errors in production scenarios. Concretely, the restarting of StatefulSet containers, which are meant to preserve IP addresses, is a common scenario wherein a container's networking stack might, unfortunately, resemble the previous scenario. The following code illustrates what a container has for a network (as contrasted with our chrooted process in the previous section):

```
$ kubectl delete -f pod.yaml ;        ◁——┐ Creates the original pod.yaml example
    kubectl create -f pod.yaml              from earlier in this chapter
$ kubectl exec -t -i core-k8s ip a                    ◁————————┐ Runs a command
                                                                to list its network
1: lo: <LOOPBACK,UP,LOWER_UP> mtu 65536 qdisc noqueue qlen 1    interfaces
```

```
     link/loopback 00:00:00:00:00:00 brd 00:00:00:00:00:00
     inet 127.0.0.1/8 scope host lo
        valid_lft forever preferred_lft forever
     inet6 ::1/128 scope host
        valid_lft forever preferred_lft forever
2: tun10@NONE: <NOARP> mtu 1480 qdisc noop qlen 1
     link/ipip 0.0.0.0 brd 0.0.0.0
3: ip6tnl0@NONE: <NOARP> mtu 1452 qdisc noop qlen 1
     link/tunnel6 00:00:00:00:00:00:00:00:00:00:00:00:00:00:00:00
     brd 00:00:00:00:00:00:00:00:00:00:00:00:00:00:00:00
5: eth0@if10: <BROADCAST,MULTICAST,UP,LOWER_UP,M-DOWN>
        mtu 1500 qdisc noqueue
     link/ether 4a:9b:b2:b7:58:7c brd ff:ff:ff:ff:ff:ff
     inet 10.244.0.7/24 brd 10.244.0.255 scope global eth0
        valid_lft forever preferred_lft forever
     inet6 fe80::489b:b2ff:feb7:587c/64 scope link
        valid_lft forever preferred_lft forever
```

We see a stark contrast here. In the previous process namespace, where we couldn't even run a simple curl command, we had no eth0 device, but in this container, we clearly do. You can delete this pod.yaml file if you want. And, as usual, there's no need for any hard feelings—BusyBox containers don't take themselves too seriously.

We'll revisit some networking concepts again in the context of iptables and IP routing later in this chapter. First, let's finish our initial tour of Linux container creation primitives. Then we'll look at the most commonly toggled parameter for typical Kubernetes applications in production: cgroup's limits.

3.4.6   Adjusting CPU with cgroups

Control groups (abbreviated as *cgroups*) are those knobs we all know and love. These allow us to give more or less CPU and memory to applications running in our clusters, which need that extra boost of vigor. If you run Kubernetes at work, you've likely turned these knobs on and off before. We can easily amend our earlier BusyBox container to use more or less CPU by issuing the following:

```
$ cat << EOF > greedy-pod.yaml
apiVersion: v1
kind: Pod
metadata:
  name: core-k8s-greedy
spec:
  containers:
    - name: any-old-name-will-do
      image: docker.io/busybox:latest
      command: ['sleep','10000']
      resources:          ←——  Tells Kubernetes to create
       limits:                  a cgroup to limit (or not)
          memory: "200Mi"       available CPU
        requests:
          memory: "100Mi"
EOF
```

3.4.7 *Creating a resources stanza*

We'll manually walk through the steps that the kubelet goes through when we define a cgroup's limits. Note that the actual way that this is defined can be configured in any given Kubernetes distribution by the `--cgroup-driver` flag. (*Cgroup drivers* are the architectural components in Linux that are used to allocate cgroup resources, and typically, we use systemd as the Linux driver.) Nevertheless, the core logical steps of running a container in Kubernetes, which involve making a suitable sandbox for the process to execute inside of, are essentially the same, even if you deviate from a traditional containerd/Linux architecture. In fact, with Windows kubelets, the same `resources` stanza is honored using an entirely different set of implementation details. To define the cgroup's limits, use these steps:

1 Create a PID (we already did this). This is called the Pod sandbox in Kubernetes.
2 Write the limits for that PID to the OS.

First, from inside your running chroot0 script, get its PID by running `echo $$`. Jot this number down. For us, the value was 79455. Next, we'll go through a series of steps to put this particular process in a situation where it can only use a small number of bytes. In doing so, we'll be able to estimate how much memory the `ls` command needs to execute:

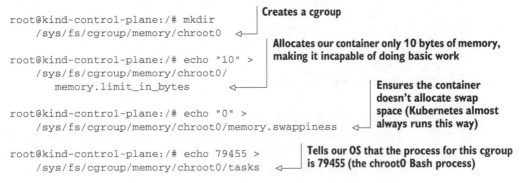

```
root@kind-control-plane:/# mkdir              Creates a cgroup
    /sys/fs/cgroup/memory/chroot0

root@kind-control-plane:/# echo "10" >        Allocates our container only 10 bytes of memory,
    /sys/fs/cgroup/memory/chroot0/            making it incapable of doing basic work
        memory.limit_in_bytes
                                              Ensures the container
                                              doesn't allocate swap
root@kind-control-plane:/# echo "0" >         space (Kubernetes almost
    /sys/fs/cgroup/memory/chroot0/memory.swappiness    always runs this way)

root@kind-control-plane:/# echo 79455 >       Tells our OS that the process for this cgroup
    /sys/fs/cgroup/memory/chroot0/tasks       is 79455 (the chroot0 Bash process)
```

Note that, in the example, creating the /chroot0 directory triggers an OS action to make a full cgroup that contains memory, CPU, and so on. Now, going back into your Bash terminal started in the chroot0.sh script, a simple command like `ls` will fail. Depending on your OS, you may get another equally dismal response as the one that follows; however, either way, this command should fail:

```
bash-5.0# ls
bash: fork: Cannot allocate memory
```

That's it! You've now created your own process that is isolated from other files, limited in its memory footprint, and also runs in an isolated process space, where it thinks it's the only process in the entire world. This is the natural state of being for any Pod in a Kubernetes cluster. From here on out, we'll explore how Kubernetes expands this baseline of functionality to enable a complex, dynamic, and resilient distributed system.

3.5   *Using our Pod in the real world*

A real container is depicted in figure 3.4. Although we've learned a lot in this chapter, it's best to keep in mind that a typical microservice might need to communicate with a lot of other services, which often means mounting new certificates to those. Additionally, discovering other services using internal DNS is always tricky and is an enormous part of the benefit of the Kubernetes model for managing microservices at scale. Because we didn't have a chance to add the ability to query an API for internal services and we didn't explore the automated injection of credentials to talk to such services in a secure manner, we can't say that our tiny prototypical cgroup and namespaces example can be used in the real world.

In figure 3.4, you'll note that our container is able to talk to other containers in our cluster. In order for this to happen, it needs an IP address. Because our Pod was created without a properly configured network namespace and distinct IP address, however, it will not be able to make any kind of direct TCP connections to its downstream dependent services.

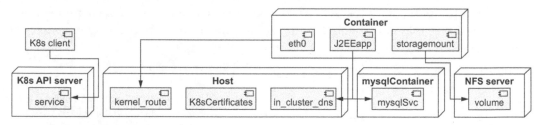

Figure 3.4   An example of a real container

We'll now dive a little bit into what it means to have a networked container. Recall that earlier, when we attempted to look at this aspect of our Bash process, we saw that it only had one IP address, and it wasn't specific to our container. This means that there will be no way to route incoming traffic to any service that we run in that process over a port. (Note that we're not suggesting anyone run a web server in Bash, but we used Bash as a metaphor for any program, including the most common type of containers, TCP services.)

To begin to illuminate this part of the puzzle, we'll now briefly learn about some basic Linux networking primitives. This sets the stage for the various aspects of Kubernetes networking that we'll cover later.

3.5.1   *The networking problem*

Any Kubernetes container might need to have

- Traffic routed directly to it for in-cluster or Pod-to-Pod connectivity
- Traffic routed out of it to access another Pod or the internet
- Traffic load balanced to it to serve as an endpoint behind a service with a static IP address

To allow these operations, we need metadata about Pods to be published to other parts of Kubernetes (this is the API Server's job), and we need to constantly monitor their state (the kubelet's job) so that this state is updated and populated over time. Pods, thus, have a lot more than a container command and a Docker image. They have *labels* and well-defined *specifications* for how their state is published, so they can be recreated on the fly alongside a cast of kubelet-provided functionality. This ensures IP addresses and DNS rules are always up to date. Labels are self-evident in the schema of a Pod. By specifications, we mean to say that Pods have well-defined states, restart logic, and guarantees around IP address reachability within a cluster.

Note that we'll again use a Linux environment to explore these aspects. You are welcome to rebuild your `kind` cluster if you want, in case you broke something in the furious hacking in the previous sections. You can do this by running `kind delete cluster --name=kind` followed by `kind create cluster`.

3.5.2 *Utilizing iptables to understand how kube-proxy implements Kubernetes services*

Kubernetes services define an API contract that says, "If you access this IP address, you'll forward to one of many possible endpoints automatically." They are, thus, the backbone of the Kubernetes user experience when it comes to deploying microservices. In most clusters, these networking rules are entirely implemented by the `kube-proxy` that's most often configured to use the iptables program to do low-level network routing.

The iptables program adds rules to the kernel, which are then processed linearly to deal with network traffic, and it is the most common way that Kubernetes services are implemented in order to route traffic to Pods. Note that iptables is not required for basic Pod networking (that is handled by the CNI; however, almost any real-world Kubernetes cluster is consumed by the end users through services). Thus, the iptables and its various incantations are one of the most fundamental primitives required for reasoning about a Kubernetes network. In a traditional setting (outside of Kubernetes), each iptables rule is appended to the kernel's networking stack by using the `-A` … syntax like so:

```
iptables -A INPUT -s 10.1.2.3 -j DROP
```

This command says to drop any traffic coming from 10.1.2.3. However, a Pod needs a lot more than a few firewall rules. It needs at least

- The ability to accept traffic as a service endpoint
- The ability to send traffic to the outside world from its own endpoint
- The ability to track ongoing TCP connections (in Linux, this is done with the conntrack module, a part of the Linux kernel)

Let's see how real service networking rules (running in `kind`) are implemented. We won't be reusing our Pod anymore because to attach it to an IP address, we would actually need a running, routable software-defined network. Instead, we'll keep it simple.

Let's look at the `iptables-save | grep hostnames` command, which shows all of the glue being used to hold our network together.

3.5.3 *Using the kube-dns Pod*

The `kube-dns` Pod is a good example to study because it represents the type of Pod you would typically run in a Kubernetes app. The `kube-dns` Pod

- Runs in any Kubernetes cluster
- Has no special privileges and uses the regular old Pod network rather than the host network
- Sends traffic to port 53, which is universally known as the DNS port standard
- Already runs in your `kind` cluster by default

Just as the Pod we made earlier was incapable of accessing the internet, it was also unable to receive any traffic. When we ran `ip a`, the Pod didn't have its own IP address. In Kubernetes, a CNI provider provides a unique IP address and routing rules to access this address. We can investigate these routes with the `ip route` command like so:

```
root@kind-control-plane:/# ip route
default via 172.18.0.1 dev eth0
10.244.0.2 dev vethfc5287fa scope host
10.244.0.3 dev veth31aba882 scope host
10.244.0.4 dev veth1e578a9a scope host
172.18.0.0/16 dev eth0 proto kernel scope link src 172.18.0.2
```

In the code snippet, IP routes are defined to send traffic to specific veth devices. These devices are made for us by our networking plugin. How do the Kubernetes Services route traffic to them? For this, we can look at the iptables program's output. If we run `iptables-save`, we can grep out the `10.244.0.*` addresses (the specific addresses will vary depending on your cluster and on how many Pods it might have) and see that there are egress rules, which enable these to make outgoing TCP connections.

ROUTING TRAFFIC INTO OUR DNS PODS WITH SERVICE RULES

Internal traffic is routed to our DNS Pods by the following rules, using the `-j` option that tells the Kernel "if something is trying to access the KUBE-SVC-ERIFX rule, send it to the KUBE-SEP-IT2Z rule." The `-j` option in an iptables rule stands for *jump* (as in "jump to another rule"). The jump rule forwards network traffic to a service endpoint (a Pod) as in the next example:

```
-A KUBE-SVC-ERIFXISQEP7F7OF4 -m comment --comment
                             "kube-system/kube-dns:dns-tcp"
                             -m statistic
                             --mode random
                             --probability 0.50000000000
                             -j KUBE-SEP-IT2ZTR26TO4XFPTO
```

DEFINING RULES FOR OUR INDIVIDUAL PODS WITH ENDPOINT RULES

When traffic from a service is received, it is routed using the following KUBE-SEP rules. These Pods access the external internet or receive traffic. For example:

```
-A KUBE-SEP-IT2Z.. -s 10.244.0.2/32
    -m comment --comment "kube-system/kube-dns:dns-tcp"
    -j KUBE-MARK-MASQ

-A KUBE-SEP-IT2Z.. -p tcp
    -m comment --comment "kube-system/kube-dns:dns-tcp"
    -m tcp -j DNAT --to-destination 10.244.0.2:53
```

In case it isn't obvious from the example, the final destination port for any traffic headed to these IP addresses goes to port 53. This is the endpoint where the kube-dns Pod serves its traffic (the IP address of the CoreDNS Pod that is running). If one of these Pods becomes unhealthy, then the specific rule for KUBE-SEP-IT2Z will be reconciled by the network proxy, kube-proxy, so that traffic only forwards to the healthy copies of our DNS Pods. Note that kube-dns is the name of our service, and CoreDNS is the Pod that implements our kube-dns service endpoint.

The network proxy's entire purpose in life is to continually update and manage these simple rulesets so that any node in a Kubernetes cluster can forward traffic into Kubernetes services, which is why we often refer to it generically as the Kubernetes network proxy or the Kubernetes service proxy.

3.5.4 *Considering other issues*

Storage, scheduling, and restarts are all issues that we haven't discussed yet. Each one of these issues affects any enterprise application. For example, a traditional data center might require migration of a database from one server to another and then need migration of application servers connecting to that database in a way that is complimentary to the new data center topology. In Kubernetes, we also need to take into account these age-old primitives.

STORAGE

In addition to issues with networking, our Pod also might need access to many different kinds of storage. For example, what if we had a large Network Attached Storage (NAS) that all of our containers need to use, and we needed to periodically change the way this NAS was mounted? In our previous example, this would mean modifying our shell commands and changing the way we mount volumes, one at a time. Doing this for hundreds or thousands of processes without extra infrastructure tooling to automate the process would be untenable for obvious reasons. However, even with such tooling, we would need a way to define these storage types and to report if attachments to these mounted storage volumes were failing. This is managed by Kubernetes StorageClasses, PersistentVolumes, and PersistentVolumeClaims.

SCHEDULING

We discussed in the previous chapter how the scheduling of Pods is a complex process in and of itself. Remember when we set the cgroups up previously? Imagine what might happen if we made the memory too high or if we ran our container in an environment where there wasn't enough memory to allocate its memory requests. In either of these cases, we might actually bring down an entire node in our Kubernetes cluster. Having a scheduler that is smart enough to put a Pod in a place where the cgroup hierarchy is able to match the resource requirements of our Pod is another key feature that requires Kubernetes.

Scheduling is a generic problem in computer science, so we should note here that there are alternative scheduling tools, such as Nomad (https://www.nomadproject .io/), that solve the scheduling problem in a Kubernetes-agnostic manner for data centers. That said, the Kubernetes scheduler specializes in simple, container-centric, and predictable choices of nodes for Pods we want to run, based on parameters such as affinity, CPU, memory, storage availability, data center topology, and so on.

UPGRADES AND RESTARTS

The Bash commands we ran to create our Pod won't work well if the PID of our Pod keeps changing or if we forget to record it in the first place. As you might recall, we need to write down the PID for certain operations. If we want to run a more sophisticated app than bin or Bash, we may find that we need to delete data from a folder, add new data to a folder, and then restart our script. Again, this process is essentially impossible to do at scale with shell scripts due to the high volume of concurrency and locking required to manage directories, processes, and mounts for several applications at a time.

Managing the stale processes and/or cgroups associated with a Pod that might no longer be running is an important part of running containerized workloads at large scales, especially in the context of microservices that are meant to be portable and ephemeral. The Kubernetes data model for applications, which most often is thought of in terms of Deployments, StatefulSets, Jobs, and DaemonSets, accounts for upgrading in a graceful manner.

Summary

- Kubernetes itself is a union of various Linux primitives.
- You can build a Pod-like construct in any Linux distribution using `chroot`.
- Storage, scheduling, and networking need to be managed in a sophisticated way if we want our Pod to run in a production scenario.
- `iptables` is a Linux primitive that can be used to forward traffic or create firewalls in a flexible manner.
- Kubernetes services are implemented by the `kube-proxy`, which is usually running in `iptables` mode.

Using cgroups for processes in our Pods

4

This chapter covers

- Exploring the basics of cgroups
- Identifying Kubernetes processes
- Learning how to create and manage cgroups
- Using Linux commands to investigate cgroup hierarchies
- Understanding cgroup v2 versus cgroup v1
- Installing Prometheus and looking at Pod resource usage

The last chapter was pretty granular, and you might have found it a little bit theoretical. After all, nobody really needs to build their own Pods from scratch nowadays (unless you're Facebook). Never fear, from here on out, we will start moving a little bit further up the stack.

In this chapter, we'll dive a bit deeper into *cgroups*: the control structures that isolate resources from one another in the kernel. In the previous chapter, we actually implemented a simple cgroup boundary for a Pod that we made all by ourselves. This time around, we'll create a "real" Kubernetes Pod and investigate how the kernel manages that Pod's cgroup footprint. Along the way, we'll go through some silly, but nevertheless instructive, examples of why cgroups exist. We'll conclude with a look at Prometheus, the time-series metrics aggregator that has become the de facto standard for all metrics and observation platforms in the cloud native space.

The most important thing to keep in mind as you follow along in this chapter is that cgroups and Linux Namespaces aren't any kind of dark magic. They are really just ledgers maintained by the kernel that associates processes with IP addresses, memory allocations, and so on. Because the kernel's job provides these resources to programs, it's then quite evident why these data structures are also managed by the kernel itself.

4.1   Pods are idle until the prep work completes

In the last chapter, we touched briefly on what happens when a Pod starts. Let's zoom in a little bit on that scenario and look at what the kubelet *actually* needs to do to create a real Pod (figure 4.1). Note that our app is idle until the pause container is added to our namespace. After that, the actual application we have finally starts.

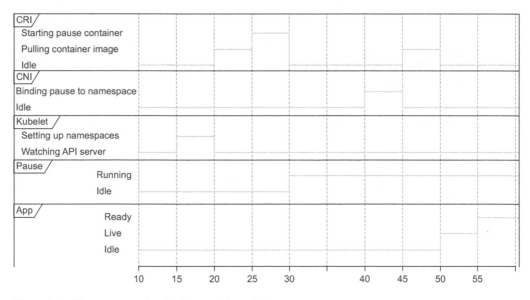

Figure 4.1   The processes involved in container startup

Figure 4.1 shows us the states of various parts of the kubelet during the creation of a container. Every kubelet will have an installed CRI, responsible for running containers, and a CNI, responsible for giving containers IP addresses, and will run one or many *pause containers* (placeholders where the kubelet creates namespaces and cgroups for a container to run inside of). In order for an app to ultimately be ready for Kubernetes to begin load balancing traffic to it, several ephemeral processes need to run in a highly coordinated manner:

- If the CNI were to run before the CNI's pause container, there would be no network for it to use.
- If there aren't any resources available, the kubelet won't finish setting up a place for a Pod to run, and nothing will happen.
- Before every Pod runs, a pause container runs, which is the placeholder for the Pod's processes.

The reason we chose to illustrate this intricate dance in this chapter is to drive home the fact that programs need resources, and resources are finite: orchestrating resources is a complex, ordered process. The more programs we run, the more complex the intersection of these resource requests. Let's look at a few example programs. Each of the following programs has different CPU, memory, and storage requirements:

- *Calculating Pi*—Calculating Pi needs access to a dedicated core for continuous CPU usage.
- *Caching the contents of Wikipedia for fast look ups*—Caching Wikipedia into a hash table for our Pi program needs little CPU, but it could call for about 100 GB or so of memory.
- *Backing up a 1 TB database*—Backing up a database into cold storage for our Pi program needs essentially no memory, little CPU, and a large, persistent storage device, which can be a slow spinning disk.

If we have a single computer with 2 cores, 101 GB of memory, and 1.1 TB of storage, we could theoretically run each program with the equivalent CPU, memory, and storage access. The result would be

- The Pi program, if written incorrectly (if it wrote intermediate results to a persistent disk, for example) could eventually overrun our database storage.
- The Wikipedia cache, if written incorrectly (if its hashing function was too CPU-intensive, for example) might prevent our Pi program from rapidly doing mathematical calculations.
- The database program, if written incorrectly (if it did too much logging, for example) might prevent the Pi program from doing its job by hogging all of the CPU.

Instead of running all processes with complete access to all of our system's (limited) resources, we could do the following—that is, if we have the ability to portion out our CPU, memory, and disk resources:

- Run the Pi process with 1 core and 1 KB of memory
- Run the Wikipedia caching with half a core and 99 GB of memory
- Run the database backup program with 1 GB of memory and the remaining CPU with a dedicated storage volume not accessible by other apps

So that this can be done in a predictable manner for all programs controlled by our OS, cgroups allow us to define hierarchically separated bins for memory, CPU, and other OS resources. All threads created by a program use the same pool of resources initially granted to the parent process. In other words, no one can play in someone else's pool.

This is, in and of itself, the argument for having cgroups for Pods. In a Kubernetes cluster, you might be running 100 programs on a single computer, many of which are low-priority or entirely idle at certain times. If these programs reserve large amounts of memory, they make the cost of running such a cluster unnecessarily high. The creation of new nodes to provide memory to starving processes leads to administrative overhead and infrastructure costs that compound over time. Because the promise of containers (increased utilization of data centers) is largely predicated on being able to run smaller footprints per service, careful usage of cgroups is at the heart of running applications as microservices.

4.2   Processes and threads in Linux

Every process in Linux can create one or more threads. An execution *thread* is an abstraction that programs can use to create new processes that share the same memory with other processes. As an example, we can inspect the use of various independent scheduling threads in Kubernetes by using the `ps -T` command:

```
root@kind-control-plane:/# ps -ax | grep scheduler        ⌐──   Gets the PID of the
631 ?  Ssl 60:14 kube-scheduler                           │     Kubernetes scheduler Pod
  --authentication-kubeconfig=/etc/kubernetes/...

root@kind-control-plane:/# ps -T 631     ⌐──── Finds the threads in the Pod

root@kind-control-plane:/# ps -T 631
  PID  SPID TTY        STAT   TIME COMMAND
  631   631 ?          Ssl    4:40 kube-scheduler --authentication-kube..
  631   672 ?          Ssl   12:08 kube-scheduler --authentication-kube..
  631   673 ?          Ssl    4:57 kube-scheduler --authentication-kube..
  631   674 ?          Ssl    4:31 kube-scheduler --authentication-kube..
  631   675 ?          Ssl    0:00 kube-scheduler --authentication-kube..
```

This query shows us parallel scheduler threads that share memory with one another. These processes have their own subprocess IDs, and to the Linux kernel, they are all just regular old processes. That said, they have one thing in common: a parent. We can investigate this parent/child relationship by using the `pstree` command in our kind cluster:

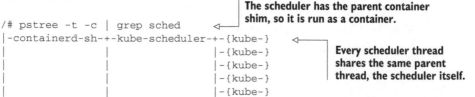

```
/# pstree -t -c | grep sched       ⌐── The scheduler has the parent container
|-containerd-sh-+-kube-scheduler-+-{kube-}      shim, so it is run as a container.
|               |                 |-{kube-}   ⌐──
|               |                 |-{kube-}       Every scheduler thread
|               |                 |-{kube-}       shares the same parent
|               |                 |-{kube-}       thread, the scheduler itself.
```

```
|              |              |-{kube-}
|              |              |-{kube-}
|              |              |-{kube-}
|              |              |-{kube-}
|              |              |-{kube-}
|              |              |-{kube-}
|              |              |-{kube-}
|              |              |-{kube-}
|              |              |-{kube-}
```

> ### containerd and Docker
>
> We haven't spent time contrasting containerd and Docker, but it's good to note that our `kind` clusters are *not* running Docker as their container runtime. Instead, they use Docker to create nodes, and then every node uses containerd as a run time. Modern Kubernetes clusters do not typically run Docker as the container runtime for Linux for a variety of reasons. Docker was a great on-ramp for developers to run Kubernetes, but data centers require a lighter-weight container runtime solution that is more deeply integrated with the OS. Most clusters execute `runC` as the container runtime at the lowest level, where `runC` is called by containerd, CRI-O, or some other higher-level command-line executable that is installed on your nodes. This causes systemd to be the parent of your containers rather than the Docker daemon.

One of the things that makes containers so popular is the fact that, especially in Linux, they don't create an artificial boundary between a program and its host. Rather, they just allow for scheduling programs in a way that is lightweight and easier to manage than a VM-based isolation.

4.2.1 systemd and the init process

Now that you've seen a process hierarchy in action, let's take a step back and ask what it *really* means to be a process. Back in our trusty `kind` cluster, we ran the following command to see who started this whole charade (look at the first few lines of systemd's status log). Remember, our `kind` node (which we exec into in order to do all of this) is really just a Docker container; otherwise, the output of the following command might scare you a little:

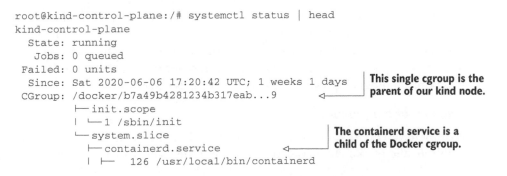

```
root@kind-control-plane:/# systemctl status | head
kind-control-plane
   State: running
    Jobs: 0 queued
  Failed: 0 units
   Since: Sat 2020-06-06 17:20:42 UTC; 1 weeks 1 days        This single cgroup is the
  CGroup: /docker/b7a49b4281234b317eab...9    ◄──────────    parent of our kind node.
          ├─ init.scope
          │ └─1 /sbin/init
          └─ system.slice                                    The containerd service is a
            ├─ containerd.service    ◄──────────             child of the Docker cgroup.
            │ ├─   126 /usr/local/bin/containerd
```

If you happen to have a regular Linux machine, you can see the following output. This gives you a more revealing answer:

```
State: running
    Jobs: 0 queued
  Failed: 0 units
   Since: Thu 2020-04-02 03:26:27 UTC; 2 months 12 days
  cgroup: /
          ├─docker
          │ ├─ae17db938d5f5745cf343e79b8301be2ef7
          │ │ ├─init.scope
          │ │ │ └─20431 /sbin/init
          │ │ └─system.slice
```

And, under the `system.slice`, we'll see

```
├─containerd.service
├─ 3067 /usr/local/bin/containerd-shim-runc-v2
      -namespace k8s.io -id db70803e6522052e
├─ 3135 /pause
```

In a standard Linux machine or in a kind cluster node, the root of all cgroups is /. If we really want to know what cgroup is the ultimate parent of all processes in our system, it's the / cgroup that is created at startup. Docker itself is a child of this cgroup, and if we run a kind cluster, our kind nodes are the child of this Docker process. If we run a regular Kubernetes cluster, we would likely not see a Docker cgroup at all, but instead, we would see that containerd itself was a child of the systemd root process. If you have a handy Kubernetes node to ssh into, this might be a good follow-up exercise.

   If we traverse down these trees far enough, we'll find the available processes, including any process started by any container, in our entire OS. Note that the process IDs (PIDs), such as 3135 in the previous snippet, are actually high numbers if we inspect this information in our host machine. That is because the PID of a process *outside* of a container is *not* the same as the PID of a process *inside* a container. If you're wondering why, recall how we used the unshare command in the first chapter to separate our process namespaces. This means that processes started by containers have no capacity to see, identify, or kill processes running in other containers. This is an important security feature of any software deployment.

   You may also be wondering why there are pause processes. Each of our containerd-shim programs has a pause program that corresponds to it, which is initially used as a placeholder for the creation of our network namespace. The pause container also helps clean up processes and serves as a placeholder for our CRI to do some basic process bookkeeping, helping us to avoid zombie processes.

4.2.2   cgroups for our process

We now have a pretty good idea of what this scheduler Pod is up to: it has spawned several children, and most likely, it was created by Kubernetes because it's a child of containerd, which is the container runtime that Kubernetes uses in kind. As a first look at how processes work, you can kill the containerd process, and you'll naturally see the scheduler and its subthreads come back to life. This is done by the kubelet itself, which has a /manifests directory. This directory tells the kubelet about a few processes that should always run even before an API server is able to schedule containers. This, in fact, is how Kubernetes installs itself via a kubelet. The life cycle of a Kubernetes installation, which uses kubeadm (now the most common installation tool), looks something like this:

- The kubelet has a manifests directory that includes the API server, scheduler, and controller manager.
- The kubelet is started by systemd.
- The kubelet tells containerd (or whatever the container runtime is) to start running all the processes in the manifests directory.
- Once the API server comes up, the kubelet connects to it and then runs any containers that the API server asks it to execute.

Mirror Pods sneak up on the API server

The kubelet has a secret weapon: the /etc/kubernetes/manifests directory. This directory is continuously scanned, and when Pods are put inside of it, they are created and run by the kubelet. Because these aren't scheduled via the Kubernetes API server, they need to mirror themselves so that the API server can be aware of their existence. Hence, the Pods created outside the knowledge of the Kubernetes control plane are known as *mirror Pods*.

Mirror Pods can be viewed by listing them like any other Pod, via kubectl get pods -A, but they are created and managed by a kubelet on an independent basis. This allows the kubelet, alone, to bootstrap an entire Kubernetes cluster that runs inside the Pods. Pretty sneaky!

You might ask, "What does this all have to do with cgroups?" It turns out that the scheduler we've been spelunking is actually identified as a mirror Pod, and the cgroups that it is assigned to are named using this identity. The reason it has this special identity is that, originally, the API server doesn't actually have any knowledge of the mirror Pod because it was created by the kubelet. To be a little less abstract, let's poke around with the following code and find its identity:

```
apiVersion: v1
kind: Pod
metadata:
  annotations:
    kubernetes.io/config.hash: 155707e0c1919c0ad1
    kubernetes.io/config.mirror: 155707e0c19147c8        ◄──┐ The mirror Pod ID
    kubernetes.io/config.seen: 2020-06-06T17:21:0           │ of the scheduler
    kubernetes.io/config.source: file
  creationTimestamp: 2020-06-06T17:21:06Z
  labels:
```

We use the mirror Pod ID of the scheduler for finding its cgroups. You can get at these Pods to view their contents by running `edit` or `get action` against a control plane Pod (for example, `kubectl edit Pod -n kube-system kube-apiserver-calico-control-plane`). Now, let's see if we can find any cgroups associated with our processer by running the following:

```
$ cat /proc/631/cgroup
```

With this command, we used the PID we found earlier to ask the Linux kernel about what cgroups exist for the scheduler. The output is pretty intimidating (something like that shown in the following). Don't worry about the burstable folder; we will explain the burstable concept, which is a quality of service or QoS class, later, when we look at some kubelet internals. In the meantime, a *burstable Pod* is generally one that doesn't have hard usage limits. The scheduler is an example of a Pod that typically runs with the ability to use large bursts of CPU when necessary (for example, in an instance where 10 or 20 Pods need to be quickly scheduled to a node). Each of these entries has an extremely long identifier for the cgroup and Pod identity like so:

```
13:name=systemd:/docker/b7a49b4281234b31
➥ b9/kubepods/burstable/pod155707e0c19147c../391fbfc..
➥ a08fc16ee8c7e45336ef2e861ebef3f7261d
```

The kernel is thus tracking all of these processes in the /proc location, and we can keep digging further to see what each process is getting in terms of resources. To abbreviate the entire listing of cgroups for process 631, we can `cat` the cgroup file, as the following shows. Note that we've abbreviated the extra-long IDs for readability:

```
root@kind-control-plane:/# cat /proc/631/cgroup
```

```
13:name=systemd:/docker/b7a49b42.../kubepods/burstable/pod1557.../391f...
12:pids:/docker/b7a49b42.../kubepods/burstable/pod1557.../391f...
11:hugetlb:/docker/b7a49b42.../kubepods/burstable/pod1557.../391f...
10:net_prio:/docker/b7a49b42.../kubepods/burstable/pod1557.../391f...
9:perf_event:/docker/b7a49b42.../kubepods/burstable//pod1557.../391f...
8:net_cls:/docker/b7a49b42.../kubepods/burstable//pod1557.../391f...
7:freezer:/docker/b7a49b42.../kubepods/burstable//pod1557.../391f...
6:devices:/docker/b7a49b42.../kubepods/burstable//pod1557.../391f...
5:memory:/docker/b7a49b42.../kubepods/burstable//pod1557.../391f...
4:blkio:/docker/b7a49b42.../kubepods/burstable//pod1557.../391f...
3:cpuacct:/docker/b7a49b42.../kubepods/burstable//pod1557.../391f...
2:cpu:/docker/b7a49b42.../kubepods/burstable//pod1557.../391f...
1:cpuset:/docker/b7a49b42.../kubepods/burstable//pod1557.../391f...
0:::/docker/b7a49b42.../system.slice/containerd.service
```

We'll look inside these folders, one at a time, as follows. Don't worry too much about the docker folder, though. Because we're in a `kind` cluster, the docker folder is the parent of everything. But note that, actually, our containers are all running in containerd:

- *docker*—The cgroup for Docker's daemon running on our computer, which is essentially like a VM that runs a kubelet.
- *b7a49b42* . . .—The name of our Docker `kind` container. Docker creates this cgroup for us.
- *kubepods*—A division of cgroups that Kubernetes puts aside for its Pods.
- *burstable*—A special cgroup for Kubernetes that defines the quality of service the scheduler gets.
- *pod1557* . . .—Our Pod's ID, which is reflected inside our Linux kernel as its own identifier.

At the time of the writing of this book, Docker has been deprecated in Kubernetes. You can think of the docker folder in the example, not as a Kubernetes concept, but rather as "the VM that runs our kubelet," because `kind` itself is really just running one Docker daemon as a Kubernetes node and then putting a kubelet, containerd, and so on, inside this node. Thus, continue to repeat to yourself when exploring Kubernetes, "`kind` itself does not use Docker to run containers." Instead, it uses Docker to make nodes and installs containerd as the container runtime inside those nodes.

We've now seen that every process Kubernetes (for a Linux machine) ultimately lands in the bookkeeping tables of the proc directory. Now, let's explore what these fields mean for a more traditional Pod: the NGINX container.

4.2.3 *Implementing cgroups for a normal Pod*

The scheduler Pod is a bit of a special case in that it runs on all clusters and isn't something that you might directly want to tune or investigate. A more realistic scenario might be one wherein you want to confirm that the cgroups for an application you're running (like NGINX) were created correctly. In order to try this out, you can create a Pod similar to our original pod.yaml, which runs the NGINX web server with resource requests. The specification for this portion of the Pod looks like the following (which is probably familiar to you):

```
spec:
    containers:
    - image: nginx
      imagePullPolicy: Always
      name: nginx
      resources:
        requests:
          cpu: "1"
          memory: 1G
```

In this case, the Pod defines a core count (1) and a memory request (1 GB). These both go in to the cgroups defined under the /sys/fs directory, and the kernel enforces the cgroup rules. Remember, you need to ssh into your node to do this or, if you're using kind, use `docker exec -t -i 75 /bin/sh` to access the shell for the `kind` node.

The result is that now your NGINX container runs with dedicated access to 1 core and 1 GB of memory. After creating this Pod, we can actually take a direct look at its cgroup hierarchy by traversing its cgroup information for the memory field (again running the ps -ax command to track it down). In doing so, we can see how Kubernetes *really* responds to the memory request we give it. We'll leave it to you, the reader, to experiment with other such limits and see how the OS expresses them.

If we now look into our kernel's memory tables, we can see that there is a marker for how much memory has been carved up for our Pod. It's about 1 GB. When we made the previous Pod, our underlying container runtime was in a cgroup with a limited amount of memory. This solves the exact problem we originally discussed in this chapter—isolating resources for memory and CPU:

```
$ sudo cat /sys/fs/memory/docker/753../kubepods/pod8a58e9/d176../
    memory.limit_in_bytes
999997440
```

Thus, the magic of Kubernetes isolation really can just be viewed on a Linux machine as regular old hierarchical distribution of resources that are organized by a simple directory structure. There's a lot of logic in the Kernel to "get this right," but it's all easily accessible to anyone with the courage to peer under the covers.

4.3   *Testing the cgroups*

We now know how to confirm that our cgroups are created correctly. But how do we *test* that the cgroups are being honored by our processes? It's a well-known fact that container runtimes and the Linux kernel itself may have bugs when it comes to isolating things in the exact way we expect. For example, there are instances where the OS might allow a container to run above its allotted CPU allocation if the other processes aren't starving for resources. Let's run a simple process with the following code to test whether our cgroups are working properly:

```
$ cat /tmp/pod.yaml
apiVersion: v1
kind: Pod
metadata:
  name: core-k8s
  labels:
    role: just-an-example
    app: my-example-app
    organization: friends-of-manning
    creator: jay
spec:
  containers:
    - name: an-old-name-will-do
      image: busybox:latest
      command: ['sleep', '1000']      Ensures our Pod has
      resources:                      plenty of opportunity
        limits:             ◁———————  to use lots of CPU
          cpu:  2
```

```
    requests:
        cpu: 1
    ports:
       - name: webapp-port
         containerPort: 80
         protocol: TCP
```

Ensures our Pod won't start until it has a full core of CPU to access

Now, we can execute into our Pod and run a (nasty) CPU usage command. We'll see in the output that the `top` command blows up:

```
$ kubectl create -f pod.yaml
$ kubectl exec -t -i core-k8s /bin/sh
```

Creates a shell into your container

```
#> dd if=/dev/zero of=/dev/null
```

Consumes CPU with reckless abandon by running dd

```
$ docker exec -t -i 75 /bin/sh
```

Runs the top command to measure CPU usage in our Docker kind node

```
root@kube-control-plane# top
PID USER       PR  NI    VIRT      RES    SHR S   %CPU   %MEM    TIME+ COMMAND
91467 root     20   0    1292        4      0 R   99.7    0.0   0:35.89 dd
```

What happens if we fence this same process and rerun this experiment? To test this, you can change the `resources` stanza to something like this:

```
resources:
        limits:
            cpu:  .1
        requests:
            cpu:  .1
```

Limits CPU usage to .1 core as a maximum

Reserves the whole .1 core, guaranteeing this CPU share

Let's rerun the following command. In this second example, we can actually see a much less stressful scenario for our `kind` node taking place:

This time only 10% of the CPU is used for the node.

```
root@kube-control-plane# top
PID USER       PR  NI    VIRT      RES    SHR S   %CPU  %MEM TIME+COMMAND
93311 root     20   0    1292        4      0   R   10.3   0.0  0:03.61 dd
```

4.4 *How the kubelet manages cgroups*

Earlier in this chapter we glossed over the other cgroups like `blkio`. To be sure, there are many different kinds of cgroups, and it's worth understanding what they are, even though 90% of the time, you will only be concerned about CPU and memory isolation for most containers.

At a lower level, clever use of the cgroup primitives listed in /sys/fs/cgroup exposes control knobs for managing how these resources are allocated to processes. Some such groups are not readily useful to a Kubernetes administrator. For example, the `freezer` cgroup assigns groups of related tasks to a single stoppable or freezable control point. This isolation primitive allows for efficient scheduling and descheduling of gang processes (and, ironically, some have criticized Kubernetes for its poor handling of this type of scheduling).

Another example is the `blkio` cgroup, which is also a lesser-known resource that's used to manage I/O. Looking into the /sys/fs/cgroup, we can see all of the various quantifiable resources that can be allocated hierarchically in Linux:

```
$ ls -d /sys/fs/cgroup/*
/sys/fs/cgroup/blkio freezer perf_event
/sys/fs/cgroup/cpu hugetlb pids
/sys/fs/cgroup/cpuacct memory rdma
/sys/fs/cgroup/cpu,cpuacct net_cls systemd
/sys/fs/cgroup/cpuset net_cls,net_prio unified
/sys/fs/cgroup/devices net_prio
```

You can read about the original intent of cgroups at http://mng.bz/vo8p. Some of the corresponding articles might be out of date, but they provide a lot of information about how cgroups have evolved and what they are meant to do. For advanced Kubernetes administrators, understanding how to interpret these data structures can be valuable when it comes to looking at different containerization technologies and how they affect your underlying infrastructure.

4.5   *Diving into how the kubelet manages resources*

Now that you understand where cgroups come from, it is worth taking a look at how cgroups are used in a kubelet; namely, by the `allocatable` data structure. Looking at an example Kubernetes node (again, you can do this with your `kind` cluster), we can see the following stanza in the output from `kubectl get nodes -o yaml`:

```
...
   allocatable:
     cpu: "12"
     ephemeral-storage: 982940092Ki
     hugepages-1Gi: "0"
     hugepages-2Mi: "0"
     memory: 32575684Ki
     pods: "110"
```

Do these settings look familiar? By now, they should. These resources are the amount of cgroup budget available for allocating resources to Pods. The kubelet calculates this by determining the total capacity on the node. It then deducts how much CPU bandwidth is required for itself as well as for the underlying node and subtracts this from the amount of allocatable resources for containers. The equations for these numbers are documented at http://mng.bz/4jJR and can be toggled with parameters, including `--system-reserved` and `--kubelet-reserved`. This value is then used by the Kubernetes scheduler to decide whether to request a running container on this particular node.

Typically, you might launch `--kubelet-reserved` and `--system-reserved` with half of a core each, leaving a 2-core CPU with ~ 1.5 cores free to run workloads, because a kubelet is not an incredibly CPU-hungry resource (except in times of burst scheduling or startup). At large scales, all of these numbers break down and depend on a variety of performance factors related to workload types, hardware types, network latency, and so on. As an equation, when it comes to scheduling, we have the following implementation (`system-reserved` refers to the quantity of resources a healthy OS needs to run):

Allocatable = node capacity - kube-reserved - system-reserved

As an example, if you have

- 16 cores of CPU reserved for a node
- 1 CPU core reserved for a kubelet and system processes in a cluster

the amount of allocatable CPU is 15 cores. To contextualize how all of this relates to a scheduled, running container

- The kubelet creates cgroups when you run Pods to bound their resource usage.
- Your container runtime starts a process inside the cgroups, which guarantees the resource requests you gave it in the Pod specification.
- systemd usually starts a kubelet, which broadcasts the total available resources to the Kubernetes API periodically.
- systemd also typically starts your container runtime (containerd, CRI-O, or Docker).

When you start a kubelet, there is parenting logic embedded in it. This setting is configured by a command-line flag (that you should leave enabled), which results in the kubelet itself being a top-level cgroup parent to its children's containers. The previous equation calculates the total amount of allocatable cgroups for a kubelet. It is called the *allocatable resource budget*.

4.5.1 Why can't the OS use swap in Kubernetes?

To understand this, we have to dive a little deeper into the specific cgroups that we saw earlier. Remember how our Pods resided under special folders, such as guaranteed and burstable? If we allowed our OS to swap inactive memory to disk, then an idle process might suddenly have slow memory allocation. This allocation would violate the *guaranteed* access to memory that Kubernetes provides users when defining Pod specifications and would make performance highly variable.

Because the scheduling of large amounts of processes in a predictable manner is more important than the health of any one process, we disable swapping entirely on Kubernetes. To avoid any confusion around this, the Kubernetes installers, such as `kubeadm`, fail instantly if you bootstrap your kubelets on machines with swap enabled.

> **Why not enable swap?**
>
> In certain cases, thinly provisioning memory might benefit an end user (for example, it might allow you to pack containers on a system more densely). However, the semantic complexity associated with accommodating this type of memory facade isn't proportionally beneficial to most users. The maintainers of the kubelet haven't decided (yet) to support this more complex notion of memory, and such API changes are hard to make in a system such as Kubernetes, which is being used by millions of users.
>
> Of course, like everything else in tech, this is rapidly evolving, and in Kubernetes 1.22, you'll find that, in fact, there are ways you can run with swap memory enabled (http://mng.bz/4jY5). This is not recommended for most production deployments, however, because it would result in highly erratic performance characteristics for workloads.

That said, there is a lot of subtlety at the container runtime level when it comes to resource usage such as memory. For example, cgroups differentiate between soft and hard limits as follows:

- A process with *soft* memory limits has varying amounts of RAM over time, depending on the system load.
- A process with *hard* memory limits is killed if it exceeds its memory limit for an extended period.

Note that Kubernetes relays an exit code and the OOMKilled status back to you in the cases where a process has to be killed for these reasons. You can increase the amount of memory allocated to a high-priority container to reduce the odds that a noisy neighbor causes problems on a machine. Let's look at that next.

4.5.2 *Hack: The poor man's priority knob*

HugePages is a concept that initially was not supported in Kubernetes because it was a web-centric technology at inception. As it moved to a core data-center technology, more subtle scheduling and resource allocation strategies became relevant. HugePages configuration allows a Pod to access memory pages larger than the Linux kernel's default memory page size, which is usually 4 KB.

Memory, like CPU, can be allocated explicitly for Pods and is denoted using units for kilobytes, megabytes, and gigabytes (Kis, Mis, and Gis, respectively). Many memory-intensive applications like Elasticsearch and Cassandra supports using HugePages. If a node supports HugePages and also sustains 2048 KiB page sizes, it exposes a schedulable resource: HugePages - 2 Mi. In general, it is possible to schedule against HugePages in Kubernetes using a standard `resources` directive as follows:

```
resources:
  limits:
    hugepages-2Mi: 100Mi
```

Transparent HugePages are the optimization of HugePages that can have highly variable effects on Pods that need high performance. You'll want to disable them in some cases, especially for high-performance containers that need large, contiguous blocks of memory at the bootloader or OS level, depending on your hardware.

4.5.3 Hack: Editing HugePages with init containers

We've come full circle now. Remember how at the beginning of this chapter we looked at the /sys/fs directory and how it managed various resources for containers? The rigging of HugePages can be done in `init` containers if you can run these as root and mount /sys using a container to edit these files.

The configuration of HugePages can be toggled by merely writing files to and from the sys directory. For example, to turn off transparent HugePages, which might make a performance difference for you on specific OSs, you would typically run a command such as `echo 'never' > /sys/kernel/mm/redhat_transparent_hugepage/enabled`. If you need to set up HugePages in a specific way, you could do so entirely from a Pod specification as follows:

1 Declare a Pod, which presumably has specific performance needs based around HugePages.
2 Declare an `init` container with this Pod, which runs in privileged mode and mounts the /sys directory using the volume type of `hostPath`.
3 Have the `init` container execute any Linux-specific commands (such as the previous `echo` statement) as its only execution steps.

In general, `init` containers can be used to bootstrap certain Linux features that might be required for a Pod to run properly. But keep in mind that any time you mount a hostPath, you need special privileges on your cluster, which an administrator might not readily give you. Some distributions, such as OpenShift, deny hostPath volume mounts by default.

4.5.4 QoS classes: Why they matter and how they work

We've seen terms such as *guaranteed* and *burstable* throughout this chapter, but we haven't defined these terms yet. To define these concepts, we first need to introduce QoS.

When you go to a fancy restaurant, you expect the food to be great, but you also expect the wait staff to be responsive. This responsiveness is known as *quality of service* or *QoS*. We hinted at QoS earlier when we looked at why swap is disabled in Kubernetes to guarantee the performance of memory access. QoS refers to the availability of resources at a moment's notice. Any data center, hypervisor, or cloud has to make a tradeoff around resource availability for applications by

- Guaranteeing that critical services stay up, but you're spending lots of money because you have more hardware than you need
- Spending little money and risking essential services going down

QoS allows you to walk the fine line of having many services performing suboptimally during peak times without sacrificing the quality of critical services. In practice, these critical services might be payment-processing systems, machine-learning or AI jobs that are costly to restart, or real-time communications processes that cannot be interrupted. Keep in mind that the eviction of a Pod is heavily dependent on how much above its resource limits it is. In general

- Nicely-behaved applications with predictable memory and CPU usage are less likely to be evicted in times of duress than others.
- Greedy applications are more likely to get killed during times of pressure when they attempt to use more CPU or memory than allocated by Kubernetes, unless these apps are in the Guaranteed class.
- Applications in the BestEffort QoS class are highly likely to get killed and rescheduled in times of duress.

You might be wondering how we decide which QoS class to use. In general, you don't directly decide this, and instead, you influence this decision by determining whether your app needs guaranteed access to resources by using the `resource` stanza in your Pod specification. We'll walk through this process in the following section.

4.5.5   *Creating QoS classes by setting resources*

Burstable, Guaranteed, and BestEffort are the three QoS classes that are created for you, depending on how you define a Pod. These settings can increase the number of containers that you can run on your cluster, where some may die off at times of high utilization and can be rescheduled later. It's tempting to make global policies for how much CPU or memory you should allocate to end users but, be warned, rarely does one size fit all:

- If all the containers on your system have a Guaranteed QoS, your ability to handle dynamic workloads with modulating resources needs is hampered.
- If no containers on your servers have a Guaranteed QoS, then a kubelet won't be able to make certain critical processes stay up.

The rules for QoS determination are as follows (these are calculated and displayed as a `status` field in your Pod):

- *BestEffort Pods are those that have no CPU or memory requests.* They are easily killed and displaced (and are likely to pop up on a new node) when resources are tight.
- *Burstable Pods are those that have memory or CPU requests but do not have limits defined for all classes.* These are less likely to be displaced than BestEffort Pods.
- *Guaranteed Pods are those that have both CPU and memory requests.* These are less likely to be displaced than Burstable Pods.

Let's see this in action. Create a new deployment by running `kubectl create ns qos;` `kubectl -n qos run --image=nginx myapp`. Then, edit the deployment to include a container specification that states a request but does not define a limit. For example:

```
spec:
    containers:
    - image: nginx
      imagePullPolicy: Always
      name: nginx
      resources:
        requests:
          cpu: "1"
          memory: 1G
```

You will now see that when you run `kubectl get Pods -n qos -o yaml`, you will have a Burstable class assigned to the `status` field of your Pod, as the following code snippet shows. In crunch time, you might use this technique to ensure that the most critical processes for your business all have a Guaranteed or Burstable status.

```
hostIP: 172.17.0.3
    phase: Running
    podIP: 192.168.242.197
    qosClass: Burstable
    startTime: "2020-03-08T08:54:08Z"
```

4.6 Monitoring the Linux kernel with Prometheus, cAdvisor, and the API server

We've looked at a lot of low-level Kubernetes concepts and mapped them to the OS in this chapter, but in the real world, you won't be manually curating this data. Instead, for system metrics and overall trends, people typically aggregate container and system-level OS information in a single, time-series dashboard so that, in case of emergencies, they can ascertain the timescale of a problem and drill into it from various perspectives (application, OS, and so forth).

To conclude this chapter, we'll up-level things a little bit and use Prometheus, the industry standard for monitoring cloud native applications, as well as monitoring Kubernetes itself. We'll look at how Pod resource usage can be quantified by direct inspection of cgroups. This has several advantages when it comes to an end-to-end system visibility:

- It can see sneaky processes that might overrun your cluster that aren't visible to Kubernetes.
- You can directly map resources that Kubernetes is aware of with kernel-level isolation tools, which might uncover bugs in the way your cluster is interacting with your OS.
- It's a great tool for learning more about how containers are implemented at scale by the kubelet and your container runtime.

Before we get into Prometheus, we need to talk about metrics. In theory, a *metric* is a quantifiable value of some sort; for example, how many cheeseburgers you ate in the last month. In the Kubernetes universe, the myriad of containers coming online and offline in a data center makes application metrics important for administrators as an objective and app-independent model for measuring the overall health of a data center's services.

Sticking with the cheeseburger metaphor, you might have a collection of metrics that look something like the following code snippet, which you can jot down in a journal. There are three fundamental types of metrics that we'll concern ourselves with—histograms, gauges, and counters:

- *Gauges:* Indicate how many requests you get per second at any given time.
- *Histograms:* Show bins of timing for different types of events (e.g., how many requests completed in under 500 ms).
- *Counters:* Specify continuously increasing counts of events (e.g., how many total requests you've seen).

As a concrete example that might be a little closer to home, we can output Prometheus metrics about our daily calorie consumption. The following code snippet shows this output:

```
meals_today 2          The total number of
                       meals you had today
cheeseburger 1
salad 1                The number of cheeseburgers
dinner 1               you've eaten today
lunch 1                                              The amount of calories you've
calories_total_bucket_bucket[1e=1024] 1             had, binned into buckets of 2,
                                                     4, 8, 16, and so on, up to 2,048
```

You might publish the total number of meals once a day. This is known as a *gauge*, as it goes up and down and is updated periodically. The amount of cheeseburgers you've eaten today would be a *counter*, which continually gets incremented over time. With the amount of calories you've had, the metric says you had one meal with less than 1,024 calories. This gives you a discrete way to bin how much you ate without getting bogged down in details (anything above 2,048 is probably too much and anything below 1,024 is most likely too few).

Note that buckets like this are commonly used to monitor etcd over long time periods. The amount of writes above 1 second are important for predicting etcd outages. Over time, if we aggregated the daily journal entries that you made, you might be able to make some interesting correlations as long as you logged the time of these metrics. For example:

```
meals_today 2
cheeseburger 50
salad 99
dinner 101
lunch 99

calories_total_bucket_bucket[1e=512] 10
calories_total_bucket_bucket[1e=1024] 40
calories_total_bucket_bucket[1e=2048] 60
```

If you plotted these metrics on their own individual y-axes with the x-axis being time, you might be able to see that

- Days where you ate cheeseburgers were inversely correlated to days you ate breakfast.
- The amount of cheeseburgers you've been eating is increasing steadily.

4.6.1   *Metrics are cheap to publish and extremely valuable*

Metrics are important for containerized and cloud-based applications, but they need to be managed in a lightweight and decoupled manner. *Prometheus* gives us the tools to enable metrics at scale without creating any unnecessary boilerplate or frameworks that get in our way. It is designed to fulfill the following requirements:

- Hundreds or thousands of different processes might publish similar metrics, which means that a given metric needs to support metadata labels to differentiate these processes.
- Applications should publish metrics in a language-independent manner.
- Applications should publish metrics without being aware of how those metrics are being consumed.
- It should be easy for any developer to publish metrics for a service, regardless of the language they use.

Programmatically, if we were to journal our diet choices in the previous analogy, we would declare instances of `cheeseburger`, `meals_today`, and `calories_total` that would be of the type `counter`, `gauge`, and `histogram`, respectively. These types would be Prometheus API types, supporting operations that automatically store local values to memory, which could be scraped as a CSV file from a local endpoint. Typically, this is done by adding a Prometheus handler to a REST API server, and this handler serves only one meaningful endpoint: metrics/. To manage this data, we might use a Prometheus API client like so:

- Periodically, to observe a value for how many `meals_today` we've had as that is a Gauge API call
- Periodically, to increment a value for the `cheeseburger` right after lunch
- Daily, to aggregate the value of `calories_total`, which can be fed in from a different data source

Over time, we could possibly correlate whether eating cheeseburgers related to a higher total calorie consumption on a per day basis, and we might also be able to tie in other metrics (for example, our weight) to these values. Although any time-series database could enable this, Prometheus, as a lightweight metrics engine, works well well in containers because it is entirely published by processes in a way that is independent and stateless, and it's emerged as the modern standard for adding metrics to any application.

Don't wait to publish metrics

Prometheus is often mistakenly thought of as a heavyweight system that needs to be centrally installed to be useful. Actually, it's really just an open source *counting tool* and an API that can be embedded in any application. The fact that a Prometheus master can scrape and integrate this information is obviously central to that story, but it's not a requirement to begin publishing and collecting metrics for your app.

Any microservice can publish metrics on an endpoint by importing a Prometheus client. Although your cluster may not consume these metrics, there's no reason not to make these available on the container side, if for no other reason than that you can use this endpoint to manually inspect counts of various quantifiable aspects of your application, and you can spin up an ad hoc Prometheus master if you want to observe it in the wild.

There are Prometheus clients for all major programming languages. Thus, for any microservice, it is simple and cheap to journal the daily goings-on of various events as a Prometheus metric.

4.6.2   *Why do I need Prometheus?*

In this book, we focus on Prometheus because it is the de facto standard in the cloud native landscape, but we'll try to convince you that it deserves this status with a simple, powerful example of how to quickly do a health check on the inner workings of your API server. As an example, you can take a look at whether requests for Pods has put a lot of strain on your Kubernetes API server by running the following commands in your terminal (assuming that you have your `kind` cluster up and running). In a separate terminal, run a `kubectl proxy` command, and then `curl` the API server's metrics endpoint like so:

```
$ kubectl proxy   ◀──────  Allows you to access the Kubernetes
                           API server on localhost:8001

$> curl localhost:8001/metrics |grep etcd   ◀──────  curls the API server's
                                                      metrics endpoint
etcd_request_duration_seconds_bucket{op="get",type="*core.Pod",le="0.005"}
174
etcd_request_duration_seconds_bucket{op="get",type="*core.Pod",le="0.01"}
194
etcd_request_duration_seconds_bucket{op="get",type="*core.Pod",le="0.025"}
201
etcd_request_duration_seconds_bucket{op="get",type="*core.Pod",le="0.05"}
203
```

Anyone with a `kubectl` client can immediately use the `curl` command to ingest real-time metrics about the response times for a certain API endpoint. In the previous snippet, we can see that almost all `get` calls to the Pod's API endpoint return in less than .025 seconds, which is generally considered as reasonable performance. For the remainder of this chapter, we'll set up a Prometheus monitoring system for your `kind` cluster from scratch.

4.6.3   *Creating a local Prometheus monitoring service*

We can use a Prometheus monitoring service to inspect the way cgroups and system resources are utilized under duress. The architecture of a Prometheus monitoring system (figure 4.2) on `kind` includes the following:

- A Prometheus master
- A Kubernetes API server that the master monitors
- Many kubelets (in our case, 1), each a source of metric information for the API server to aggregate

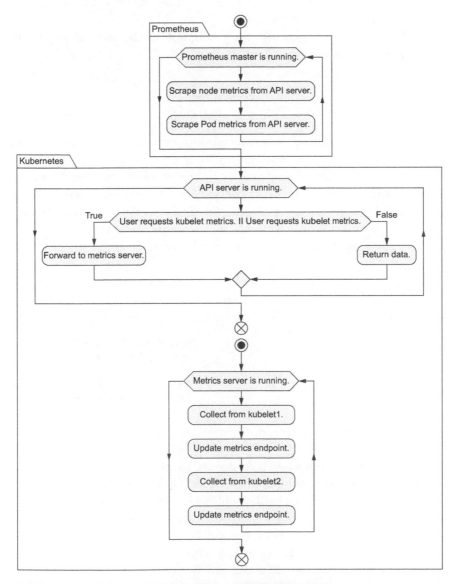

Figure 4.2   Architecture of a Prometheus monitoring deployment

Note that, in general, a Prometheus master might be scraping metrics from many different sources, including API servers, hardware nodes, standalone databases, and even standalone applications. Not all services conveniently get aggregated into the Kubernetes API server for use, however. In this simple example, we want to look at how to use Prometheus for the specific purpose of monitoring cgroup resource usage on Kubernetes, and conveniently, we can do this by simply scraping data from all of our nodes directly from the API server. Also, note that our kind cluster in this example has only one node. Even if we had more nodes, we could still scrape all of this data directly from the API server by adding more target fields to our scrape YAML file (which we will introduce shortly).

We will launch Prometheus with the configuration file that follows. Then we can store the configuration file as prometheus.yaml:

```
$ mkdir ./data
$ ./prometheus-2.19.1.darwin-amd64/prometheus \
    --storage.tsdb.path=./data --config.file=./prometheus.yml
```

The kubelet uses the cAdvisor library to monitor cgroups and to collect quantifiable data about them (for example, how much CPU and memory a Pod in particular group uses). Because you already know how to browse through cgroup filesystem hierarchies, reading the output of a kubelet collected by cAdvisor metrics will yield an "aha" moment for you (in terms of your understanding how Kubernetes itself connects to the lower-level kernel resource accounting). To scrape up these metrics, we'll tell Prometheus to query the API server every 3 seconds like so:

```
global:
  scrape_interval: 3s
  evaluation_interval: 3s

scrape_configs:
  - job_name: prometheus
    metrics_path:                              The kind control plane node is
      /api/v1/nodes/kind-control-plane/        the only node in our cluster.
      proxy/metrics/cadvisor    ◄──────┐
    static_configs:                            Add more nodes in our cluster or more
      - targets: ['localhost:8001']  ◄──┘      things to scrape in subsequent jobs here.
```

Real-world Prometheus configurations have to account for real-world constraints. These include data size, security, and alerting protocols. Note that time-series databases are notoriously greedy when it comes to disk usage and that metrics can reveal a lot about a threat model for your organization. These may not be important in your initial prototyping, as we noted earlier, but it's better to start by publishing your metrics at the application level and to then add the complexity of managing a heavyweight Prometheus installation later. For our simple example, this will be all we need to configure Prometheus to explore our cgroups.

Again, remember that the API server receives data from the kubelet periodically, which is why this strategy of only needing to scrape one endpoint works. If this was not the case, we could collect this data directly from the kubelet itself or even run our own cAdvisor service. Now, let's take a look at the *container CPU user seconds total* metric. We'll make it spike by running the following command.

> **WARNING** This command immediately creates a lot of network and CPU traffic on your computer.

```
$ kubectl apply -f \
https://raw.githubusercontent.com/
➥ giantswarm/kube-stresscheck/master/examples/node.yaml
```

This command launches a series of resource-intensive containers that suck up network assets, memory, and CPU cycles in your cluster. If you're on a laptop, the giant swarm container produced by running this command will probably cause a lot of CPU spiking, and you might hear some fan noise.

In figure 4.3, you'll see what our `kind` cluster looks like under duress. We'll leave it as an exercise for you to map the various container cgroups and metadata (found by

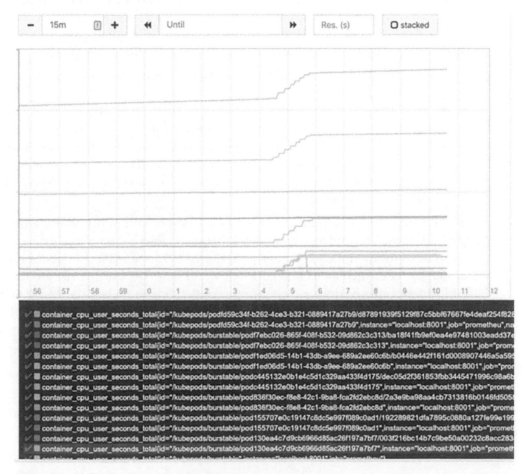

Figure 4.3 Plotting metrics in a busy cluster

hovering your mouse over the Prometheus metrics) back to processes and containers that are running in your system. In particular, it's worth looking at the following metrics to get a feel for CPU-level monitoring in Prometheus. Exploring these metrics, along with the hundreds of other metrics in your system when running your favorite workloads or containers, gives you a good way to create important monitoring and forensics protocols for your internal systems engineering pipelines:

- `container_memory_usage_bytes`
- `container_fs_writes_total`
- `container_memory_cache`

4.6.4   *Characterizing an outage in Prometheus*

Let's look in more detail at the three metric types before closing up shop for this chapter, just for good measure. In figure 4.4, we compare the general topology of how these three metrics give you different perspectives on the same situation in your data center. Specifically, we can see that the gauge gives us a Boolean value indicating whether our cluster is up. Meanwhile, the histogram shows us fine-grained information on how requests are trending until we lose our application entirely. Finally, the counters show us the overall number of transactions leading to an outage:

- The gauge readout would be most valuable to someone who might be on pager duty for application up time.
- The histogram readout may be most valuable to an engineer doing "day after" forensics on why a microservice went down for an extended time.
- The counter metric would be a good way to determine how many successful requests were served before an outage. For example, in case of a memory leak, we might find that after a certain number of requests (say, 15,000 or 20,000), a web server predictably fails.

It's ultimately up to you to decide which metrics you want to use to make decisions, but in general, it's good to keep in mind that your metrics should not just be a dumping ground for information. Rather, they should help you tell a story about how your services behave and interact with each other over time. Generic metrics are rarely useful for debugging intricate problems, so take the time to embed the Prometheus client into your applications and collect some interesting, quantifiable application metrics. Your administrators will thank you! We'll look back at metrics again in our etcd chapter, so don't worry—there will be more Prometheus to come!

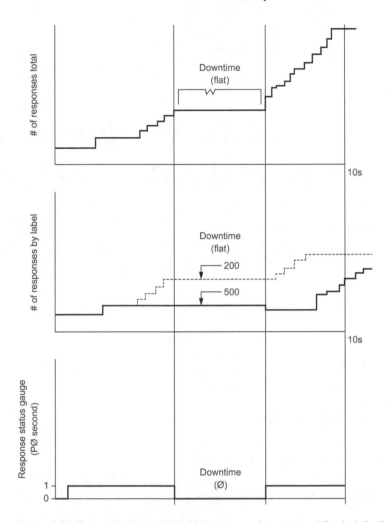

Figure 4.4   Comparing how gauge, histogram, and counter metrics look in the same scenario cluster

Summary

- The kernel expresses cgroup limitations for containers.
- A kubelet starts the scheduler processes and mirrors it for the API server.
- We can use simple containers to inspect how cgroups implement a memory limitation.
- The kubelet has QoS classes that nuance the quota for process resources in your Pods.
- We can use Prometheus to view real-time metrics of a cluster under duress.
- Prometheus expresses three core metric types: gauges, histograms, and counters.

CNIs and providing the Pod with a network

This chapter covers

- Defining the Kubernetes SDN in terms of the kube-proxy and CNI
- Connecting between traditional SDN Linux tools and CNI plugins
- Using open source technologies to govern the way CNIs operate
- Exploring the Calico and Antrea CNI providers

Software-Defined Networking (SDN) traditionally manages load balancing, isolation, and security of VMs in the cloud, as well as in many on-premise data centers. SDNs are a convenience which eases the burden on system administrators, allowing reconfiguration of large data center networks every week, or maybe every day, when new VMs are created or destroyed. Fast-forwarding into the age of containers, the concept of SDN takes on a whole new meaning because our networks change constantly (every second, in a large Kubernetes cluster), and so it must, by definition, be automated by software. The Kubernetes network is entirely software-defined and is constantly in flux due to the ephemeral and dynamic nature of the Kubernetes Pod and service endpoints.

In this chapter, we'll look at Pod-to-Pod networking and, in particular, how hundreds or thousands of containers on a given machine can have unique, cluster-routable IP addresses. Kubernetes delivers this functionality in a modular and extensible way by using a Container Network Interface (CNI) standard, which can be implemented by a broad range of technologies to give each Pod a unique routable IP address.

> **The CNI specification doesn't specify the details of container networking**
>
> The CNI specification is a generic definition for the high-level operations to add a container to a network. Reading too deeply into it might cause a little difficulty at first if you approach it in terms of how you think about Kubernetes CNI providers. For example, some CNI plugins, such as the IPAM plugin (https://www.cni.dev/plugins/current/ipam/), are only responsible for finding a valid IP address for a container, while other CNI plugins, such as Antrea or Calico, operate at a higher level, delegating functionality as needed to other plugins. Some CNI plugins, in fact, do not actually attach a Pod to a network at all, but rather play a minute role in the broader "let's add this container to a network" workflow. (Understanding that, the IPAM plugin is a good way to grok this concept.)
>
> Keep in mind that any CNI plugin you'll encounter in the wild is a snowflake that might operate at a different time in the overall progression of connecting your container to a network. Also, some CNI plugins are only meaningful in the context of the other plugins that reference them.

Let's revisit our Pods from earlier and look back at their core networking requirement. As part of exploring this concept, we previously discussed the way iptables rules for nftables, IPVSs (IP virtual servers), and other network proxy implementations are managed by the kube-proxy. We also looked at various KUBE-SEP rules that tell the Linux kernel to "masquerade" traffic so that the traffic leaving a container is post-marked as coming from a node or to NAT traffic via a service IP. This traffic is then forwarded to a running Pod, which often might be on a different node in our cluster.

The kube-proxy is great for routing services to backend Pods and is usually the first piece of software-defined networking that users interact with. For example, when you first run and expose a simple Kubernetes application with a node port, you are accessing a Pod through a routing rule that's created by the kube-proxy running on your Kubernetes nodes. The kube-proxy, however, is not particularly useful unless there is a robust Pod network on your cluster. This is because, ultimately, its only job is to map a service IP address into a Pod's IP address. If that Pod's IP address is not routable between two nodes, then the kube-proxy's routing decisions do not result in an application that is usable to the end user. That is to say, a load balancer is only as reliable as its slowest endpoint.

The kpng project and the future of `kube-proxy`

As Kubernetes grows, the CNI landscape expands to actually implement the `kube-proxy` service routing functionality at the CNI level. This allows CNI providers like Antrea, Calico, and Cilium, to provide high performance and extended feature sets to the Kubernetes service proxy (for example, monitoring and native integration with other load balancing technologies).

To address the need for a "pluggable" network proxy that can retain some of the core logic from Kubernetes, while allowing vendors to extend other parts, the kpng project (https://github.com/kubernetes-sigs/kpng) was created and is incubating as a new `kube-proxy` alternative. It's extremely modular and lives completely outside of the Kubernetes codebase. If you are interested in Kubernetes load-balancing services, it's a great project to dig into and learn more about, but it is not ready for production workloads at the time of this writing.

As an example of an alternative CNI-provided network proxy that might someday be able to be fully implemented as a kpng extension, you can look at projects such as the Antrea proxy (currently a new feature in Antrea) that can be turned on or off, based on user preference. You'll find more information at http://mng.bz/AxGQ.

5.1   *Why we need software-defined networks in Kubernetes*

The container networking puzzle can be defined as follows: given hundreds of Pods, some of which correspond to the same service, how can we consistently route traffic into and out of a cluster so that all traffic always goes to the right place, even if our Pods are moving? This is the obvious Day 2 operations problem facing anyone who has tried to run a non-Kubernetes container solution in production (for example, Docker). To solve this, Kubernetes gives us two fundamental networking tools:

- *The service proxy*—Ensures that Pods can be load balanced behind services with stable IPs and routes Kubernetes Service objects
- *The CNI*—Ensures that Pods can be reborn continually inside a network that is flat and easy to access from inside the cluster

At the heart of this solution is the Kubernetes Service object with the type `ClusterIP`. A ClusterIP service is a Kubernetes Service that is routable inside your Kubernetes cluster, but it is not accessible outside your cluster. It is a fundamental primitive on top of which other services can be built. It's also a simple way for applications inside your cluster to access one another without needing to directly route to a Pod IP address (remember, Pod IPs can change if they move or die).

As an example, if we create the same service three times in a `kind` cluster, we will see that it has three random IP addresses in the 10.96 IP space. To verify this, we can recreate the same three services by running `kubectl create service clusterip my-service-1 --tcp="100:100"` three times in a row (changing the name of `my-service-1`, of course). Afterward, we could list the service IPs like so:

```
$ kubectl get svc -o wide
svc-1 ClusterIP 10.96.7.53    80/TCP 48s app=MyApp
svc-2 ClusterIP 10.96.152.223 80/TCP 33s app=MyApp
svc-3 ClusterIP 10.96.43.92   80/TCP 5s  app=MyApp
```

Similarly for Pods, we have a single network and subnet. We can see that new IP addresses are easily provisioned when making new Pods. Because our kind cluster already has two CoreDNS Pods running, we can check their IP addresses to confirm this:

```
$ kubectl get pods -A -o wide | grep coredns
kube-system coredns-74ff55c5b-nlxrs 1/1  Running 0 4d16h 192.168.71.1
➥ calico-control-plane <none> <none>
kube-system coredns-74ff55c5b-t4p6s 1/1  Running 0 4d16h 192.168.71.3
➥ calico-control-plane <none> <none>
```

We just saw the first important lessons of the Kubernetes SDN: Pod and Service IP addresses are managed for us and are in different IP subnets. This is (generally) a constant in almost any cluster we'll encounter in the real world. In fact, if we do encounter a cluster where this is *not* the case, there is a chance that some other behavior of Kubernetes has been severely compromised. This behavior may include the ability for the kube-proxy to route traffic or the ability of the node to route Pod traffic.

> **The Kubernetes control plane charts the course for Pod and Service IP ranges**
> It's a common misconception in Kubernetes that CNI providers are responsible for service as well as Pod IP addresses. Actually, when you make a new ClusterIP Service, the Kubernetes control plane creates a new IP from the CIDR you give it on startup as a command-line option (for example, --service-cluster-ip-range), which is used with the --allocate-node-cidrs option. CNI providers often rely on the node CIDRs that are also allocated by the API server if specified. Thus, CNI and the network proxy act at a highly localized level, issuing the directives of the overall cluster configuration that is coordinated by the Kubernetes control plane.

5.2 Implementing the service side of the Kubernetes SDN: The kube-proxy

There are three primary types of Kubernetes Service API objects that we can create (as you likely know by now): ClusterIPs, NodePorts, and LoadBalancers. These Services define which backend Pod we'll connect to by the use of *labels*. For example, in the previous cluster, we have ClusterIP services in our 10 subnet, and those Services route traffic to Pods in our 192 subnet. How does traffic destined for a service IP get routed into another subnet? It gets routed by the kube-proxy (or, more formally, the Kubernetes network or service proxy).

In the previous example, we ran kubectl create service my-service-1 --tcp= "100:100" three times and got three services of type ClusterIP. If we were to make these services as type NodePort, then the IP of these Services would be any node in our entire cluster. If we were to make these Services a LoadBalancer type, then our cloud (if we were in a cloud) would provide an external IP, such as 35.1.2.3. This would be accessible on the wider internet or on a network outside our Pod, node, or service IP range, depending on the cloud provider.

Is the `kube-proxy` a proxy?

In the early days of Kubernetes, the `kube-proxy` itself opened up a new Golang routine for incoming requests; thus, services were actually implemented as userspace processes that continue to respond to traffic. The creation of the Kubernetes iptables proxy (and later, the IPVS proxy) and the Windows kernel proxy led to the `kube-proxy` being much more scalable and CPU-efficient.

Some such use cases for userspace proxying still exist but are far and few between. For example, VMware's Tanzu Kubernetes Grid uses userspace proxying to support Windows clusters because it cannot rely on kernel-space proxying. This is due to a difference in architecture in the way that it uses Open vSwitch (OVS). In any case, the `kube-proxy`, in general, typically tells other proxying tools about Kubernetes endpoints, but it is usually not considered a proxy in the traditional sense.

Figure 5.1 shows the flow of traffic from a LoadBalancer into a Kubernetes cluster. It depicts how

- The `kube-proxy` uses a low-level routing technology like iptables or IPVS to send traffic from services into and out of Pods.
- We get an IP address from the outside world when we have a service of type LoadBalancer. This then routes into our internal service IP.

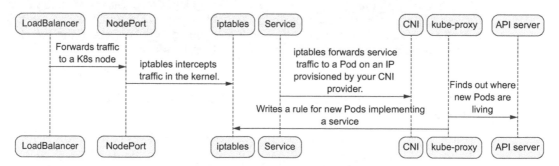

Figure 5.1   The flow of traffic from a LoadBalancer into a Kubernetes cluster

NodePort vs. ClusterIP services

NodePorts are Services in Kubernetes that are exposed on all ports outside of the internal Pod network. They allow a primitive on which you can build a load balancer. For example, you might have a web app that serves on a ClusterIP of say, 100.1.2.3:443.

(continued)

If you want to access that app from outside your cluster, every node might forward to this service from a NodePort. The value of a NodePort is random; for example, it might be something like 50491. Thus, you could access your web app on node_ip_ 1:50491, node_ip_2:50491, node_ip_3:50491, and so on.

If you are interested in more optimal ways to set up routing by annotating services using the `externalTrafficPolicy` annotation, this might not work the same on all OSs and cloud types. Make sure to dig into the details if you decide to get fancy with service routing.

NodePorts are built on top of *ClusterIP* services. ClusterIP services have an internal IP address that (usually) does not overlap with your Pod network, which is synchronous with your API server.

Reading `kube-proxy`'s iptables rules just for fun

If you are interested in seeing a fully annotated iptables configuration in a real cluster, you can look at the iptables-save-calico.md file at http://mng.bz/enV9. We put together this file as a way to see all iptables rules that normally might be output from a Kubernetes cluster running in the wild.

In particular, in this file we note that there are three main iptables tables, and the most important one for Kubernetes is the NAT table. This is where the highly dynamic ebb and flow of services and Pods takes its toll on large clusters. As mentioned in other parts of this book, there are tradeoffs between different `kube-proxy` configurations, but by far, the most commonly used proxy is the iptables `kube-proxy`.

5.2.1 The kube-proxy's data plane

The `kube-proxy` needs to be able to handle ongoing TCP traffic going to and from Pods that are backed by services. An IP packet has certain fundamental properties including the source and destination IP addresses. In a sophisticated network, these may get changed because a packet moves through a series of routers, and we consider a Kubernetes node (due to the `kube-proxy`) to be one such router. In general, the manipulation of a packet's destination is known as *NAT* (referring to network address translation) and is a fundamental aspect of almost any network architecture solution at some level. *SNAT* and *DNAT* refer to the translation of source and destination IP addresses, respectively.

The data plane of the `kube-proxy` can accomplish this task in a variety of ways, and this is specified to the `kube-proxy` by its `mode` configuration at startup. If we dig into the details, we find that the `kube-proxy` itself is organized into two separate control paths: server_windows.go and server_others.go (both located here: http://mng.bz/ EWxl). The server_windows.go binary is compiled into a kube-proxy.exe file and makes native calls to underlying Windows system APIs (such as the `netsh` command for the userspace proxy and the hcsshim and HCN [http://mng.bz/N6x2] containerization APIs for the Windows kernel proxy).

The more common case is that we run the kube-proxy on Linux. In this case, a different binary program (which is called kube-proxy) runs. This program doesn't compile the Windows functionality into its code path. In the Linux scenario, we usually run the iptables proxy. In your kind clusters, the kube-proxy just runs in the default iptables mode. You can confirm this by looking at the configuration of the kube-proxy by running kubectl edit cm kube-proxy -n kube-system and looking at its mode field:

- ipvs uses the kernel load balancer to write routing rules for services (Linux).
- iptables uses the kernel firewall to write routing rules for services (Linux).
- The userspace creates a process using a Golang go func worker that manually proxies traffic to a Pod (Linux).
- The Windows kernel relies on the hcsshim and HCN APIs for load balancing, which is incompatible with OVS-related CNI implementations but works with other CNIs like Calico (similar to the Linux userspace option).
- The Windows userspace also uses netsh for certain aspects of routing. This is useful for people who, for some reason, can't use the regular Windows kernel's APIs. Note that if you install an OVS extension on Windows, you may need to use the userspace proxy because the kernel's HCN APIs do not work in the same way.

NOTE   Throughout this book, we will mention the notion of informers, controllers, and Operators and how their behavior is not always uniformly implemented with respect to the configuration changes that occur. Although the network proxy is implemented with a Kubernetes controller, it doesn't dynamically respond to configuration changes. Thus, if you want to play with your kind cluster to modify the way that service load balancing is done, you'll need to edit configMap for the network proxy and then restart its DaemonSet. (If you want, you can do this by killing a Pod in your DaemonSet and then view the Pod's logs as it is reborn. You should see the new kube-proxy mode.)

The kube-proxy is, however, just one way to define how the Kubernetes SDN routes traffic. To be comprehensive, we can think of Kubernetes routing in three separate layers:

- *External load balancers or ingress/gateway routers*—Forward traffic into a Kubernetes cluster.
- *The* kube-proxy—Manages forwarding between services to Pods. As you may know by now, the term *proxy* is a bit of a misnomer because, typically, the kube-proxy just maintains static routing rules that are implemented by a kernel or other data plane technology, such as iptables rules.
- *CNI providers*—Route traffic to and from Pods regardless of whether we are accessing them through a service endpoint or directly (Pod-to-Pod networking).

Ultimately, a CNI provider (like the kube-proxy) also configures some kind of rule engine (such as a routing table) or an OVS switch to ensure that traffic between nodes or from the outside world can route to Pods. If you're wondering why the technology for the `kube-proxy` is different from that of CNIs, you're not alone! Many CNI providers are endeavoring to implement a full-blown `kube-proxy` themselves so that the `kube-proxy` from Kubernetes is no longer required.

5.2.2 *What about NodePorts?*

We've demonstrated the ClusterIP services in the first part of this chapter, but we haven't yet looked at NodePort services. Let's do that now by getting our feet wet and creating a new Kubernetes service. This will ultimately demonstrate how easy it is to add and modify load-balancing rules. For this example, let's make a NodePort service that points to a CoreDNS container running inside a Pod in our cluster. We can quickly cobble one together by looking at the contents of `kubectl get svc -o yaml kube-dns -n kube-system`. We can then change the type of service from `ClusterIP` to `NodePort` like so:

```
# save the following file to my-nodeport.yaml
apiVersion: v1
kind: Service
metadata:
  annotations:
    prometheus.io/port: "9153"
    prometheus.io/scrape: "true"
  labels:
    k8s-app: kube-dns
    kubernetes.io/cluster-service: "true"
    kubernetes.io/name: CoreDNS
  name: kube-dns-2           ◁─────────  Names the service kube-dns-2 to
  namespace: kube-system                 differentiate it from the already
spec:                                    existing kube-dns service
  ipFamilies:
  - IPv4
  ipFamilyPolicy: SingleStack
  ports:
  - name: dns
    port: 53
    protocol: UDP
    targetPort: 53
  - name: dns-tcp
    port: 53
    protocol: TCP
    targetPort: 53
  - name: metrics
    port: 9153
    protocol: TCP
    targetPort: 9153
  selector:
    k8s app: kube-dns
  sessionAffinity: None
  type: NodePort            ◁──────  Changes the type of this
status:                             service to a NodePort
  loadBalancer: {}
```

Now, if we run `kubectl create -f my-nodeport.yaml`, we'll see that a random port was allocated for us. This is now forwarding traffic to CoreDNS for us:

```
kubectl get pods -o wide -A
kube-system   kube-dns     ClusterIP   10.96.0.10
              53/UDP,53/TCP,9153/TCP k8s-app=kube-dns
kube-system   kube-dns-2   NodePort    10.96.80.7
              53:30357/UDP,53:30357/TCP,9153:31588/TCP      Maps the random ports
              2m33s   k8s-app=kube-dns              ◁────── 30357 and 31588 to port 53
```

The random ports 30357 and 31588, mapped to port 53 from our DNS service Pods, open on all the nodes of our cluster. That's because all nodes are running the `kube-proxy`. These random ports were not allocated earlier when we created the ClusterIP services.

If you are feeling brave, we'll leave it as an exercise for you to run `iptables-save` on your `kind` Docker nodes and fish out the handy work that the `kube-proxy` has done to write rules for your newly created service IP addresses. (If you are interested in exercising NodePorts, you'll enjoy our later chapter about how to install and test Kubernetes applications locally. There, we'll create several services for testing the famous Guestbook application in Kubernetes.)

Now that you've got a little bit of a refresher on how services ultimately plumb routing rules between internal Pod ports and the external world, let's look at CNI providers. These provide the next layer below the service proxy in the overall Kubernetes SDN networking stack. Ultimately, all our service is really doing is routing traffic from 10.96.80.7 to the Pods that are living inside our cluster. How do these Pods get attached to a valid IP address, and how do they receive this traffic? The answer is . . . the CNI interface.

5.3   *CNI providers*

CNI providers implement the CNI specification (http://mng.bz/RENK), which defines a contract that allows container runtimes to request a working IP address for a process on startup. They also add other fancy features outside this specification (like implementing network policies or third-party network monitoring integrations). For example, VMware users will find that they can use Antrea as a CNI proxy for free and plug it into things like VMware's NSX platform for real-time container monitoring and logging features that some of the current open source CNI providers include. Although CNI providers, theoretically, only need to route Pod traffic, many provide extra bells and whistles. A quick rundown of the major, on-premise CNIs includes

- *Calico*—A BGP-based CNI provider that makes new Border Gateway Protocol (BGP) routing rules to implement the data plane. Calico additionally supports XDP, NAND, and VXLAN routing options (for example, on Windows, it's not uncommon to run Calico in VXLAN mode). As an advanced CNI, it has the ability to replace the `kube-proxy`, using technology similar to Cilium's.

- *Antrea*—An OVS data plane CNI provider that uses a bridge to route all Pod traffic. It is similar to Calico in that it has many advanced routing and network proxy replacement options (AntreaProxy).
- *Flannel*—A bridge-based IP CNI provider that is no longer commonly used. It was one of the original major CNIs for production Kubernetes clusters.
- *Google, EC2, and NCP*—These cloud-based CNIs use proprietary software to make cloud-aware traffic routing decisions. For example, they are capable of creating rules that route traffic directly between containers without needing to travel over node network paths.
- *Cilium*—A XDP-based CNI provider that uses modern Linux APIs to route traffic without requiring any Kernel traffic management. This allows for faster and more secure IP communication between containers in some cases. Cillium uses its advanced data path tooling to provide a network proxy alternative as well.
- *KindNet*—A simple CNI plugin that is used in `kind` clusters by default, but it's only designed to work in simple clusters with only one subnet.

There are many other CNIs that might be specific to other vendors or open source technologies, as well as proprietary CNI providers for various cloud environments such as VMware, Azure, EKS, and so on. These proprietary CNIs only run inside a given vendor's infrastructure and, thus, are less portable but often more performant or better integrated with cloud features. Some CNIs, like Calico and Antrea, provide both vendor-specific and vendor-neutral functionality (such as Tigera or NSX specific integrations, for example).

5.4 Diving into two CNI networking plugins: Calico and Antrea

Figure 5.2 shows how CNI networking works in the Calico and Antrea plugins. Both of these plugins accomplish the same end state using a series of routing rules and open source technologies. The CNI interface defines a few core functional aspects of any networking solution for containers, and all CNI plugins (BGP and OVS, for example) implement that functionality in different ways. As figure 5.2 shows, different CNIs use different underlying technology stacks.

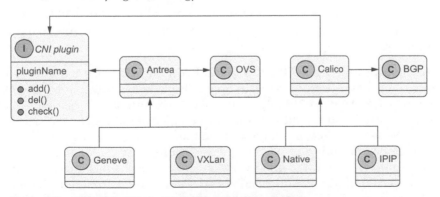

Figure 5.2   CNI networking in the Calico and Antrea plugins

Is `kube-proxy` a requirement?

We talk about `kube-proxy` as being a requirement, but increasingly, network vendors are beginning to propose technologies such as Extended Berkeley Packet Filter (eBPF), provided by the Cilium CNI, or the OVS proxy, provided by the Antrea CNI, which shortcut the need for running `kube-proxy`. These typically borrow `kube-proxy`'s inner logic and attempt to reproduce and implement it in a way that uses a different underlying data plane. The majority of clusters at the time of this book's publication, however, use the traditional iptables or Windows kernel proxy. Thus, we refer to the `kube-proxy` as a constant feature in a modern Kubernetes cluster. But look out on the horizon for fancy alternatives as the cloud native landscape expands.

5.4.1   The architecture of a CNI plugin

Both Calico and Antrea have similar architectures: a DaemonSet and a coordination container. To set these up, a CNI installation includes four steps (fully automated for you by your CNI provider, usually, so that this can be done in a snappy one-liner in simple Linux clusters):

1. Install the `kube-proxy` because it's likely that your CNI provider's coordination controller will need the ability to query the Kubernetes API server. This is usually done for you ahead of time by any Kubernetes installer.
2. Install a binary CNI program on the node (usually in a directory such as /opt/cni/bin) that can be called by the container runtime to create a Pod with a CNI-provided IP address.
3. Deploy a DaemonSet to your cluster, where one container sets up networking primitives for its resident node. This DaemonSet does the previous install step for its host on startup.
4. Deploy a coordination container to your cluster that either aggregates or proxies metadata from Kubernetes; for example, aggregating NetworkPolicy information in a single place so that it can easily be consumed and deduplicated by the DaemonSet Pods.

There's no one mandated architecture for a CNI plugin, but the overall DaemonSet plus controller pattern is pretty robust. It is generally a good pattern to follow in Kubernetes for any agent-oriented process that is designed to be integrated with the Kubernetes API.

> **NOTE** CNI providers give IP addresses to Pods, but a lot of the assumptions around how this process works were originally made in a way that is biased to the Linux OS. Thus, we'll look at the Calico and Antrea CNI providers, but when doing this, you should note that the behavior of these CNIs varies across other OSs. For example, in Windows, both Calico and Antrea are not typically run as Pods but rather as Windows services using tools such as `nssm`. Currently, some of the more battle-hardened, open source CNIs for Kubernetes that support both Linux and Windows are Calico and Antrea, but there are many others as well.

The CNI specification is implemented by the binary program installed by our agent. In particular, it implements three fundamental CNI operations: ADD, DELETE, and CHECK, which are called when the containerd starts a new Pod or deletes one. Respectively, these operations

- Add a container to a network
- Delete a container from a network
- Check that the container is properly set up

5.4.2 Let's play with some CNIs

Finally, we get to do some hacking! Let's start by installing a Calico CNI provider in our kind cluster. Calico uses Layer 3 routing (as opposed to bridging, which is a Layer 2 technology) to broadcast routes for Pods in a cluster. End users won't generally notice this difference, but it's an important distinction to administrators because some administrators might want to use Layer 3 concepts (like BGP peering) or Layer 2 concepts (like OVS-based traffic monitoring) for broader infrastructure design goals in their clusters:

- *BGP* stands for Border Gateway Protocol, which is a Layer 3 routing technology used commonly in the overall internet.
- *OVS* stands for Open vSwitch, which is a Linux kernel-based API for programming a switch inside your OS to create virtual IP addresses.

The first step in making our kind cluster is to disable its default CNI. Then we'll recreate it from a YAML specification. For example:

Disables the kind-net CNI

```
$ cat << EOF > kind-Calico-conf.yaml
kind: Cluster
apiVersion: kind.sigs.k8s.io/v1alpha4
networking:
  disableDefaultCNI: true
  podSubnet: 192.168.0.0/16
nodes:
- role: control-plane
- role: worker
EOF
$ kind create cluster --name=calico --config=./kind-Calico-conf.yaml
```

Divides the 192.168 subnet so that it's orthogonal to our service subnet

Adds a second node to our cluster

The kind-net CNI is a minimal CNI that only works for a one node cluster. We disable it so we can use a real CNI provider. All our Pods will be on a large swath of the 192.168 subnet. Calico divides this up for each node, and it should be orthogonal to our service subnet. Additionally, having a second node in our cluster helps us to understand how Calico separates local traffic from traffic destined for another node.

Setting a kind cluster up with a real CNI plugin is not significantly different from what we've already done. Once this cluster comes up, it's worth pausing for a moment to see what happens when a Pod's CNI isn't yet available. This leads to unschedulable

Pods that aren't defined in the kubelet/manifests directory. You'll see this by running the following `kubectl` commands:

```
$ kubectl get pods --all-namespaces
NAMESPACE     NAME                        READY   STATUS    RESTARTS   AGE
kube-system   coredns-66bff467f8-86mgh    0/1     Pending   0          7m47s
kube-system   coredns-66bff467f8-nfzhz    0/1     Pending   0          7m47s

$ kubectl get nodes
NAME                    STATUS     ROLES     AGE     VERSION
Calico-control-plane    NotReady   master    2m4s    v1.18.2
Calico-worker           NotReady   <none>    85s     v1.18.2
```

5.4.3   Installing the Calico CNI provider

At this point, our CoreDNS Pod will not be able to start because the Kubernetes scheduler sees that all nodes are `NotReady`, as the previous commands show. If that's not the case, check that your CNI provider is up and running. This state is determined based on the fact that the CNI provider hasn't been set yet. CNIs are configured once a CNI container writes a /etc/cni/net.d file on a kubelet's local filesystem. In order to get our cluster going, we'll now install Calico:

```
$ wget https://docs.projectCalico.org/manifests/Calico.yaml
$ kubelet create -f Calico.yaml
```

> ### Kubernetes security matters, most of the time
>
> This book is focused on learning Kubernetes internals, but we don't spend much time making every command "airtight." The previous command, for example, pulls a manifest file from the internet and installs several containers in your cluster. Make sure that you are running these commands in a sandbox (such as `kind`) if you don't fully understand their consequences!
>
> Chapters 13 and 14 provide a guide to Pod and node security. Beyond that, if you you are interested in application-centric security, projects such as https://sigstore.dev/ and https://github.com/bitnami-labs/sealed-secrets have evolved over time to address various security concerns around Kubernetes binaries, artifacts, manifests, and even secrets. If you are interested in implementing the convenient Kubernetes idioms used in this book in a more secure manner, it's worth delving into these (and other) tools in the Kubernetes ecosystem. For more information on general Kubernetes security concepts, consult https://kubernetes.io/docs/concepts/security/ or feel free to join the Kubernetes security mailing list (http://mng.bz/QWz1).

The previous step creates two container types: a Calico-node Pod on each node and a Calico-kube-controllers Pod, which run on arbitrary nodes. Once these containers come up, your nodes should be in the `Ready` state, and you'll also see that the CoreDNS Pod is now running:

```
$ kubectl get pods --all-namespaces                    Coordinates the Calico
NAMESPACE            NAME                               node containers
kube-system          Calico-kube-cntrlrs-57-m5   ◄──┘
kube-system          Calico-node-4mbc5       ◄──┐
kube-system          Calico-node-gpvxm              Sets up various BGP and IP
kube-system          coredns-66bff467f8-98t8j       routes on a per node basis
kube-system          coredns-66bff467f8-m7lj5
kube-system          etcd-Calico-control-plane
kube-system          kube-apiserver-Calico-control-plane
kube-system          kube-controller-mgr
kube-system          kube-proxy-8q5zq
kube-system          kube-proxy-zgrjf
kube-system          kube-scheduler-Calico-control-plane
local-path-storage   local-path-provisioner-b5-fsr
```

In this code example, the kube controller container coordinates the Calico node containers. Each Calico node container sets up various BGP and IP routes on a per node basis for all containers running on a given node. There are two because we have two nodes.

Both Calico and Antrea mount what are known as *hostPath* volume types. The CNI binary for the Calico-node process then accesses this hostPath, which connects to /etc/cni/net.d/ on your kubelet. The kubelet uses this binary to call the CNI API when an IP address is needed for a new Pod, and thus, it can be thought of as the *installation mechanism* for the host's CNI provider. Remember that hostPath volume types are (most of the time) an anti-pattern, unless you are configuring a low-level OS functionality such as CNI.

In figure 5.2, we looked at the DaemonSet functionality as an interface that both Calico and Antrea implement. Let's take a look at what Calico created by running `kubectl get ds -n kube-system`. We'll see that there is a Calico DaemonSet for running a CNI Pod on all nodes. When we run Antrea later, we'll see a similar DaemonSet for the Antrea agent.

Because Linux CNI plugins usually shovel a CNI binary file into the host's system path, we can think of CNI plugins as implementing a `MountCniBinary` method. This might not be a part of the formal CNI interface, but it will ultimately be a part of almost any CNI plugin you'll see in the wild.

Great! We now have a CNI. Let's take a look at what has been created for us by Calico by running `docker exec` to get into our nodes and poke around. After running `docker exec -t -i <your kind node> /bin/bash`, we can start looking at what routes have been created by Calico. For example:

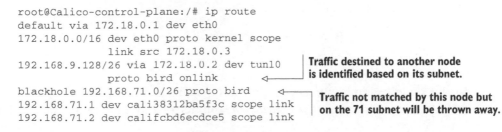

```
root@Calico-control-plane:/# ip route
default via 172.18.0.1 dev eth0
172.18.0.0/16 dev eth0 proto kernel scope
              link src 172.18.0.3
192.168.9.128/26 via 172.18.0.2 dev tunl0          Traffic destined to another node
              proto bird onlink           ◄──┘     is identified based on its subnet.
blackhole 192.168.71.0/26 proto bird       ◄──┐
192.168.71.1 dev cali38312ba5f3c scope link        Traffic not matched by this node but
192.168.71.2 dev califcbd6ecdce5 scope link        on the 71 subnet will be thrown away.
```

We can see that there are two IP addresses here: 192.168.71.1 and 71.2. These IP addresses are associated with two devices prefixed with the string *cali* that our Calico-node containers created. How do these devices work? We can see how they're defined by running the ip a command:

```
root@Calico-control-plane:/# ip a | grep califc
5: califcbd6ecdce5@if4: <BROADCAST,MULTICAST,UP,LOWER_UP>
➥ mtu 1440 qdisc noqueue state UP group default
```

Now we can see that the node has an interface created for Calico-related Pods with a recognizable name. For example:

```
root@Calico-control-plane:/# apt-get update -y;
➥ apt-get install tcpdump              ←  Installs tcpdump in the container
root@Calico-control-plane:/# tcpdump -s 0
➥ -i cali38312ba5f3c -v | grep 192     ←  Runs tcpdump against the Calico device
tcpdump: listening on cali38312ba5f3c, link-type EN10MB (Ethernet),
➥ capture size 262144 bytes

    10.96.0.1.443 > 192.168.71.1.59186: Flags [P.],
                    cksum 0x14d2 (incorrect -> 0x7189),
                    seq 520038628:520039301, ack 2015131286, win 502,
                    options [nop,nop,TS val 1110809235 ecr 1170831911],
                    length 673
    192.168.71.1.59186 > 10.96.0.1.443: Flags [.],
                    cksum 0x1231 (incorrect -> 0x9f10),
                    ack 673, win 502,
                    options [nop,nop,TS val 1170833141 ecr 1110809235],
                    length 0
    10.96.0.1.443 > 192.168.71.1.59186:
                    Flags [P.], cksum 0x149c (incorrect -> 0xa745),
                    seq 673:1292, ack 1, win 502,
                    options [nop,nop,TS val 1110809914 ecr 1170833141],
                    length 619
    192.168.71.1.59186 > 10.96.0.1.443:
                    Flags [.], cksum 0x1231 (incorrect -> 0x9757),
                    ack 1292, win 502,
                    options [nop,nop,TS val 1170833820 ecr 1110809914],
                    length 0
    192.168.71.1.59186 > 10.96.0.1.443:
                    Flags [P.], cksum 0x1254 (incorrect -> 0x362c),
                    seq 1:36, ack 1292, win 502,
                    options [nop,nop,TS val 1170833820 ecr 1110809914],
                    length 35
    10.96.0.1.443 > 192.168.71.1.59186:
                    Flags [.], cksum 0x1231 (incorrect -> 0x9734),
                    ack 36, win 502, options [nop,nop,TS val 1110809914
                    ecr 1170833820],
                    length 0
```

In our code example, we can see incoming traffic to the 71.1 IP address from the 10.96 subnet. This subnet is actually the subnet of our Kubernetes service for the

CoreDNS container, which is the point where our DNS containers powered by our CNI are contacted from. The previous cali3831... device is something that is directly attached (like any other device) via an Ethernet cable (of sorts) to our node. This is known as a *veth* pair, wherein our containers themselves have one end of a virtual Ethernet cable (named cali3831) directly plugged into them from our kubelet. This means anyone attempting to reach this device from our kubelet can easily do so.

Now, let's go back and look at the IP route table we showed earlier. The dev entries are now clear. These correspond to routes that plug into our containers directly. But what about the blackhole and 192.168.9.128/26 routes? These routes correspond to

- Containers that belong to another node (the 192.168.9.128/26 route)
- Containers that belong to no node at all (the blackhole route)

This is BGP in action. Every node in our cluster that runs a Calico-node daemon has a range of IPs that are routed to it. As new nodes come up, these routes are added to our IP route table over time. If you run kubectl scale deployment coredns -n kube-system --replicas=6, you'll find that all IP addresses come up in one of two different subnets:

- *Some Pods come up in the 192.168.9 subnet.* These correspond to one of our nodes.
- *Other Pods come up in the 192.168.71 subnet.* These correspond to the other node.

The more nodes you see in your cluster, the more subnets you'll have. Each node has its own IP range, and your CNI provider uses that IP range to allocate the IP addresses of the Pods on a given node to avoid collisions of Pod IP addresses across nodes. This also is a performance optimization because there is no need for global coordination of Pod IP address space. Thus, we can see that Calico is managing IP address ranges for us by carving up IP pools for individual nodes and then coordinating these pools with the route tables in the Kernel.

5.4.4 Kubernetes networking with OVS and Antrea

To the casual user, Antrea and Calico appear to do the same thing: route traffic between containers on a multi-node cluster. However, there's a lot of subtlety in how this is accomplished when you peek under the covers.

OVS is what Antrea uses to power its CNI capabilities. Unlike BGP, it doesn't use an IP address as the mechanism for routing directly from node to node as we saw with Calico. But, rather, it creates a *bridge* that runs locally on our Kubernetes node. This bridge is created using OVS. OVS is, literally, a software-defined switch (like the ones you buy at any computer store). OVS is then the interface between our Pods and the rest of the world when running Antrea.

The pros and cons between bridged (also known as Layer 2) and IP (also known as Layer 3) routing are beyond the scope of this book and are hotly debated among academics and software companies alike. In our case, we'll just say that these are different technologies that both work quite well and can scale to handle thousands of Pods quite readily.

Let's try making our `kind` cluster again, this time using Antrea as our CNI provider. First, delete your last cluster with `kind delete cluster --name=calico`, and then we'll recreate it with the code snippet that follows:

```
$ cat << EOF > kind-Antrea-conf.yaml
kind: Cluster
apiVersion: kind.sigs.k8s.io/v1alpha3
networking:
  disableDefaultCNI: true
  podSubnet: 192.168.0.0/16
nodes:
- role: control-plane
- role: worker
EOF
$ kind create cluster --name=Calico --config=./kind-Antrea-conf.yaml
```

Once your cluster comes up, run

```
kubectl apply -f https://github.com/vmware-tanzu/Antrea/
➡ releases/download/v0.8.0/Antrea.yml -n kube-system
```

Then, run `docker exec` again and take a look at the IP situation in your kubelets. This time, we see that there are a few different interfaces created for us. Note that we omit the `tun0` interface that you'll see in both CNIs. This is the network interface where encapsulated traffic between nodes flows.

Interestingly, when we run `ip route`, we don't see a new route for every Pod we have running. This is because OVS uses a bridge, and thus, the Ethernet cables still exist, but they are all plugged directly into our locally running OVS instance. Running the following command, we can see subnet logic in Antrea that is similar to what we saw earlier in Calico:

**Defines traffic destined for our
local subnet by the 0.0 suffix**

```
root@Antrea-control-plane:/# ip route
172.18.0.0/16 dev eth0 proto kernel scope link src 172.18.0.3
192.168.0.0/24 dev Antrea-gw0 proto kernel scope link
              src 192.168.0.1
192.168.1.0/24 via 192.168.1.1 dev
              Antrea-gw0 onlink
```

**The Antrea gateway manages traffic destined
to another subnet with the 1.0 suffix.**

Now, to confirm this, let's run the `ip a` command. This will show us all the different IP addresses that our machine understands:

```
$ docker exec -t -i ba133 /bin/bash
root@Antrea-control-plane:/# ip a
# ip a
3: ovs-system: <BROADCAST,MULTICAST> mtu 1500 qdisc noop state
    DOWN group default qlen 1000
    link/ether 2e:24:a8:d8:a3:50 brd ff:ff:ff:ff:ff:ff
4: genev_sys_6081: <BROADCAST,MULTICAST,UP,LOWER_UP> mtu 65000 qdisc
    noqueue master ovs-system state
```

```
   UNKNOWN group default qlen 1000
   link/ether 76:82:e1:8b:d4:86 brd ff:ff:ff:ff:ff:ff
5: Antrea-gw0:<BROADCAST,MULTICAST,UP,LOWER_UP> mtu 1450 qdisc noqueue state
   UNKNOWN group default qlen 1000
   link/ether 02:09:36:d3:cf:a4 brd ff:ff:ff:ff:ff:ff
   inet 192.168.0.1/24 brd 192.168.0.255 scope global Antrea-gw0
      valid_lft forever preferred_lft forever
```

One of the interesting things to note when we run the `ip a` command is that we can see several unfamiliar devices floating around. These include

- `genev_sys_6081`—The interface for Genev, which is the tunneling protocol Antrea uses
- `ovs-system`—An OVS interface
- `Antrea-gw0`—An Antrea interface that sends traffic to Pods

Antrea, unlike Calico, actually routes traffic to a gateway IP address, which is on the Pod subnet that uses the podCIDR of our cluster. Thus, the algorithm for how Antrea sets up Pod IP addresses for a given node is something like this:

1 Allocates a subnet of Pod IP addresses to every node
2 Allocates the first IP address in the subnet to an OVS switch for the given node
3 Allocates all new Pods to the remaining free IP addresses in the subnet

The routing table for such a cluster would follow a pattern where we order nodes so that they come up chronologically. Note that each node receives traffic on an x.y.z.1 IP address (the first Pod in its allocated subnet). The way that subnets are calculated per Pod relies on both your implementation of Kubernetes and how your CNI provider logic works. In some CNIs, there might not be a distinct subnet for every node, but in general, this is an intuitive way for a CNI to manage IP addresses over time, so it's pretty common.

Keep in mind that *both* Calico and Antrea create distinct subnets for a nodes' Pod network, and from that subnet, Pods are provisioned IP addresses. If you ever need to debug a network path in a CNI, knowing which Pods are going to which nodes might help you to reason about which machines you should reboot, `ssh` into, or delete entirely, depending on your DevOps practices.

The following snippet shows us the `antrea-gw0` device. This is the gateway IP address for all the Pods on your cluster:

Forwards Pods destined for the second node in your cluster to that OVS instance

All local Pods go directly to the local Antrea-gw0 device.

```
192.168.0.0/24 dev Antrea-gw0 proto kernel scope
               link src 192.168.0.1
192.168.1.0/24 via 192.168.1.1 dev Antrea-gw0 onlink
192.168.2.0/24 via 192.168.2.1 dev Antrea-gw0 onlink
```

Forwards Pods destined for the third node in your cluster to that OVS instance

Thus, we can see that in the bridged model for networking, there are a few differences between what sorts of devices are created:

- There is no blackhole route, as it is handled by OVS.
- The only routes that our kernel manages are for the Antrea gateway (`Antrea-gw0`) itself.
- All of this Pod's traffic go directly to the `Antrea-gw0` device. There is no global routing to other devices as is done in the BGP protocol that is used by our Calico CNI.

5.4.5   *A note on CNI providers and kube-proxy on different OSs*

It's worth noting here that the trick of using DaemonSets to manage host networking for Pods is a Linux-specific approach. In other OSs (Windows Kubernetes nodes, for instance), when running containerd, you actually need to install your CNI provider using a service manager, and the CNI provider runs as a host process. Although this may change in the future (again using Windows as an example, there is work underway to enable privileged containers for Windows Kubernetes nodes), it's instructive to note that the Linux networking stack is ideally suited for the Kubernetes networking model. This is largely due to the architecture of cgroups, namespaces, and the concept of the Linux *root user*, which can run as a highly privileged process even while running in a container.

Although the complexity of Kubernetes networking may seem daunting at first because of the rapid evolution of service meshes, CNI, and network/server proxies, as long as you can understand the basic process of routing between Pods, the principles remain constant across many CNI implementations.

Summary

- Kubernetes networking architecture has a lot of parallels with generic SDN concepts.
- Antrea and Calico are both CNI providers that overlay a cluster network on a real network for Pods.
- Basic Linux commands (like `ip a`) can be used to reason about how your Pods are networked.
- CNI providers manage Pod networks typically in DaemonSets that run a privileged Linux container on each node.
- Border Gateway Protocol (BGP) and Open vSwitch (OVS) are both CNI provider core technologies that solve the same fundamental problems of broadcasting and sharing overlay routing information for Pods.
- Other OSs like Windows currently don't have all of the same native conveniences for Pod networking that Linux does.

Troubleshooting large-scale network errors

6

This chapter covers

- Confirming cluster functionality with Sonobuoy
- Tracing a Pod's data path
- Using the `arp` and `ip` commands to inspect CNI routing
- A deeper look at kube-proxy and iptables
- An introduction to Layer 7 networking (the ingress resource)

In this chapter, we'll go over a few touchpoints for troubleshooting large-scale network errors. We also introduce *Sonobuoy*, a Swiss Army knife for certifying, diagnosing, and testing the functionality of live Kubernetes clusters, which is a commonly used diagnosis tool for Kubernetes.

Sonobuoy compared with the Kubernetes e2e (end-to-end) tests

Sonobuoy runs the Kubernetes e2e testing suite in a container and makes it easy to retrieve, store, and archive the overall results.

> **(continued)**
> For advanced Kubernetes users that commonly work on Kubernetes from the source
> tree, you can directly use the test/e2e/ directory (found at http://mng.bz/Dgx9) as
> an alternative to Sonobuoy. We recommend it as an entry point to learn more about
> how to run specific Kubernetes tests.

Sonobuoy is based on the Kubernetes e2e testing library. Sonobuoy is used to verify
Kubernetes releases and validate whether the software correctly follows the Kubernetes API specification. After all, Kubernetes is ultimately just an API, and so the way that
we define a Kubernetes cluster is as a set of nodes that can successfully pass the Kubernetes conformance test suite.

> **Trying out kind-local-up.sh**
> Exploring different CNIs is a great way to practice troubleshooting real-world network
> issues that you might hit in the wild. You can use the kind recipes at http://
> mng.bz/2jg0 to run different variants of Kubernetes clusters that have different CNI
> providers. For example, if you clone this project, you can run `CLUSTER=calico`
> `CONFIG=calico-conf.yaml ./kind-local-up.sh` to create a Calico-based cluster.
> Other CNI options (Antrea and Cillium, for instance) are also available and readable
> from the kind-local-up.sh script as well. As an example, to create an Antrea cluster to
> follow along with the examples in this chapter, you can run
>
> ```
> CLUSTER=antrea CONFIG=kind-conf.yaml ./kind-local-up.sh
> ```
>
> You can then modify the `CLUSTER` option to use a different CNI type, such as `calico`
> or `cillium`. Once your cluster is created, if you check all the Pods in the `kube-`
> `system` namespace, you should see the CNI Pods running happily.

NOTE   Feel free to file an issue on the repo (https://github.com/jayunit100/
k8sprototypes) if you would like to see a new CNI recipe added or if a particular version is causing problems for you in a `kind` environment.

6.1   *Sonobuoy: A tool for confirming your cluster is functioning*

The conformance test suite consists of hundreds of tests to confirm everything from
storage volumes, networking, Pod scheduling, and the ability to run a few basic applications. The Sonobuoy project (https://sonobuoy.io/) packages a set of Kubernetes
e2e tests that we can run on any cluster. This tells us specifically which parts of our
clusters might not be working properly. In general, you can download Sonobuoy and
then run the following command:

```
$ wget https://github.com/vmware-tanzu/sonobuoy/releases/
          download/v0.51.0/sonobuoy_0.51.0_darwin_amd64.tar.gz
$ tar -xvf sonobuoy
$ chmod +x sonobuoy ; cp sonobuoy /usr/loca/bin/
$ sonobuoy run e2e --focus=Conformance
```

This example installs on MacOS, so please use the appropriate binary for your operating system. Tests generally take anywhere from 1 to 2 hours on a healthy cluster. After this, you can run `sonobuoy status` to get a readout of whether your cluster is working or not. To test networking specifically, a good test to run is

```
$ sonobuoy run e2e --e2e-focus=intra-pod
```

This test confirms that every node in your cluster can communicate to Pods on other nodes in your cluster. It confirms that your CNI's core functionality and that of your network proxy (`kube-proxy`) are working correctly. For example:

```
$ sonobuoy status
PLUGIN      STATUS      RESULT    COUNT
e2e         complete    passed    1
```

6.1.1 *Tracing data paths for Pods in a real cluster*

The NetworkPolicy API allows you to create application-centric firewall rules in a Kubernetes native manner and is a central part of planning for secure cluster communication. It operates at the Pod level, meaning that a connection from one Pod to another is blocked or allowed by a NetworkPolicy rule that exists in a specific namespace. NetworkPolicies, services, and CNI providers have a delicate interplay, which we attempt to illustrate in figure 6.1. The logical data path between any two Pods in a production cluster might be generalized like that shown in the figure, where:

- A Pod from 100.96.1.2 sends traffic to a service IP that it receives via a DNS query (not shown in the figure).
- The service then routes the traffic from the Pod to an IP determined by iptables.
- The iptables rule routes the traffic to a Pod on a different node.
- The node receives the packet, and an iptables (or OVS) rule determines if it is in violation of a network policy.
- The packet is delivered to the 100.96.1.3 endpoint.

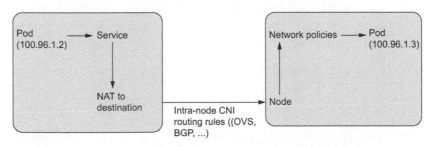

Figure 6.1 **The logical data path between any two Pods in a production cluster**

The data path does not take into account several caveats that can go wrong. For example, in the real world

- The first Pod can also be subject to network policy rules.
- There may be a firewall at the interface between nodes 10.1.2.3 and 10.1.2.4.
- The CNI may be down or malfunctioning, meaning that the routing of the packet between nodes might go to the wrong place.
- Often, in the real world, a Pod's access to other Pods might require mTLS (mutual TLS) certificates.

As you likely know by now, iptables rules consist of *chains* and *rules*. Each iptables table has different chains, and those chains consist of rules that determine the overall flow of packets. The following chains are managed by the `kube-proxy` service during a typical flow of a packet through a cluster. (In the next section, we'll look at what exactly we mean by a *route device*.)

```
KUBE_MARK_MASQ -> KUBE-SVC -----> KUBE_MARK_DROP
|-----> KUBE_SEP -> KUBE_MARQ_MASK -> NODE -> route device
```

6.1.2 *Setting up a cluster with the Antrea CNI provider*

In the previous chapter, we talked about network traffic with Calico. In this chapter, we'll do this again. We'll also look at the Antrea CNI provider that uses OpenVSwitch (OVS) as an alternative to the technologies used by Calico for IP routing. This means

- Instead of BGP broadcasting of IPs that are routable on all nodes, OVS runs a switch on every node, which routes traffic as it comes in.
- Instead of using iptables to create network policy rules, the OVS router makes rules to implement the Kubernetes NetworkPolicy API.

We'll repeat some concepts here because, in our opinion, seeing the same material from a different angle greatly aids your understanding of production networking in the real world. This time, however, we're going to go a little faster because we assume that you understand some of the concepts from the previous networking chapters. These concepts include services, iptables rules, CNI providers, and Pod IP addresses.

To set up a cluster with the Antrea provider, we'll use `kind` similarly to what we did with Calico; however, this time, we'll directly use the "recipes" provided by the Antrea project. To create an Antrea-enabled `kind` cluster, run the following steps:

```
$ git clone https://github.com/vmware-tanzu/antrea/
$ cd antrea
$ cd ci/kind
$ ./kind-setup.sh
```

WARNING The tutorial in this chapter is somewhat advanced. To reduce verbosity, we're going to assume that you are able to switch contexts between clusters. If you don't have both an Antrea and a Calico cluster up and running, reading along and trying some of these commands along the way might be easier than attempting to follow this section verbatim. As always, when hacking around with networking internals, you might need to run `apt-get update; apt-get install net-tools` in your kind cluster if you haven't already done so.

6.2   Inspecting CNI routing on different providers with the arp and ip commands

> **This time we skipped Kind**
>
> Although you can run Antrea in a `kind` cluster, for this chapter, we will show examples from a VMware Tanzu cluster. If you are interested in reproducing this content using Antrea on `kind`, you can run the recipes at http://mng.bz/2jg0, which enable either Calico, Cillium, or Antrea on a `kind` cluster. Cillium and Antrea are both CNI providers that require a little finagling to get them to work properly on a `kind` cluster due to their reliance on advanced Linux networking that needs a small amount of extra configuration (eBPF and OVS, respectively).

The entire concept of IP networking is based on the idea that IP addresses ultimately send you to a hardware device of some sort, which operates one layer below (Layer 2) the abstraction of IP (Layer 3) and is, thus, only addressable on machines that understand information about each other's MAC addresses. Often, the first step to inspecting how your network is operating is to run `ip a`. This gives you a bird's-eye view of what network interfaces your host is aware of and the devices that are ultimately targeted as the network endpoints in your cluster.

In an Antrea cluster, we can exec into any node using the same `docker exec` commands from our previous chapters and issue the `arp -na` command to look at what devices a given node is aware of. In this chapter's examples, we'll show real VMs so that you can use this as a reference for looking at Antrea networks, which will be (virtually) identical to the output that you'll get from your local cluster.

To start, let's exec into a node and look at the IP addresses it knows by running the `arp` command. For addresses of Pods that the node can reach, we'll grep IP addresses out with the `100` filter, as in this case. We're running this demo in a bare metal cluster with machines in the 100 subnet:

```
antrea_node> arp -na | grep 100
? (100.96.26.15) at 86:55:7a:e3:73:71 [ether] on antrea-gw0
? (100.96.26.16) at 4a:ee:27:03:1d:c6 [ether] on antrea-gw0
? (100.96.26.17) at <incomplete> on antrea-gw0
? (100.96.26.18) at ba:fe:0f:3c:29:d9 [ether] on antrea-gw0
? (100.96.26.19) at e2:99:63:53:a9:68 [ether] on antrea-gw0
? (100.96.26.20) at ba:46:5e:de:d8:bc [ether] on antrea-gw0
? (100.96.26.21) at ce:00:32:c0:ce:ec [ether] on antrea-gw0
? (100.96.26.22) at e2:10:0b:60:ab:bb [ether] on antrea-gw0
? (100.96.26.2) at 1a:37:67:98:d8:75 [ether] on antrea-gw0
```

The addresses that are local to the node include

```
antrea_node> arp -na | grep 192
? (192.168.5.160) at 00:50:56:b0:ee:ff [ether] on eth0
? (192.168.5.1) at 02:50:56:56:44:52 [ether] on eth0
? (192.168.5.207) at 00:50:56:b0:80:64 [ether] on eth0
```

```
? (192.168.5.245) at 00:50:56:b0:e2:13 [ether] on eth0
? (192.168.5.43) at 00:50:56:b0:0f:52 [ether] on eth0
? (192.168.5.54) at 00:50:56:b0:e4:6d [ether] on eth0
? (192.168.5.93) at 00:50:56:b0:1b:5b [ether] on eth0
```

6.2.1   *What is an IP tunnel and why do CNI providers use them?*

You might be wondering what that antrea-gw0 device is. If you ran these commands on a Calico cluster, you may have seen a tun0 device as well. In any event, these are known as *tunnels,* and they are the construct that allow *flat* networking between Pods in a cluster. In the previous example, the antrea-gw0 devices correspond to the OVS gateway that manages traffic for the Antrea CNI. This gateway traffic is smart enough to "mask" the traffic from one Pod to another, so that the traffic flows to a node first. In Calico clusters, you will see a similar pattern, wherein a protocol (such as IPIP) is used to mask such traffic. Both the Calico and Antrea CNI providers are smart enough to know *when* to mask traffic for performance reasons.

Now, let's see where Antrea and Calico CNI's begin to differ somewhat interestingly. In our Calico cluster, running ip a shows us that we have a tunl0 interface. This is created by the calico_node container via the brd service, which is responsible for routing traffic through the IPIP tunnel in the cluster. We contrast that with the ip a command for Antrea in the second code snippet.

```
calico_node> ip a
2: tunl0@NONE: <NOARP,UP,LOWER_UP>
mtu 1440 qdisc noqueue state UNKNOWN
group default qlen 1000

antrea_node> ip a
3: ovs-system: <BROADCAST,MULTICAST> mtu 1500 qdisc noop state DOWN
   group default qlen 1000
   link/ether 7e:de:21:4b:88:46 brd ff:ff:ff:ff:ff:ff
5: antrea-gw0: <BROADCAST,MULTICAST,UP,LOWER_UP> mtu 1450 qdisc
   noqueue state UNKNOWN group default qlen 1000
    link/ether 82:aa:a9:6f:02:33 brd ff:ff:ff:ff:ff:ff
    inet 100.96.29.1/24 brd 100.96.29.255 scope global antrea-gw0
       valid_lft forever preferred_lft forever
    inet6 fe80::80aa:a9ff:fe6f:233/64 scope link
```

Now, in both clusters, run kubectl scale deployment coredns --replicas=10 -n kube-system. Then rerun the previous commands. You'll see new IP entries for the containers.

6.2.2   *How many packets are flowing through the network interfaces for our CNI?*

We know that all packets may be getting shoved into special tunnels so that they end up in the right physical node before going to a Pod. Because each node is then aware of all the Pod-local traffic, we can use standard Linux tools to monitor Pod traffic without actually relying on any knowledge of Kubernetes itself. The ip command has a -s option to show us if traffic is flowing. Running this command on a node of either a

Calico or Antrea cluster tells us exactly what interface traffic is flowing into our Pod and at what rate. Here's the output:

```
10: cali3317e4b4ab5@if5: <BROADCAST,MULTICAST,UP,LOWER_UP>
    mtu 1440 qdisc noqueue state UP group default
    link/ether ee:ee:ee:ee:ee:ee brd ff:ff:ff:ff:ff:ff
    link-netns cni-abb79f5f-b6b0-f548-3222-34b5eec7c94f
    RX: bytes  packets  errors  dropped overrun mcast
    150575     1865     0       2       0       0
    TX: bytes  packets  errors  dropped carrier collsns
    839360     1919     0       0       0       0


5: antrea-gw0: <BROADCAST,MULTICAST,UP,LOWER_UP> mtu 1450 qdisc
⮕ noqueue state UNKNOWN group default qlen 1000
    link/ether 82:aa:a9:6f:02:33 brd ff:ff:ff:ff:ff:ff
    inet 100.96.29.1/24 brd 100.96.29.255 scope global antrea-gw0
       valid_lft forever preferred_lft forever
    inet6 fe80::80aa:a9ff:fe6f:233/64 scope link
       valid_lft forever preferred_lft forever
    RX: bytes  packets  errors  dropped overrun mcast
    89662090   1089577  0       0       0       0
    TX: bytes  packets  errors  dropped carrier collsns
    108901694  1208573  0       0       0       0
```

At this point, we now have a high-level view of how network connectivity is working in our clusters. If no traffic goes into a Calico- or Antrea-related interface, then (obviously) our CNI is broken because most Kubernetes clusters will have at least *some* traffic flowing between Pods during steady state operations. For example, even without a user creating any Pods in a `kind` cluster, you'll see that `kube-proxy` Pod and CoreDNS Pod will be actively communicating about network traffic via the CoreDNS service endpoint. Seeing these Pods in the Running state is a good sanity test (especially with CoreDNS, which requires a Pod network to function) and also will be a good way to verify that your CNI provider is healthy.

6.2.3 Routes

The next level of our journey into the Pod network path involves seeing how these devices are wired to IP addresses. In figure 6.2, we again depict the architecture of a Kubernetes network. This time, however, we include the tunneling information that was revealed in the previous commands.

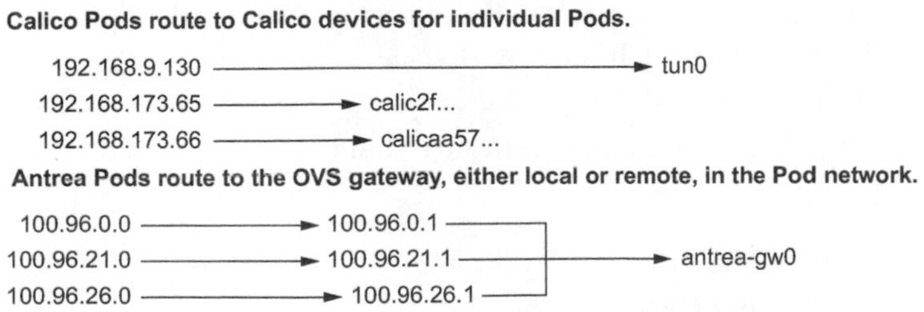

Calico Pods route to Calico devices for individual Pods.

192.168.9.130 ──────────────────────────────▶ tun0
192.168.173.65 ────────────▶ calic2f...
192.168.173.66 ────────────▶ calicaa57...

Antrea Pods route to the OVS gateway, either local or remote, in the Pod network.

100.96.0.0 ────────▶ 100.96.0.1 ──┐
100.96.21.0 ───────▶ 100.96.21.1 ─┼──▶ antrea-gw0
100.96.26.0 ───────▶ 100.96.26.1 ─┘

Figure 6.2 Tunneling information added to the architecture of a Kubernetes network

Now that we know what a tunnel is, let's see how our CNI manages routing traffic to tunnels via programming the Linux routing table. Running `route -n` in our Calico cluster shows the following routing table in the kernel, where the `cali` interfaces are Pods local to a node, and the tunl0 interfaces are special interfaces created by Calico itself for sending traffic to a gateway node:

```
# route -n
Kernel IP routing table
Destination       Gateway       Genmask           Flags Metric Ref Use Iface
0.0.0.0           172.18.0.1    0.0.0.0           UG    0      0   0   eth0
172.18.0.0        0.0.0.0       255.255.0.0       U     0      0   0   eth0
192.168.9.128     172.18.0.3    255.255.255.192   UG    0      0   0   tunl0
192.168.71.0      172.18.0.5    255.255.255.192   UG    0      0   0   tunl0
192.168.88.0      172.18.0.4    255.255.255.192   UG    0      0   0   tunl0
192.168.143.64    172.18.0.2    255.255.255.192   UG    0      0   0   tunl0
192.168.173.64    0.0.0.0       255.255.255.192   U     0      0   0   *
192.168.173.65    0.0.0.0       255.255.255.255   UH    0      0   0   calicd2f3
192.168.173.66    0.0.0.0       255.255.255.255   UH    0      0   0   calibaa57
```

In this table for Calico, we can see that

- 172 nodes are gateways for some of our Pods.
- 192 IP addresses within specific ranges (shown in the Genmask column) are routed to specific nodes.

What about on our Antrea CNI provider? On a similar cluster, we won't see a new destination IP for every device. Instead, we'll see that there is a `.1` Antrea gateway:

```
root [ /home/capv ]# route -n
Kernel IP routing table
Destination    Gateway       Genmask           Flags Ref Use Iface
0.0.0.0        192.168.5.1   0.0.0.0           UG    0   0   eth0
100.96.0.0     100.96.0.1    255.255.255.0     UG    0   0   antrea-gw0
100.96.21.0    100.96.21.1   255.255.255.0     UG    0   0   antrea-gw0
100.96.26.0    100.96.26.1   255.255.255.0     UG    0   0   antrea-gw0
100.96.28.0    100.96.28.1   255.255.255.0     UG    0   0   antrea-gw0
```

In this table for Antrea, we can see that

- *Any traffic destined for the 100.96.0.0 IP range gets routed directly to IP address 100.96.0.1.* This is a *reserved* IP address on the CNI network that Antrea uses for its OVS-routing mechanism. Thus, instead of sending things directly to a node IP address, it sends all traffic to an IP address on the Pod network on which Antrea itself manages a switch service.
- *Unlike Calico, all traffic (including local traffic) goes directly to the Antrea gateway device.* The only thing that differentiates its final destination is the gateway IP.

Thus, we can see that

- Antrea has one routing table entry *per node*.
- Calico has one routing table entry *per Pod*.

6.2.4 *CNI-specific tooling: Open vSwitch (OVS)*

Antrea and Calico CNI plugins both run as Pods in our clusters. This isn't necessarily true for all CNI providers, but when it is, we will be able to use a lot of nice Kubernetes features to debug the networking data path if necessary. Once we start getting into the internals of CNIs, we will need to actually look at tools such as `ovs-vsctl`, `antctl`, `calicoctl`, and so on. We're not going to go over all of these here, but we will introduce you to the `ovs-vsctl` tool that can be run easily from inside an Antrea container on your clusters. We can then ask OVS to tell us more about this interface via the `ovs-vsctl` tool. In order to use this tool, you can directly execute into an Antrea container with `kubectl  exec -t -i antrea-agent-1234 -n kube-system /bin/bash`, create a shell, and then run a command such as the following:

```
# ovs-vsctl list interface|grep -A 5 antrea
name                : antrea-gw0
ofport              : 2
ofport_request      : 2
options             : {}
other_config        : {}
statistics          : {collisions=0, rx_bytes=1773391201,
            rx_crc_err=0, rx_dropped=0, rx_errors=0,
            rx_frame_err=0, rx_missed_errors=0, rx_over_err=0,
            rx_packets=16392260, tx_bytes=6090558410,
            tx_dropped=0, tx_errors=0, tx_packets=17952545}
```

There are several command-line tools that give you the ability to diagnose low-level CNI issues in clusters. For CNI specific debugging, you can use `antctl` or `calicoctl`:

- `antctl` lists enabled Antrea features, gets debugging information about agents, and does fine-grained analysis of Antrea NetworkPolicy targets.
- `calicoctl` analyzes NetworkPolicy objects, prints information about network diagnostics, and turns off common networking features (as an alternative to manually editing YAML files).

If you are interested in a generic Linux-centric debugging of clusters, you can use tools like Sonobuoy to run a gamut of e2e tests on a cluster. You can also consider using the https://github.com/sarun87/k8snetlook tool, which runs realistic cluster diagnostics for fine-grained networking features (for example, API server connectivity, Pod connectivity, and so on).

Depending on how sophisticated your networking configuration is, the amount of troubleshooting you need to do in the real world will vary. It's quite common to have 100+ Pods per node, and some level of inspection or reasoning about these concepts will be increasingly important.

6.2.5 *Tracing the data path of active containers with tcpdump*

Now that you have some intuition around how a packet flows from one place to another in various CNIs, let's pop back up the stack and look at one of our favorite traditional network diagnostic tools: tcpdump. Because we have traced the relationship between our host to the underlying Linux networking tools that route traffic, we may want to look at things from the container's perspective. The most common tool for doing this is tcpdump. Let's grab one of our CoreDNS containers and look at its traffic. In Calico, we can directly sniff the packets on the cali devices like so:

```
192.168.173.66  0.0.0.0    255.255.255.255 UH  0   0   0 calibaa5769d671
calico_node> tcpdump -i calicd2f389598e
listening on calicd2f389598e,
link-type EN10MB (Ethernet),
capture size 262144 bytes
20:13:07.733139 IP 10.96.0.1.443 > 192.168.173.65.60684:
  Flags [P.],
  seq 1615967839:1615968486,
  ack 1173977013, win 264,
  options [nop,nop,TS val 296478
```

The 10.96.0.1 IP address is the internal Kubernetes service address. This IP (the API server) acknowledges receipt of a request from the CoreDNS server to get a DNS record. If we look at a typical node in our cluster, where we are running the CoreDNS Pod, our Antrea Pods will be named like so:

```
30: coredns--e5cc00@if3: <BROADCAST,MULTICAST,UP,LOWER_UP>
    mtu 1450 qdisc noqueue master ovs-system state UP
    group default
    link/ether e6:8a:27:05:d7:30 brd ff:ff:ff:ff:ff:ff
    link-netns cni-2c6b1bc0-cf36-132c-dfcb-88dd158f51ca
    inet6 fe80::e48a:27ff:fe05:d730/64 scope link
       valid_lft forever preferred_lft forever
```

This means we can directly sniff the packets going to this node by attaching to this veth device with tcpdump. The following code snippet shows how to do this:

```
calico_node> tcpdump -i coredns--29244a -n
```

When you run this command, you should see traffic from different Pods that are attempting to resolve Kubernetes DNS records. We often use the -n option so that our IP addresses don't get hidden from us when using tcpdump.

If you specifically want to see if one Pod is talking to another, you can go to the node on the Pod where you are receiving traffic and scrape all TCP traffic, which includes one of the Pod's IP addresses. Let's say a Pod that sends traffic is 100.96.21.21. Running this command gives you a raw dump of anything with, for example, a 192 address and a 9153 port:

```
calico_node> tcpdump host 100.96.21.21 -i coredns--29244a
listening on coredns--29244a, link-type EN10MB (Ethernet),
capture size 262144 bytes

21:59:36.818933 IP 100.96.21.21.45978 > 100.96.26.19.9153:
```

```
    Flags [S], seq 375193568, win 64860, options [mss 1410,sackOK,TS
    val 259983321 ecr 0,nop,wscale 7], length 0

21:59:36.819008 IP 100.96.26.19.9153 > 100.96.21.21.45978: Flags [S.],
    seq 3927639393, ack 375193569, win 64308, options [mss 1410,
    sackOK,TS val 2440057191 ecr 259983321,nop,wscale 7], length 0

21:59:36.819928 IP 100.96.21.21.45978 > 100.96.26.19.9153:
    Flags [.], ack 1, win 507, options [nop,nop,TS val
    259983323 ecr 2440057191], length 0
```

The `tcpdump` tool is often used for live debugging of traffic from one container to another. In particular, if you don't see an `ack` from the receiving Pod to the sending Pod, this might mean that your Pod is not receiving traffic. This might be due to something such as a network policy or an iptables rule that is interfering with normal kube-proxy forwarding information.

> **NOTE** Traditional IT shops often use tools such as Puppet to configure and manage iptables rules. It is difficult to combine `kube-proxy` with iptables rules managed by other IT-based networking rules, and often, it's best to just run your nodes in an environment that is isolated from the regular rules maintained by your network administrators.

6.3 *The kube-proxy and iptables*

The most important thing to remember about the network proxy is that its operations are, generally speaking, independent of the operations of your CNI provider. Of course, like all other things in Kubernetes, this statement is not without a caveat: some CNI providers have considered implementing their own service proxy as an alternative to the iptables (or IPVS) service proxying that Kubernetes comes with out of the box. That said, this is not the typical way most clusters run. In most clusters, you should conceptually separate the concepts of service proxying, which is done by the `kube-proxy`, from the concept of traffic routing, which is done by your CNI provider (such as OVS) that manages Linux primitives.

This deep dive has reiterated a few basic Kubernetes networking concepts. So far, we have seen

- How the host maps Pod traffic with the IP and routes commands
- How you can verify incoming Pod traffic and look up IP tunneling information from the host
- How to sniff traffic on specific IP addresses using `tcpdump`

Let's now take a look at `kube-proxy`. Even though it's not part of your CNI, understanding `kube-proxy` is integral when diagnosing networking issues.

6.3.1 *iptables-save and the diff tool*

The simplest thing you can do when looking for all service endpoints is to run `iptables-save` on a cluster. This command stores every iptables rule at some point in time. Along with tools such as `diff`, it can be used to measure the delta between two Kubernetes networking states. From here, you can look for the comment rules, which tell you the services that are associated with a rule. A typical run of `iptables-save` results in several lines of rules like so:

```
-A KUBE-SVC-TCOU7JCQXEZGVUNU -m comment
   --comment "kube-system/kube-dns:dns" -m statistic --mode random
   --probability 0.10000000009 -j KUBE-SEP-QIVPDYSUOLOYQCAA

-A KUBE-SVC-TCOU7JCQXEZGVUNU -m comment
   --comment "kube-system/kube-dns:dns" -m statistic --mode random
   --probability 0.11111111101 -j KUBE-SEP-N76EJY3A4RTXTN2I

-A KUBE-SVC-TCOU7JCQXEZGVUNU -m comment
   --comment "kube-system/kube-dns:dns" -m statistic --mode random
   --probability 0.12500000000 -j KUBE-SEP-LSGM2AJGRPG672RM
```

After looking at these services, you'll want to find the corresponding `SEP` rules for them. We can use `grep` to find all rules associated with a specific service. In this case, `SEP-QI…` corresponds to the CoreDNS container in our cluster.

> **NOTE** We use CoreDNS in many examples because it is a standard Pod that can be scaled up and down, and likely runs in almost any cluster. You can complete this exercise with any other Pod that is available behind an internal Kubernetes service and that is using a CNI plugin for its IP address (it isn't using the host network).

```
calico_node> iptables-save | grep SEP-QI
:KUBE-SEP-QIVPDYSUOLOYQCAA - [0:0]
### Masquerading happens here for outgoing traffic...
-A KUBE-SEP-QIVPDYSUOLOYQCAA -s 192.168.143.65/32
   -m comment
   --comment "kube-system/kube-dns:dns" -j KUBE-MARK-MASQ

-A KUBE-SEP-QIVPDYSUOLOYQCAA -p udp -m comment
   --comment "kube-system/kube-dns:dns" -m udp -j DNAT
   --to-destination 192.168.143.65:53

-A KUBE-SVC-TCOU7JCQXEZGVUNU -m comment
   --comment "kube-system/kube-dns:dns" -m statistic
   --mode random --probability 0.10000000009 -j KUBE-SEP-QIVPDYSUOLOYQCAA
```

This step is the same in any CNI provider. Because of that, we don't provide an Antrea/Calico comparison.

6.3.2 *Looking at how network policies modify CNI rules*

Ingress rules and NetworkPolicies are two of the sharpest features of Kubernetes networking, largely because these are both defined by the API but implemented by external services that are considered optional in a cluster. Ironically, NetworkPolicies and ingress routing are table stakes for most IT administrators. So, although these features are theoretically optional, you likely are going to use them if you're reading this book.

NetworkPolicies in Kubernetes support blocking traffic for ingress/egress calls or both on any Pod. In general, Pods are not secured at all in a Kubernetes cluster, so NetworkPolicies are considered essential as part of a secure Kubernetes production cluster. The NetworkPolicy API can be quite difficult to use for beginners, so we'll keep it simple to get you started:

- NetworkPolicies are created in a specific namespace and target Pods by label.
- NetworkPolicies must define a type (ingress is the default).
- NetworkPolicies are additive and are *allow-only*, meaning that they deny things by default and can be layered to allow more and more traffic whitelisting
- Both Calico and Antrea implement the Kubernetes NetworkPolicy API differently. Calico creates new iptables rules, whereas Antrea creates OVS rules.
- Some CNIs, like Flannel, don't implement the NetworkPolicy API at all.
- Some CNIs, like Cillium and OVN, (Open Virtual Network) Kubernetes, don't implement the entire Kubernetes API's NetworkPolicy specification (for example, Cillium doesn't implement the recently added PortRange policy, which is Beta at the time of this publication, and OVN Kubernetes doesn't implement the NamedPort functionality).

It's important to realize that Calico does not use iptables for anything other than network policies. All other routing is done via the BGP routing rules, which we saw in a previous section. In this section, we'll create a network policy and see how it affects the routing rules in both Calico and Antrea. To begin looking at how network policies might affect traffic, we'll run a NetworkPolicy test where we block all traffic to a Pod named web:

```
kind: NetworkPolicy
apiVersion: networking.k8s.io/v1
metadata:
  name: web-deny-all
spec:                          This NetworkPolicy acts on the app:web
  podSelector:                 container in the default namespace.
    matchLabels:
        app: web   ←────────   Denies all traffic because we haven't
  ingress: []      ←────────   actually defined any ingress rules
```

If we wanted to define an ingress rule, our policy might look something like this:

```
kind: NetworkPolicy
apiVersion: networking.k8s.io/v1
metadata:
  name: web
spec:
  podSelector:
    matchLabels:
        app: web
  ingress:
  - ports:                     Allows traffic, but we limit it to the
    - port: 80   ←────────     port our web server serves on, 80
```

```
- from:
  - podSelector:
      matchLabels:
        app: web2  ◁──┐  Allows the web Pod's to respond to
                       │  incoming traffic from our web2 Pod
```

Note that in the second snippet, the web2 Pod would also be able to receive traffic from the web Pod. That's because the web Pod has not defined any egress policies, which means all egress is allowed by default. Thus, in order to fully lock down the web Pod, we would want to

- Define an *egress* NetworkPolicy that only allows outgoing traffic to essential services
- Define an *ingress* NetworkPolicy that only allows incoming traffic from essential services
- Add port numbers to both of the preceding policies so that only essential ports are allowed

Defining these sorts of YAML policies can be very painstaking. If you want to deeply explore this area, see http://mng.bz/XWEl, which has several tutorials to introduce you to crafting specific network policies for different use cases.

A good way to uniformly test these policies created by our CNI is to define a DaemonSet running the same container in all nodes. Note that the fact that our CNI provider creates rules for NetworkPolicies is a feature of the CNI provider itself. This is not part of the CNI interface. Because most CNI providers are built for Kubernetes, the implementation of the Kubernetes NetworkPolicy API is an obvious add-on that they provide.

Now, let's test our policy by creating a Pod that it can target. The following DaemonSet runs a Pod on every node. Each Pod is secured by the policy above it, which results in a specific set of iptables rules written by the Calico CNI (or, alternatively, OVS rules written by our Antrea CNI). We can test our policy with the code in this snippet:

```
apiVersion: apps/v1
kind: DaemonSet
metadata:
  name: nginx-ds
spec:
  selector:
    matchLabels:
      app: web    ◁──── Runs a Pod on every node
  template:
    metadata:
      labels:
        app: web
    spec:
      containers:
      - name: nginx
        image: nginx
```

6.3.3 *How are these policies implemented?*

We can use `diff` or `git diff` to compare iptables rules before and after our policy is created. In Calico, you'll see policies such as this. This is where the `drop` rule for a policy is implemented. To do this

1 Create the DaemonSet in the previous code snippet and then run `iptables-save > a1` on any node.
2 Create the network policy that blocks this traffic, again running `iptables-save > a2`, and save it to a different file.
3 Run a command such as `git diff a1 a2` and look at the difference.

In this case, you'll see the following new rules for policies:

```
> -A cali-tw-calic5cc839365a -m comment
  --comment "cali:Uv2zkaIvaVnFWYI9" -m comment
  --comment "Start of policies" -j MARK --set-xmark 0x0/0x20000

> -A cali-tw-calic5cc839365a -m comment
  --comment "cali:7OLyCb9i6s_CPjbu" -m mark --mark 0x0/0x20000
  -j cali-pi-_IDb4Gbl3P1MtRtVzfEP

> -A cali-tw-calic5cc839365a -m comment --comment "cali:DBkU9PXyu2eCwkJC"
  -m comment --comment "Return if policy accepted" -m mark
  --mark 0x10000/0x10000 -j RETURN

> -A cali-tw-calic5cc839365a -m comment --comment "cali:tioNk8N7f4P5Pzf4"
  -m comment --comment "Drop if no policies passed packet" -m mark
  --mark 0x0/0x20000 -j DROP

> -A cali-tw-calic5cc839365a -m comment --comment "cali:wcGG1iiHvTXsj5lq"
  -j cali-pri-kns.default

> -A cali-tw-calic5cc839365a -m comment --comment "cali:gaGDuGQkGckLPa4H"
  -m comment --comment "Return if profile accepted" -m mark
  --mark 0x10000/0x10000 -j RETURN

> -A cali-tw-calic5cc839365a -m comment --comment "cali:B61_lueEhRWiWwnn"
  -j cali-pri-ksa.default.default

> -A cali-tw-calic5cc839365a -m comment --comment "cali:McPS2ZHiShhYyFnW"
  -m comment --comment "Return if profile accepted" -m mark
  --mark 0x10000/0x10000 -j RETURN
> -A cali-tw-calic5cc839365a -m comment --comment "cali:1ThI2kHuPODjvF4v"
  -m comment --comment "Drop if no profiles matched" -j DROP
```

Antrea also implements network policies but uses OVS flows and writes these flows to table 90. Running a similar workload in Antrea, you'll see these policies created. An easy way to do this is to call `ovs-ofctl`. Typically, this is done from inside a container because Antrea agents are fully configured with all OVS administrative binaries. This can also work from the host as well, if needed, just by installing the OVS utilities. To run the following example in an Antrea cluster, you can use the `kubectl` client. This command line shows us how Antrea implements network policies:

```
$ kubectl -n kube-system exec -it antrea-agent-2kksz
⮡ ovs-ofctl dump-flows br-int | grep table=90
...
Defaulting container name to antrea-agent.
 cookie=0x2000000000000, duration=344936.777s, table=90, n_packets=0,
 n_bytes=0, priority=210,ct_state=-new+est,ip actions=resubmit(,105)

 cookie=0x2000000000000, duration=344936.776s, table=90, n_packets=83160,
 n_bytes=6153840, priority=210,ip,nw_src=100.96.26.1 actions=resubmit(,105)

 cookie=0x2050000000000, duration=22.296s, table=90, n_packets=0,
 n_bytes=0, priority=200,ip,reg1=0x18 actions=conjunction(1,2/2)

 cookie=0x2050000000000, duration=22.300s, table=90, n_packets=0, n_bytes=0,
 priority=190,conj_id=1,ip actions=load:0x1->NXM_NX_REG6[],resubmit(,105)

 cookie=0x2000000000000, duration=344936.782s, table=90, n_packets=149662,
 n_bytes=11075281, priority=0 actions=resubmit(,100)
```

> Antrea uses the conjunction rules written by OVS when it sees that it needs to apply a network policy to a specific Pod.

OVS, similar to iptables, defines rules that designate the flow of packets. There are several OVS flow tables that Antrea uses, and each of these tables have specific logic programming for different Pods. The number of flows that are actively in use by OVS can be monitored in real time using a tool like Prometheus if you want to run Antrea at large scales and confirm any specific details around the use of OVS in your data center.

Remember, both OVS and iptables are integrated within the Linux kernel, so you don't have to do anything special to your data center in order to use these technologies. For more information on how to monitor OVS with Prometheus, a companion blog post to this book exists at http://mng.bz/1jaj. There we walk you through the details of setting up Prometheus as a monitoring tool for Antrea.

Cyclonus and the NetworkPolicy e2e tests

If you are interested in learning more about NetworkPolicies, you can run the Kubernetes e2e tests for them using Sonobuoy. You'll get a beautiful list of tables that print exactly which Pods can (and can't) talk to each other, given a policy specification. Another even more powerful tool for investigating the NetworkPolicy features of your CNI provider is Cyclonus, which can be easily run from a source (see https://github.com/mattfenwick/cyclonus).

Cyclonus generates hundreds of network policy scenarios and probes whether your CNI provider properly implements them. From time to time, CNI providers might regress in their implementation of the complex NetworkPolicy API, so it's a great idea to run this in production to verify the conformance of your CNI provider to the Kubernetes API specification.

6.4   *Ingress controllers*

Ingress controllers allow you to route all traffic to your cluster through a single IP address (and are a great way to save money on cloud IP addresses). However, they can be tricky to debug, largely because they are add-on components. As a way to deal with this, the Kubernetes community has discussed shipping a default ingress controller.

> ### NGINX, Contour, and the Gateway API
>
> The original ingress API for Kubernetes was implemented by NGINX as a canonical standard. However, soon after, two large shifts occurred:
>
> - Contour (https://projectcontour.io/) emerged as an alternative CNCF (Cloud Native Computing Foundation) ingress controller.
> - The Gateway API emerged as an alternative way to provide a better multi-tenant solution to the problem of exposing routes from a Kubernetes cluster.
>
> At the time of publication, the ingress API is "on the ropes" and soon to be replaced by the Gateway API, which is much more descriptive and capable of describing different types of Layer 7 resources to developers in a way that is more flexible. Thus, although we encourage you to learn the material in this section, we note that you should use this material as a springboard to begin researching the Gateway API and how it might be able to suit your needs in the future. To read more about the Gateway API, you can spend some time at https://gateway-api.sigs.k8s.io/.

To implement an ingress controller (or a Gateway API), you need to decide how to route traffic to it because the IP addresses for it are not regular ClusterIP services. If your ingress controller goes down, all traffic into your cluster will also break, so you will likely want to run it as a DaemonSet (if running it in the cluster) on all nodes.

Contour uses a technology, called the *Envoy* proxy, under the hood as the basis for its service proxying. Envoy can be used to build ingress controllers, service meshes, and other sorts of networking technologies that transparently forward or manage traffic for you. As you read this, note that the Kubernetes Services API is an ongoing area of innovation in the upstream Kubernetes community. As clusters become larger and larger, the need for increasingly sophisticated models for routing traffic will emerge over the next few years.

6.4.1   *Setting up Contour and kind to explore ingress controllers*

The purpose of ingress controllers is to provide named access to the outside world for the myriad of Kubernetes services you'll run. If you're on a cloud with limitless public IPs, this might have slightly less value than otherwise, but an ingress controller also serves the purpose of allowing you to cleanly set up HTTPS passthrough, monitor all services being exposed, and create policies around externally accessible URLs.

To explore how you add an ingress controller to your existing Kubernetes cluster, we'll create a trusty `kind` cluster. This time, however, we'll set it up to forward ingress traffic to port 80. This traffic will be resolved by the Contour ingress controller, which allows us to bind multiple services by name to port 80 on our cluster:

```
kind: Cluster
apiVersion: kind.sigs.k8s.io/v1alpha3
networking:
  disableDefaultCNI: true # disable kindnet
  podSubnet: 192.168.0.0/16 # set to Calico's default subnet
nodes:
- role: control-plane
- role: worker
  extraPortMappings:          ⟵──┐  Defines extraPortMappings to reach port
  - containerPort: 80                  80 from our local terminal and to forward
    hostPort: 80                       into port 80 on our kind nodes
    listenAddress: "0.0.0.0"
  - containerPort: 443
    hostPort: 443
    listenAddress: "0.0.0.0"
```

The extra port mappings in this code snippet allow us to reach port 80 on our local terminal and to get forwarded into that port from our kind nodes. Note that this configuration only works with single-node clusters because you only have one port to expose when running Docker-based Kubernetes nodes on a local machine. After we create our _kind_ cluster, we will then install Calico, as shown in the following example. You will have a working, basic Pod-to-Pod network:

```
$ kubectl create -f
  https://docs.projectcalico.org/archive/v3.16/manifests/
  tigera-operator.yaml

$ kubectl -n kube-system set env daemonset/calico-node
        FELIX_IGNORELOOSERPF=true
$ kubectl -n kube-system set env daemonset/calico-node
        FELIX_XDPENABLED=false
```

OK, now our infrastructure is all set up. Let's start learning about ingress! In this section, we'll expose a Kubernetes service from bottom to top. As always, we'll use our trusty kind cluster to do the dirty work. This time, however, we will

- Access a service from inside the cluster as a sanity check
- Use the Contour ingress controller as a way to manage this service by its hostname, along with a fleet of other services

6.4.2   *Setting up a simple web server Pod*

To get started, let's create our kind cluster as done in previous chapters. Once we're up and running, we'll then create a simple web application. Because NGINX is often used as an ingress controller, this time, we'll create a Python web app like so:

```
apiVersion: v1
kind: Pod
metadata:
  name: example-pod
  labels:
    service: example-pod      <—— Our service selects this label.
spec:
  containers:
    - name: frontend
      image: python
      command:
        - "python"
        - "-m"
        - "SimpleHTTPServer"
        - "8080"
      ports:
        - containerPort: 8080
```

Next, we'll expose the `containerPort` via a standard ClusterIP service. This is the simplest of all Kubernetes services; it does nothing other than tell the `kube-proxy` to create a single virtual IP address (the `KUBE_SEP` endpoints we saw earlier) in one of our Python Pods:

```
apiVersion: v1
kind: Service
metadata:
  name: my-service
spec:
  selector:                              Specifies this Pod as an
    service: example-pod      <——┘        endpoint of our service
  ports:
    - protocol: TCP
      port: 8080
      targetPort: 8080
```

Thus far, we've created a little web app that receives traffic from a service. The web app that we've created serves traffic internally on port 8080, and our service uses that port as well. Let's try to access it locally. We'll create a simple Docker image that we can use to poke around in our cluster services (this image is forked from https://github.com/arunvelsriram/utils):

```
apiVersion: v1
kind: Pod
metadata:
  name: sleep
spec:
  containers:
    - name: check
      image: jayunit100/ubuntu-utils
      command:
        - "sleep"
        - "10000"
```

Now, from inside this image, let's see if we can `curl` down our service. The following `curl` command outputs all the lines of the /etc/passwd file in our container. You can also write a file, such as hello.html, to the / directory of your container if you prefer something a little friendlier:

```
$ kubectl exec -t -i sleep curl my-service:8080/etc/passwd
root:x:0:0:root:/root:/bin/bash
```
◄———| **Outputs all lines in the /etc/passwd file**

It worked! For this to work, we know that

- The Pod is running and serving all files in the OS on port 8080.
- Every Pod in the cluster is capable of accessing this service via port 8080 because of the `my-service` service we created previously.
- The `kube-proxy` forwards traffic from `my-service` to the `example-pod` and writes relevant iptables forwarding rules.
- Our CNI provider *is* capable of making necessary routing rules (which we explored earlier in the chapter) and forwarding traffic between the IP address of the `check` Pod to the `example-pod` once the iptables rule forwards this packet.

Let's say we want to access this service from the outside world. To do this, we need to

1 Add it to an ingress resource so that the Kubernetes API can tell an ingress controller to forward traffic to it
2 Run an ingress controller that forwards traffic from the outside world to the internal service

There are a few different ingress controllers out there. The popular ones are NGINX and Contour. In this case, we'll use Contour to access this service:

```
$ git clone https://github.com/projectcontour/contour.git
$ kubectl apply -f contour/examples/contour
```

Now you have an ingress controller installed that will manage all external traffic for you. Next, we'll add an entry to our /etc/hosts file on our local machine, which tells us to access the previous service on localhost:

```
$ echo "127.0.0.1  my-service.local" >> /etc/hosts
```

Now, we'll create an ingress resource:

```
apiVersion: networking.k8s.io/v1
kind: Ingress
metadata:
  name: example-ingress
spec:
  rules:
  - host: my-service.local        ◄———| Names the service we put
    http:                              into our laptop at 127.0.0.1
```

```
      paths:
    - path: /
      backend:
          serviceName: my-service      ⟵┐  Names the internal
          servicePort: 8080                Kubernetes service
```

We can issue a `curl` command from our local computer to the `kind` cluster. The way this will work is as follows:

1 Locally, our client tries to issue `curl  my-service.local` on port 80. This resolves the IP address to 127.0.0.1.

2 The traffic to our localhost gets intercepted by the Docker node in our `kind` cluster listening on 80.

3 The Docker node forwards the traffic to the Contour ingress controller, which sees that we are trying to access my-service.local.

4 Contour's ingress controller forwards the my-service.local traffic to the my-service backend.

When this process is complete, we'll see the same output that we got in our sleep container in an earlier example. The following code snippet shows this process, using the Envoy server to listen on the other end. That's because the ingress controller uses Envoy (a service proxy used by Contour under the hood) as a gateway into the cluster:

```
curl -v http://my-service.local/etc/passwd
*    Trying 127.0.0.1...
* TCP_NODELAY set
* Conn to my-service.local (127.0.0.1) port 80    ⟵┐  Resolves my-service.local
> GET / HTTP/1.1                                       to localhost
> Host: my-service.local
> User-Agent: curl/7.64.1
> Accept: */*
>
< HTTP/1.1 200 OK                         ┌ The Envoy server responding
< server: envoy                    ⟵──────┘ to the HTTP request
< date: Sat, 26 Sep 2020 18:32:36 GMT
< content-type: text/html; charset=UTF-8
< content-length: 728
< x-envoy-upstream-service-time: 1
<
root:x:0:0:root:/root:/bin/bash
```

We now can access content hosted by the Python SimpleHTTPServer using both internal `curl` commands on the ClusterIP as well as `curl` commands from our local machine by running an ingress controller service that forwards to the ClusterIP under the hood. As mentioned earlier, the ingress API is going to eventually be subsumed by a newer Gateway API.

The Gateway API in Kubernetes allows for sophisticated decoupling of different tenants in a cluster, replacing the ingress resource with gateways, gateway classes, and routes that can be configured by different personas in an enterprise. Nevertheless, the concepts from the Gateway and ingress APIs are functionally similar and most of what we've learned in this chapter transfers to the Gateway API naturally.

Summary

- Traffic forwarding in CNI plugins involves routing Pod traffic between nodes through networking interfaces.
- CNI plugins can be bridged or unbridged, and in each case, the way they forward traffic is different.
- Network policies can be implemented using many different underlying technologies, such as Antrea OpenVSwitch (OVS) and Calico iptables.
- Layer 7 network policies are implemented with ingress controllers.
- Contour is an ingress controller that solves the same problems that CNIs solve for Pods at the Layer 7 level and works with any CNI provider.
- In the future, the Gateway API will replace the Ingress API with a more flexible API schema, but what you learn in this chapter transfers to the Gateway API naturally.

Pod storage and the CSI

Storage is complex, and this book won't cover all the storage types available to the modern app developer. Instead, we'll start with a concrete problem to solve: our Pod needs to store a file. The file needs to persist between container restarts, and it needs to be schedulable to new nodes in our cluster. In this case, the default baked-in storage volumes that we've already covered in this book won't "cut the mustard":

- Our Pod can't rely on `hostPath` because the node itself may not have a unique writeable directory on its host disk.
- Our Pod also can't rely on `emptyDir` because it is a database, and databases can't afford to lose information stored on an ephemeral volume.

135

- Our Pod might be able to use Secrets to retain its certificate or password credentials to access services like databases, but this Pod is generally not considered a volume when it comes to applications running on Kubernetes.
- Our Pod has the ability to write data on the top layer of its container filesystem. This is generally slow and not recommended for high-volume write traffic. And, in any case, this simply won't work: this data disappears as soon as the Pod is restarted!

Thus, we've stumbled upon an entirely new dimension of Kubernetes storage for our Pod: fulfilling the needs of the application developer. Kubernetes applications, like regular cloud applications, often need to be able to mount EBS volumes, NFS shares, or data from S3 buckets inside containers and read from or write to these data sources. To solve this application storage problem, we'll need a cloud-friendly data model and API for storage. Kubernetes represents this data model using the concepts of PersistentVolume (PV), PersistentVolumeClaim (PVC), and StorageClass:

- PVs give administrators a way to manage disk volumes in a Kubernetes environment.
- PVCs define a claim to these volumes that can be requested by an application (by a Pod) and fulfilled by the Kubernetes API under the hood.
- StorageClass gives application developers a way to get a volume without knowing exactly how it is implemented. It gives applications a way to request a PVC without knowing exactly which type of PersistentVolume is being used under the hood.

StorageClasses allow applications to request volumes or storage types that fulfill different end-user requirements in a *declarative* way. This allows you to design StorageClasses for your data center that might fulfill various needs, such as

- Complex data SLAs (what to keep, how long to keep it, and what not to keep)
- Performance requirements (batch-processing applications versus low-latency applications)
- Security and multi-tenancy semantics (for users to access particular volumes)

Keep in mind that many containers (for example, a CFSSL server for managing application certificates) might not need a lot of storage, but they will need some storage in case they restart and need to reload basic caching or certificate data, for example. In the next chapter, we'll dig further into the high-level concepts of how you might manage StorageClasses. If you're new to Kubernetes, you might be wondering if Pods can maintain any state without a volume.

Do Pods retain state?

In short, the answer is no. Don't forget that a Pod is an ephemeral construct in almost all cases. In some cases (for example, with a StatefulSet) some aspects of a Pod (such as the IP address or, potentially, a locally mounted host volume directory) might persist between restarts.

If a Pod dies for any reason, it will be recreated by a process in the Kubernetes controller manager (KCM). When new Pods are created, it is the Kubernetes scheduler's job to make sure that a given Pod lands on a node capable of running it. Hence, the ephemeral nature of Pod storage that allows this real-time decision making is integral to the flexibility of managing large fleets of applications.

7.1 A quick detour: The virtual filesystem (VFS) in Linux

Before going head-on into the abstractions that Kubernetes offers for Pod storage, it's worth noting that the OS itself also provides these abstractions to programs. In fact, the *filesystem* itself is an abstraction for a complicated schematic that connects applications to a simple set of APIs that we've seen before. You likely know this already, but recall that accessing a file is like accessing any other API. A file in a Linux OS supports a variety of obvious and basic commands (as well as some more opaque ones not listed here):

- `read()`—Reads a few bytes from a file that is open
- `write()`—Writes a few bytes from a file that is open
- `open()`—Creates and/or opens a file so that reads and writes can take place
- `stat()`—Returns some basic information about a file
- `chmod()`—Changes what users or groups can do with a file and reads, writes, and executes permissions

All of these operations are called against what is known as the *virtual filesystem* (VFS), which ultimately is a wrapper around your system's BIOS in most cases. In the cloud, and in the case of FUSE (Filesystem in Userspace), the Linux VFS is just a wrapper to what is ultimately a network call. Even if you are writing data to a disk outside of your Linux machine, you are still accessing that data via the Linux kernel through the VFS. The only difference is that, because you are writing to a remote disk, the VFS uses its NFS client, FUSE client, or whatever other filesystem client it needs, based on your OS, to send this write over the wire. This is depicted in figure 7.1, where all of the various container write operations are actually talking through the VFS API:

- In the case of Docker or CIR storage, the VFS sends filesystem operations to a device mapper or OverlayFS, which ultimately sends traffic to local devices through your system's BIOS.
- In the case of Kubernetes infrastructure storage, the VFS sends filesystems operations to locally attached disks on your node.
- In the case of applications, the VFS often sends writes over the network, especially in "real" Kubernetes clusters running in the cloud or in a data center with many computers. This is because you are not using the local volume types.

> **What about Windows?**
>
> In Windows nodes, the kubelet mounts and provides storage to containers in a similar way as does Linux. Windows kubelets typically run the CSI Proxy (https://github .com/kubernetes-csi/csi-proxy) that makes low-level calls to the Windows OS, which mounts and unmounts volumes when the kubelet instructs it to do so. The same concepts around filesystem abstraction exist in the Windows ecosystem (https://en .wikipedia.org/wiki/Installable_File_System).

In any case, you don't need to understand the Linux storage API in order to mount PersistentVolumes in Kubernetes. It is, however, helpful to understand the basis for filesystems when creating Kubernetes solutions because, ultimately, your Pods will interact with these low-level APIs. Now, let's get back to our Kubernetes-centric view of Pod storage.

7.2   *Three types of storage requirements for Kubernetes*

The term *storage* is overloaded. Before we go down the rabbit hole, let's distinguish the types of storage that typically cause problems in Kubernetes environments:

- *Docker/containerd/CRI storage*—The copy-on-write filesystem that runs your containers. Containers require special filesystems on their resident run times because they need to write to a VFS layer (this is why, for example, you can run `rm -rf /tmp` on a container without actually deleting anything from your host). Typically, the Kubernetes environment uses a filesystem such as btrfs, overlay, or overlay2.
- *Kubernetes infrastructure storage*—The hostPath or Secret volumes that are used on individual kubelets for local information sharing (for example, as a home for a secret that is going to be mounted in a Pod or a directory from where a storage or networking plugin is called).
- *Application storage*—The storage volumes that Pods use in a Kubernetes cluster. When Pods need to write data to disk, they need to mount a storage volume, and this is done in a Pod specification. Common storage volume filesystems are OpenEBS, NFS, GCE, EC2 and vSphere persistent disks, and so on.

In figure 7.1, which is extended by figure 7.2, we visually depict how all three types of storage are fundamental steps in starting a Pod. Previously, we only looked at the CNI-related Pod startup sequence steps. As a reminder, there are several checks done by the scheduler before a Pod starts to confirm storage is ready. Then, before a Pod is started, the kubelet and the CSI provider mount external application volumes on a node for the Pod to use. A Pod that is running might write data to its own OverlayFS, and this is completely ephemeral. For example, it might have a /tmp directory that it uses for scratch space. Finally, once a Pod is running, it reads local volumes and might write other remote volumes.

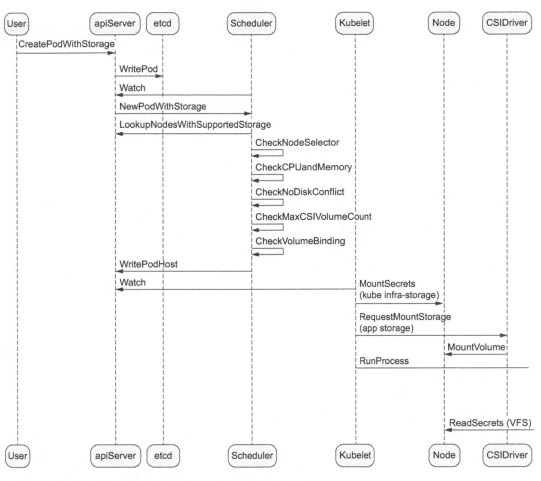

Figure 7.1   The three types of storage in the startup of a Pod

Now, the first figure ends with the CSIDriver, but there are many other layers to the sequence diagram that it depicts. In figure 7.2, we can see that the CSIDriver, containerd, layered filesystem, and CSI volume itself are all targeted downstream from the processes of the Pod. Specifically, when the kubelet starts a process, it sends a message to containerd, which then creates a new writeable layer in the filesystem. Once the containerized process starts, it needs to read secrets from files that are mounted to it. Thus, there are many different types of storage calls made in a single Pod. In a typical production scenario, each has its own semantics and purpose in the life cycle of an app.

The CSI volume mounting step is one of the final events occurring before a Pod starts. To understand this step, we need to take a quick detour and look at how Linux organizes its filesystems.

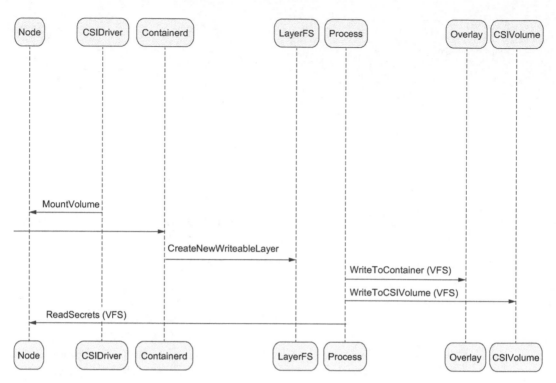

Figure 7.2   The three types of storage in the startup of a Pod, part 2

7.3 *Let's create a PVC in our kind cluster*

Enough with the theory; let's give some application storage to a simple NGINX Pod. We defined PVs, PVCs, and StorageClasses earlier. Now, let's see how they are used to provide a real Pod with a scratch directory to store some files:

- The PV is created by a dynamic storage provisioner that runs on our kind cluster. This is a container that provides Pods with storage by fulfilling PVCs on demand.
- The PVC will not be available until the PersistentVolume is ready because the scheduler needs to ensure that it can mount storage into the Pod's namespace before starting it.
- The kubelet will not start the Pod until the VFS has successfully mounted the PVC into the Pod's filesystem namespace as a writable storage location.

Luckily, our kind cluster comes out of the box with a storage provider. Let's see what happens when we ask for a Pod with a new PVC, one that hasn't been created yet and that has no associated volume already in our cluster. We can check which storage providers are available in a Kubernetes cluster by running the kubectl get sc command as follows:

```
$ kubectl get sc
NAME                      PROVISIONER            RECLAIMPOLICY
standard (default)        rancher.io/local-path  Delete

VOLUMEBINDINGMODE         ALLOWVOLUMEEXPANSION   AGE
WaitForFirstConsumer      false                  9d
```

In order to demonstrate how Pods share data between containers, as well as mount multiple storage points with different semantics, this time around we'll run a Pod with two containers and two volumes. In summary,

- The containers in a Pod can share information with each other.
- Persistent storage can be created on the fly in kind by its dynamic hostPath provisioner.
- Any container can have multiple volume mounts in a Pod.

```
apiVersion: v1
kind: PersistentVolumeClaim
metadata:
  name: dynamic1
spec:
  accessModes:
  - ReadWriteOnce
  resources:
    requests:
      storage: 100k        ⟵  Shares a folder with
---                            the second container
apiVersion: v1
kind: Pod
metadata:
  name: nginx
spec:                          Specifies a dynamic storage volume for
  containers:                  the second container, in addition to
  - image: busybox         ⟵  sharing a folder with the first container
    name: busybox
    volumeMounts:
      - mountPath: /shared
        name: shared           Mounts the volume that
  - image: nginx           ⟵  was previously created
    imagePullPolicy: Always
    name: nginx
    ports:
    - containerPort: 80
      protocol: TCP            Because the volume stanza is outside
    volumeMounts:              of our container's stanza, multiple
      - mountPath: /var/www    Pods can read the same data.
        name: dynamic1     ⟵
      - mountPath: /shared
        name: shared
  volumes:                     Accesses the shared volume
  - name: dynamic1             by both containers if needed
    persistentVolumeClaim:
      claimName: dynamic1  ⟵
  - name: shared               The amount of storage requested; our
    emptyDir: {}           ⟵  PVC determines if it can be fulfilled.
```

```
$ kubectl create -f simple.yaml
pod/nginx created

$ kubectl get pods
NAME      READY    STATUS      RESTARTS    AGE
nginx     0/1      Pending     0           3s
```

The first state, Pending, occurs because the volume for our Pod doesn't exist yet.

```
$ kubectl get pods
NAME      READY    STATUS            RESTARTS    AGE
nginx     0/1      ContainerCreating 0           5s

$ kubectl get pods
NAME      READY    STATUS      RESTARTS    AGE
nginx     1/1      Running     0           13s
```

The final state, Running, means that the volume for our Pod exists (via a PVC), and the Pod can access it; thus, the kubelet starts the Pod.

Now, we can create a file in our first container by running a simple command, such as echo a > /shared/ASDF. We can easily see the results of this in the second container in the emptyDir folder named /shared/ for both containers:

```
$ kubectl exec -i -t nginx -t busybox -- /bin/sh
Defaulting container name to busybox.
Use kubectl describe pod/nginx -n default to see the containers in this pod.
/ # cat /shared/a
ASDF
```

We now have a Pod that has two volumes: one ephemeral and one permanent. How did this happen? If we look at the logs that come with our kind cluster for the local-path-provisioner, it becomes obvious:

```
$ kubectl logs local-path-provisioner-77..f-5fg2w
    -n local-path-storage
controller.go:1027] provision "default/dynamic2" class "standard":
    volume "pvc-ddf3ff41-5696-4a9c-baae-c12f21406022"
        provisioned
controller.go:1041] provision "default/dynamic2" class "standard":
        trying to save persistentvolume "pvc-ddf3ff41-5696-4a9c-baae-
        c12f21406022"
controller.go:1048] provision "default/dynamic2" class "standard":
        persistentvolume "pvc-ddf3ff41-5696-4a9c-baae-c12f21406022" saved
controller.go:1089] provision "default/dynamic2" class "standard": succeeded
event.go:221] Event(v1.ObjectReference{Kind:"PersistentVolumeClaim",
        Namespace:"default", Name:"dynamic2",
        UID:"ddf3ff41-5696-4a9c-baae-
    c12f21406022", APIVersion:"v1", ResourceVersion:"11962",
        FieldPath:""}
    ): type: 'Normal' reason:
        'ProvisioningSucceeded'
    Successfully provisioned volume
        pvc-ddf3ff41-5696-4a9c-baae-c12f21406022
```

The container continues to run as a controller at all times in our cluster. When it sees that we want a volume called dynamic2, it creates it for us. Once this succeeds, the volume itself is bound to the PVC by Kubernetes itself. In the Kubernetes core, if a volume exists that satisfies the needs of a PVC, then a binding event occurs.

At this point, the Kubernetes scheduler confirms that this particular PVC is now deployable on a node, and if this check passes, the Pod moves from the Pending state to the ContainerCreating state, as we saw earlier. As you know by now, the Container-Creating state is simply the state wherein cgroups and mounts are set up by the kubelet for a Pod before it enters the Running state. The fact that this volume was made for us (we did not manually make a PersistentVolume) is an example of *dynamic storage* in a cluster. We can take a look at the dynamically generated volumes like so:

```
$ kubectl get pv
NAME                                          CAPACITY   ACCESS
pvc-74879bc4-e2da-4436-9f2b-5568bae4351a      100k       RWO


RECLAIM POLICY    STATUS    CLAIM              STORAGECLASS
Delete            Bound     default/dynamic1   standard
```

Looking a little closer, we can see that the StorageClass standard is used for this volume. In fact, that storage class is the way that Kubernetes was able to make this volume. When a standard or default storage class is defined, a PVC that has no storage class is automatically configured to receive the default PVC if one exists. This actually happens via an *admission controller* that premodifies new Pods coming into the API server, adding a default storage class label to them. With this label in place, the volume provisioner that runs in your cluster (in our case, this is called local-path-provisioner, and comes bundled with kind) automatically detects the new Pod's storage request and immediately creates a volume:

```
$ kubectl get sc -o yaml
apiVersion: v1
items:
- apiVersion: storage.k8s.io/v1
  kind: StorageClass
  metadata:
    annotations:
      kubectl.kubernetes.io/last-applied-configuration: |
        {"apiVersion":"storage.k8s.io/v1",
          "kind":"StorageClass","metadata":{
        "annotations":{
              "storageclass.kubernetes.io/is-default-class": "true"}
            ,"name":"standard"
          },
          "provisioner":"rancher.io/local-path",
          "reclaimPolicy":"Delete",
        "volumeBindingMode":"WaitForFirstConsumer"}
      storageclass.kubernetes.io/is-default-class: "true"
    name: standard
  provisioner: rancher.io/local-path
kind: List
```

The is-default-class makes this the go-to volume for Pods wanting storage without needing to explicitly request a storage class.

You can have many different storage classes in a cluster.

Once we realize that Pods can have many different types of storage, it becomes clear that we need a pluggable storage provider for Kubernetes. That is the purpose of the CSI interface (https://kubernetes-csi.github.io/docs/).

7.4   *The container storage interface (CSI)*

The Kubernetes CSI defines an interface (figure 7.3) so that vendors providing storage solutions can easily plug themselves into any Kubernetes cluster and provide applications with a broad range of storage solutions to meet different needs. It is the alternative to in-tree storage, where the kubelet itself bakes the drivers for a volume type into its startup process for a Pod.

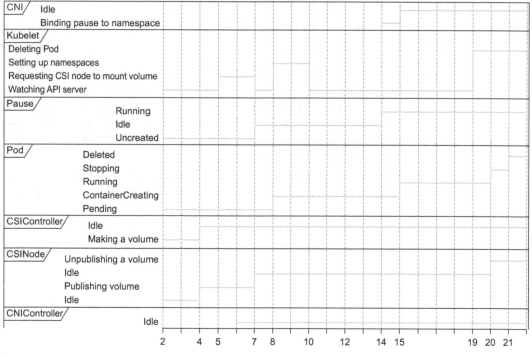

Figure 7.3   The architecture of the Kubernetes CSI model

The purpose of defining the CSI is to make it easy to manage storage solutions from a vendor's perspective. To frame this problem, let's consider the underlying storage implementation for a few Kubernetes PVCs:

- vSphere's CSI driver can create VMFS- or vSAN-based PersistentVolume objects.
- Filesystems such as GlusterFS have CSI drivers that allow you to run volumes in a distributed fashion in containers if you want.
- Pure Storage has a CSI driver that directly creates volumes on a Pure Storage disk array.

Many other vendors also provide CSI-based storage solutions for Kubernetes. Before we describe how the CSI makes this easy, we'll take a quick look at the in-tree provider problem in Kubernetes. This CSI was largely a response to the challenges associated with managing storage volumes, posed by the in-tree storage model.

7.4.1 The in-tree provider problem

Since the inception of Kubernetes, vendors have spent a lot of time putting interoperability into its core codebase. The consequence of this was that vendors of different storage types had to contribute operability code into the Kubernetes core itself! There are still remnants of this in the Kubernetes codebase, as we can see at http://mng.bz/J1NV:

```
package glusterfs

import (
    "context"
          ...
    gcli "github.com/heketi/heketi/client/api/go-client"
    gapi "github.com/heketi/heketi/pkg/glusterfs/api"
```

The importation of the GlusterFS's API package (Heketi is the REST API for Gluster) actually implies that Kubernetes is aware of and dependent on GlusterFS. Looking a little further, we can see how this dependency is manifested:

```
func (p *glusterfsVolumeProvisioner) CreateVolume(gid int)
    (r *v1.GlusterfsPersistentVolumeSource, size int,
     volID string, err error) {
  ...
    // GlusterFS/heketi creates volumes in units of GiB.
    sz, err := volumehelpers.RoundUpToGiBInt(capacity)
  ...
    cli := gcli.NewClient(p.url, p.user, p.secretValue)
  ...
```

The Kubernetes volume package ultimately makes calls to the GlusterFS API to create new volumes. This can also be seen for other vendors as well, such as VMware's vSphere. In fact, many vendors, including VMware, Portworx, ScaleIO, and so on, have their own directories under the pkg/volume file in Kubernetes. This is an obvious anti-pattern for any open source project because it conflates vendor-specific code with that of the broader open source framework. This comes with obvious baggage:

- Users have to align their version of Kubernetes with specific storage drivers.
- Vendors have to continually commit code to Kubernetes itself to keep their storage offerings up to date.

These two scenarios are obviously unsustainable over time. Hence, the need for a standard to define externalized volume creation, mounting, and life cycle capabilities was born. Similarly to our look at CNI earlier, the CSI standard typically results in a DaemonSet running on all nodes that handle mounting (much like the CNI agents that handled IP injection for a namespace). Also, the CSI allows us to easily swap out one storage type for another and to even run multiple storage types at once (something not easily done with networks) because it specifies a specific volume-naming convention.

Note that the in-tree problem isn't specific to storage. The CRI, CNI, and CSI are all born of polluted code that's lived in Kubernetes for a long time. In the first versions of Kubernetes, the codebase was coupled to tools such as Docker, Flannel, and many other filesystems. These couplings are being moved out over time, and the CSI is just one prominent example of how code can move from in-tree to out-of-tree once the proper interfaces are in place. In practice, however, there is still quite a bit of vendor-specific life cycle code that lives in Kubernetes, and it will potentially take years to truly decouple these add-on technologies.

7.4.2   *CSI as a specification that works inside of Kubernetes*

Figure 7.4 demonstrates the workflow for provisioning a PVC with a CSI driver. It's much more transparent and decoupled than what we see with GlusterFS, where different components accomplish different tasks in a discrete manner.

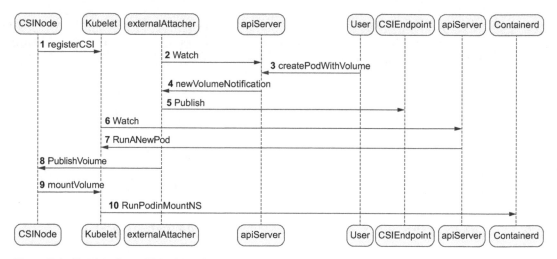

Figure 7.4   Provisioning a PVC with a CSI driver

The CSI specification abstractly defines a generic set of functionality that allows a storage service to be defined without specifying any implementation. In this section, we'll go through some aspects of this interface in the context of Kubernetes itself. The operations it defines are in three general categories: identity services, controller services, and node services. At its heart is the notion of, as you might have guessed, a controller that negotiates the need for storage with a backend provider (your expensive NAS solution) and the Kubernetes control plane by fulfilling a dynamic storage request. Let's take a quick peek at these three categories:

- *Identity services*—Allow a plugin service to self-identify (provide metadata about itself). This allows the Kubernetes control plane to confirm that a particular type of storage plugin is running and available for a volume type.
- *Node services*—Allow the kubelet itself to talk to a local service, which can do operations for the kubelet that are specific to a storage provider. For example, a CSI provider's node service might call a vendor-specific binary when it is prompted to mount a particular type of storage. This is requested over a socket, communicating via the GRPC protocol.
- *Controller services*—Implement the creation, deletion, and other life cycle-related events for a vendor's storage volume. Keep in mind that in order for the Node-Service to be of any value, the backend storage system being used needs to first *create* a volume that can be attached at the right moment to a kubelet. Thus, the controller services play a "glue" role, connecting Kubernetes to the storage vendor. As you might expect, this is implemented by running a watch against the Kubernetes API for volume operations.

The following code snippet provides a brief overview of the CSI specification. We don't show all the methods here as they are available at http://mng.bz/y4V7:

```
service Identity {
  rpc GetPluginInfo(GetPluginInfoRequest)        <─┐  The Identity service tells Kubernetes
  rpc GetPluginCapabilities(GetPluginCapabilitiesRequest)  what type of volumes can be created by
  rpc Probe (ProbeRequest)                            the controllers running in a cluster.
}

service Controller {
  rpc CreateVolume (CreateVolumeRequest)
  rpc DeleteVolume (DeleteVolumeRequest)        <─┐  The Create and Delete methods are
  rpc ControllerPublishVolume (ControllerPublishVolumeRequest)  called before a node can mount a
}                                                   volume into a Pod, implementing
                                                    dynamic storage.

service Node {
  rpc NodeStageVolume (NodeStageVolumeRequest)   <─┐  The Node service is the part of CSI
  rpc NodeUnstageVolume (NodeUnstageVolumeRequest)  that runs on a kubelet, mounting
  rpc NodePublishVolume (NodePublishVolumeRequest)  the volume created previously into
  rpc NodeUnpublishVolume (NodeUnpublishVolumeRequest)  a specific Pod on demand.
  rpc NodeGetInfo (NodeGetInfoRequest)
  ...
}
```

7.4.3 CSI: How a storage driver works

A *CSI storage plugin* decomposes the operations necessary for mounting a Pod's storage into three distinct phases. This includes registering a storage driver, requesting a volume, and publishing a volume.

Registering a storage driver is done via the Kubernetes API. This involves telling Kubernetes how to deal with this particular driver (whether certain things need to happen before a storage volume is writable) and letting Kubernetes know that a particular type of storage is available for the kubelet. The name of a CSI driver is important, as we will see shortly:

```
type CSIDriverInfoSpec struct {
    Name string `json:"name"`
```

When requesting a volume (by making an API call to your $200,000 NAS solution, for instance), the vendor storage mechanism is called upon to create a storage volume. This is done using the CreateVolume function we introduced previously. The call to Create-Volume is actually made by (typically) a separate service that is known as an *external provisioner*, which probably isn't running in the DaemonSet. Rather, it's a standard Pod that watches the Kubernetes API server and responds to volume requests by calling another API for a storage vendor. This service looks at created PVC objects and then calls CreateVolume against a registered CSI driver. It knows what driver to call because this information is provided to it by the volume name. (Hence, it is important to get the name field right.) In this scenario, the request for a volume in a CSI driver is separate from the mounting of that volume.

When publishing a volume, the volume is attached (mounted) to a Pod. This is done by a CSI storage driver that typically lives on every node of your cluster. Publishing a volume is a fancy way to say mounting a volume to a location the kubelet requests so a Pod can write data to it. The kubelet is in charge of making sure the Pod's container is launched with the correct mount namespaces to access this directory.

7.4.4   *Bind mounting*

You might recall that earlier we defined mounts as simple Linux operations that expose a directory to a new place under the / tree. This is a fundamental part of the contract between the attacher and the kubelet, which is defined by the CSI interface. In Linux, the specific operation that we refer to when we make a directory available to a Pod (or any other process via mirroring a directory) is called a *bind mount*. Thus, in any CSI-provisioned storage environment, Kubernetes has several services running that coordinate the delicate interplay of API calls back and forth to reach the ultimate end goal of mounting external storage volumes into Pods.

Because CSI drivers are a set of containers often maintained by vendors, the kubelet itself needs to be able to accept that mounts might be created from inside a container. This is known as *mount propagation* and is an important part of the low-level Linux requirements for certain aspects of Kubernetes to work properly.

7.5   *A quick look at a few running CSI drivers*

We'll conclude with a few concrete examples of real CSI providers. Because this may require a running cluster, rather than creating a walkthrough where we reproduce CSI behavior step by step (as we did with CNI providers), we'll instead just share the running logs of the various components of a CSI provider. That way, you can see how the interfaces in this chapter are implemented and monitored in real time.

7.5.1 The controller

The *controller* is the brains of any CSI driver, connecting requests for storage with back-end storage providers, such as vSAN, EBS, and so on. The interface it implements needs to be able to create, delete, and publish volumes on the fly for our Pods to use. We can see the continuous monitoring of the Kubernetes API server if we look directly at the logs of a running vSphere CSI controller:

```
I0711 05:38:07.057037      1 controller.go:819] Started provisioner
    controller csi.vsphere.vmware.com_vsphere-csi-controller-...-
I0711 05:43:25.976079      1 reflector.go:389] sigs.k8s.io/sig-
    storage-lib-external-provisioner/controller/controller.go:807:
      Watch close - *v1.StorageClass total 0 items received
I0711 05:45:13.975291      1 reflector.go:389] sigs.k8s.io/sig-
    storage-lib-external-provisioner/controller/controller.go:804:
      Watch close - *v1.PersistentVolume total 3 items received
I0711 05:46:32.975365      1 reflector.go:389] sigs.k8s.io/sig-
    storage-lib-external-provisioner/controller/controller.go:801:
      Watch close - *v1.PersistentVolumeClaim total 3 items received
```

Once these PVCs are perceived, the controller can request storage from vSphere itself. The volumes created by vSphere can then synchronize metadata across PVCs and PVs to confirm that a PVC is now mountable. After this, the CSI node takes over (the scheduler first will confirm that a CSI node for vSphere is healthy on the Pod's destination).

7.5.2 The node interface

The *node interface* is responsible for communicating with kubelets and mounting storage to Pods. We can concretely see this by looking at the running logs of volumes in production. Previously, we attempted to run the NFS CSI driver in a hostile environment as a way to uncover lower-level VFS utilization by Linux. Now that we've covered the CSI interface, let's again look back at how the NFS CSI driver looks in production.

The first thing we'll look at is how both the NFS and vSphere CSI plugins use a socket for communicating with the kubelet. This is how the node components of the interface are called. When we look into the details of a CSI node container, we should see something like this:

```
$ kubectl logs
➥ csi-nodeplugin-nfsplugin-dbj6r  -c nfs
I0711 05:41:02.957011  1 nfs.go:47]
➥ Driver: nfs.csi.k8s.io version: 2.0.0        ⟵──┤ Name of the CSI driver
I0711 05:41:02.963340  1 server.go:92] Listening for connections on address:
    &net.UnixAddr{
      Name:"/plugin/csi.sock",    │ The channel for the kubelet to talk to
      Net:"unix"}      ⟵────┤ the CSI plugins it uses for storage

$ kubectl logs csi-nodeplugin-nfsplugin-dbj6r
    -c node-driver-registrar
I0711 05:40:53.917188   1 main.go:108] Version: v1.0.2-rc1-0-g2edd7f10
I0711 05:41:04.210022   1 main.go:76] Received GetInfo call: &InfoRequest{}
```

The naming of CSI drivers is important because it is part of the CSI protocol. The csi-nodeplugin prints its exact version on startup. Note that the csi.sock plugin directory is the common channel that the kubelet uses to talk to the CSI plugins:

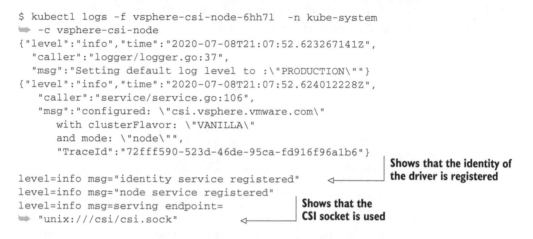

```
$ kubectl logs -f vsphere-csi-node-6hh7l  -n kube-system
➥ -c vsphere-csi-node
{"level":"info","time":"2020-07-08T21:07:52.623267141Z",
  "caller":"logger/logger.go:37",
  "msg":"Setting default log level to :\"PRODUCTION\""}
{"level":"info","time":"2020-07-08T21:07:52.624012228Z",
  "caller":"service/service.go:106",
  "msg":"configured: \"csi.vsphere.vmware.com\"
    with clusterFlavor: \"VANILLA\"
    and mode: \"node\"",
    "TraceId":"72fff590-523d-46de-95ca-fd916f96a1b6"}

level=info msg="identity service registered"    ◀———————  Shows that the identity of
level=info msg="node service registered"                  the driver is registered
level=info msg=serving endpoint=
➥ "unix:///csi/csi.sock"    ◀———————  Shows that the
                                       CSI socket is used
```

This concludes our treatment of the CSI interface and why it exists. Unlike other components of Kubernetes, this is not easy to discuss or reason about without a cluster with real workloads running in front of you. As a follow-up exercise, we highly recommend installing the NFS CSI provider (or any other CSI driver) on a cluster of your choice (VMs or bare metal). One exercise worthy of running through is measuring whether the creation of volumes slows over time and, if so, what the bottlenecks are.

We don't include a live example of a CSI driver in this chapter because most of the current CSI drivers that are used in production clusters aren't runnable inside of a simple `kind` environment. In general, as long as you understand that the provisioning of volumes is distinct from the mounting of those volumes, you should be well prepared to debug CSI failures in a production system by treating these two independent operations as distinct failure modes.

7.5.3 *CSI on non-Linux OSs*

Similar to CNI, the CSI interface is OS-agnostic; however, its implementation is quite natural for Linux users with the ability to run privileged containers. As with networking outside of Linux, the way CSI is implemented in a Linux process is a little different by tradition. For example, if you are running Kubernetes on Windows, you might find a lot of value in the CSI proxy project (https://github.com/kubernetes-csi/csi-proxy) that runs a service on every kubelet of your cluster, which abstracts away many of the PowerShell commands that implement CSI node functionality. This is because, on Windows, the concept of *privileged* containers is quite new and only works on certain, more recent versions of containerd.

In time, we expect that many people running Windows kubelets will also be able to run their CSI implementations as Windows DaemonSets, with behavior similar to that of the Linux DaemonSets we've demoed in this chapter. Ultimately the need to abstract storage happens at many levels of the computing stack, and Kubernetes is just one more abstraction on top of an ever increasing ecosystem of storage and persistence support for applications.

Summary

- Pods can acquire storage dynamically at run time when they are created by mount operations that the kubelet executes.
- The simplest way to experiment with Kubernetes storage providers is to make a PVC in a Pod in a `kind` cluster.
- The CSI provider for NFS is one of many CSI providers, all of which conform to the same CSI standard for container storage mounting. This decouples Kubernetes source code from storage vendor source code.
- When implemented, the CSI-defined identity controller and node services, each of which includes several abstract functions, allow providers to dynamically provide storage to Pods through the CSI API.
- The CSI interface can be made to work on non-Linux OSs, with the CSI proxy for Windows kubelets as the leading example of this type of implementation.
- The Linux virtual filesystem (VFS) includes anything that can be opened, read, and written to. Operations on disks happen beneath its API.

Storage implementation and modeling

This chapter covers

- Exploring how dynamic storage works
- Utilizing emptyDir volumes in workloads
- Managing storage with CSI providers
- Using hostPath values with CNI and CSI
- Implementing storageClassTemplates for Cassandra

Modeling storage in a Kubernetes cluster is one of the most important tasks that an administrator needs to do before going to production. This entails asking yourself questions about what your storage needs are for a production application, and there are several dimensions to this. You'll want to generally ask yourself the following questions for any application that needs persistent storage:

- Does the storage need to be durable or just best effort? Durable storage often means NAS, NFS, or something like GlusterFS. All of these have performance tradeoffs that you'll need to vet.

- Does the storage need to be fast? Is I/O a bottleneck? If speed is important, emptyDir running in memory or a special storage class with a storage controller suited for this is often a good choice.
- How much storage is used per container, and how many containers do you expect to run? A storage controller might be needed for large container numbers.
- Do you need a dedicated disk for security? If so, local volumes may possibly fit your needs.
- Are you running AI workloads with model or training caches? These might need rapidly recycled volumes that stick around for a few hours at a time.
- Are you in the range of 1–10 GB for storage? If so, local storage or emptyDir might work in most cases.
- Are you implementing something like Hadoop Distributed File System (HDFS) or Cassandra that replicates and backs up data for you? If so, you can exclusively use local disk volumes, but recovery is complicated this way.
- Are you okay with downtime and cold storage? If so, maybe an object storage model on top of cheap distributed volumes will work. Technologies like NFS or GlusterFS are a good use case here.

8.1   A microcosm of the broader Kubernetes ecosystem: Dynamic storage

Once you have a feel for your application's storage needs, you can look at the primitives that Kubernetes provides. There are quite a few personas in the storage workflow with different motives. This is because storage, unlike networking, is an extremely finite and expensive resource due to the physical constraints (its requirement of persisting between machine reboots) and various legal and procedural aspects of storage in an enterprise. To keep these actors straight in our heads, let's take a quick look at a 1,000-foot representation of the overall storage story in figure 8.1.

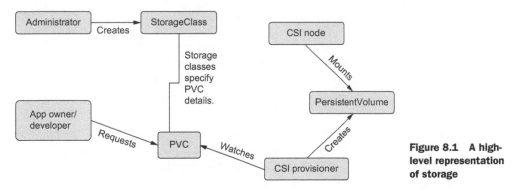

Figure 8.1   A high-level representation of storage

In figure 8.1, you'll notice that users *request* storage, administers *define* storage via storage classes, and the CSI provisioners typically are responsible for *provisioning* storage for a user to write against. If we think back to our chapter on networking, this multi-tenant view of storage provisioning can be thought of as analogous to the emerging Gateway API for Layer 7 load balancing:

- GatewayClasses are analogous in some ways to StorageClasses for CSI in that they define a type of entry point to a network.
- Gateways are analogous to PersistentVolumes (PVs) for CSI in that they represent provisioned Layer 7 load balancers.
- Routes are analogous to PersistentVolumeClaims (PVCs) for CSI in that they allow individual developers to ask for an instance of a GatewayClass for a specific application.

Thus, as we deep dive into storage, it's helpful to keep in mind that much of Kubernetes itself is, as time goes on, increasingly devoted to the idea of putting vendor-neutral APIs around infrastructure resources that developers and administrators can asynchronously and independently manage. With that said, let's jump into looking at dynamic storage and what it means for developers in various common use cases.

8.1.1 Managing storage on the fly: Dynamic provisioning

The ability to manage storage on the fly in a cluster means that we need to be able to provision volumes on the fly as well. This is known as *dynamic provisioning*. Dynamic provisioning, in the most generic sense, is a feature of many cluster solutions (for example, Mesos has had a PersistentVolume offering for quite some time, which reserves persistent, reclaimable local storage for processes). Anyone who has used a product like VSan knows that an EBS cloud provider must provide some kind of API-driven storage model.

Dynamic provisioning in Kubernetes stands out because of its highly pluggable (PVCs, CSI) and declarative nature (PVCs alongside dynamic provisioning). This allows you to build your own semantics for different types of storage solutions and provides indirection between a PVC and a corresponding PersistentVolume.

8.1.2 Local storage compared with emptyDir

An *emptyDir* volume is well-known to most Kubernetes novices. It's the simplest way to mount a directory into a Pod and has basically no security or resource costs that need to be monitored closely. However, there are quite a few subtleties around its use that can prove a powerful security and performance booster when you move an application into production.

In table 8.1, we compare local and empty volume types. When it comes to local and emptyDir, we have a totally different storage life cycle, even though all the data is local. For example, a local volume could be reliably used to recover data from a running database in case of disasters, whereas an emptyDir would not support this use case. The use of third-party volumes and volume controllers for PVCs is a third use case that generally implies that storage can be portable and mounted on new nodes if the Pods need to migrate.

Table 8.1   Comparing local, emptyDir, and PVC storage

Storage type 1	Lifespan	Durable	Implementation	Typical consumer
Local	Life of local disk	Yes	Local disk on your node	A heavy-weight data intensive or legacy app
emptyDir	As long as your Pod is on the same node	No	Local folder in your node	Any Pod
PVC	Forever[a]	Yes	Third-party storage vendor	A light-weight database app

[a]Data persistence depends on the reclaim policy for the PersistentVolume.

In general, we consume PVCs for applications that require persistence as a preference. In cases where we have complex persistent storage requirements, we might implement a local storage volume (for example, an app that needs to run in the same place and needs to be attached to a huge disk for legacy purposes). An emptyDir volume has no specific use case, and it's used as a Swiss army knife in Pods for a variety of purposes. The `emptyDir` type is generally used when two containers need a scratchpad to write data to. You might wonder why anyone would use an `emptyDir` type instead of just mounting a real PersistentVolume directly to two containers. There are several reasons:

- *PersistentVolumes are typically expensive.* They require a distributed storage controller to provision a volume with specific amounts of storage, and this storage might be limited. If you don't need to keep the data around for a Pod, there's no value in wasting storage resources.
- *PersistentVolumes can be an order of magnitude or more slower then emptyDir volumes.* This is because they often require network traffic and writing to a disk of some sort. An emptyDir volume, however, can write to temporary file storage (tmpfs) or even be pure memory-mapped volumes, which are as fast as RAM by definition.
- *PersistentVolumes are less secure by nature then emptyDir volumes.* The data Persistent-Volumes might stick around and be re-read in different places on a cluster. In comparison, the emptyDir volumes are not mountable by Kubernetes to anything outside of the Pod that declares them.
- *emptyDir can be used with scratch containers to create directories.* This includes /var/log and /etc/ when an application wants to write log files or configuration files to a specific point throughout its life cycle.
- *You need to add a /tmp or /var/log directory to a container for performance or functional reasons.*

An emptyDir volume can be used as a performance optimization or as a way to monkey patch container directory structures. In a functional sense, a container may require an emptyDir volume when it lacks the default filesystem paths, containing only a single binary executable. Sometimes a container is built with a scratch image to reduce its security footprint, but this comes at the cost of having nowhere to cache or store simple files (like logging or caching data).

Even if you have the /var/log directory available in your container image, you still may want emptyDir as a performance optimization for writing data to disk. This is common because containers that write files to a predefined directory (for example, /var/log) might take a performance hit due to the slow nature of copy-on-write filesystem operations. Container layers usually have such filesystems, which allow a process to write data to the top layer of a filesystem without actually affecting the underlying container image. This allows you to do almost anything in a running container without damaging the underlying Docker image, but it comes at a performance cost. Copy-on-write filesystems are often slow (and potentially CPU-intensive) compared with other native filesystem operations. This depends on the storage driver that you are running for your container runtime.

As you can see, there's quite a bit of sophistication in an emptyDir volume in terms of how it might be used in production. But, in general, if you are interested in Kubernetes storage, you probably are going to spend a lot more time working on problems related to PersistentVolumes then ephemeral ones.

8.1.3 *PersistentVolumes*

A *PersistentVolume* is the Kubernetes reference to a storage volume that can be mounted to a Pod. Storage is mounted by the kubelet, which invokes, creates, and mounts various types of volumes and/or potentially a CSI driver (which we will discuss next). A PersistentVolumeClaim (PVC) is therefore a named reference to a PersistentVolume. This claim ties up a volume if the volume is of type RWO (which stands for read-write-once) so that other Pods may not be able to use it again until that volume is no longer mounted. The following chain of events typically occurs when you create a Pod that requires persistent storage:

1 You request creation of a Pod that requires a PVC.
2 The Kubernetes scheduler begins looking for a home for your Pod, waiting for a node with the appropriate storage topology, CPU, and memory attributes.
3 You create a valid PVC that your Pod can access.
4 The volume claim is fulfilled by the Kubernetes control plane.

   This involves the creation of a PersistentVolume via a dynamic storage controller. Most production Kubernetes installations come with at least one such controller (or many, which are differentiated via the StorageClass name), and this is usually a vendor add-on. These controllers simply watch for the creation of standard PVC objects in the API server and then create a volume that those claims will then use for storage.

5 The scheduler proceeds with deciding that your Pod is ready now that its storage claim is fulfilled.
6 A Pod that depends on this claim can be scheduled, and the Pod is started.
7 While the Pod is being started, the kubelet mounts local directories corresponding to this claim.

8 The locally mounted volume is made writable to the Pod.

9 The Pod you requested is now running and reading or writing to the storage that exists inside the PersistentVolume.

The Kubernetes scheduler and attaching volumes to Pods

The Kubernetes scheduler is intricately woven into the logic of how volumes are attached to Pods. The scheduler defines several extensions where we can implement logic from different Pod requirements, such as storage. The extensions are PreFilter, Filter, PostFilter, Reserve, PreScore, PreBind, Bind, PostBind, Permit, and QueueSort. The PreFilter extension point is one of the places where storage logic is implemented by the scheduler.

The ability to intelligently decide whether a Pod is ready to start is partially determined by the storage parameters that the scheduler is aware of. For example, the scheduler proactively avoids scheduling a Pod that depends on a volume, which only allows one concurrent reader in cases where an existing Pod already has access to such a volume. This prevents Pod startup errors, where a volume never binds, but you can't find out why.

You may wonder why the scheduler needs access to information about storage. (After all, it's really the kubelet's job to attach storage to a Pod, as you might imagine.) The reason is performance and predictability. For various reasons, you may want to limit the amount of volumes on a node. Additionally, if specific nodes have specific constraints around storage, the scheduler might want to avoid placing Pods on these nodes proactively so as not to create "zombie" Pods that, although scheduled, never properly start because of a lack of access to storage resources.

Thanks to recent advances in the Kubernetes API to support storage capacity logic, the CSI API includes the ability to describe storage constraints, and this is in a manner that can be queried and used by the scheduler so that Pods are placed in nodes that are best suited to their storage requirements. To learn more about this, you can peruse http://mng.bz/M2pE.

8.1.4 CSI (container storage interface)

You might be wondering how the kubelet is capable of mounting arbitrary storage types. For example, a filesystem like NFS requires an NFS client to be YUM-installed on typical Linux distributions. Indeed, storage mounting is highly platform-dependent, and the kubelet doesn't magically solve that problem for you.

Until Kubernetes 1.12, common filesystem types like NFS, GlusterFS, Ceph, and many others were included as part of the kubelet itself. CSI has changed this, however, and the kubelet now is increasingly unaware of platform-specific filesystems. Instead, users interested in mounting a particular type of storage usually run a CSI driver as a DaemonSet on their clusters. These drivers use a socket to communicate with the kubelet and to do the necessary low-level filesystem mounting operations. The movement to CSI makes it easy for vendors to evolve storage clients and publish updates to those clients frequently, without needing to put their vendor-specific logic into particular Kubernetes releases.

> **NOTE** A common pattern in the CNCF is to initially publish an open source project including many dependencies and then slowly break those dependencies out over time. This helps to create a simple user experience for early adopters. Once the adoption of something is commonplace, however, work is done after the fact to decouple such dependencies to clean up the architecture. The CNI, CSI, and CRI interfaces are all examples of this.

CSI is the container storage interface that has evolved so that PersistentVolume code no longer has to be compiled into your Kubernetes release. The CSI storage model means that you only have to implement a few Kubernetes concepts (a DaemonSet and a storage controller) so that the kubelet can provision any kind of storage you want. CSI is not Kubernetes-specific. To be fair, Mesos also supports CSI, as well as Kubernetes itself, so we're not picking on anyone here.

8.2 *Dynamic provisioning benefits from CSI but is orthogonal*

Dynamic provisioning, the ability to magically make a PersistentVolume when a PVC is created, is not the same as *CSI*, which gives you the ability to dynamically mount any kind of storage into a container. These two technologies are, however, quite synergistic. By combining them, you allow developers to continue using the same declaration via StorageClasses (described later) to mount potentially different kinds of storage that expose the same high-level semantics. As an example, a `fast` storage class might initially be implemented using solid state disks that are exposed through a NAS:

```
kind: StorageClass
apiVersion: storage.k8s.io/v1
metadata:
  name: fast
parameters:
  type: pd-ssd
```

Later on, you might pay a company (such as Datera) to provide fast storage on a different storage array. In either case, using a dynamic provisioner, your developers can continue using the exact same API requests for new storage volumes with only the CSI drivers that run on your cluster and the storage controllers changing under the hood.

In any case, dynamic provisioning is implemented by most cloud providers for Kubernetes with a simple cloud-attached disk type as the default. In many small apps, a slow PersistentVolume that is automatically selected by your cloud provider is enough. However, for heterogeneous workloads, being able to choose between different storage models and to implement policies (or, better yet, Operators) around PVC fulfillment becomes increasingly important.

8.2.1　*StorageClasses*

StorageClasses enable sophisticated storage semantics to be specified in a declarative way. Although there are several parameters that can be sent to different types of storage classes, one that is common to all of them is the *binding mode*. This is where building a custom, dynamic provisioner might be extremely important.

Dynamic provisioning is not just a way to provide naive storage, but also a powerful tool for enabling high performance workloads in a data center with heterogeneous storage requirements. Every different workload you care about in production might benefit from a different StorageClass for the binding mode, retention, and performance (which we'll explain shortly).

A HYPOTHETICAL STORAGE CLASS PROVIDER FOR A DATA CENTER

StorageClasses seem mostly theoretical, until we consider a use case of a Kubernetes administrator fending off scores of developers who are hungry to deploy their applications to production and who also know little about how storage works. Consider, for a moment, such a scenario wherein you have applications in three categories: batch data processing, transactional web-style applications, and AI applications. In this scenario, one might make a single volume provisioner with three storage classes. An application could then request specific storage types declaratively like so:

```
apiVersion: v1
kind: PersistentVolumeClaim
metadata:
  name: my-big-data-app-vol
spec:
  storageClassName: bigdata
  accessModes:
    - ReadWriteOnce
  resources:
    requests:
      storage: 100G
```

This PVC would live inside of a Pod like so:

```
apiVersion: v1
kind: Pod
metadata:
  name: my-big-data-app
spec:
  volumes:
    - name: myvol
      persistentVolumeClaim:
        claimName: my-big-data-app-vol
  containers:
    - name: my-big-data-app
      image: datacruncher:0.1
      volumeMounts:
        - mountPath: "/mybigdata-app-volume"
          name: myvol
```

A QUICK REMINDER OF HOW PVCs WORK

Kubernetes looks at the metadata of a PVC (for example, how much storage it asks for) and then finds PV objects that match your claim. Thus, you do not explicitly assign storage to a claim. Rather, you create a claim that requests certain attributes (for example, 100 G of storage) and asynchronously create a volume that fulfills those attributes.

8.2.2   Back to the data center stuff

What happens in our dynamic provisioner that we've envisioned here? Let's take a look at that:

1 We write a control loop that watches for volume claims.
2 When we see a request, we summon a volume on a persistent spinning disk of size 100 G by making an API call (for example, to a storage provider on our NAS). Note that an alternative way to do this is to precreate many storage directories in a NAS or NFS share.
3 We then define a Kubernetes PV object to back the PVC. This volume type might be anything, such as an NFS or `hostPath` PV type.

From here on, Kubernetes does the work, and once the PVC is fulfilled with a backing PersistentVolume, our Pods are schedulable. In this scenario, we mention three steps: the control loop, the request for a volume, and the creation of that volume. Our decision on what kind of low-level storage volumes to create hinges on what type of storage is requested by one of our developers. In a previous code snippet, we used `bigdata` as a StorageClass type. In a data center, we might typically support three storage classes:

- `bigdata` (as mentioned)
- `postgres`
- `ai`

Why three classes? There's no specific reason for having three storage class implementations. We easily might have four or more classes.

For BigData/HDFS/ETL-style workloads, and for storage-intensive work, data locality is important. Thus, in this case, you might want to store your data on a bare metal disk and read from that disk as if it were a host volume mount. The binding mode for this type might benefit from the WaitForFirstConsumer strategy, allowing for a volume to be created and attached directly on a node that runs the workload, as opposed to creating it beforehand, potentially in a place with lower data locality.

Because Hadoop data nodes are a persistent feature of a cluster and HDFS itself maintains replication for you, your retention policy for this model might be Delete. With cold storage workloads (for example, in GlusterFS), you'll want to automate a policy of implementing specific translators for storage volumes into workloads running in certain labeled namespaces. Either way, all provisioning might be done on demand in the cheapest disks available at the time.

For Postgres/RDBMS-style workloads, you'll need dedicated, solid-state drives that can be several terabytes. As soon as storage is requested, you'll want to know where your Pod is running, so you can reserve an SSD in the same rack or on the same node. Because disk locality and scheduling can significantly affect the performance of these workloads, your storage class for Postgres might use the WaitForFirstConsumer strategy. Because a Postgres database in production often has important transactional history, you may choose a retention policy of Retain for it.

Finally, with AI workloads, your data scientists may not care about storage; they just want to crunch numbers and probably need a scratchpad. You'll want to put indirection between your developers and the type of storage that is provided to them so that you can continually change the StorageClass and volume types in your cluster without affecting things like YAML API definitions, Helm charts, or application code. Similar to the cold storage scenario, because AI workloads suck a lot of things into memory for a short period of time before dumping them out, data locality isn't always important. Immediate binding could be done for faster Pod startups, and similarly, a retention policy of Delete would probably be appropriate.

Given the complexity of these processes, you may need custom logic for fulfilling volume claims. You can simply name these volume types `hdfs`, `coldstore`, `pg-perf`, and `ai-slow`, respectively.

8.3 *Kubernetes use cases for storage*

We've now looked at the importance of modeling your end-user use cases for storage. Now, let's take a look at a few other topics that will give you a broader feel for how Kubernetes often uses storage volumes to do basic housekeeping for Secrets and networking functionality.

8.3.1 *Secrets: Sharing files ephemerally*

The design pattern of sharing a file as a way to distribute credentials to containers or VMs is pretty common. As an example, the cloud-init language, which bootstraps VMs in cloud environments such as AWS, Azure, and vSphere has a `write_files` directive that is commonly used outside of Kubernetes environments, as seen in the following:

```
# This is taken from https://cloudinit.readthedocs.io/en/latest/topics
# /examples.html#writing-out-arbitrary-files
write_files:
- encoding: b64
  content: CiMgVGhpcyBmaWxlIGNvbnRyb2xzIHRoZSBzdGF0ZSBvZiBTRUxpbnV4...
  owner: root:root
  path: /etc/sysconfig/selinux
  permissions: '0644'
- content: |
    # My new /etc/sysconfig/samba file
    SMBDOPTIONS="-D"
  path: /etc/sysconfig/samba
```

In the same sense that system administrators use tools such as `cloud-init` to bootstrap virtual machines, Kubernetes uses the API server and the kubelet to bootstrap Secrets or files into Pods using an almost identical design pattern. If you've administered a cloud environment that has to access a database of any sort, you've probably solved this problem in one of three ways:

- *Injecting credentials as environment variables*—This requires that you have some control over the context a process runs in.
- *Injecting credentials as files*—This means that a process can be restarted using different options or argument contexts without needing to get its password environment variables updated.
- *Using the Secret API object*—This is a Kubernetes construct for doing essentially the same types of things we do with ConfigMaps, with a few minor caveats that differentiate them from ConfigMaps:
  - We can use different types of algorithms for encrypting and decrypting Secrets but not ConfigMaps.
  - We can encrypt Secrets with the API server at rest in etcd but not ConfigMaps, making Secrets easier to read or debug but less secure.
  - By default, any data in a Secret is Base64-encoded rather than stored as plain text. This is due to the common use case of storing certificates or other complex data types in Secrets (as well as the obvious benefit that, in passing, it's hard to read a Base64-encoded string).

Over time, it is expected that vendors will provide sophisticated Secret rotation APIs that are targeted at the Secrets API type in Kubernetes. That said, at the time of this writing, Secrets and ConfigMaps are largely the same in terms of how we use them in Kubernetes.

WHAT DOES A SECRET LOOK LIKE?

A Secret in Kubernetes looks like this:

```
apiVersion: v1
kind: Secret
metadata:
  name: mysecret
type: Opaque
data:
  val1: YXNkZgo=
  val2: YXNkZjIK
stringData:
  val1: asdf
```

In this Secret, we have multiple values: `val1` and `val2`. The `StringData` field actually stores `val` as a plain text string that is easy to read. A common misconception is that Secret data in Kubernetes is secured via Base64 encoding. This is *not* the case, as Base64 encoding doesn't secure anything at all! Rather, the security of Secrets in

Kubernetes comes with the care with which an administrator takes to regularly audit and rotate Secrets. In any case, Secrets in Kubernetes are secure because they are only given to the kubelet to mount into Pods that are authorized to read them via RBAC. The `val1` value might be later mounted into a Pod like so:

```
apiVersion: v1
kind: Pod
metadata:
  name: mypod
spec:
  containers:
  - name: mypod
    image: my-webapp
    volumeMounts:
    - name: myval
      mountPath: "/etc/myval"
      readOnly: true
  volumes:
  - name: myval
    secret:
      secretName: val1
```

Thus, the `asdf` value would then be the contents of the /etc/myval file in this Pod when it runs. This can be done by the kubelet's clever on-demand creation of a special ephemeral tmpfs volume specifically for the containers that need to access this Secret. The kubelet also can handle updating this file when the Secret value changes in the Kubernetes API because it's really just a file that lives on the host, shared through the magic of, you guessed it, filesystem namespaces.

CREATING A SIMPLE POD WITH AN EMPTYDIR VOLUME FOR FAST WRITE ACCESS

A canonical example of an emptyDir Pod might be something like an application that needs to write temporary files to /var/tmp. Ephemeral storage is typically mounted into Pod as

- A volume with one or more files, which is common with ConfigMaps that have configuration data (for example, for an application's various knobs and dials)
- An environment variable, which is common with Secrets

If you have an app that uses a file as a lock or semaphore between different containers, or you need to inject some ephemeral configuration into an app (for example, via a ConfigMap), local storage volumes managed by the kubelet are sufficient. Secrets can use an emptyDir volume under the hood to mount a password (for example, as a file into a container). Similarly, an emptyDir volume can be shared by two Pods so that you can build a simple work or signaling queue between two containers.

An emptyDir is the simplest type of storage to implement. It doesn't need an actual volume implementation and is guaranteed to work on any cluster. For concreteness, in a Redis database, where long-term persistence doesn't matter, you might mount ephemeral storage as a volume like so:

```
apiVersion: v1
kind: Pod
metadata:
  name: redis
spec:
  containers:
  - name: redis
    image: redis
    volumeMounts:
    - name: redis-storage
      mountPath: /data/redis
  volumes:
  - name: redis-storage
    emptyDir: {}
```

Why bother with emptyDir? Because, as we mentioned earlier, performance of empty-Dirs might be much faster than that of a containerized directory. Remember, the way that your container runtime writes to a file is through a copy-on-write filesystem, which has a different write path than that of regular files on your disk. Thus, for folders that need high performance in production containers, you may deliberately choose an emptyDir or hostPath volume mount. In some container runtimes, it is not uncommon to see speedups up to ten times faster when comparing writing to the host filesystem to that of a container filesystem.

8.4   *What does a dynamic storage provider typically look like?*

Unlike emptyDir volumes, storage providers are implemented outside of Kubernetes, often by vendors. Implementing a storage solution ultimately involves implementing the provisioning step of the CSI specification. As an example, we could make a NAS storage provider that cycles through a list of predefined folders. In the following, we only support six volumes as a way to keep the code easy to read and concrete. However, in the real world, you might need a more complex way of managing underlying storage directories for a volume provisioner. For example:

```
var storageFolder1 = "/opt/NAS/1"     ◄──┐  Supports six
var storageFolder2 = "/opt/NAS/2"        │  different mounts
var storageFolder3 = "/opt/NAS/3"
var storageFolder4 = "/opt/NAS/4"
var storageFolder5 = "/opt/NAS/5"
var storageFolder6 = "/opt/NAS/6"
var storageFoldersUsed = 0

// Provision creates a storage asset, returning a PV object to represent it.
func (p *hostPathProvisioner) Provision
    (options controller.VolumeOptions) (*v1.PersistentVolume, error) {
    glog.Infof("Provisioning volume %v", options)
    path := path.Join(p.pvDir, options.PVName)

    // Implement our artificial constraint in the simplest way possible...
    if storageFoldersUsed == 0 {
        panic("Cant store anything else !")
```

```
    }
    if err := os.MkdirAll(path, 0777); err != nil {
        return nil, err
    }

    // Explicitly chmod created dir so we know that
    // mode is set to 0777 regardless of umask
    if err := os.Chmod(path, 0777); err != nil {
        return nil, err
    }

    // Example of how you might call to your NAS
    folders := []string{
            storageFolder1, storageFolder2, storageFolder3,
            storageFolder4, storageFolder5, storageFolder6
    }
```

Round robins against these mounts by storing them in an array

```
    // Now let's make the folder ...
    mycompany.ProvisionNewNasResourceToLocalFolder
                (folders[storageFoldersUsed++]);

    // This is taken straight from the minikubes controller, mostly...
    pv := &v1.PersistentVolume{
        ObjectMeta: metav1.ObjectMeta{
            Name: options.PVName,
            Annotations: map[string]string{
                // Change this
                "myCompanyStoragePathIdentity": string(p.identity),
            },
        },
        Spec: v1.PersistentVolumeSpec{
```

Creates the PV YAML, similar to what we've done in other places

```
            PersistentVolumeReclaimPolicy:
              options.PersistentVolumeReclaimPolicy,
            AccessModes:            options.PVC.Spec.AccessModes,
            Capacity: v1.ResourceList{
                v1.ResourceName(v1.ResourceStorage):
                            options.PVC.Spec.Resources.Requests[
                                v1.ResourceName(v1.ResourceStorage...
            },
            PersistentVolumeSource: v1.PersistentVolumeSource{
                HostPath: &v1.HostPathVolumeSource{

                    Path: storageFolder,
                },
            },
        },
    }
    return pv, nil
}
```

Uses hostPath under the hood, except we mount it to a directory in our NAS

To clarify, this code is just a hypothetical example of how one could write a custom provisioner by borrowing from the logic of the hostPath provisioner in minikube. The remaining code for the storage controller in minikube can be found at http://mng.bz/wn5P. If you are interested in understanding PersistentVolumeClaims or

StorageClasses and how they work, you should definitely read it, or better yet, try compiling it on your own!

8.5 *hostPath for system control and/or data access*

Kubernetes hostPath volumes are similar to Docker volumes because they allow a container running in a Pod to write directly to a host. This is a powerful feature that is often abused by microservice novices, so be careful when you use it. The `hostPath` volume type has a broad range of use cases. These are generally split into two categories:

- *Utility functionality*—Provided by containers that can only be achieved by accessing host file resources (we'll walk through an example of this).
- *Using the host as a persistent file store*—In this way, when a Pod disappears, its data persists in a predictable location. Note that this is almost always an anti-pattern because it means that applications behave differently when a Pod dies and is later rescheduled to a new node.

8.5.1 *hostPaths, CSI, and CNI: A canonical use case*

CNI and CSI, which are the backbone for Kubernetes networking and storage, both rely heavily on the use of hostPath. The kubelet itself runs on every node mount and unmounts storage volumes, making these calls through a CSI driver and a UNIX domain socket shared on the host by using, you guessed it, a hostPath volume. There is also a second UNIX domain socket that the node-driver-registrar uses to register the CSI driver to a kubelet.

As mentioned, many use cases for hostPath that involve applications are anti-patterns. However, one common and critical use case for hostPath is the implementation of a CNI plugin. Let's look at that next.

A CNI HOSTPATH EXAMPLE

As an example of how heavily reliant CNI providers can be on the hostPath functionality, let's look at the volume mounts in a running Calico node. The Calico Pod is responsible for many system-level actions, like manipulating XDP rules, iptables rules, and so on. Additionally, these Pods need to make sure that BGP tables across Linux kernels are synchronized properly. Thus, as you can see, there are many hostPath volume declarations to access various host directories. For example:

```
volumes:
  - hostPath:
      path: /run/xtables.lock
      type: FileOrCreate
    name: xtables-lock
  - hostPath:
      path: /opt/cni/bin
      type: ""
...
```

On Linux, CNI providers install themselves onto a kubelet by literally writing their own binaries from inside a container onto the node itself, usually in the /opt/cni/bin directory. This is one of the most popular use cases for hostPaths—using Linux containers to do administrative actions on a Linux node. Many applications that are administrative in nature use this feature, including

- Prometheus, a metrics and monitoring solution, for mounting /proc and other system resources to check resource usage
- Logstash, a logging integration solution, for mounting various logging directories into containers
- CNI providers that, as mentioned, self-install binaries into /opt/cni/bin
- CSI providers, which use hostPaths to mount vendor-specific utilities for storage

The Calico CNI provider is one many such examples of low-level Kubernetes system processes that wouldn't be possible if we couldn't directly mount devices or directories from a host into a container. In fact, other CNIs (such as Antrea or Flannel) and even CSI storage drivers also require this functionality to bootstrap and manage hosts.

At first, this type of self-installation can be counterintuitive, so you might want to take a moment to noodle on it. Timothy St. Claire, an early Kubernetes maintainer and contributor, has referred to this behavior as "reaching inside your own belly button." However, it's at the heart of how Kubernetes is designed to work in Linux. (We say in Linux specifically because in other OSs, such as Windows, this level of container privilege isn't yet possible. With Windows HostProcess containers emerging in Kubernetes 1.22, we may begin to see this paradigm take root in non-Linux environments as well.) Thus, hostPath volumes aren't just a feature for enabling containerized workloads, but actually, a feature that allows containers to administer complex aspects of a Linux server outside of the realm of developer-centric containerized applications.

WHEN SHOULD YOU USE HOSTPATH VOLUMES?

In your storage travels, keep in mind that you can use hostPath for all sorts of things, and although it's considered an anti-pattern, it can get you out of a tight jam pretty easily. hostPath can allow you do to things like quick-and-easy backups, fulfilling compliance policies (where nodes are authorized for storage but distributed volumes are not), and providing high performance storage without relying on deep cloud-native integration. In general, when considering how you should implement storage for a given backend, consider the following:

- Is there a native Kubernetes volume provider? If so, that might be the easiest approach and require the least automation on your end.
- If not, is your volume vendor providing a CSI implementation? If so, you can run that, and most likely, it comes with a dynamic provisioner.

If neither of these are an option, you can use tools such as hostPath or Flex volumes to rig any type of storage as a volume that can be bound into any Pod on a case-by-case basis. You may have to add scheduling information to the Pod if only certain hosts in your cluster have access to this storage provider, which is why the former choices are often ideal.

8.5.2 *Cassandra: An example of real-world Kubernetes application storage*

Persistent applications on Kubernetes need to scale dynamically, although there are still predictable ways to access named volumes with mission critical data volumes. Let's take a look at a sophisticated storage use case in detail—Cassandra.

Cassandra Pods typically are managed in a StatefulSet. The concept behind a StatefulSet is that a Pod is continually recreated on the same node. In this case, rather than simply having a volume definition, we have a VolumeClaimTemplate. This template is named differently for each volume.

VolumeClaimTemplates are a construct in the Kubernetes API that tells Kubernetes how to declare PersistentVolumes for a StatefulSet. This is so they can be made on the fly, based on the size of the StatefulSet, by an operator who is installing this StatefulSet for the first time or one that is scaling it. In this code snippet

```
volumeClaimTemplates:
  - metadata:
      name: cassandra-data
```

Pod cassandra-1, for example, will have a volumeClaimTemplate cassandra-data-1. That claim lives on the same node, and the StatefulSet is rescheduled to the same node over and over again.

Make sure not to confuse a StatefulSet with a DaemonSet. The latter guarantees that the same Pod is running on *all* nodes of a cluster. The former guarantees that Pods will restart on the same node but does not imply anything about how many such Pods are running nor where they will run. To make this differentiation even clearer, DaemonSets are used for security tools, network or storage providers that are containerized, and so forth. Now, let's take a quick look at what a StatefulSet for Cassandra looks like alongside its volumeClaimTemplate:

```
apiVersion: apps/v1
kind: StatefulSet
metadata:
  name: cassandra
  labels:
    app: cassandra
spec:
  serviceName: cassandra
  replicas: 1
  selector:
    matchLabels:
    ...
        volumeMounts:
        - name: cassandra-data
          mountPath: /cassandra_data
  # These are converted to volume claims by the controller
  # and mounted at the paths mentioned in our discussion, and don't
  # use in production until ssd GCEPersistentDisk or other ssd pd
```

```
    volumeClaimTemplates:
   - metadata:
       name: cassandra-data
     spec:
       accessModes: [ "ReadWriteOnce" ]
       storageClassName: fast
       resources:
         requests:
           storage: 1Gi
---
kind: StorageClass
apiVersion: storage.k8s.io/v1
metadata:
  name: fast
parameters:
  type: pd-ssd
```

From this point forward, every time that your Cassandra Pod restarts on this same node, it accesses the same predictably named volume. Thus, you can easily add more copies of a Cassandra replica to a cluster and guarantee that the eighth Pod always starts on the eighth node in your Cassandra quorum. Without such a template, you would have to handcraft unique storage VolumeClaimTemplate names every time you expanded the number of Pods in your Cassandra quorum. Note that if the Pod needs rescheduling to another node and the storage can be mounted to another node, the Pod's storage will move, and the Pod will start on that node.

8.5.3 *Advanced storage functionality and the Kubernetes storage model*

Unfortunately, all the native functionality of a particular storage type can never be entirely expressed in Kubernetes. For example, different types of storage volumes might have different read and write semantics when it comes to low-level storage options. Another example is the concept of *snapshots*. Many cloud vendors allow you to back up, restore, or take snapshots of disks. If a storage vendor supports snapshots and has appropriately implemented snapshot semantics in their CSI specification, then you can use this feature.

As of Kubernetes 1.17, snapshots and cloning (which can be implemented entirely in Kubernetes) are emerging as new operations in the Kubernetes API. For example, the following PVC is defined as originating from a data source. This data source itself is, in turn, a VolumeSnapshot object, which means that it is a specific volume loaded from a particular point in time:

```
apiVersion: v1
kind: PersistentVolumeClaim
metadata:
  name: restore-pvc
spec:
  storageClassName: csi-hostpath-sc
```

```
dataSource:
  name: new-snapshot-test
  kind: VolumeSnapshot
  apiGroup: snapshot.storage.k8s.io
accessModes:
  - ReadWriteOnce
resources:
  requests:
    storage: 10Gi
```

Because we've now covered the importance of the CSI specification, you may have guessed that plugging the Kubernetes client into a vendor-specific snapshot logic is entirely unnecessary. Instead, in order to support this feature, a storage vendor only needs to implement a few CSI API calls like

- CreateSnapshot
- DeleteSnapshot
- ListSnapshots

Once these are implemented, the Kubernetes CSI controllers can generically manage snapshots. If you are interested in snapshots for your production data volumes, check with your specific CSI drivers or your storage providers for your Kubernetes cluster. Make sure that they implement the snapshot components of the CSI API.

8.6   *Further reading*

J. Eder. "The Path to Cloud-Native Trading Platforms." http://mng.bz/p2nE (accessed 12/24/21).

The Kubernetes Authors. "PV controller changes to support PV Deletion protection finalizer." http://mng.bz/g46Z (accessed 12/24/21).

The Kubernetes Authors. "Remove docker as container runtime for local-up." http://mng.bz/enaw (accessed 12/24/21).

Kubernetes documentation. "Create static Pods." http://mng.bz/g4eZ (accessed 12/24/21).

Kubernetes documentation. "Persistent Volumes." http://mng.bz/en9w (accessed 12/24/21).

"PostgreSQL DB Restore: unexpected data beyond EOF." http://mng.bz/aDQx (accessed 12/24/21).

"Shared Storage." https://wiki.postgresql.org/wiki/Shared_Storage (accessed 12/24/21).

Z. Zhuang and C. Tran. "Eliminating Large JVM GC Pauses Caused by Background IO Traffic." http://mng.bz/5KJ4 (accessed 12/24/21).

Summary

- StorageClasses are similar to other multi-tenant concepts such as Gateway-Classes in Kubernetes.
- Administrators model storage requirements using StorageClasses to accommodate common developer scenarios in a generic manner.
- Kubernetes itself uses emptyDir and hostPath volumes to accomplish daily activities.
- For predictable volume names across Pod restarts, you can use VolumeClaim-Templates, which creates named volumes for Pods in a StatefulSet. This can enable high performance or stateful workloads when maintaining a Cassandra cluster, for example.
- Volume snapshots and cloning are emerging popular storage options that can be implemented with newer CSI implementations.

Running Pods:
How the kubelet works

This chapter covers

- Learning what the kubelet does and how it's configured
- Connecting container runtimes and launching containers
- Controlling the Pod's life cycle
- Understanding the CRI
- Looking at the Go interfaces inside the kubelet and CRI

The kubelet is the workhorse of a Kubernetes cluster, and there can be thousands of kubelets in a production data center, as every node runs the kubelet. In this chapter, we'll go through the internals of what the kubelet does and precisely how it uses the CRI (Container Runtime Interface) to run containers and manage the life cycle of workloads.

One of the kubelet's jobs is to start and stop containers, and the CRI is the interface that the kubelet uses to interact with container runtimes. For example, *contain-*

erd is categorized as a container runtime because it takes an image and creates a running container. The *Docker engine* is a container runtime, but it is now depreciated by the Kubernetes community in favor of containerd, runC, or other runtimes.

> **NOTE** We want to thank Dawn Chen for allowing us to interview her about the kubelet. Dawn is the original author of the kubelet binary and is currently one of the leads of the Node Special Interest Group for Kubernetes. This group maintains the kubelet codebase.

9.1 The kubelet and the node

At a high level, the kubelet is a binary, started by systemd. The kubelet runs on every node and is a Pod scheduler and node agent, but only for the local node. The kubelet monitors and maintains information about the server it runs on for the node. The binary updates the Node object via calls to the API server, based on changes to the node.

Let's start by looking at a Node object, which we get by executing `kubectl get nodes <insert_node_name> -o yaml` on a running cluster. The next few code blocks are snippets produced by the `kubectl get nodes` command. You can follow along by executing `kind create cluster` and running the `kubectl` commands. For example, `kubectl get nodes -o yaml` produces the following output, which is shortened for the sake of brevity:

```
kind: Node
metadata:
  annotations:
    kubeadm.alpha.kubernetes.io/cri-socket:
      /run/containerd/containerd.sock
    node.alpha.kubernetes.io/ttl: "0"
    volumes.kubernetes.io/controller-managed-attach-detach: "true"
  labels:
    beta.kubernetes.io/arch: amd64
    kubernetes.io/hostname: kind-control-plane
    node-role.kubernetes.io/master: ""
  name: kind-control-plane
```

> **The kubelet uses this socket to communicate with the container runtime.**

The metadata in the Node object in this code tells us what its container runtime is and what Linux architecture it runs. The kubelet interacts with the CNI provider. As we have mentioned in other chapters, the CNI provider's job is to allocate IP addresses for Pods and to create the Pod's network, which allows networking inside a Kubernetes cluster. The Node API object includes the CIDR (an IP address range) for all Pods. Importantly, we also specify an internal IP address for the node itself, which is necessarily different from that of the Pod's CIDR. The next source block displays part of the YAML produced by `kubectl get node`:

```
spec:
  podCIDR: 10.244.0.0/24
```

Now we get to the status portion of the definition. All Kubernetes API objects have spec and status fields:

- spec—Defines an object's specifications (what you want it to be)
- status—Represents the current state of an object

The status stanza is the data that the kubelet maintains for the cluster, and it also includes a list of conditions that are heartbeat messages communicated to the API server. All additional system information is acquired automatically when the node starts. This status information is sent to the Kubernetes API server and is updated continually. The following code block displays part of the YAML produced by kubectl get node that shows the status fields:

```
status:
  addresses:
  - address: 172.17.0.2
    type: InternalIP
  - address: kind-control-plane
    type: Hostname
```

Further down in the YAML document, you'll find the allocatable fields for this node. If you can explore these fields, you'll see that there is information about CPU and memory:

```
allocatable:
  ...
  capacity:
    cpu: "12"
    ephemeral-storage: 982940092Ki
    hugepages-1Gi: "0"
    hugepages-2Mi: "0"
    memory: 32575684Ki
    pods: "110"
```

There are other fields available in a Node object, so we encourage you to look at the YAML for yourself when your nodes report back as you inspect them. You can have anywhere from 0–15,000 nodes (15,000 nodes is considered the current limit of nodes on a cluster due to endpoints and other metadata-intensive operations that become costly at scale). The information in the Node object is critical for things like scheduling Pods.

9.2 The core kubelet

We know that the kubelet is a binary that is installed on every node, and we know that it is critical. Let's get into the world of the kubelet and what it does. Nodes and kubelets are not useful without a container runtime, which they rely on to execute containerized processes. We'll take a look at container runtimes next.

9.2.1 Container runtimes: Standards and conventions

Images, which are tarballs, and the kubelet need well-defined APIs for executing binaries that run these tarballs. This is where standard APIs come into play. Two specifications, CRI and OCI, define the *how* and the *what* for the kubelet's goal of running containers:

- *The CRI defines the how.* These are the remote calls used to start, stop, and manage containers and images. Any container runtime fulfills this interface in one way or another as a remote service.
- *The OCI defines the what.* This is the standard for container image formats. When you start or stop a container via a CRI implementation, you are relying on that container's image format to be standardized in a certain way. The OCI defines a tarball that contains more tarballs with a metadata file.

If you can, start a `kind` cluster so that you can walk through these examples with us. The kubelet's core dependency, the CRI, must be provided as a startup argument to the kubelet or configured in an alternative manner. As an example of a containerd's configuration, you can look for /etc/containerd/config.toml inside a running `kind` cluster and observe the various configuration inputs, which include the hooks that defined the CNI provider. For example:

```
# explicitly use v2 config format
version = 2

# set default runtime handler to v2, which has a per-pod shim
[plugins."io.containerd.grpc.v1.cri".containerd]
  default_runtime_name = "runc"
[plugins."io.containerd.grpc.v1.cri".containerd.runtimes.runc]
  runtime_type = "io.containerd.runc.v2"

# setup a runtime with the magic name ("test-handler") for k8s
# runtime class tests ...
[plugins."io.containerd.grpc.v1.cri"
    .containerd.runtimes.test-handler]
  runtime_type = "io.containerd.runc.v2"
```

In the next example, we use `kind` to create a Kubernetes v1.20.2 cluster. Note that this output may vary between Kubernetes versions. To view the file on a `kind` cluster, run these commands:

```
$ kind create cluster     ◀── Creates a Kubernetes cluster

$ export \
KIND_CONTAINER=\
$(docker ps | grep kind | awk '{ print $1 }')    ◀──┐

$ docker exec -it "$KIND_CONTAINER" /bin/bash    ◀────┘

root@kind-control-plane:/# \
  cat /etc/containerd/config.toml     ◀──┘
```

Finds the Docker container ID of the running kind container

Executes into the running container and gets an interactive command line

Displays the containerd configuration file

We're not going to be diving into container implementation details here. Still, you need to know that it is the underlying runtime that the kubelet usually depends on under the hood. It takes a CRI provider, image registry, and runtime values as inputs, meaning that the kubelet can accommodate many different containerization implementations (VM containers, gVisor containers, and so on). If you are in the same shell running inside the kind container, you can execute the following command:

```
root@kind-control-plane:/# ps axu | grep /usr/bin/kubelet
root         653 10.6   3.6 1881872 74020 ?
   Ssl  14:36    0:22 /usr/bin/kubelet
   --bootstrap-kubeconfig=/etc/kubernetes/bootstrap-kubelet.conf
   --kubeconfig=/etc/kubernetes/kubelet.conf
   --config=/var/lib/kubelet/config.yaml
   --container-runtime=remote
   --container-runtime-endpoint=unix:///run/containerd/containerd.sock
   --fail-swap-on=false --node-ip=172.18.0.2
   --provider-id=kind://docker/kind/kind-control-plane
   --fail-swap-on=false
```

This prints the list of configuration options and command-line flags provided to the kubelet running inside the kind container. These options are covered next; however, we do not cover all the options because there are a lot.

9.2.2   *The kubelet configurations and its API*

The kubelet is an integration point for a broad range of primitives in the Linux OS. Some of its data structures reveal the form and function of how it has evolved. The kubelet has well over 100 different command-line options in two different categories:

- *Options*—Toggle the behavior of the low-level Linux functionality used with Kubernetes, such as rules related to maximum iptables usage or DNS configuration
- *Choices*—Define the life cycle and health of the kubelet binary

The kubelet has numerous corner cases; for example, how it handles Docker versus containerd workloads, how it manages Linux versus Windows workloads, and so on. Each one of these corner cases may take weeks or even months to debate when it comes down to defining its specification. Because of this, it's good to understand the structure of the kubelet's codebase so that you can dig into it and provide yourself with some self-soothing in cases where you hit a bug or an otherwise unexpected behavior.

> **NOTE**   The Kubernetes v1.22 release introduced quite a few changes to the kubelet. Some of these changes included removal of in-tree storage providers, new security defaults via the `--seccomp-default` flag, the ability to rely on memory swapping (known as the NodeSwap feature), and memory QoS improvements. If you are interested in learning more about all the improvements in the Kubernetes v1.22 release, we highly recommend reading through http://mng.bz/2jy0. Relevant to this chapter, a recent bug in the kubelet can cause static Pod manifest changes to break long running Pods.

The kubelet.go file is the main entry point for the start of the kubelet binary. The cmd folder contains the definitions for the kubelet's flags. (Take a look at http://mng .bz/REVK for the flags, CLI options, and definitions.) The following declares the kubeletFlags struct. This struct is for the CLI flags, but we also have API values as well:

```
// kubeletFlags contains configuration flags for the kubelet.
// A configuration field should go in the kubeletFlags instead of the
// kubeletConfiguration if any of these are true:
// - its value will never or cannot safely be changed during
//   the lifetime of a node, or
// - its value cannot be safely shared between nodes at the
//   same time (e.g., a hostname);
//   the kubeletConfiguration is intended to be shared between nodes.
// In general, please try to avoid adding flags or configuration fields,
// we already have a confusingly large amount of them.

type kubeletFlags struct {
```

Previously, we had a code block where we grepped for /usr/bin/kubelet, and part of the result included --config=/var/lib/kubelet/config.yaml. The --config flag defines a configuration file. The following code block cats that configuration file:

```
$ cat /var/lib/kubelet/config.yaml        ⟵——— Outputs the config.yaml file
```

The next code block shows the output of the cat command:

```
apiVersion: kubelet.config.k8s.io/v1beta1
authentication:
  anonymous:
    enabled: false
  webhook:
    cacheTTL: 0s
    enabled: true
  x509:
    clientCAFile: /etc/kubernetes/pki/ca.crt
authorization:
  mode: Webhook
  webhook:
    cacheAuthorizedTTL: 0s
    cacheUnauthorizedTTL: 0s
clusterDNS:
- 10.96.0.10
clusterDomain: cluster.local
cpuManagerReconcilePeriod: 0s
evictionHard:
  imagefs.available: 0%
  nodefs.available: 0%
  nodefs.inodesFree: 0%
evictionPressureTransitionPeriod: 0s
fileCheckFrequency: 0s
healthzBindAddress: 127.0.0.1
healthzPort: 10248
```

```
httpCheckFrequency: 0s
imageGCHighThresholdPercent: 100
imageMinimumGCAge: 0s
kind: kubeletConfiguration
logging: {}
nodeStatusReportFrequency: 0s
nodeStatusUpdateFrequency: 0s
rotateCertificates: true
runtimeRequestTimeout: 0s
staticPodPath: /etc/kubernetes/manifests
streamingConnectionIdleTimeout: 0s
syncFrequency: 0s
volumeStatsAggPeriod: 0s
```

All of the kubelet API values are defined in the types.go file at http://mng.bz/wnJP. This file is an API data structure holding input configuration data for the kubelet. It defines many of the configurable aspects of the kubelet referenced via http://mng.bz/J1YV.

> **NOTE** Although we reference Kubernetes version 1.20.2 in the URLs, when you read this information, keep in mind that although the code location may vary, the API objects change quite slowly.

Kubernetes API machinery is the mechanism or standard for how API objects are defined within Kubernetes and the Kubernetes source base.

You will notice in the types.go file that many low-level networking and process control knobs are sent directly to the kubelet as input. The following example shows the ClusterDNS configuration that you probably can relate to. It is important for a functioning Kubernetes cluster:

```
// ClusterDNS is a list of IP addresses for a cluster DNS server. If set,
// the kubelet will configure all containers to use this for DNS resolution
// instead of the host's DNS servers.

ClusterDNS []string
```

When a Pod is created, multiple files are also produced dynamically. One of those files is /etc/resolv.conf. It is used by the Linux networking stack to perform DNS lookups because the file defines DNS servers. We'll see how to create this next.

9.3   Creating a Pod and seeing it in action

Run the following commands to create a NGINX Pod running on a Kubernetes cluster. Then, from the command line, you can cat the file with the next code block:

```
$ kubectl run nginx --generator=run-pod/v1 \
    --image nginx          ←┐  Starts the Pod

$ kubectl exec -it nginx -- /bin/bash   ←┘  Executes into the shell of the
                                            running NGINX container
```

```
root@nginx:/# cat /etc/resolv.conf                    ◁─────────────┐
search default.svc.cluster.local svc.cluster.local cluster.local   │
nameserver 10.96.0.10              Use cat to inspect the resolv.conf file.
options ndots:5
```

You can now see how the kubelet, when creating a Pod (as in the previous section), creates and mounts the resolv.conf file. Now your Pod can do a DNS lookup and, if you want, you can ping google.com. Other interesting structs in the types.go file include

- `ImageMinimumGCAge` (for image garbage collection)—In long-running systems, images might fill up drive space over time.
- `kubeletCgroups` (for Pod cgroup roots and drivers)—The ultimate upstream pool for Pod resources can be systemd, and this struct unifies the administration of all processes along with the administration of containers.
- `EvictionHard` (for hard limits)—This struct specifies when Pods should be deleted, which is based on system load.
- `EvictionSoft` (for soft limits)—This struct specifies how long the kubelet waits before evicting a greedy Pod.

These are just a few of the types.go file options; the kubelet has hundreds of permutations. All of these values are set via command-line options, default values, or YAML configuration files.

9.3.1 *Starting the kubelet binary*

When a node starts, several events occur that ultimately lead to its availability as a scheduling target in a Kubernetes cluster. Note that the ordering of events is approximate due to changes in the kubelet codebase and the asynchrony of Kubernetes in general. Figure 9.1 shows the kubelet at startup. Looking at the steps in the figure, we notice that

- Some simple sanity checks occur to make sure that Pods (containers) are runnable by the kubelet. (`NodeAllocatable` inputs are checked, which defines how much CPU and memory are allocated.)
- The `containerManager` routine begins. This is the kubelet's main event loop.
- A cgroup is added. If necessary, it's created with the `setupNode` function. The Scheduler and ControllerManager both "notice" that there is a new node in the system. They "watch" it via the API server so that it can run processes that need homes (it can even run new Pods) and ensure that it is not skipping periodic heartbeats from the API server. If the kubelet skips a heartbeat, the node eventually is removed from the cluster by the ControllerManager.
- The deviceManager event loop starts. This takes external plugin devices into the kubelet. These devices are then sent as part of the continuous updates (mentioned in the previous step).
- Logging, CSI, and device-plugin functionality are attached to the kubelet and registered.

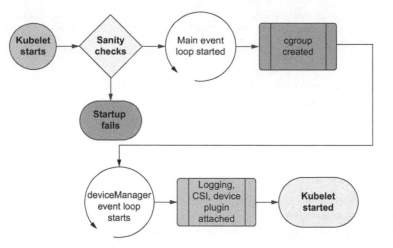

Figure 9.1   The kubelet startup cycle

9.3.2   *After startup: Node life cycle*

In earlier versions of Kubernetes (before 1.17), the Node object was updated in a status loop every 10 seconds via the kubelet making a call to the API server. By design, the kubelet is a bit chatty with the API server because the control plane in a cluster needs to know if nodes are healthy or not. If you watch a cluster starting, you will notice the kubelet binary attempting to communicate with the control plane, and it will do so multiple times until the control plane is available. This control loop allows the control plane to not be available, and the nodes are aware of this. When the kubelet binary starts, it configures the network layer as well, having the CNI provider create the proper networking features, such as a bridge for CNI networking to function.

9.3.3   *Leasing and locking in etcd and the evolution of the node lease*

To optimize the performance of large clusters and decrease network chattiness, Kubernetes versions 1.17 and later implement a specific API server endpoint for managing the kubelets via etcd's *leasing mechanism*. etcd introduced the concept of a lease so that HA (highly available) components that might need failovers can rely on a central leasing and locking mechanism rather than implementing their own.

Anyone who has taken a computer science course on semaphores can identify with why the creators of Kubernetes did not want to rely on a myriad of home-grown locking implementations for different components. Two independent control loops maintain the kubelet's state:

- *The NodeStatus object is updated by the kubelet every 5 minutes to tell the API server about its state.* For example, if you reboot a node after upgrading its memory, you will see this update in the API server's view of the NodeStatus object of the kubelet 5 minutes later. If you're wondering how big this data structure is, run `kubectl get nodes -o yaml` on a large production cluster. You will likely see tens of thousands of lines of text amounting to at least 10 KB per node.

- *Independently, the kubelet updates a Lease object (which is quite tiny) every 10 seconds.* These updates allow the controllers in the Kubernetes control plane to evict a node within a few seconds if it appears to have gone offline, without incurring the high cost of sending a large amount of status information.

9.3.4 *The kubelet's management of the Pod life cycle*

After all of the preflight checks are complete, the kubelet starts a big sync loop: the `containerManager` routine. This routine handles the Pod's life cycle, which consists of a control loop of actions. Figure 9.2 shows the Pod's life cycle and the steps to managing a Pod:

1. Starts the Pod life cycle
2. Ensures the Pod can run on the node
3. Sets up storage and networking (CNI)
4. Starts the containers via CRI
5. Monitors the Pod
6. Performs restarts
7. Stops the Pod

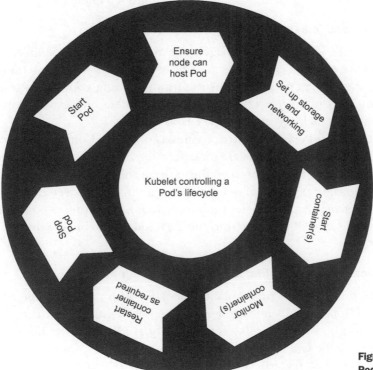

Figure 9.2 A kubelet's Pod life cycle

Figure 9.3 illustrates the life of a container hosted on a Kubernetes node. As depicted in the figure

1   A user or the replica set controller decides to create a Pod via the Kubernetes API.
2   The scheduler finds the right home for the Pod (e.g., a host with the IP Address of 1.2.3.4).
3   The kubelet on host 1.2.3.4 gets new data from its watch on the API server's Pods, and it notices that it is not yet running the Pod.
4   The Pod's creation process starts.
5   The pause container has a sandbox where the requested one or more containers will live, defining the Linux namespaces and IP address created for it by the the kubelet and the CNI (container networking interface) provider.
6   The kubelet communicates with the container runtime, pulling the layers of a container, and runs the actual image.
7   The NGINX container starts.

If something goes wrong, such as if the container dies or its health check fails, the Pod itself may get moved to a new node. This is known as *rescheduling*. We mentioned the pause container, which is a container that is used to create the Pod-shared Linux namespaces. We'll cover the pause container later in this chapter.

9.3.5   *CRI, containers, and images: How they are related*

Part of the kubelet's job is image management. You probably are familiar with this process if you have ever run `docker rm -a -q` or `docker images --prune` on your laptop. Although the kubelet only concerns itself with running containers, to come to life, these containers ultimately rely on *base images*. These images are pulled from image registries. One such registry is Docker Hub.

A new layer on top of existing images creates a container. Commonly used images use the same layers, and these layers are cached by the container runtime running on the kubelet. The caching time is based on the garbage collection facility in the kubelet itself. This functionality expires and deletes old images from the ever-growing registry cache, which ultimately is the kubelet's job to maintain. This process optimizes container startup while preventing disks from getting flooded with images that are no longer utilized.

9.3.6   *The kubelet doesn't run containers: That's the CRI's job*

A container runtime provides functionality associated with managing the containers you need to run from the kubelet. Remember, the kubelet itself can't run containers on its own: it relies on something like containerd or runC under the hood. This reliance is managed via the CRI interface.

The chances are that, regardless of what Kubernetes release you are running, you have runC installed. You can efficiently run any image manually with runC. For example,

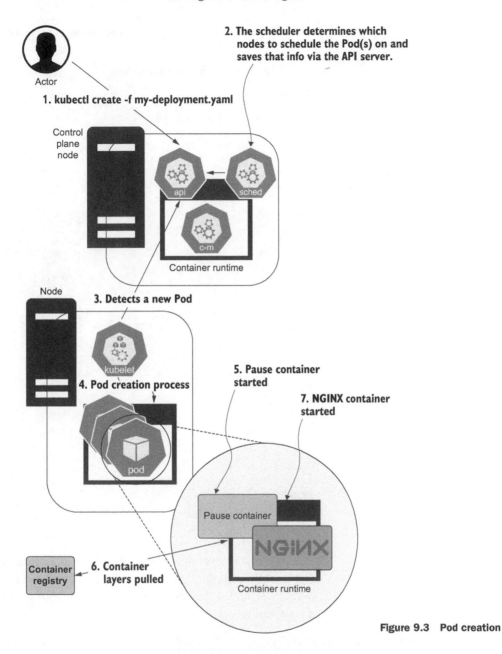

Figure 9.3   Pod creation

run `docker ps` to list a container that is running locally. You could export the image as a tarball as well. In our case, we can do the following:

```
$  docker ps          ⟵── Gets the image ID
d32b87038ece kindest/node:v1.15.3
"/usr/local/bin/entr…" kind-control-plane
```

```
$ docker export d32b > /tmp/whoneedsdocker.tar    ⟵——— Exports the image to a tarball
$ mkdir /tmp/whoneedsdocker
$ cd /tmp/whoneedsdocker
$ tar xf /tmp/whoneedsdocker.tar    ⟵——— Extracts the tarball
$ runc spec        ⟵——┐
                       └─ Starts runC
```

These commands create a config.json file. For example:

```
{
        "ociVersion": "1.0.1-dev",
        "process": {
                "terminal": true,
                "user": {
                        "uid": 0,
                        "gid": 0
                },
                "args": [
                  "sh"
                ]
        },
        "namespaces": [
            {
              "type": "pid"
            },
            {
              "type": "network"
            },
            {
              "type": "ipc"
            },
            {
              "type": "uts"
            },
            {
              "type": "mount"
            }
        ]
}
```

Typically, you will want to chat the args section sh, which is the default command created by runC, to do something meaningful (such as python mycontainerizedapp.py). We omitted most of the boilerplate from the preceding config.json file, but we kept an essential part: the namespaces section.

9.3.7 *Pause container: An "aha" moment*

Every container in a Pod corresponds to a runC action. We therefore need a pause container, which precedes all of the containers. A pause container

- Waits until a network namespace is available so all containers in a Pod can share a single IP and talk over 127.0.0.1
- Pauses until a filesystem is available so all containers in a Pod can share data over emptyDir

Once the Pod is set up, each runC call takes the same namespace parameters. Although the kubelet does not run the containers, there is a lot of logic that goes into creating Pods, which the kubelet needs to manage. The kubelet ensures that Kubernetes has the networking and storage guarantees for containers. This makes it easy to run in distributed scenarios. Other tasks precede running a container, like pulling images, which we will walk through later in this chapter. First, we need to back up and look at the CRI so that we can understand the boundary between the container runtime and the kubelet a little more clearly.

9.4 The Container Runtime Interface (CRI)

The runC program is one small part of the puzzle when it comes to what Kubernetes needs for running containers at scale. The whole mystery is primarily defined by the CRI interface, which abstracts runC along with other functionality to enable higher-order scheduling, image management, and container runtime functionality.

9.4.1 Telling Kubernetes where our container runtime lives

How do we tell Kubernetes where our CRI service is running? If you look inside a running `kind` cluster, you will see that the kubelet runs with the following two options:

```
--container-runtime=remote
--container-runtime-endpoint=/run/containerd/containerd.sock
```

The kubelet communicates via gRPC, a remote procedure call (RPC) framework, with the container runtime endpoint; containerd itself has a CRI plugin built into it. By `remote`, what is meant is that Kubernetes can use the containerd socket as a minimal implementation of an interface to create and manage Pods and their life cycles. The CRI is a minimal interface that any container runtime can implement. It was mainly designed so that the community could quickly innovate different container runtimes (other than Docker) and plug those into and unplug from Kubernetes.

> **NOTE** Although Kubernetes is modular in how it runs containers, it is still stateful. You cannot "hot" unplug a container runtime from a running Kubernetes cluster without also draining (and potentially removing) a node from a live cluster. This limitation is due to metadata and cgroups that the kubelet manages and creates.

Because the CRI is a gRPC interface, the `container-runtime` option in Kubernetes ideally should be defined as `remote` for newer Kubernetes distributions. The CRI describes all container creation through an interface, and like storage and networking, Kubernetes aims to move container runtime logic out of the Kubernetes core over time.

9.4.2   *The CRI routines*

The CRI consists of four high-level go interfaces. This unifies all the core functionality Kubernetes needs to run containers. CRI's interfaces include

- *PodSandBoxManager*—Creates the setup environment for Pods
- *ContainerRuntime*—Starts, stops, and executes containers
- *ImageService*—Pulls, lists, and removes images
- *ContainerMetricsGetter*—Provides quantitative information about running containers

These interfaces provide pausing, pulling, and sandboxing functions. Kubernetes expects this functionality to be implemented by any remote CRI and invokes this functionality using gRPC.

9.4.3   *The kubelet's abstraction around CRI: The GenericRuntimeManager*

The CRI's functionality does not necessarily cover all the bases for a production container orchestration tool, such as garbage collecting old images, managing container logs, and dealing with the life cycle of image pulls and image pull backoffs. The kubelet provides a Runtime interface, implemented by kuberuntime.NewKubeGeneric-RuntimeManager, as a wrapper for any CRI provider (containerd, CRI-O, Docker, and so on). The runtime manager (inside of http://mng.bz/lxaM) manages all calls to the four core CRI interfaces. As an example, let's see what happens when we create a new Pod:

```
imageRef, msg, err := m.imagePuller.EnsureImageExists(
        pod, container, pullSecrets,
        podSandboxConfig)                    <——  Pulls the image
        containerID, err := m.runtimeService.CreateContainer(
        podSandboxID, containerConfig,
        podSandboxConfig)                         Performs network or device
        err = m.internalLifecycle.PreStartContainer(   configuration, which is cgroup-
        pod, container, containerID)          <——  or namespace-dependent
        err = m.runtimeService.StartContainer(
        containerID)                         <—— Starts the container
        events.StartedContainer, fmt.Sprintf(
        "Started container %s", container.Name))
```

Creates the container's cgroups without starting the container

You might wonder why we need a prestart hook in this code. A few common examples of where Kubernetes uses prestart hooks include certain networking plugins and GPU drivers, which need to be configured with cgroups-specific information before a GPU process starts.

9.4.4   *How is the CRI invoked?*

Several lines of code obfuscate the remote calls to the CRI in the previous code snippet, and we've removed a lot of the bloat. We will go through the EnsureImageExists function in detail in a few moments, but let's first look at the way Kubernetes abstracts the low-level CRI functionality into the two main APIs that are internally utilized by the kubelet to work with containers.

9.5 The kubelet's interfaces

In the source code of the kubelet, various Go interfaces are defined. The next few sections will walk through the interfaces in order to provide an overview of the inner workings of the kubelet.

9.5.1 The Runtime internal interface

The CRI in Kubernetes is broken into three parts: Runtime, StreamingRuntime, and CommandRunner. The KubeGenericRuntime interface (located at http://mng.bz/BMxg) is managed inside of Kubernetes, wrapping core functions in the CRI runtime. For example:

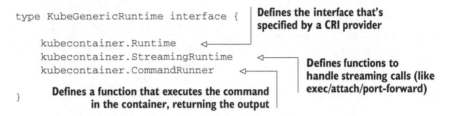

```
type KubeGenericRuntime interface {          Defines the interface that's
                                             specified by a CRI provider

    kubecontainer.Runtime           ←

    kubecontainer.StreamingRuntime  ←
                                                Defines functions to
    kubecontainer.CommandRunner     ←           handle streaming calls (like
                                                exec/attach/port-forward)
}       Defines a function that executes the command
        in the container, returning the output
```

For vendors, this means that you first implement the Runtime interface and then the StreamingRuntime interface because the Runtime interface describes most of the core functionality of Kubernetes (see http://mng.bz/1jXj and http://mng.bz/PWdn). The gRPC service clients are the functions that let you get your head around how the kubelet interacts with CRI. These functions are defined in the `kubeGeneric-RuntimeManager` struct. Specifically, `runtimeService internalapi.RuntimeService` interacts with the CRI provider.

Within the RuntimeService, we have the ContainerManager, and this is where the magic happens. This interface is part of the actual CRI definition. The function calls in the next code snippet allow the kubelet to use a CRI provider to start, stop, and remove containers:

```
// ContainerManager contains methods to manipulate containers managed
// by a container runtime. The methods are thread-safe.

type ContainerManager interface {
    // CreateContainer creates a new container in specified PodSandbox.
    CreateContainer(podSandboxID string, config
        *runtimeapi.ContainerConfig, sandboxConfig
        *runtimeapi.PodSandboxConfig) (string, error)
    // StartContainer starts the container.
    StartContainer(containerID string) error
    // StopContainer stops a running container.
    StopContainer(containerID string, timeout int64) error
    // RemoveContainer removes the container.
    RemoveContainer(containerID string) error
    // ListContainers lists all containers by filters.
    ListContainers(filter *runtimeapi.ContainerFilter)
        ([]*runtimeapi.Container, error)
```

```
    // ContainerStatus returns the status of the container.
    ContainerStatus(containerID string)
        (*runtimeapi.ContainerStatus, error)
    // UpdateContainerResources updates the cgroup resources
    // for the container.
    UpdateContainerResources(
        containerID string, resources *runtimeapi.LinuxContainerResources)
            error
    // ExecSync executes a command in the container.
    // If the command exits with a nonzero exit code, an error is returned.
    ExecSync(containerID string, cmd []string, timeout time.Duration)
            (stdout []byte, stderr []byte, err error)
    // Exec prepares a streaming endpoint to exe..., returning the address.
    Exec(*runtimeapi.ExecRequest) (*runtimeapi.ExecResponse, error)
    // Attach prepares a streaming endpoint to attach to
    // a running container and returns the address.
    Attach(req *runtimeapi.AttachRequest)
            (*runtimeapi.AttachResponse, error)
    // ReopenContainerLog asks runtime to reopen
    // the stdout/stderr log file for the container.
    // If it returns error, the new container log file MUST NOT
    // be created.
    ReopenContainerLog(ContainerID string) error
}
```

9.5.2 *How the kubelet pulls images: The ImageService interface*

Lurking in the routines for a container runtime is the ImageService interface, which defines a few core methods: PullImage, GetImage, ListImages, and RemoveImage. The concept of pulling an image, which derives from Docker semantics, is part of the CRI specification. You can see its definition in the same file (runtime.go) as the other interfaces. Thus, every container runtime implements these functions:

```
// ImageService interfaces allows to work with image service.
type ImageService interface {
    PullImage(image ImageSpec, pullSecrets []v1.Secret,
                podSandboxConfig *runtimeapi.PodSandboxConfig)
                (string, error)
    GetImageRef(image ImageSpec) (string, error)
    // Gets all images currently on the machine.
    ListImages() ([]Image, error)
    // Removes the specified image.
    RemoveImage(image ImageSpec) error
    // Returns the image statistics.
    ImageStats() (*ImageStats, error)
}
```

A container runtime could call docker pull to pull an image. Similarly, this runtime could make a call to execute docker run to create a container. The container runtime, as you'll recall, can be set on the kubelet when it starts, using the container-runtime-endpoint flag like so:

```
--container-runtime-endpoint=unix:///var/run/crio/crio.sock
```

9.5.3 Giving ImagePullSecrets to the kubelet

Let's make the connection between `kubectl`, the kubelet, and the CRI interface concrete. To do that, we will look at how you can provide information to the kubelet so that it can download images securely from a private registry. The following is a block of YAML that defines a Pod and a Secret. The Pod references a secure registry that requires login credentials, and the Secret stores the login credentials:

```
apiVersion: v1
kind: Pod
metadata:
  name: myapp-pod
  labels:
    app: myapp
spec:
  containers:
  - name: myapp-container
    image: my.secure.registry/container1:1.0
  imagePullSecrets:
  - name: my-secret
---
apiVersion: v1
data:
  .dockerconfigjson: sojosaidjfwoeij2f0ei8f...
kind: Secret
metadata:
  creationTimestamp: null
  name: my-secret
  selfLink: /api/v1/namespaces/default/secrets/my-secret
type: kubernetes.io/.dockerconfigjson
```

In the snippet, you need to generate the `.dockerconfigjson` value yourself. You can also generate the Secret interactively using `kubectl` itself like so:

```
$ kubectl create secret docker-registry my-secret
  --docker-server my.secure.registry
  --docker-username my-name --docker-password 1234
  --docker-email jay@apache.org
```

Or you can do this with the equivalent command, if you already have an existing Docker configuration JSON file:

```
$ kubectl create secret generic regcred
   --from-file=.dockerconfigjson=<path/to/.docker/config.json>
   --type=kubernetes.io/dockerconfigjson
```

This command creates an entire Docker configuration, puts it into the .dockerconfigjson filc, and then uses that JSON payload when pulling images through ImageService. More importantly, this service ultimately calls the `EnsureImageExists` function. You can then run `kubectl get secret -o yaml` to view the Secret and copy the entire Secret value. Then use Base64 to decode it to see your Docker login token, which the kubelet uses.

Now that you know how the Secret is used by the Docker daemon when pulling images, we will get back to looking at the plumbing in Kubernetes, which allows this functionality to work entirely via Secrets managed by Kubernetes. The key to all this is the ImageManager interface, which implements this functionality via an `EnsureImage-Exists` method. This method calls the `PullImage` function under the hood, if necessary, depending on the `ImagePullPolicy` defined on your Pod. The next code snippet sends the required pull Secrets:

```
type ImageManager interface {
    EnsureImageExists(pod *v1.Pod, container *v1.Container,
      pullSecrets []v1.Secret,
      podSandboxConfig *runtimeapi.PodSandboxConfig)
    (string, string, error)
}
```

The `EnsureImageExists` function receives the pull Secrets that you created in the YAML document earlier in this chapter. Then a `docker pull` is executed securely by deserializing the `dockerconfigjson` value. Once the daemon pulls this image, Kubernetes can move forward, starting the Pod.

9.6   Further reading

M. Crosby. "What is containerd ?" Docker blog. http://mng.bz/Nxq2 (accessed 12/27/21).

J. Jackson. "GitOps: 'Git Push' All the Things." http://mng.bz/6Z5G (accessed 12/27/21).

"How does copy-on-write in fork() handle multiple fork?" Stack Exchange documentation. http://mng.bz/Exql (accessed 12/27/21).

"Deep dive into Docker storage drivers." YouTube video. https://www.youtube.com/watch?v=9oh_M11-foU (accessed 12/27/21).

Summary

- The kubelet runs on every node and controls the lifecyle of Pods on that node.
- The kubelet interacts with the container runtime to start, stop, create, and delete containers.
- We have the capability to configure various functionality (such as time to evict Pods) within the kubelet.
- When the kubelet starts, it runs various sanity checks on the node, creates cgroups, and starts various plugins, such as CSI.
- The kubelet controls the life cycle of a Pod: starting the Pod, ensuring that it's running, creating storage and networking, monitoring, performing restarts, and stopping Pods.

- CRI defines the way that the kubelet interacts with the container runtime that is installed.
- The kubelet is built from various Go interfaces. These include interfaces for CRI, image pulling, and the kubelet itself.

DNS in Kubernetes

DNS has existed as long as the internet. Microservices make it hard to manage DNS records at scale because they require an explosion in the use of domain names on an internal data center. Kubernetes standards around DNS for Pods make DNS extremely easy, such that individual applications rarely need to follow complex guidelines for finding downstream services. This is generally enabled by CoreDNS (https://github.com/coredns/coredns), which is at the heart of this chapter.

10.1 A brief intro to DNS (and CoreDNS)

The job of any DNS server is to map DNS names (like www.google.com) to IP addresses (like 142.250.72.4). There are a few common mappings from DNS servers that we use every day when we browse the web. Let's look at some of those.

10.1.1 *NXDOMAINs, A records, and CNAME records*

When using Kubernetes, DNS is mostly handled for you, at least in clusters. We still need to define a few terms to contextualize this chapter, however, especially in situations where you might have a custom DNS behavior you care about (for example, with headless services, as seen in this chapter). As for our definitions, at the very least, you'll want to know about

- *NXDOMAIN responses*—DNS responses that are returned if IP addresses don't exist for domain names
- *A and AAAA mappings*—Take a hostname as input and return an IPv4 or IPv6 address (e.g., they take google.com as input and return 142.250.72.4)
- *CNAME mappings*—Return an alias for certain DNS names (e.g., they take www.google.com and return google.com)

In a homegrown environment, CNAMEs are crucial for backward compatibility of API clients and other apps depending on services. The following code snippet shows an example of how A names and CNAME records intermingle. These records live in what are known as *zone files*. A zone file resembles a long CSV file of records just like this (well, without the commas, of course):

```
my.very.old.website CNAME my.new.site.
my.old.website. CNAME my.new.site.
my.new.site. A 192.168.10.123
```

If this looks a little like /etc/hosts to you, you're right. A Linux system's /etc/hosts file is just a local DNS configuration that is checked before your computer goes out to the internet to find other hosts that might match the DNS names you enter into your browser, and ANAME and CNAME records are provided by a DNS server. Even before Kubernetes, there were many different DNS server implementations:

- Some of these are recursive; in other words, they are capable of resolving almost anything on the internet by starting at the root of a DNS record (such as .edu or .com) and working their way down. BIND is one such server that is commonly used in Linux data centers.
- Some of these are cloud-based and cloud-integrated (for example, Route53 in AWS) and aren't hosted by end users.
- In most modern installations, Kubernetes typically uses CoreDNS to provide in-cluster DNS to Pods.
- The Kubernetes Conformance test suites actually confirm that certain DNS characteristics are present, including
  - The /etc/hosts cluster entries in Pods, so they can automatically access the API server through an internal host name, kubernetes.default
  - Pods that are allowed to inject their own DNS records

   – Arbitrary services and headless services that must resolve to A records by the Pods

   – Pods that have their own DNS records

Using CoreDNS to implement this behavior is by no means required in Kubernetes, but it sure does make things easier. All that really matters is that your Kubernetes distribution adheres to the DNS specification for Kubernetes. In any case, CoreDNS is likely what you use in your clusters, and for good reason. It is the only widely available open source DNS service with baked-in Kubernetes support. It is capable of

- Connecting to the Kubernetes API server and slurping in IP addresses for Pods and Services where needed.
- Resolving DNS service records to service IP addresses for Pods and in-cluster services.
- Caching DNS entries so that large Kubernetes clusters, where hundreds of Pods need to resolve Services, can work in a performant manner.
- Plugging in new functionality at compile time (not run time).
- Scaling horizontally and performing with extremely low latency even in high-load environments.
- Forwarding requests (via the https://coredns.io/plugins/forward/ plugin) for external cluster addresses to other upstream resolvers.

Although CoreDNS can handle a lot, it doesn't forward requests for external cluster addresses to other upstream servers that provide recursive DNS capabilities. CoreDNS allows you to resolve the IP addresses of services that live in your cluster networks as well as Pods, in some cases (as we'll see in a few moments).

Figure 10.1 depicts the relationship between CoreDNS and other DNS servers (such as BIND). Any DNS server must implement the baseline functionality for resolving internet hosts. CoreDNS was built after Kubernetes and, thus, has explicit support for the Kubernetes DNS as well.

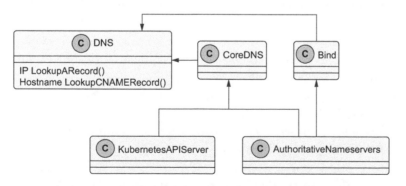

Figure 10.1   The relationship between CoreDNS and other DNS servers

10.1.2 *Pods need internal DNS*

Because every Pod in a microservice environment is usually accessed over a service, and Pods can come and go (which means they have changing IPs), DNS is the primary way that any service is accessed. This is true for the internet and the cloud, in general. Gone are the days that someone would give you an IP address with the destination of a specific server or database. Let's take a look at how Pods can reach each other over DNS in a cluster by firing up a multicontainer service and probing it:

```
apiVersion: v1
kind: Service
metadata:
  name: nginx4
  labels:
    app: four-of-us
spec:
  ports:
  - port: 80          ⟵⎤ Provides a port
    name: web              for our service
  clusterIP: None
  selector:
    app: four-of-us
---
apiVersion: apps/v1
kind: StatefulSet
metadata:
  name: web-ss
spec:
  serviceName: "nginx"
  replicas: 2
  selector:
    matchLabels:
      app: four-of-us
  template:
    metadata:
      labels:
        app: four-of-us
    spec:
      containers:                    An old NGINX version that
      - name: nginx                  allows for a shell inside our
        image: nginx:1.7    ⟵⎤       NGINX Pod
        ports:
        - containerPort: 80
          name: web
---
apiVersion: apps/v1     ⎤ For comparison of how DNS works
kind: Deployment    ⟵⎦ in different types of Pods
metadata:
  name: web-dep
spec:
  replicas: 2
  selector:
    matchLabels:
```

```
      app: four-of-us
template:
  metadata:
    labels:
      app: four-of-us
  spec:
    containers:
    - name: nginx
      image: nginx:1.7
      ports:
      - containerPort: 80
        name: web
```

Having a port in place for a service is important in our example because we're interested in exploring how DNS resolves. Also note that we're using an old NGINX version so that we can have a shell inside of our NGINX Pod. Newer NGINX containers don't have a shell for security reasons. And, finally, this time we use a StatefulSet to compare how DNS works in different types of Pods.

> **NOTE** The NGINX container we're using allows us to poke around in the shell, but we don't have this convenience with newer NGINX containers. We've mentioned scratch containers a few times in this book (the really lean kind that don't have a full-blown OS base, thus being more secure, but also lacking a shell to access and hack around in). More and more, you'll find that for security reasons, containers are published without a shell that you can enter. Another increasingly common image base is the *distroless* base image for containers. If you want to securely build containers with a few reasonable defaults, we recommend using the distroless image, which has most of the defaults you need for a microservices app without the extra bloat that can increase your vulnerability footprint in terms of CVEs. This concept is also covered in chapter 13. To learn more about how to build your apps from distroless base images, you can peruse https://github.com/GoogleContainerTools/distroless.

Before we start hacking, we'll quickly go over the concept of StatefulSets and where they are used in Kubernetes. These often have the most interesting DNS properties and requirements.

10.2   *Why StatefulSets Instead of Deployments?*

In this chapter, we'll create a Pod that runs in what is known as a *StatefulSets*. StatefulSets have interesting properties when it comes to DNS, so we'll use this Pod to probe the capabilities and limitations of Kubernetes when it comes to running HA processes with reliable DNS endpoints. StatefulSets are extremely important for applications that need to have firm identities. For example:

- Apache ZooKeeper
- MinIO or other storage-related applications
- Apache Hadoop

- Apache Cassandra
- Bitcoin mining applications

StatefulSets are intimately related to advanced DNS use cases in Kubernetes because they both are typically used in scenarios where the canonical microservices model begins to break down, and external entities (services, applications, legacy systems) begin to influence the way applications are deployed. In theory, you should rarely, if ever, need to use a StatefulSet for a modern stateless application, unless there are critical performance requirements that you cannot attain otherwise. StatefulSets are inherently harder to administer, extending and scaling over time, rather than "dumb" deployments that have no carryover baggage between Pod restarts.

10.2.1 *DNS with headless services*

When we use a StatefulSet to deploy an application, we often do so with a headless service. A *headless service* is one that doesn't have a `ClusterIP` field, and instead, directly returns an A record from a DNS server. This has some important implications for DNS. To take a look at such a service, run the following code snippet:

```
$ kubectl create -f https://github.com/jayunit100/k8sprototypes/
➥ blob/master/smoke-tests/nginx-pod-svc.yaml
```

The previous command returns a YAML file. That file defines a service like so:

```
apiVersion: v1
kind: Service
metadata:
  name: headless-svc
spec:
  clusterIP: None
  selector:
    app: nginx
  ports:
    - protocol: TCP
      port: 80
      targetPort: 80
  # Change this to true if you NEVER want an NXDOMAIN response!
  publishNotReadyAddresses: false
```

> **publishNotReadyAddresses decides whether you get NXDomain records or not.**

This service selects from a set of Pods running a web server that's also defined in this file. Once this service is up

- You can issue a query to `wget headless-svc:80` in the BusyBox Pod that we co-deployed.
- Your BusyBox Pod queries the CoreDNS (which we talk about in this chapter) to get the IP address of the headless service.
- CoreDNS will then, upon checking if the headless service is up (based on its `readinessProbe`), return the IP addresses of the corresponding Pods.

> **NOTE** If set to `true`, `publishNotReadyAddresses` always returns backend Pods for NGINX, even if they are not ready. Interestingly, this means that if the Pod for NGINX is not ready according to its `readinessProbe`, your underlying CoreDNS services returns NXDOMAIN records instead of IP addresses. This is often mischaracterized by Kubernetes novices as a DNS bug, but actually, it points to potential problems in your kubelet or application.

Why use a headless service? It turns out that many applications build up quorums and other network-specific behavior by directly connecting to one another over a Pod IP, as opposed to relying on the network proxy (`kube-proxy`) for load-balanced connections. In general, you should try to use ClusterIP services whenever possible because they're much easier to reason about from a DNS perspective, unless you really need some kind of network-specific behavior related to IP preservation, quorum decision making, or specific IP-to-IP performance guarantees.

If you're interested in learning more about the way headless services and DNS works, you can walk through the steps at http://mng.bz/q2Rz.

10.2.2 *Persistent DNS records in StatefulSets*

Let's recreate the original StatefulSet example. As a shortcut, you can run `kubectl create -f https://raw.githubusercontent.com/jayunit100/k8sprototypes/master/smoke-tests/four-of-us.yaml`. The name of this service can be used to see its endpoints, as in this code snippet:

```
$ kubectl get endpoints -o yaml | grep ip
    - ip: 172.18.0.2
      ip: 10.244.0.13
    - ip: 10.244.0.14
    - ip: 10.244.0.15
      ip: 10.244.0.16
```

Here, we can see that we have four consecutive endpoints in the 13–16 range. This comes from our two StatefulSet replicas and our two Deployment replicas.

10.2.3 *Using a polyglot deployment to explore Pod DNS properties*

In this section, we'll look at two different ways to use Kubernetes DNS. We'll then compare the DNS properties of our StatefulSet and Deployment Pods.

First, let's look at how DNS works for these Pods. The most obvious test we can run is to check their service endpoints. Let's do this from inside our cluster so that we don't have to worry about exposing or forwarding any ports. First, create a bastion Pod that we can use to _wget_ against different apps that we've created:

```
$ cat << EOF > bastion.yml
apiVersion: v1
kind: Pod
metadata:
  name: core-k8s
```

```
    namespace: default     <------  The default namespace
spec:
  containers:
    - name: bastion
      image: docker.io/busybox:latest
      command: ['sleep','10000']
EOF
$ kubectl create -f bastion.yml
```

Note that the default namespace is the easiest one to use for this example, but you can also create this Pod in a different namespace. If so, you need to make sure to fully qualify DNS names when probing the four-of-us services. Now, let's exec into this Pod and use it for all of the experiments in the remainder of this chapter:

```
$ kubectl get pods
NAME                          READY   STATUS    AGE
core-k8s                      1/1     Running   9m56s   <------  This is the Pod we'll
web-dep-58db7f9644-fjtp6      1/1     Running   12h              access as a way to explore
web-dep-58db7f9644-gxddt      1/1     Running   12h              DNS inside our cluster.
web-ss-0                      1/1     Running   12h
web-ss-1                      1/1     Running   12h


$ kubectl exec -t -i core-k8s /bin/sh
```

The first obvious thing we can do is to wget down our endpoints. The following code snippet shows the command for this:

```
#> wget nginx4:80
   Connecting to nginx4:80 (10.96.123.164:80)
   saving to 'index.html'
```

That's a relief. We now know that our service is up. Now, if we look closely at our IP address, we'll see that it's not in the 10.244 range. That's because we're accessing a Service, not a Pod. Typically, the DNS name that you will use to access a service inside a cluster will be a service name, but what if we want to access a specific Pod? Then we can use something like this:

```
#> wget nginx:80
   Connecting to nginx:80 (10.96.123.164:80)
   saving to 'index.html'
                                                          The Pod name plus service
#> wget web-ss-0.nginx                   <------          name combination
   Connecting to web-ss-0.nginx (10.244.0.13:80)

#> wget web-dep-58db7f9644-fjtp6         <------  Get the IP address for a Pod
   bad address 'web-dep-58db7f9644-fjtp6'         in a deployment by name.
```

In the example, the Pod name plus the service name combination is accessible like any web server, and there's no equivalent DNS name for a Pod created from a deployment.

Inside our container, we can not only access our Pods by their service, but some of our Pods, the ones created by StatefulSet, can also be accessed directly over DNS.

When we run `wget` against the web-ss-0.nginx endpoint (or, in general, against any *<name>*-0.*<serviceName>* endpoint), we will directly resolve this address to the IP address of the first replica of a given StatefulSet. To access the second replica, we can replace the 0 with a 1, and so on. We've thus learned our first lesson on DNS for clusters: Services and StatefulSet Pods both are first-class, stable DNS endpoints in a Kubernetes cluster. Now, how does the extremely convenient web-ss-0.nginx name get resolved?

10.3   *The resolv.conf file*

Let's look at how these different DNS requests are resolved (or, in some cases, not resolved) by starting with a peek into the resolv.conf file itself. This will ultimately lead us to the CoreDNS service.

10.3.1   *A quick note about routing*

This chapter is not about Pod IP networking, but it's a good chance to ensure that there is a clear connection in your mental model between DNS and Pod network infrastructure because these two aspects of a cluster are intricately dependent. After a host is resolved to an IP

- If that host's IP is a service, it is the network proxy's job to make sure this IP routes to a Pod endpoint.
- If that host is a Pod, it is your CNI provider's job to make sure that the IP is directly routable.
- If that host is on the internet, then your Pod's outgoing traffic needs to be NAT'd via iptables so that the TCP connection that is made to the outside world flows back to your Pod from the node that the request originated on.

Figure 10.2 depicts the way that Pod DNS resolution for an incoming hostname works. The key functionality here is that multiple versions of a DNS query will be sent to 10.96.0.10 until a match is found.

The resolv.conf file is a standard way to configure DNS for a container. In any scenario where you are attempting to figure out how your Pod is configured with regard to DNS, this is the first place to look. If you are running a modern Linux server, you might use `resolvctl` instead, but the principal is the same. We can now take a quick look at how DNS is set up inside our Pod with this code snippet:

```
/ # cat /etc/resolv.conf          Appends the following
search                            to the end of a query
  default.svc.cluster.local
  svc.cluster.local
  cluster.local
nameserver 10.96.0.10      ◁──── Specifies a DNS server
options ndots:5
```

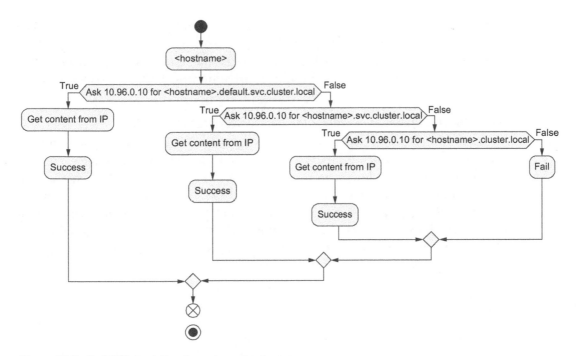

Figure 10.2   Pod DNS resolution for an incoming hostname

In this code snippet, the search field in this file is basically saying "append these attributes to the end of a query, until a query returns." In other words, first see if a URL resolves without any modification. If that fails, try adding `default.svc.cluster.local` to the DNS request. If that fails, try adding `svc.cluster.local`, and so on. Next, note the `nameserver` field. This tells your resolver that it can rectify external DNS names (those not in /etc/hosts) by asking a DNS server that lives at 10.96.0.10, which is the address of your kube-dns service.

We can see how, for example, the DNS for our StatefulSet Pods resolves to a Pod IP inside our cluster network by running `wget`. Let's `kubectl exec` into our NGINX Pod and run the following command:

```
/ # wget web-ss-0.nginx.default.svc.cluster.local
Connecting to web-ss-0.nginx.default.svc.cluster.local
   (10.244.0.13:80)
```

We'll leave it as an exercise for the reader to try this out from a different Namespace. Rest assured, resolving `web-ss-0` works from any namespace in your cluster if you include the entire DNS name. For that matter, so will `wget web-ss-0.nginx.default`. You can now envision various ways to share services across different Namespaces using this trick. One of the most obvious use cases for this might be

- A user (Joe) makes an application in the namespace `joe`, which normally accesses the database using the URL my-db from inside the `joe` Namespace.
- Another user (Sally), who has an app in the namespace `sally`, wants to access the my-db service, which she can do by using the URL my-db.joe.svc.cluster .local.

10.3.2 CoreDNS: The upstream resolver for the ClusterFirst Pod DNS

CoreDNS is the mysterious nameserver lurking behind the 10.96.0.10 endpoint. We can confirm this by running `kubectl get services` locally if we want. What exactly is CoreDNS doing that allows it to resolve hosts from the internet, from the internal cluster, and so on? We can see how it is set up by looking at its configuration map.

CoreDNS is powered by plugins, and you read a CoreDNS configuration from the top down, with each plugin being a new line in the file. To view the configuration map for CoreDNS, you can run `kubectl get cm coredns -n kube-system -o yaml` on any cluster. In our example, this returns

```
apiVersion: v1
data:
  Corefile: |
    .:53 {
        errors
        health {
            lameduck 5s
        }
        ready
        kubernetes
            cluster.local in-addr.arpa ip6.arpa {     ◁────  Resolves the cluster's
            pods insecure                                    local IP hosts
            fallthrough in-addr.arpa ip6.arpa
            ttl 30
        }
        prometheus :9153                         ┌─────  Resolves internet addresses
        forward . /etc/resolv.conf     ◁─────┘         if the K8s plugin fails
        cache 30     ◁───┐
        loop             │  Keep a close eye on this
        reload           │  plugin; we'll use it later.
        loadbalance
        log {
          class all     ◁───┐
        }                   │  Enables verbose logging of
    }                       │  CoreDNS responses and errors
kind: ConfigMap
```

In this code example, the first thing we try to do is to resolve the cluster's local IP hosts using the Kubernetes plugin for CoreDNS. Then we use the kubelet's resolv.conf to resolve addresses on the internet if the Kubernetes plugin fails at resolving them.

You might be wondering, if CoreDNS is running in a container, isn't its resolv.conf going to depend on CoreDNS? It turns out that the answer to that is no! To see why, let's look at the cluster's `dnsPolicy` field, which is set for any Pod in a Kubernetes cluster:

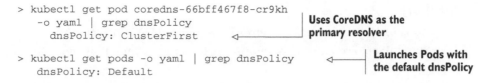

```
> kubectl get pod coredns-66bff467f8-cr9kh
    -o yaml | grep dnsPolicy
        dnsPolicy: ClusterFirst
```
Uses CoreDNS as the primary resolver

```
> kubectl get pods -o yaml | grep dnsPolicy
    dnsPolicy: Default
```
Launches Pods with the default dnsPolicy

ClusterFirst policies use CoreDNS as their primary resolver, which is why our resolv.conf file in our Pod basically had CoreDNS and nothing else. Pods launched with the default dnsPolicy actually get a /etc/resolv.conf file injected into them, which resolves entries from the Kubelet itself. Thus, on most Kubernetes clusters, you'll find that

- Even though CoreDNS runs in the regular Pod network, it has a different DNS policy than other "normal" Pods in your cluster.
- The Pods in your cluster first try to contact a Kubernetes internal service before reaching out to the internet via the flow configured in your Corefile.
- The CoreDNS Pod itself forwards noncluster internal IP addresses to the same place that its host forwards these IP addresses. In other words, it inherits internet host-resolution properties from your kubelet.

10.3.3 *Hacking the CoreDNS plugin configuration*

The cache plugin for CoreDNS tells CoreDNS that it can cache results for 30 seconds. This means that if we were to

- Scale down our StatefulSet (by running `kubectl scale statefulset web-ss --replicas=0`)
- Start a `wget` for the web-ss-0.nginx Pod
- Scale our StatefulSet back up (by running `kubectl scale statefulset web-ss --replicas=3`)

we would actually see that we can get a long hang in our `wget` command, even though three replicas run almost immediately. This is because the default for CoreDNS, which is to run its cache plugin with a 30-second response, means that DNS requests to the web-ss-0.nginx Pod fail for several seconds, even after this Pod is happily up and running.

To fix this, you can run the `kubectl edit cm coreDNS -n kube-system` command and modify this `cache` value to a smaller number, such as 5. This then guarantees that DNS queries will rapidly refresh their results. The larger this number is, the less load you will create on the underlying Kubernetes control plane over time, but of course, in our small `kind` cluster, this overhead is not important.

Note that DNS tuning is a deep subject in any data center, regardless of Kubernetes. If you are interested in further tuning DNS for larger clusters, you can launch the kubelet with NodeLocalDNS policies in newer versions of Kubernetes. This policy makes DNS extremely fast by running a DaemonSet across all nodes in a cluster, which caches all DNS requests for all Pods. There are also many other CoreDNS plugin tunings you can look into, as well as Prometheus metrics, which you can monitor over time.

Summary

- A major Kubernetes feature gives Pods internal DNS to access Services.
- StatefulSets are extremely important for applications that need to have firm identities.
- Headless Services return Pod IPs directly and don't have a stable ClusterIP, which means they can sometimes return NXDOMAIN if a Pod is down.
- Services and StatefulSet Pods both are first class, stable DNS endpoints in a Kubernetes cluster.
- The resolv.conf file is a standard way to configure DNS for a container. In any scenario where you are attempting to figure out how your Pod is configured with regard to DNS, this is the first place to look.
- CoreDNS is powered by plugins, and you read a CoreDNS configuration from the top down, with each plugin being a new line in the file.
- The cache plugin for CoreDNS tells CoreDNS that it can cache results for 30 seconds.

11

The core
of the control plane

This chapter covers

- Investigating core components of the control plane
- Reviewing API server details
- Exploring scheduler interfaces and its inner workings
- Walking through the controller manager and cloud manager

Previously, we provided a high-level overview of Pods, a web application outlining why we need Pods, and how Kubernetes is built with Pods. Now that we've covered all of our requirements for the use case, let's dive into the details of the control plane. Typically, all of the control plane components are installed in the kube-system namespace, a namespace where you, as an operator, should install very few components.

> **NOTE** You should just not use kube-system! One of the main reasons is that noncontroller applications running inside kube-system increase the security blast radius, which refers to the breadth and depth of a security

intrusion. Further, if you are on a hosted system like GKE or EKS, you cannot see all of the control plane components. We talk more about blast radius and security best practices in chapter 13.

11.1 Investigating the control plane

One of the easiest ways to start and poke at the control plane is to use `kind`, which is Kubernetes in a container (see the following link for install instructions: http:// mng.bz/lalM). To use `kind` to view the control plane, run the following commands:

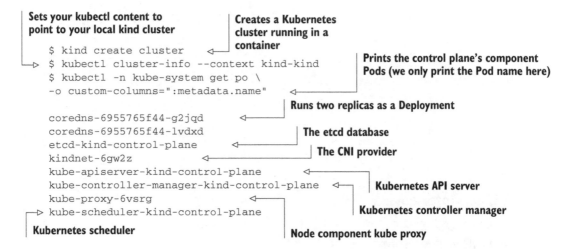

Sets your kubectl content to point to your local kind cluster

Creates a Kubernetes cluster running in a container

```
$ kind create cluster
$ kubectl cluster-info --context kind-kind
$ kubectl -n kube-system get po \
-o custom-columns=":metadata.name"
```

Prints the control plane's component Pods (we only print the Pod name here)

```
coredns-6955765f44-g2jqd
coredns-6955765f44-lvdxd
etcd-kind-control-plane
kindnet-6gw2z
kube-apiserver-kind-control-plane
kube-controller-manager-kind-control-plane
kube-proxy-6vsrg
kube-scheduler-kind-control-plane
```

Runs two replicas as a Deployment

The etcd database

The CNI provider

Kubernetes API server

Kubernetes controller manager

Kubernetes scheduler

Node component kube proxy

You'll notice that the kubelet is not running as a Pod. Some systems run the kubelet inside a container, but in systems such as `kind`, the kubelet is just run as a binary. To see the kubelet running in a `kind` cluster, issue the following commands:

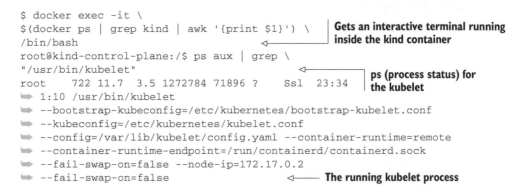

```
$ docker exec -it \
$(docker ps | grep kind | awk '{print $1}') \
/bin/bash
root@kind-control-plane:/$ ps aux | grep \
"/usr/bin/kubelet"
root    722 11.7  3.5 1272784 71896 ?    Ssl  23:34
  1:10 /usr/bin/kubelet
  --bootstrap-kubeconfig=/etc/kubernetes/bootstrap-kubelet.conf
  --kubeconfig=/etc/kubernetes/kubelet.conf
  --config=/var/lib/kubelet/config.yaml --container-runtime=remote
  --container-runtime-endpoint=/run/containerd/containerd.sock
  --fail-swap-on=false --node-ip=172.17.0.2
  --fail-swap-on=false
```

Gets an interactive terminal running inside the kind container

ps (process status) for the kubelet

The running kubelet process

Type `exit` to get out of the interactive terminal inside the container. To truly get a feel of what comprises a control plane, take a look at the various Pods. For instance, you can print the API server Pod with this command:

```
$ kubectl -n kube-system get po kube-apiserver-kind-control-plane -o yaml
```

11.2 API server details

Now, it's time to dive into the details regarding the API server. That's because it's not only a RESTful web server, but it is also a critical component of the control plane. What is important to note is not only the API objects, but also the custom API objects. Later in the book, we will cover the authentication, authorization, and admission controllers, but first, let's look in a bit more detail at Kubernetes API objects and custom resources.

11.2.1 API objects and custom API objects

The essence of Kubernetes is an open platform, meaning open APIs. Opening up a platform is what provides additional innovation and creation. The following lists a number of API resources associated with a Kubernetes cluster. You will recognize some of these API objects (like Deployments and Pods):

```
$ kubectl api-resources -o name | head -n 20     ◁——  Shows the available APIs,
bindings                                                just looking at the first 20
componentstatuses                                       using head
configmaps
endpoints
events
limitranges
namespaces
nodes
persistentvolumeclaims
persistentvolumes
pods
podtemplates
replicationcontrollers
resourcequotas
secrets
serviceaccounts
services
mutatingwebhookconfigurations.admissionregistration.k8s.io
validatingwebhookconfigurations.admissionregistration.k8s.io
customresourcedefinitions.apiextensions.k8s.io
```

When we define a YAML manifest with a ClusterRoleBinding, part of that definition is the API version. For instance:

```
apiVersion: rbac.authorization.k8s.io/v1     ◁——  The apiVersion matches
kind: ClusterRoleBinding                            the API group in the
metadata:                                           previous code snippet.
  name: cockroach-operator-default
  labels:
    app: cockroach-operator
roleRef:
  apiGroup: rbac.authorization.k8s.io
  kind: ClusterRole
  name: cockroach-operator-role
subjects:
  - name: cockroach-operator-default
    namespace: default
    kind: ServiceAccount
```

The `apiVersion` stanza in the previous YAML defines the API's version. Versioning APIs is a complex problem. In order to allow for APIs to move through different versions, Kubernetes has the capability to have a version and levels. For instance, in the previous YAML definition, you'll notice that we have `v1beta1` in our `apiVersion` definition. This designates that the ClusterRoleBinding is a *beta* API object.

API objects have the following levels: alpha, beta, and GA (general availability). Objects marked as alpha are ones that are never to be used in production because they cause serious upgrade path problems. Alpha API objects are going to change and are only for development and experimentation. Beta is really not beta! Beta software is often thought of as unstable and not for production, but beta API objects in Kubernetes *are* ready for production, and support for these objects is guaranteed, unlike alpha objects. For example, DaemonSets were beta for years, and virtually everyone ran them in production.

The *v1* prefix allows the Kubernetes developers to number the version of the API object. For instance, in Kubernetes v1.17.0, the autoscaling APIs are

- /apis/autoscaling/v1
- /apis/autoscaling/v2beta1
- /apis/autoscaling/v2beta2

Notice that this list is in a URI layout. You can view the URI layout of the API objects by first starting a `kind` Kubernetes cluster locally:

```
$ kind cluster start
```

Then, run a `kubectl` command on a system that also has a web browser. For example:

```
$ kubectl proxy --port=8181
```

Now go to the URL http://127.0.0.1:8181/. For brevity sake we're not going to show the 120-line response from the API server, but if you do this locally, it will give you a graphical view of the API endpoints.

11.2.2 *Custom resource definitions (CRDs)*

In the ClusterRoleBinding code snippet, we defined CRDs to communicate with the cockroach database operator. It's time to discuss why CRDs exist. In Kubernetes v1.17.0, we have 54 API objects. The following command will provide some insight:

```
$ kubectl api-resources | wc
      54     230    5658
```
← **Pipes the result of the kubectl command into wc to count the number of lines, words, and characters**

You can understand how much development time it requires to maintain a system that contains 54 different objects (frankly, we need more). In order to decouple non-core API objects from the API server, CRDs were created. These allow developers to create their own API object definition and then, with `kubectl`, apply that definition to the API server. The following command creates a CRD object within the API server:

```
$ kubectl apply -f https://raw.githubusercontent.com/cockroachdb/
➥ cockroach-operator/v2.4.0/config/crd/bases/
➥ crdb.cockroachlabs.com_crdbclusters.yaml
```

As with a Pod or other stock API objects within the API server, CRD objects extend the Kubernetes API platform programmatically with zero programmer interaction. Operators, custom admission controllers, Istio, Envoy, and other technologies now use the API server by defining their own CRDs. But these custom objects are not tightly coupled to the Kubernete's API object implementation. Moreover, many new core components of Kubernetes are not being added to the stock definitions of the API server, but rather are added as CRDs. This, then, is the API server. Next, we'll discuss the first controller that we will cover: the Kubernetes scheduler.

11.2.3 Scheduler details

The *scheduler*, like other controllers, is comprised of various control loops that handle different events. As of Kubernetes v1.15.0, the scheduler was refactored to use a scheduling framework and, additionally, custom plugins. Kubernetes supports using custom schedulers that do not run in the actual scheduler but in another Pod. However, the problem with custom schedulers is often poor performance.

The first component of the scheduler framework is QueueSort. It sorts the Pods that require scheduling into a queue. The framework is then broken into two cycles: the scheduling cycle and the binding cycle. First, the scheduling cycle chooses which node a Pod runs on. Once the scheduling cycle is complete, the binding cycle takes over.

The scheduler chooses which node the Pod can live on, and actually determining if the Pod can live there can take some time. For instance, a Pod needs a volume, so that volume needs to be created. What happens if the creation of the required volume fails? Then the Pod cannot run on the node and the scheduling for that Pod is requeued.

We'll walk through this to get an understanding of when the scheduler, for instance, handles Pod NodeAffinity during its scheduling process. Each of the cycles has individual components that are laid out in the following structure in the Scheduler API. The following code is from the Kubernetes v1.22 release, and as of v1.23, it has been refactored, moving to allow plugins to be enabled via multipoint. The scheduler itself and plugin fundamentals have not changed as of the writing of this book. This code snippet (located at http://mng.bz/d2oX) defines the various sets of plugins that are registered inside a running scheduling instance. Here is the base API definition:

```
// Plugins include multiple extension points. When specified, the list of
// plugins for a particular extension point are the only ones enabled. If
// an extension point is omitted from the config, then the default set of
// plugins is used for that extension point. Enabled plugins are called in
// the order specified here, after the default plugins. If they need to be
// invoked before the default plugins, the default plugins must be disabled
// and re-enabled here in the desired order.
type Plugins struct {
    // QueueSort is a list of plugins that should be invoked when
    // sorting pods in the scheduling queue.
    QueueSort *PluginSet              ⟵── Sorts the Pods in a Queue
```

```
// PreFilter is a list of plugins that should be invoked at the
// PreFilter extension point of the scheduling framework.
PreFilter *PluginSet
```
◁─── **The scheduling cycle plugins start here and end at the Permit plugin.**

```
// Filter is a list of plugins that should be invoked when filtering
// nodes that cannot run the Pod.
Filter *PluginSet

// PostFilter is a list of plugins that are invoked after filtering
// phase, no matter whether filtering succeeds or not.
PostFilter *PluginSet

// PreScore is a list of plugins that are invoked before scoring.
PreScore *PluginSet

// Score is a list of plugins that should be invoked when ranking nodes
// that have passed the filtering phase.
Score *PluginSet

// Reserve is a list of plugins invoked when reserving/unreserving
// resources after a node is assigned to run the pod.
Reserve *PluginSet

// Permit is a list of plugins that control binding of a Pod. These
// plugins can prevent or delay binding of a Pod.
Permit *PluginSet

// PreBind is a list of plugins that should be invoked before a pod
// is bound.
PreBind *PluginSet

// Bind is a list of plugins that should be invoked at the Bind
// extension point of the scheduling framework. The scheduler calls
// these plugins in order and skips the rest of these plugins as soon
// as one returns success.
Bind *PluginSet

// PostBind is a list of plugins that should be invoked after a pod
// is successfully bound.
PostBind *PluginSet
}
```

These last three plugins are the binding cycle.

The struct in the previous code snippet is instantiated in http://mng.bz/rJaZ (after 1.21 this code was refactored and moved). In the following code, you will recognize scheduling plugins that handle configurations like Pod NodeAffinity, which impacts a Pod's scheduling. The first phase in this process is the QueueSort, but note that QueueSort is extendable and thus replaceable:

```
func getDefaultConfig() *schedulerapi.Plugins {        ◁──── Calls getDefaultConfig()
    return &schedulerapi.Plugins{
        QueueSort: &schedulerapi.PluginSet{          ◁──── Calls getDefaultConfig()
```

```
        Enabled: []schedulerapi.Plugin{
            {Name: queuesort.Name},
        },
    },
```

The private function, getDefaultConfig(), is called by NewRegistry in the same Go file. This returns an algorithm provider registry instance. The next members that are returned define the scheduling cycle. First, the Prefilter, which is a list of plugins run in serial:

```
PreFilter: &schedulerapi.PluginSet {
        Enabled: []schedulerapi.Plugin {

            {Name: noderesources.FitName},

            {Name: nodeports.Name},

            {Name: podtopologyspread.Name},

            {Name: interpodaffinity.Name},

            {Name: volumebinding.Name},
        },
    },
```

Checks if a node has sufficient resources

Determines if a node has free ports to host the Pod

Checks that the PodTopologySpread is met, which allows for the spreading of Pods evenly across zones

This is not actually a filter but creates a cache that is used later during the reserve and prebind phases.

Handles interpod affinity that, like Pod anti-affinity, repels Pods from nodes based on user-defined rules

Next, the filter phase. Note that *Filter* is a list of plugins that determines whether a Pod can run on a specific node:

```
Filter: &schedulerapi.PluginSet {
    Enabled: []schedulerapi.Plugin {
        {Name: nodeunschedulable.Name},

        {Name: noderesources.FitName},

        {Name: nodename.Name},

        {Name: nodeports.Name},

        {Name: nodeaffinity.Name},

        {Name: volumerestrictions.Name},

        {Name: tainttoleration.Name},

        {Name: nodevolumelimits.EBSName},
        {Name: nodevolumelimits.GCEPDName},
        {Name: nodevolumelimits.CSIName},
        {Name: nodevolumelimits.AzureDiskName},

        {Name: volumebinding.Name},

        {Name: volumezone.Name},
```

Ensures that Pods are not scheduled on a node marked as unschedulable in the pastschedulable (for instance, the nodes in the control plane)

Executes the plugin again

The PodSpec API lets you set a nodeName, which identifies the node where you want the Pod.

Plugin executed a second time

Checks if the Pod node selector matches the node label

Checks if various volume restrictions are met

Checks that the node has the capacity to add more volumes (for instance, a node can mount 16 volumes in GCP).

Checks if a Pod tolerates node taints

Repeats a filter in PreFilter

Checks that a volume exists in the zone that the node resides in

```
        {Name: podtopologyspread.Name},          These two filters
        {Name: interpodaffinity.Name},           are repeated.
    },
},
```

In the filtering phase, the scheduler checks various constraints around mounting different volumes in GCP, AWS, Azure, ISCI, and RBD. For instance, Pod anti-affinity ensures that StatefulSet Pods reside on different nodes. You are probably starting to notice that the filters are scheduling Pods from settings that you may have already created on a Pod in the past. Now, let's move on to the PostFilter. This plugin runs even if filtering is unsuccessful:

```
PostFilter: &schedulerapi.PluginSet{
  Enabled: []schedulerapi.Plugin{
    {Name: defaultpreemption.Name},      ◁─── Handles Pod preemption
  },
},
```

A user can set a priority class for a Pod. If so, the default preemption plugin allows the scheduler to determine if it can set another Pod for eviction to make room for the scheduled Pod in the priority class. Note that these plugins do all of the filtering to determine if a Pod can run on a specific node.

Next comes the scoring. The scheduler builds a list of which nodes the Pod can run on, so now it's time to rank the list of nodes that can host the Pod by scoring the nodes. Because the scoring component is also part of the plugins that filter the nodes, you will notice a lot of repeated plugin names. The scheduler first prescores in order to create a shareable list for the score plugins:

```
PreScore: &schedulerapi.PluginSet{        ◁─
  Enabled: []schedulerapi.Plugin{           All the defined plugins have already
    {Name: interpodaffinity.Name},          run during the filtering process.
    {Name: podtopologyspread.Name},
    {Name: tainttoleration.Name},
  },
},
```

The next code snippet defines the reuse of various repeated plugins, but also some new ones. The scheduler defines a weight value, which impacts the scheduling. All nodes that are scored have passed the different filtering phases:

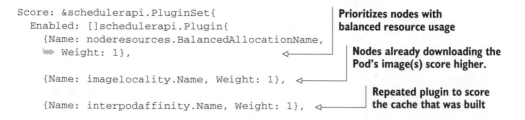

```
Score: &schedulerapi.PluginSet{              Prioritizes nodes with
  Enabled: []schedulerapi.Plugin{            balanced resource usage
    {Name: noderesources.BalancedAllocationName,
    ➡ Weight: 1},                            ◁───    Nodes already downloading the
                                                     Pod's image(s) score higher.
    {Name: imagelocality.Name, Weight: 1},   ◁───
                                                     Repeated plugin to score
    {Name: interpodaffinity.Name, Weight: 1}, ◁───  the cache that was built
```

```
{Name: noderesources.LeastAllocatedName,
   Weight: 1},                                  ◄──  Nodes with fewer
                                                      requests are favored.

{Name: nodeaffinity.Name, Weight: 1},          ◄──  Repeated plugin, again scoring
                                                      the cache that was built

{Name: nodepreferavoidpods.Name,
   Weight: 10000},                              ◄──  Lowers a node score if
// Weight is doubled because:                        preferAvoidPods is set
// - This is a score coming from user preference.
// - It makes its signal comparable to NodeResourcesLeastAllocated.
{Name: podtopologyspread.Name, Weight: 2},      Repeats these two plugins
{Name: tainttoleration.Name, Weight: 1},
   },
},
```

When prioritizing nodes with balanced resource usage, the scheduler calculates CPU, memory, and volume fractions. The algorithm is as follows:

```
(cpu((capacity • sum(requested)) * MaxNodeScore/capacity) +
  memory((capacity • sum(requested)) * MaxNodeScore/capacity)) / weightSum
```

This algorithm scores the nodes with fewer requests. The node label, preferAvoid-Pods, denotes that a node should be avoided for scheduling.

The last step in the filtering process is the reserve phase. In the reserve phase, we reserve a volume for a Pod to use during the binding cycle. In the following code, note that volumebinding is a repeated plugin:

```
Reserve: &schedulerapi.PluginSet{
  Enabled: []schedulerapi.Plugin{          The cache reserves a
    {Name: volumebinding.Name},       ◄──  volume for the Pod.
  },
},
```

The scheduling cycle, which mostly filters nodes, determines which node the Pod should run on. But ensuring that the Pod actually runs on that node is a much longer process, and you may find the Pod requeued for scheduling. Let's now look at the binding cycle in the scheduler framework, starting with a prebind phase. The following snippet shows the code for the PreBind plugin:

```
PreBind: &schedulerapi.PluginSet{
  Enabled: []schedulerapi.Plugin{          Binds the volume
    {Name: volumebinding.Name},       ◄──  to the Pod
  },
},

Bind: &schedulerapi.PluginSet{             Saves a Bind object via the
  Enabled: []schedulerapi.Plugin{          API server, updating the
    {Name: defaultbinder.Name},       ◄──  node a Pod will start on
  },

},
```

Through all of this, the scheduler has multiple queues: an active queue, which is the scheduling Pod, and a backoff queue, which includes Pods that are not schedulable. The registry in the scheduler does not instantiate plugins for two different phases: Permit and PostBind. These entry points are used by other plugins, such as the batch scheduler, which soon will be an external plugin for the scheduler. Because we now have a scheduling framework, we can use and register other custom scheduler plugins. An example of these custom plugins can be found in the GitHub repository at http://mng.bz/oaBN.

11.2.4 Recap of scheduling

Figure 11.1 shows the three components that make up the scheduler framework. These include

- *Queue builder*—Maintains a queue of Pods
- *Scheduling cycle*—Filters nodes to find one to run the Pod
- *Binding cycle*—Saves data to the API server, along with binding information

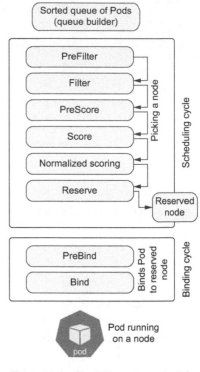

Figure 11.1   The Kubernetes scheduler

11.3   The controller manager

A lot of the functionality that was contained within KCM (the Kubernetes controller manager) was moved into CCM (the cloud controller manager). This binary is a combination of four components that are controllers themselves or just simply control loops. We'll look at these in the following sections.

11.3.1 Storage

Storage in Kubernetes is a bit of a moving target. As functionality moves out of KCM and into the CCM, there are also major changes with how storage functions inside of the Kubernetes control plane. Before the move, KCM storage adapters existed in the main repository, kubernetes/kubernetes. A user created a PVC (PersistentVolume-Claim) in the cloud, and the KCM called code that was inside the Kubernetes project. Then, there were flex volume controllers, which are still in existence today. But, looping back to KCM, it drives the creation of storage objects as of Kubernetes v1.18.x.

When a user creates a PV or a PVC, or a PVC/PV combination that is required by the creation of a StatefulSet, a component on the control plane must initiate and control the creation of a storage volume. That storage volume can be hosted by a cloud provider or created in another virtual environment. The point to hold on to is that the KCM controls the creation and deletion of storage. Let's go through the controllers that make up KCM.

The Node controller watches for when a node goes down. It then updates the node status in the Nodes API object.

The Replication controller maintains the correct number of Pods for every replication controller object in the system. Replication controller objects, for the most part, have been replaced by deployments that use ReplicaSets.

The Endpoint controller is the last controller, which manages Endpoint objects. The Endpoint object is defined within the Kubernetes API. These objects are typically not maintained manually, but are created to provide `kube-proxy` the information to join a Pod to a service. A Service may have one or more Pods that handle traffic from said Service. Here is an example of the endpoints created for `kube-dns` on a `kind` cluster:

```
$ kubectl -n kube-system describe endpoints kube-dns
Name:           kube-dns
Namespace:      kube-system
Labels:         k8s-app=kube-dns
                kubernetes.io/cluster-service=true
                kubernetes.io/name=KubeDNS
Annotations:    endpoints.kubernetes.io/last-change-trigger-time:
➥ 2020-09-30T00:21:28Z
Subsets:
  Addresses:            10.244.0.2,10.244.0.4      ⟵   The IP addresses of the Pods
  NotReadyAddresses:    <none>                         that are a member of the
  Ports:                                               kube-dns service
    Name      Port   Protocol
    ----      ----   --------
    dns       53     UDP
    dns-tcp   53     TCP
    metrics   9153   TCP
```

11.3.2 Service accounts and tokens

When a new Namespace is generated, the Kubernetes controller manager creates a default ServiceAccount and API access tokens for the new Namespace. If you do not name a specific ServiceAccount when you define a Pod, it joins the default ServiceAccount created in the Namespace. The ServiceAccount, not surprisingly, is used when a Pod accesses the cluster's API server. When the Pod is started, the API access token is mounted to the Pod, unless a user disables the mounting of the token.

TIP If a Pod does not need the ServiceAccount token, disable the mounting of the token by setting `automountServiceAccountToken` to `false`.

11.4 *Kubernetes cloud controller managers (CCMs)*

Say we have a Kubernetes cluster running on a cloud service, or we are running Kubernetes on top of a virtualization provider. Either way, these different hosting platforms maintain different cloud controllers that interact with the API layer where Kubernetes is hosted. If you wanted to write a new cloud controller, you would need to include functionality for the following components:

- *Nodes*—For virtual instances
- *Routing*—For traffic between nodes
- *External LoadBalancers*—To create a load balancer that is external to the nodes in the cluster

The code behind interacting with these components inside of a cloud provider is specific to the provider via their APIs. The cloud controller interface now defines a common interface for different cloud providers. In order for Omega, for example, to build a cloud provider for Kubernetes, we need to build a controller that utilizes the following interface:

```
// Interface is an abstract, pluggable interface for cloud providers.
type Interface interface {

    // Initialize provides the cloud with a Kubernetes client builder and
    // can spawn goroutines to perform housekeeping or run custom
    // controllers specific to the cloud provider. Any tasks started here
    // should be cleaned up when the stop channel closes.
    Initialize(clientBuilder ControllerClientBuilder, stop <-chan struct{})

    // LoadBalancer returns a balancer interface. It also returns true if
    // the interface is supported; otherwise, it returns false.
    LoadBalancer() (LoadBalancer, bool)

    // Instances returns an instances interface. It also returns true if
    // the interface is supported; otherwise, it returns false.
    Instances() (Instances, bool)

    // InstancesV2 is an implementation for instances and should only be
    // implemented by external cloud providers. Implementing InstancesV2
    // is behaviorally identical to Instances but is optimized to
    // significantly reduce API calls to the cloud provider when registering
    // and syncing nodes. It also returns true if the interface is supported
    // and false otherwise.
    // WARNING: InstancesV2 is an experimental interface and is subject to
    // change in v1.20.
    InstancesV2() (InstancesV2, bool)

    // Zones returns a zones interface. It also returns true if the
    // interface is supported and false otherwise.
    Zones() (Zones, bool)
```

```
    // Clusters returns a clusters interface. It also returns true if the
    // interface is supported and false otherwise.
    Clusters() (Clusters, bool)

    // Routes returns a routes interface along with whether the interface
    // is supported.
    Routes() (Routes, bool)

    // ProviderName returns the cloud provider ID.
    ProviderName() string

    // HasClusterID returns true if a ClusterID is required and set.
    HasClusterID() bool
}
```

The recommended design pattern for a CCM is to implement three control loops (controllers). These are then typically deployed as a single binary.

In order to mount a cloud volume onto a node, we have to find the node in the cloud, and the Node controller provides this functionality. The controller has to know which nodes are in a cluster, and this is beyond the information that the kubelet provides when a node starts. When running in a cloud environment, Kubernetes needs specific information (for example, zone information) about the node and how it is deployed in the cloud environment. Also, there is a layer that determines if a node has been completely deleted from a cloud environment. The node controller provides a bridge between the cloud API layer and stores that information in the API server.

Kubernetes has to route traffic between nodes and this is handled by the Route controller. If a cloud requires configuration to route data between nodes, the CCM makes the API calls to all network traffic between nodes.

The name *service controller* is a bit of a misnomer. The service controller is only a controller that facilitates the creation of LoadBalancer type services within a cluster. It does not facilitate anything with ClusterIP services within a Kubernetes cluster.

11.5 *Further reading*

Acetozi. "Kubernetes Master Components: Etcd, API Server, Controller Manager, and Scheduler." http://mng.bz/doKX (accessed 12/29/2021).

Summary

- The Kubernetes control plane provides the functionality to orchestrate and host Pods in a Kubernetes cluster.
- The scheduler is comprised of various control loops that handle different events.
- The scheduling cycle, which mostly filters nodes, determines which node the Pod should run on.

- Beta API objects in Kubernetes are ready for production. Support for these objects is guaranteed, unlike alpha objects.
- KCM and CCM work together to provision storage, Services, LoadBalancers, and other components via the different controllers that comprise the KCM and the CCM.

etcd and the
control plane

This chapter covers

- Comparing etcd v2 and v3
- Looking at a watch in Kubernetes
- Exploring the importance of strict consistency
- Load balancing against etcd nodes
- Looking at etcd's security model in Kubernetes

As discussed in chapter 11, etcd is a key/value store with strong consistency guarantees. It's similar to ZooKeeper, which is used for popular technologies like HBase and Kafka. A Kubernetes cluster at its core consists of

- The kubelet
- The scheduler
- The controller managers (KCM and CCM)
- The API server

These components all speak to one another by updating the API server. For example, if the scheduler wants to run a Pod on a specific node, it does so by modifying the Pod's definition in the API server. If, during the process of starting a Pod, the kubelet needs to broadcast an event, it does so by sending the API server a message. Because the scheduler, kubelet, and controller manager all communicate through the API server, this makes them strongly *decoupled*. For example, the scheduler doesn't know how a kubelet runs Pods, and the kubelet doesn't know how the API server schedules Pods. In other words, Kubernetes is a giant machine that stores the state of your infrastructure at all times in the API server.

When nodes, controllers, or API servers fail, your data center's applications need to be reconciled, such that a container can be scheduled to new nodes, the volumes can be bound to those containers, and so on. All of the state modifications that are made via the Kubernetes API are actually backed up in etcd. This is nothing new in the world of scale-out computing. You've probably heard of tools like ZooKeeper that are used in the same manner. In fact, HBase, Kafka, and many other distributed platforms use ZooKeeper under the hood. The etcd database is just a modern version of ZooKeeper with a few different opinions on how to store highly critical data and reconcile records in cases of failure scenarios.

12.1   *Notes for the impatient*

It can be quite overwhelming once you begin looking at the theoretical internals of distributed consensus scenarios and disaster recovery for etcd databases. Before we dip our toe into that universe, let's cover some practical details around etcd in Kubernetes:

- If you lose your etcd data, your cluster will be crippled. Back up etcd!
- You will need fast disk access via a solid state disk and a high performance network to run etcd v3 in production.

  A single write in etcd that takes more than 1 second to serialize to disk can slowly bring a large cluster to a halt. Given that you might have many writes occurring at any given time, this implies network and disk requirements that roughly correspond to a 10 GB network and solid state disks. From etcd's own documentation (https://etcd.io/docs/v3.3/op-guide/hardware/): "Typically 50 sequential IOPS (e.g., a 7200 RPM disk) is required." And often etcd requires even more IOPS

- There will be periodic failures in most data centers or cloud environments for a given compute node, and thus, you need redundant etcd nodes. This means running three or more etcd nodes in a given installation.
- For a clustered etcd environment, understanding how its Raft implementation works, why disk I/O matters for Raft consensus, and how etcd uses CPU and memory is going to be important.
- All events, in addition to cluster state, are stored in etcd. You should, however, decide to store cluster events (of which there are many) in a different etcd endpoint so that your core cluster data is not competing with the unimportant event metadata.

- A command-line tool for interacting with the etcd server, `etcdctl`, has its own embedded performance test for quick etcd performance verification: `etcdctl check perf`.
- If you need to rescue an etcd instance, you can follow the guidelines at http://mng.bz/6Ze5 to manually recover an etcd snapshot.

12.1.1 *Visualizing etcd performance with Prometheus*

Much of the information in this section will be anecdotal, as there is a lot of theory involved in tuning and managing etcd inside of Kubernetes. To offset that, we'll start with an applied journey of how etcd tuning and observation might work in a production scenario. These examples are advanced, and you're welcome to follow along, but it isn't required to produce this data independently in order to benefit from this section.

Figure 12.1 shows the canonical flow of processes that occur when any event happens in a Kubernetes cluster. All writes ultimately coincide with a quorum of multiple etcd servers agreeing that the writes are complete. This will give us some context for the real-world scenario that we'll go through in a moment.

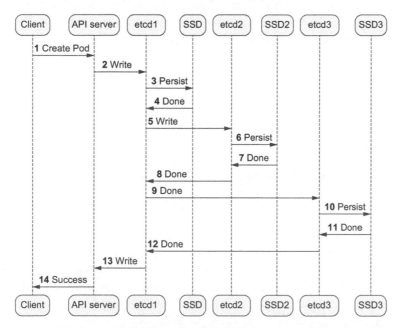

Figure 12.1 **Flow of processes when an event happens in a Kubernetes cluster**

Every API server action (for example, any time you make a simple Pod via `kubectl create -f mypod.yaml`) results in a synchronous write to etcd. This ensures that the request to create the Pod is stored on disk in case the API server dies at some point (which, by the law of large numbers, it eventually will). The API server sends information to a "leader" etcd server, and from there, the magic of distributed consensus takes over to set that write in stone. In figure 12.1, we can see that

- This cluster has three etcd instances. Normally, this can be three, five, or seven. The number of etcd instances is always odd so that a vote on electing a new leader (we'll look at etcd leadership towards the end of this chapter) is always possible.
- A single API server can receive a write, at which point it stores data in its designated etcd endpoint, which is specific to your etcd server on startup as `--etcd-servers`.
- A write operation actually is slowed down by the slowest etcd node. If a single node's round trip to serialize data to disk is slow, then that time dominates the total round trip time for a transaction.

Now, let's take a look from an etcd perspective at what happens when our cluster is healthy. First, you'll need to install Prometheus. (Although we went over this quite a while ago, in this case, there's a slight deviation: we're going to configure Prometheus running in Docker to specifically scrape an etcd instance.) You may recall that starting Prometheus requires giving it a YAML file so that it knows from which targets it needs to scrape information. To customize this file for analyzing the three etcd clusters in our example diagram, you would create the following:

```
global:
  scrape_interval:      15s
  external_labels:
    monitor: 'myetcdscraper'
scrape_configs:
  - job_name: 'prometheus'
    scrape_interval: 5s
    static_configs:
      - targets: ['10.0.0.217:2381']
      - targets: ['10.0.0.251:2381']
      - targets: ['10.0.0.141:2381']
```

For this process, the key metric that we will look at is the *fsync* metric. This tells us how long the writes to etcd (disk) are taking. This metric is divided into buckets (it's a histogram). Any write taking close to 1 second is an indicator that our performance is at risk. If we see that there's a positive trend in the number of writes that happen in more than, say, .25 seconds, we might start to get concerned that our etcd cluster is slowing down because a production Kubernetes cluster may as well.

After launching Prometheus with this configuration, you can make some pretty graphs. Let's take a look at a happy Kubernetes cluster where the various etcd nodes are all functioning properly. Prometheus histograms can be counterintuitive in the beginning. The important thing to remember is that if a particular bucket changes in slope, you might be in trouble! In our first Prometheus graph, in figure 12.2, we can see that

- The amount of writes taking more than 1 seconds is negligible.
- The amount of writes taking more than .5 seconds is negligible.
- The only deviation in overall write speeds happens in high performance buckets.
- Most importantly, the slope of the lines does not change.

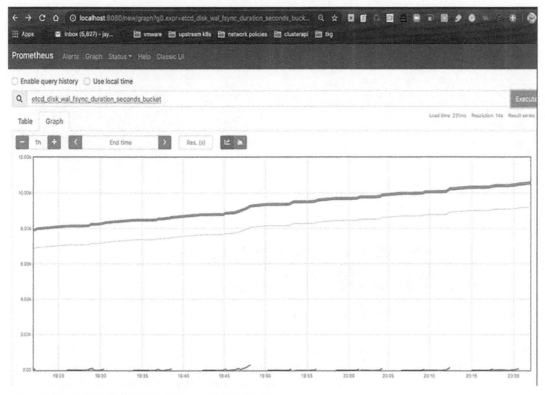

Figure 12.2   Graph of a healthy cluster and etcd metrics

Some clusters are not quite so happy. If we reinstall the same cluster on hardware that is, for example, running on a slow set of disks, we will eventually end up with a histogram that looks like figure 12.3. In contrast to figure 12.2, you'll note that there is a drastic change of slope in some of the histogram's buckets over time. The bucket with the most wildly oscillating slope represents writes that happen in less than .5 seconds. Because we normally expect almost all writes to happen below this margin, we know that over time, our cluster may be in jeopardy; however, it's not necessarily a smoking gun that our cluster is not healthy or is trending towards disaster.

Figure 12.3   Graph of an unhealthy cluster and etcd metrics

We've now seen that it's easy to monitor etcd over time in a cluster. But how can we correlate this to real problems that are happening? The performance of an etcd server's write capacity can lead to problems involving frequent leader elections if it continually degrades. Every leader election event in a Kubernetes cluster means that kubectl will be essentially useless for a period of time while the API server waits for etcd to come back online. Finally, we'll look at one more metric: leader election (figure 12.4).

To see the consequences of figure 12.3, we can look directly at the leader election event's metric, etcd_server_is_leader. By graphing this over time (figure 12.4), you can easily notice when bursts of elections happen in the data center. Next, we'll go over a few simple smoke tests that you can run using tools such as etcdctl for diagnosing individual etcd nodes quickly.

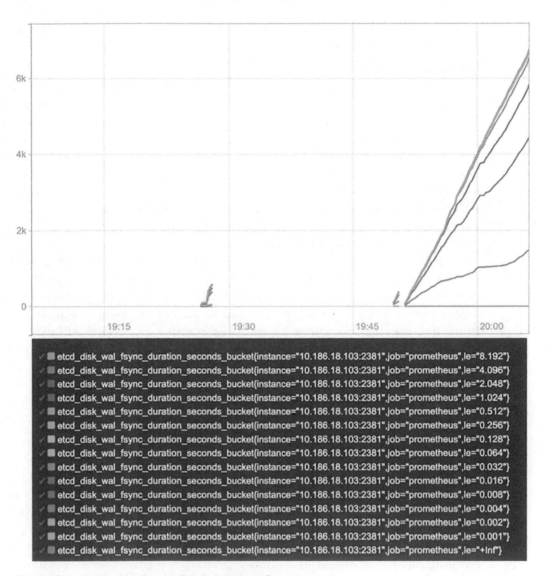

Figure 12.4 Graph of leader election and etcd metrics

12.1.2 *Knowing when to tune etcd*

As noted in the previous section, you might need to tune an etcd instance in production. There are hundreds of scenarios that might lead you to consider this path, but for concreteness, we'll briefly look at a couple. There are many Kubernetes providers that will either manage etcd for you (cluster API-based installations will do this to some extent by storing etcd on individual nodes that can be recreated) or hide etcd entirely from you (such as GKE). In other cases, you might need to think about how etcd is installed and what circumstances it is running under. Two interesting use cases in this regard are nested virtualization and raw `kubeadm`-based Kubernetes installation. Let's look at these two use cases next.

NESTED VIRTUALIZATION

Nested virtualization is common in developer and test environments. As an example, you might use a technology such as VMware Fusion to simulate a vSphere Hypervisor. In this case, you'll have VMs that run inside of other VMs. We can think of the nodes in our `kind` clusters as an analog to nested virtualization: we have Docker containers that run inside of a Docker daemon, which simulate VMs, and then inside of these Docker nodes, we run Kubernetes containers. In any case, as you might imagine, nesting a VM inside another VM creates a huge performance overhead and is not recommended for a production Kubernetes. The main reason it is such a dangerous hardware profile is that, as we virtualize multiple layers, we add latency to the write operations on a hard disk. This latency can make etcd extremely unreliable.

Nested virtualization limits IOPS (input/output operations) and leads to common write failures. Although Kubernetes itself recovers from these, many Pods will continuously lose leader status if you are using the Lease API in Kubernetes, which is increasingly common. This can lead to false alarms and/or progress starvation in long-running, consensus-driven applications. As an example, the Cluster API itself (which we'll cover later) is heavily dependent on leases for healthy functionality. If you run the Cluster API as your Kubernetes provider_and you don't have a healthy etcd for your management cluster, you may never see Kubernetes cluster requests fulfilled. Even without a cluster solution like the Cluster API, which is etcd-dependent, you still will have problems when it comes to your API server's ability to keep up with node status and to receive incoming updates from controllers.

KUBEADM

For a lot of Kubernetes providers, `kubeadm` is the default installer and is often used as a building block for a Kubernetes distribution. However, it doesn't come out of the box with an end-to-end etcd story. For production use cases, you need to bring your own etcd data store to `kubeadm` rather than using its defaults, which, although reasonable, might need to be tweaked or architected specifically for scalability requirements. For example, you may want to create an external etcd cluster with a dedicated disk drive and send this as input to your `kubeadm` installation.

12.1.3 *Example: A quick health check of etcd*

We started this chapter by looking at time-series fsync performance in Prometheus, but in production, you won't often have the ability to craft beautiful graphs and pontificate. One of the simplest ways to quickly make sure etcd is not down is to use the `etcdctl` command-line tool, which comes with an embedded performance test. As an example, go ahead and `ssh` (or `docker exec` if you are on a `kind` cluster) into your cluster node that's running etcd. Then run `find` to track down where your `etcdctl` binary is living:

```
$> find / -name etcdctl # This is obviously a bit of a hack,
                        # but will likely work on any machine
/var/lib/containerd/io.containerd.snapshotter.v1.overlayfs/
  snapshots/13/fs/usr/local/bin/etcdctl
```

From here, use this binary for etcd. Send it the necessary cacerts, which will likely be living in /etc/kubernetes/pki/ if you are using kind or Cluster API-based clusters:

```
$> /var/lib/containerd/io.containerd.snapshotter.v1
➥ .overlayfs/snapshots/13/fs/usr/local/bin/etcdctl \
 --endpoints="https://localhost:2379" \
 --cacert="/etc/kubernetes/pki/etcd/ca.crt" \
 --cert="/etc/kubernetes/pki/etcd/server.crt" \
 --key="/etc/kubernetes/pki/etcd/server.key" \
   check perf
 0 / 60 B
60 / 60 Boooooooooooo...ooooooo!
        100.00% 1m0s
PASS: Throughput is 150 writes/s
PASS: Slowest request took 0.200639s
PASS: Stddev is 0.017681s
PASS
```

This tells us, as a baseline, that etcd is fast enough for production use. Exactly what this means and why it's important will be exemplified throughout the rest of this chapter.

12.1.4 *etcd v3 vs. v2*

If you run any version of Kubernetes after 1.13.0 with etcd v2 or lower, you will get the following error message: "etcd2 is no longer a supported storage backend." Thus, etcd v2 is most likely a nonfactor, and you probably are running etcd v3 in production. This is good news because when cluster sizes become large, or the amount of cloud native tooling you have increases, you might have hundreds or thousands of clients depending on your Kubernetes API server. Once you reach this tipping point, you need etcd v3:

- etcd v3 is much better then v2 for performance purposes.
- etcd v3 uses gRPC for faster transactions.
- etcd v3 has a completely flat key space (compared with a hierarchical one) for faster concurrent access at scales that can easily support thousands of clients.
- etcd v3 watches operations, which are the basis for a Kubernetes controller, can inspect many different keys over a single TCP connection.

We've discussed etcd in other parts of this book, so we assume that you already know why it's important. Instead, we'll zero in on the *hows* of etcd's internal implementation for the purposes of this chapter.

12.2 *etcd as a data store*

Consensus algorithms have been a key part of distributed systems from day one. As early as the 1970s, Ted Codd's rules for databases were, indeed, largely a way to simplify the world of transactional programming so that any computer program did not have to waste time resolving redundant, overlapping, or inconsistent data records. Kubernetes is no different.

The decisions on the architecture of the data plane, implemented via etcd, and the control plane (the scheduler, the controller managers, and the API server) are all based on the same principle of *consistency at all costs*. etcd, therefore, solves the generic problem of reconciling global knowledge. The core functionality underlying the Kubernetes API server includes

- Creating key/value pairs
- Deleting key/value pairs
- Watching keys (with selection filters that can prevent watches from unnecessarily getting data)

12.2.1 *The watch: Can you run Kubernetes on other databases?*

Watches in Kubernetes allow you to "watch" an API resource—not several API resources, just one. This is important to note because a real-world Kubernetes-native application might need to make many watches to respond to new incoming Kubernetes events. Note here that, by API resource, we mean a specific object type, such as Pods or Services. Every time you watch a resource, you can receive events that affect it (for example, you can receive an event from your client each time a new Pod is added or deleted from a cluster). The pattern in Kubernetes for building watch-based applications is known as the *controller pattern*. We've mentioned this before in this book: controllers are the backbone of how Kubernetes manages homeostasis in clusters.

Now, let's focus on the last operation, as it is a critical differentiator for how Kubernetes works compared with other database-backed applications. Most databases do not have a watch operation. We've alluded to the importance of a watch many times in this book. Because Kubernetes itself is just a bunch of controller loops that maintain homeostasis of a distributed group of computers, a mechanism for monitoring changes in the desired state of affairs is required. A few databases that support watches, which you may have heard of, include

- Apache ZooKeeper
- Redis
- etcd

The Raft protocol is a way to manage distributed consensus, and was written as a follow-up to the Paxos protocol used by Apache ZooKeeper. Raft is easier to reason about than Paxos, and simply defines a robust and scalable way to ensure that a distributed group of computers can agree on the state of a key/value database. In short, we can define Raft like so:

1 There is a leader and several follower nodes in a database with an odd number of total nodes.
2 A client requests a write operation on a database.

3 A server receives the write request and forwards it to several follower nodes.

4 Once half of the follower nodes receive and acknowledge the write request, the server commits this request.

5 The client receives a successful write response from the server.

6 If a leader dies, the followers elect a new leader, and this same process continues with the old leader evicted from the cluster.

Of the aforementioned databases, etcd has a strict consistency model based on the Raft protocol and is much more purposely built for coordinating data centers and, thus, was the choice for Kubernetes. That said, it can be feasible to run Kubernetes on another database. There is no Kubernetes-specific functionality inside etcd. In any case, Kubernetes has the core requirement of being able to watch a data source so that it can do tasks such as scheduling Pods, creating load balancers, provisioning storage, and so on. The value of the watch semantic on a database is, however, only as meaningful as the quality of the data being reconciled.

As mentioned, etcd v3 has the ability to watch many records over a single TCP connection. This optimization makes etcd v3 a powerful companion for large Kubernetes clusters. Thus, Kubernetes has a second requirement for its database: consistency.

12.2.2 *Strict consistency*

Imagine it's Christmas, and you're running an application for a shopping site that needs extreme uptime. Now, imagine one of your etcd nodes "thinks" you needed 2 Pods for a critical service, but in actuality, you needed 10. In this case, a downscaling event might occur, interfering with your production availability requirements for this critical application. In this case, the cost of failing over from a correct etcd node to an incorrect one is higher than the cost of not failing over at all! Thus, etcd is strictly consistent. This is done by key architectural constants behind an etcd installation:

- There is only one leader in an etcd cluster, and that leader's world view is 100% correct.
- An odd-number quorum of etcd instances can always vote to decide which instance is the leader in case a new one needs to be created due to loss of an etcd node.
- No write can occur in an etcd quorum until it is persisted collectively to the quorum's disks.
- An etcd node that doesn't have an up-to-date record of all transactions will never serve any data. This is enforced by a consensus protocol called Raft, which we'll discuss later.
- An etcd cluster at any time has exactly one, and only one, leader that we can write to.
- All etcd writes are blocked on the write, cascading to at least half of the etcd nodes in a quorum.

12.2.3   *fsync operations make etcd consistent*

fsync operations block disk writes, which guarantee that etcd is consistent. When you write data to etcd, it guarantees that a real disk is actually modified before the write returns. This can make certain API operations slow, and in turn, it also guarantees that you'll never lose data about your cluster's state in a Kubernetes outage. The faster your disks (yes, your disks, not your memory or CPU), the faster an fsync operation will be:

- In production clusters, you will generally see performance slow-down (or failures) if the fsync operation duration extends beyond 1 second.
- In a typical cloud, you should expect this operation to complete within 250 ms or so.

The simplest way to understand how etcd performs is to look at its fsync performance. Let's quickly do this in one of the myriad kind clusters that you've likely spun up throughout your earlier adventures in this book. In your terminal, run docker exec -t -i <kind container> /bin/bash like so:

```
$ docker ps
CONTAINER ID      IMAGE                    COMMAND
ba820b1d7adb      kindest/node:v1.17.0     "/usr/local/bin/entr..."

$ docker exec -t -i ba /bin/bash
```

Now, let's take a look at the speed of fsync. Prometheus metrics are published by etcd for its performance, which can be curled down or viewed in a tool such as Grafana. These metrics tell us, in seconds, how long the blocking fsync calls take for writes. In a local cluster on an SSD, you'll see that this can be fast indeed. For example, on a local kind cluster running on a laptop with a solid state drive, you may see something like this:

```
root@kind-control-plane:/#
   curl localhost:2381/metrics|grep fsync
 # TYPE etcd_disk_wal_fsync_duration_seconds histogram
etcd_disk_wal_fsync_duration_seconds_bucket{le="0.001"} 1239
etcd_disk_wal_fsync_duration_seconds_bucket{le="0.002"} 2365
etcd_disk_wal_fsync_duration_seconds_bucket{le="0.004"} 2575
etcd_disk_wal_fsync_duration_seconds_bucket{le="0.008"} 2587
etcd_disk_wal_fsync_duration_seconds_bucket{le="0.016"} 2588
etcd_disk_wal_fsync_duration_seconds_bucket{le="0.032"} 2588
etcd_disk_wal_fsync_duration_seconds_bucket{le="0.064"} 2588
etcd_disk_wal_fsync_duration_seconds_bucket{le="0.128"} 2588
etcd_disk_wal_fsync_duration_seconds_bucket{le="0.256"} 2588
etcd_disk_wal_fsync_duration_seconds_bucket{le="0.512"} 2588
etcd_disk_wal_fsync_duration_seconds_bucket{le="1.024"} 2588
etcd_disk_wal_fsync_duration_seconds_bucket{le="2.048"} 2588
etcd_disk_wal_fsync_duration_seconds_bucket{le="4.096"} 2588
etcd_disk_wal_fsync_duration_seconds_bucket{le="8.192"} 2588
etcd_disk_wal_fsync_duration_seconds_bucket{le="+Inf"} 2588
etcd_disk_wal_fsync_duration_seconds_sum 3.181597084000007
etcd_disk_wal_fsync_duration_seconds_count 2588
```

The buckets in this output tell us that

- 1,239 out of 2,588 writes to disk happened in .001 seconds.
- 2,587 out or 2,588 writes to disk happened within .008 seconds or less.
- One write happened within .016 seconds.
- No writes took more than .016 seconds.

You'll notice these buckets are exponentially graded because once your writes take longer than 1 second, it doesn't matter; your cluster is likely broken. That's because there can be hundreds of watches and events firing at any given time in Kubernetes in order to do their jobs, all of which are dependent on the speed of etcd's I/O.

12.3 *Looking at the interface for Kubernetes to etcd*

The Kubernetes data store interface gives us the concrete abstraction that Kubernetes itself uses to access an underlying data store. Of course, the only popular and well-tested implementation of a Kubernetes data store is etcd. The API server in Kubernetes abstracts etcd into a few core operations—Create, Delete, WatchList, Get, GetToList, and List—as the following code snippet shows:

```
type Interface interface {
        Create(ctx context.Context, key string, obj, out runtime.Object, ...
        Delete(ctx context.Context, key string,
           out runtime.Object, preconditions...
        Get(ctx context.Context, key string,
          resourceVersion string, objPtr runtime.Object,
        GetToList(ctx context.Context, key string,
          resourceVersion string, p SelectionPredicate, ...
        List(ctx context.Context, key string,
          resourceVersion string, p SelectionPredicate ...
...
```

Next, let's look at WatchList and Watch. These functions are part of what make etcd special, compared to other databases (although other databases like ZooKeeper and Redis also implement this API):

```
WatchList(ctx context.Context, key string, resourceVersion string ...
Watch(ctx context.Context, key string, resourceVersion string, ...
```

12.4 *etcd's job is to keep the facts straight*

Strict consistency is a key component of Kubernetes in production, as we can discern from this chapter. But how can multiple database nodes all have the same view of a system at any given time? The answer is, simply, they can't. The travel of information has speed limitations, and although its speed limit is fast, it is not infinitely fast. There is always a latency between when a write happens to one location and when that write is cascaded (or backed up) into another location.

Many a PhD thesis has been written on this subject, and we will not attempt to explain the theoretical limitations of consensus and strict writes in gory detail. What we will do, however, is to define a few concepts with specific Kubernetes motivations that ultimately depend on the ability of etcd to maintain a consistent view of a cluster. For example:

- You can only accept one new fact at a time, and these facts must flow to a single node running the control plane.
- The state of the system at any given time is the sum total of all current facts.
- The Kubernetes API server provides read and write operations that are always 100% correct with regard to the existing stream of facts.
- Because entities in any database might change over time, older versions of a record might be available, and etcd supports the notion of versioned entries.

This involves two stages: establishing leadership at a given time so that a fact that is being proposed into the stream of facts is accepted by all members in a system, and then writing that fact to those members. This is a (crude) rendition of what is known as the *Paxos consensus algorithm.*

Given that the preceding logic is quite complex, imagine a scenario where cluster leaders are continually trading off and starving one another. By "starving," we mean to say that a leader election scenario reduces uptime of etcd availability for writes. If elections continue to occur, then write throughput suffers. In Raft, rather than continually getting a leadership lock for every new transaction, we continually just send facts from a single leader. That leader can change over time, and a new leader is elected.

etcd ensures that the leader's unavailability does not result in an inconsistent state of the database, and, thus, writes are aborted if a leader dies during a transaction before the writes have cascaded to 50% of the etcd nodes in a cluster. This is described in figure 12.1, where our sequence diagram returns from a write request after the second node in the cluster has acknowledged a write. Note that the third etcd node can take its sweet time to update its own internal state at this point, without slowing down the overall database speed.

This is important to consider when we look at how etcd nodes are distributed, especially if these nodes are distributed across different networks. In that case, elections may be more frequent because you can lose leaders more often in data center to data center internetworking slowness. At any time, the majority of all databases in an etcd cluster will have an up-to-date log of all transactions.

12.4.1 *The etcd write-ahead log*

Because all transactions are written to a write-ahead log (WAL), etcd is durable. To understand the importance of the WAL, let's consider what happens when we undertake a write:

1. A client sends a request to an etcd server.
2. The etcd server relies on the Raft consensus protocol to write a transaction.
3. Raft ultimately confirms that all etcd nodes that are members of a Raft cluster have synchronized WAL files. Data is, thus, always consistent in an etcd cluster,

even though you may send writes to different etcd servers at different times. That's because all etcd nodes in a cluster ultimately have a single Raft consensus of the exact state of the system over time.

Yes, we actually can load balance an etcd client, even though etcd is strictly consistent. You may wonder how a client can send writes to many different servers without potentially having some inconsistency between these locations that are temporal. The reason for this is that, again, the Raft implementation in etcd ultimately manages to forward writes to the Raft leader, regardless of origin. A write is not completed until the leader is up-to-date and one-half of the other nodes in the cluster are also current.

12.4.2 Effect on Kubernetes

Because etcd implements Raft as its consensus algorithm, the consequence of this is that, at any time, we know exactly where all Kubernetes state information is saved. No state is modified in Kubernetes unless the master etcd node has accepted a write and cascades to a majority of other nodes in a cluster. The effect this has on Kubernetes is that when etcd goes down, the API server for Kubernetes is itself, essentially, also down when it comes to most of the important operations that it implements.

12.5 The CAP theorem

The CAP theorem is a seminal theory in computer science; you can read more about it at https://en.wikipedia.org/wiki/CAP_theorem. The fundamental conclusion of the CAP theorem is that you cannot have perfect consistency, availability, and partitionability in a database all at the same time. etcd chooses consistency as its most important feature. The consequence of this is that, if a single leader in an etcd cluster is down, then the database is not available until a new leader is elected.

Comparatively, there are databases such as Cassandra, Solr, and so on, that are much more available and well partitioned; however, they don't guarantee that all nodes in a database have a consistent view of data at a given time. In etcd, we always have a clear definition of what the exact state of the database is at any given time. Compared with ZooKeeper, Consul, and other similar consistent key/value stores, etcd's performance is extremely stable at large scales, with predictable latency being its "killer" feature:

- Consul is suited for service discovery and, in general, stores megabytes of data. At high scales, latency and performance are an issue.
- etcd is suited for reliable key/value storage with predictable latency because it can handle gigabytes of data.
- ZooKeeper can be used in ways similar to etcd, generally, with the caveat that its API is lower-level, it doesn't support versioned entries, and scale is a little harder to achieve.

The theoretical basis for these tradeoffs is referred to as the *CAP theorem*, which dictates that you must pick between data consistency, availability, and partitionability. For example, if we have a distributed database, we need to exchange transaction information. We can do this immediately and strictly, in which case, we will always have a consistent record of data, until we do not.

Why can't we always have a perfect record of data in a distributed system? Because machines can go down, and when they do, we need some amount of time before we can recover them. The fact that this time is nonzero means that databases with multiple nodes, which need to always be consistent with one another, can be unavailable at times. For example, transactions must be blocked until the other data stores are capable of consuming them.

What happens if we decide that we are OK with some databases not receiving transactions at times (for example, if a netsplit happens)? In that case, we may be sacrificing consistency. In short, we have to choose between two scenarios in a distributed system that runs in the real world, so that when networks are slow or machines are misbehaving, we either

- Stop receiving transactions (sacrifice availability)
- Keep receiving transactions (sacrifice consistency)

The reality of this choice (again, the CAP theorem) limits the ability of a distributed system to ever be "perfect." As an example, a relational database is known generally as consistent and partitionable. Meanwhile, a database like Solr or Cassandra is known as partitionable and available.

CoreOS (a company that was acquired by RedHat) designed etcd to manage large fleets of machines, creating a key/value store that could provide a consistent view of the desired state of the cluster to all nodes. Servers were then able to upgrade, if needed, by looking at the state of etcd itself. Thus, Kubernetes adopted etcd as a backend for the API server, which provided a strictly consistent key/value store where Kubernetes could store all of the desired states of the cluster. In the final section of this chapter, we will go through a few of the salient aspects around etcd in production, in particular, load balancing, keepalives, and size limitations.

12.6   *Load balancing at the client level and etcd*

As mentioned, a Kubernetes cluster consists of a control plane, and the API server needs to access etcd in order to respond to events from the various control plane components. In the previous requests, we used `curl` to acquire raw JSON data. Although convenient, a real etcd client needs to have access to all members in an etcd cluster so that it can load balance queries across nodes:

- The etcd client tries to grab all connections from all endpoints, and the first one to respond is kept open.
- etcd keeps a TCP connection to an endpoint that is selected from all endpoints given to an etcd client.
- In case of connection failures, failover to other endpoints can happen.

This is a common idiom in gRPC. It is based on the pattern of using HTTPS keep-alive requests.

12.6.1 *Size limitations: What (not) to worry about*

etcd itself has size limits and is not meant to be scaled up to terabytes and petabytes of key/value content. It's baseline use case is coordination and consistency of distributed systems (hint: /etc/ is the configuration directory for software on your Linux boxes). In a production Kubernetes cluster, an extremely rough but reliable starting point for memory and disk sizing is 10 KB per namespace. This would mean that a 1,000-namespace cluster would probably work reasonably well with 1 GB of RAM. However, because etcd uses a large amount of memory for managing watches, which are the dominating factor in its RAM requirements, this minimal estimate isn't useful. In a production Kubernetes cluster with thousands of nodes, you should consider running etcd with 64 GB of RAM to service the watches of all kubelets and other API server clients efficiently.

Individual key/value pairs for etcd are generally less than 1.5 MB (the request size of an operation should generally be below this). This is quite common in key/value stores because the ability to do defragmentation and optimization of storage depends on the fact that individual values can only take up a certain amount of fixed disk space. This value is configurable, however, by the `max-request-bytes` parameter.

Kubernetes doesn't explicitly prevent you from storing arbitrarily large objects (a ConfigMap with > 2 MB of data, for example), but depending on how you've configured etcd, this may or may not be possible. Keep in mind that this is especially important given that every member of an etcd cluster has a full copy of all data, so distributing data across shards for partitioning is not possible.

VALUE SIZES ARE LIMITED

Kubernetes is not designed to store infinitely large data types, and neither is etcd: both are designed to handle small key/value pairs typical for configuration and state metadata for distributed systems. Because of this design decision, etcd has certain well-intentioned limitations:

- Larger requests will work but may increase the latency of other requests.
- By default, the maximum size of any request is 1.5 MiB.
- This limit is configurable through the `--max-request-bytes` flag for the etcd server.
- The total size of the database is limited:
  - The default storage size limit is 2 GB, and it's recommended that most etcd database stay under 8 GB.
  - The default payload maximum for etcd is 1.5 MB. Because the amount of text describing a Pod is less than a kilobyte, unless you're creating a CRD or another object that is a thousand times larger than a normal Kubernetes YAML file, this shouldn't affect you.

We can derive from this the fact that Kubernetes itself is not meant to grow infinitely large in terms of its persistent footprint. This makes sense. After all, even in a 1,000-node cluster, if you ran 300 Pods per node and each Pod consumed 1 KB of text to store its configuration, you would still have well under a megabyte of data. Even if each Pod had 10 ConfigMaps of the same size associated with it, you would still be under 50 MB.

You generally do not have to worry about etcd's total size being a limiting factor in Kubernetes' performance. You do, however, need to concern yourself with the speed of watches and load-balanced queries, especially if you have a large turnover of applications. The reason is that service endpoints and internal routing requires global knowledge of Pod IP addresses, and if this becomes obsolete, your ability to route cluster traffic can be affected in production.

12.7   *etcd encryption at rest*

If you've gotten this far, you may now realize that etcd has a lot of information inside of it that, if compromised, could lead to an enterprise-scale disaster scenario. Indeed, secrets such as database passwords are idiomatically stored in Kubernetes, and ultimately, stored at rest in etcd.

Because the traffic between the API server and its various clients is known to be secure, the ability to steal a secret from a Pod, in general, is restricted to those who already have access to a `kubectl` client that is actively audited and logged (and, thus, easily traced). etcd itself, especially due to its single-node nature, is arguably the most valuable target for any hacker in a Kubernetes cluster. Let's look at how the Kubernetes API deals with the topic of encryption:

- The Kubernetes API server itself is *encryption-aware*; it accepts an argument describing what types of API objects should be encrypted (typically, at the least, this includes Secrets). The argument for this is `--encryption-provider-config`.
- The value of `--encryption-provider-config` is a YAML file with fields for an API object type (for example, Secrets) and a list of encryption providers. There are three of these: AES-GCM, AES-CBC, and Secret Box.
- The providers previously listed are tried in descending order for decryption, and the first item in the list of providers is used for encryption.

Thus, the Kubernetes API server itself is the most important tool for managing etcd security in a Kubernetes cluster. etcd is a tool in your larger Kubernetes story, and it's important not to think of it in the same way that you would a highly secured commercial database. Although in the future, encryption technology may evolve into etcd itself, for now, storing etcd data on an encrypted drive and encrypting directly on the client side is the best way to secure its data.

12.8 Performance and fault tolerance of etcd at a global scale

A *global deployment* of etcd refers to the idea that you may want to run etcd in a geo-replicated manner. Understanding the consequences that this might have requires revisiting how etcd writes work.

Recall that etcd itself cascades write consensus via the Raft protocol, meaning that over half of all etcd nodes need to accept a write before it is official. As mentioned, consensus in etcd is the most important attribute to conserve at any scale. By default, etcd is designed to support local rather than global deployments, which means that you have to tune etcd for global scale deployments. Thus, if you have etcd distributed over separate networks, you will have to tune several of its parameters so that

- Leader election is more forgiving
- Heartbeat intervals are less frequent

12.9 Heartbeat times for a highly distributed etcd

What should you do if you are running a single etcd cluster distributed across separate data centers? In this case, you need to change your expectations on write throughput, which will be much lower. Per etcd's own documentation, "A reasonable round-trip time for the continental United States is 130ms, and the time between US and Japan is around 350-400ms." (See https://etcd.io/docs/v3.4/tuning/ for details about this.)

Based on this timeframe, we should start etcd with longer heartbeat intervals, as well as longer leader election timeouts. When a heartbeat is too fast, you waste CPU cycles sending chatty maintenance data over the wire. When a heartbeat is too long, there is a higher likelihood that a new leader might need to be elected. An example of how to set etcd's election settings for a geo-distributed deployment follows:

```
$ etcd --heartbeat-interval=100 --election-timeout=500
```

12.10 Setting an etcd client up on a kind cluster

One of the trickier aspects of accessing etcd in a running Kubernetes environment is simply that of securely making queries. As a way to remedy this, the following YAML file (originally obtained from https://mauilion.dev) can be used to quickly create a Pod that we can use to execute etcd client commands. As an example, write the following to a file (call it cli.yaml) and make sure you have a kind cluster running (or any other Kubernetes cluster). You may have to modify the value of the hostPath depending on where your etcd security credentials are located:

```
apiVersion: v1
kind: Pod
metadata:
  labels:
    component: etcdclient
    tier: debug
  name: etcdclient
  namespace: kube-system
```

```
spec:
  containers:
  - command:
    - sleep
    - "6000"
    image: ubuntu
    name: etcdclient
    volumeMounts:
    - mountPath: /etc/kubernetes/pki/etcd
      name: etcd-certs
    env:
    - name: ETCDCTL_API
      value: "3"
    - name: ETCDCTL_CACERT
      value: /etc/kubernetes/pki/etcd/ca.crt
    - name: ETCDCTL_CERT
      value: /etc/kubernetes/pki/etcd/healthcheck-client.crt
    - name: ETCDCTL_KEY
      value: /etc/kubernetes/pki/etcd/healthcheck-client.key
    - name: ETCDCTL_ENDPOINTS
      value: "https://127.0.0.1:2379"
  hostNetwork: true
  volumes:
  - hostPath:
      path: /etc/kubernetes/pki/etcd
      type: DirectoryOrCreate
    name: etcd-certs
```

> **Replace this image name with an etcd service if you want to use etcdctl to query the API server instead of curl.**

Using a file like this in a live cluster is a quick and easy way to set up a container that can be used to query etcd. For example, you can run commands such as those in the following code snippet (after running `kubectl exec -t -i etcdclient -n kube-system /bin/sh` to open a bash terminal):

```
#/ curl --cacert /etc/kubernetes/pki/etcd/ca.crt \
--cert /etc/kubernetes/pki/etcd/peer.crt \
--key /etc/kubernetes/pki/etcd/peer.key https://127.0.0.1:2379/health
```

To return etcd's health status or to get various Prometheus metrics exported by etcd, run the following commands:

```
#/ curl
--cacert /etc/kubernetes/pki/etcd/ca.crt \
--cert /etc/kubernetes/pki/etcd/peer.crt \
--key /etc/kubernetes/pki/etcd/peer.key \
  https://127.0.0.1:2379/metrics
```

12.10.1 *Running etcd in non-Linux environments*

At the time of this writing, etcd can run on both macOS and Linux, but it isn't fully supported on Windows. For this reason, Kubernetes clusters that support multiple OSs (a Kubernetes cluster with Linux and Windows nodes) typically have a management cluster control plane that is entirely Linux-based, which runs etcd in a Pod. Additionally, the

API server, scheduler, and Kubernetes controller managers are only supported on Linux as well, even though they are also capable of running on macOS in a pinch. Thus, although Kubernetes is capable of supporting non-Linux OSs for workloads (mainly, this refers to the fact that you can run a Windows kubelet for running Windows containers), you'll likely still need a Linux OS in any Kubernetes deployment to run the API server, scheduler, and controller managers (as well as, of course, etcd).

Summary

- etcd is the configuration czar for almost all Kubernetes clusters running today.
- etcd is an open source database that is in the same family as ZooKeeper and Redis in terms of its overall usage patterns. It is not meant for large data sets or application data.
- The Kubernetes API abstracts the five major API calls that etcd supports, and most importantly, it includes the ability to watch individual items or lists.
- `etcdctl` is a powerful command-line tool for inspecting key/value pairs, as well as stress testing and diagnosing problems on a given node of a cluster.
- etcd has constraint defaults of 1.5 MB for transactions and, generally, less than 8 GB for most common scenarios.
- etcd, like the other control plane elements of a Kubernetes cluster, is really only supported on Linux and is, thus, one of the reasons that most Kubernetes clusters, even those that are slanted to run Windows workloads, include at least one Linux node.

13

Container and Pod security

This chapter covers

- Reviewing security basics
- Exploring best practices for container security
- Constraining Pods with a security context and resource limits

If we try to secure our computers in a secure building, locked in a guarded vault, inside a Faraday cage, with a biometric login, not connected to the internet . . . , add up all of these precautions, and they still aren't enough for our computers to be truly secure. As Kubernetes practitioners, we need to make reasonable security decisions based on our business needs. If we lock all of our Kubernetes clusters in a Faraday cage, unplugged from the internet, we make our clusters unusable. But if we do not focus on security, we allow people (like bitcoin miners, for example) to waltz in and invade our clusters.

As Kubernetes matures and is used more widely, common vulnerabilities and exposures (CVEs) in Kubernetes become a frequent occurrence. Here is a way to think about security: there is a risk that your system will get hacked! When you do get hacked, the questions to ask are

- What can they get?
- What can they do?
- What data can they get into?

Security is a series of tradeoffs that are often hard decisions. By using Kubernetes, we introduce a system that can scare people when they realize that it can often have the capability to create an internet-facing load balancer with one API call. But by utilizing simple and basic practices, we can reduce the impact of a security risk. Admittedly, most companies do not plan for the basics, such as performing security updates on containers.

Security is a balancing act; it can slow down businesses, but businesses thrive when they operate at full speed. Security is great, but going down the security rabbit hole can burn money and slow down businesses and organizations. We have to balance practical security measures that we can automate and make judgement calls when we start going down that rabbit hole.

You do not need to build all of the security precautions yourself. There is a growing set of tools that track containers running inside of Kubernetes and determine what possible security holes exist; for example, the Open Policy Agent (OPA), which we will cover in chapter 14. At the end of the day, however, a computer on the internet is simply *not* secure.

As we talked about in the first chapter of this book, DevOps is built on automation, as is Kubernetes. In this chapter, we'll discuss what you need to do to automate your Kubernetes security. To begin, the following sections walk through some security concepts so that we get into the proper mindset.

> **NOTE** Although the following two chapters could be an entire book, our intention is to make these chapters a practical handbook and not a definitive guide. When you understand the handbook, you can then learn more about each topic.

13.1 Blast radius

When something blows up, the blast radius is the distance from the center of the explosion to the edge of the explosion. Now, how the heck does this apply to computer security (compusec or cybersecurity)? When a computer system is compromised, there is an explosion, and usually in more ways than one. Suppose you have multiple containers running inside of multiple nodes with multiple security components. How far does the explosion go?

- Can a compromised Pod access another Pod?
- Can a compromised Pod be used to create another Pod?
- Can a compromised Pod be used to control a node?
- Can you jump from node01 to node02?
- Can you go from the Pod to an external database?
- Can you get into, say, an LDAP system?
- Can a hacker get into your source control or Secrets?

Think of a security intrusion as ground zero of a big explosion. How far that explosion or intrusion travels is the blast radius. By implementing easy security standards, however, such as not running a process as a root or using RBAC, we can limit the distance when stuff goes BOOM.

13.1.1 Vulnerabilities

A *vulnerability* is where something is weak. (There is a crack in the dam.) In terms of security, we are always trying to prevent the vulnerability (or crack in the dam) instead of patching it. The next two chapters are set up to cover the vulnerabilities of Kubernetes from the inside out, as well as how we can reinforce security.

13.1.2 Intrusion

An *intrusion* is what all of us do not want! It is a break-in, where an attacker exploits a vulnerability and gets into our system. For example, a bad actor (intruder) gets control of a Pod and has access to `curl` or `wget`. Then the intruder creates another Pod that runs as a root on the host network. You now have a fully compromised cluster.

13.2 Container security

The most obvious place to start with Kubernetes security is at the container level, because, after all, every Kubernetes cluster is pretty much guaranteed to run in a few containers. As much as you can secure a cluster, your front line is your container. It's wise to keep in mind that the custom software that runs inside a container is vulnerable to attacks.

When you run an application and open it to the world, people can be malicious. For example, one time we noticed that CPU levels for a node had gone nuts. A developer had deployed an application that had a known bug! Bitcoin miners utilized that Pod for mining, and it all happened within a few hours. Never forget that, as secure as you can make your container, if you are running a software application that has a critical issue, you leave yourself wide open to an attack. It takes a short amount of time, maybe minutes, for a hacker to find a cluster and seconds to put a bitcoin miner inside a container running software with a known CVE. With that in mind, let's outline some best practices for securing containers.

13.2.1 Plan to update containers and custom software

Updating is the number one thing that we consistently see companies *not* doing. Frankly, this is scary, scarier than the worst horror movie you have ever seen. Large companies leak data because they have not updated software dependencies or even overhauled the base image.

It's best to build the capacity for updates into your software pipelines early on, just in case a security vulnerability occurs. If you get pushback, you can gently remind the pushers about the bad publicity linked to companies who leak customer information. Also, a leak often costs companies millions of dollars.

Update your containers as new base container versions are released and when new CVEs come out. The CVE Program houses cybersecurity vulnerability notices that are created when those issues are found. You can review these issues at https://cve .mitre.org/. Also, plan to update custom software dependencies. You need to not only update the container around the software but also the software itself.

13.2.2 Container screening

Container screening is a system that reports if your containers have a vulnerability (as an example, think of when OpenSSL contained the Heartbleed bug back in 2014). A system that screens your images is not a nice to have, but a *must* in today's landscape. You really need to screen the software in your containers for vulnerabilities and update the image.

The software consists of what is installed, including OpenSSL and Bash. Not only must the software be updated, but the base images must also be defined with the FROM element. It is a lot of work. We personally know how much time and money this costs. Set up CI/CD and other tooling to quickly build, test, and deploy your containers. Many commercial container registries contain systems that screen your containers, but admittedly, if nobody is looking at those notifications, then they are ignored. Build a system to watch for those notifications, or get commercial software that can help with this.

13.2.3 Container users—do not run as root

Don't run as the root user inside a container. There is the notion of *popping a shell*, which means that you escape the container's Linux namespace and have access to a command-line shell. From the shell, you can access the API server and possibly the node. If you have access to a shell, you may have the permissions to download a script from the internet and run it. Running as the root user gives you the same root permission on the container and maybe root on the host system if you pop the container.

You can define a new user when you define a container and create a specific user and group with `adduser`. Then run your application as that user. The following is an example from a Debian container that creates a user:

```
$ adduser --disabled-password --no-create-home --gecos '' \
--disabled-login my-app-user
```

Now, you can run your application using that user:

```
$ su my-app-user -c my-application
```

Running as the root user within a container has many of the same consequences as operating as the root user on the host system: root is root. Also, in a Pod manifest, you are able to define the `runAsUser` and `fsGroup`. We will cover both later.

13.2.4 *Use the smallest container*

It is a good idea to use a lightweight container OS that is built to run only as a container. This limits the number of binaries in a container, and thus, limits your vulnerabilities. Projects like Google's distroless provide lightweight container options that are language-specific.

> *Restricting what's in your runtime container to precisely what's necessary for your app is a best practice employed by Google and other tech giants that have used containers in production for many years. It improves the signal to noise of scanners (e.g., CVE) and reduces the burden of establishing provenance to just what you need.*
>
> —Open Web Application Foundation's Security Cheat Sheet
> (http://mng.bz/g42v)

Google's distroless project includes a base layer, as well as containers for running different programming languages, like Java. The following shows an example of a Go application using the golang container to build our software, followed by a distroless container:

```
# Start by building the application.
FROM golang:1.17 as build

WORKDIR /go/src/app
COPY . .

RUN go get -d -v ./...
RUN go install -v ./...

# Now copy it into our base image.
FROM gcr.io/distroless/base
COPY --from=build /go/bin/app /
CMD ["/app"]
```

And then there is extra software. Say that you install cURL to download a binary during the creation process of a container. cURL then needs to be removed. The Alpine distribution handles this elegantly by removing components used in the build automatically, but Debian and others do not. If your application does not need it, don't install it. The more you have installed, the greater your number of possible vulnerabilities. Even the example missed creating a new user to run the binary. Only run as root if you have to.

13.2.5 *Container provenance*

One of the key security concerns for running Kubernetes clusters is knowing what container images are running inside each Pod and being able to account for their origins. Establishing *container provenance* means having the ability to trace the source of a container to a trusted point of origin and ensuring your organization follows the desired processes during artifact (container) creation.

Do not deploy a container from a container registry that your company does not control. Open source projects are amazing, but build and push those containers into your repository after you construct them locally. Container tags are not immutable; only the SHAs are. There is zero guarantee that the container is actually the container that you think it is. Container provenance allows for a user or a Kubernetes cluster to ensure that a deployed container can be identified, thus guaranteeing the source.

The Kubernetes team builds an image base layer for all of the containers that run inside a Kubernetes cluster. Doing this allows the team to know that the image has a safe origin, is consistent and validated, and has a specific provenance. A safe origin also means that all images come from a known source. Consistency and validation ensure that specific steps are completed when we build an image and provide a more hermetic environment. Lastly, provenance guarantees that the container's source is known and that it does not change before running.

13.2.6 Linters for containers

Automation is key to reducing workload and improving systems. Security is a lot of work, let's be honest, but you can run a linter like hadolint to find common problems with containers and custom software that can cause security vulnerabilities. The following is a short list of linters that we have used in the past:

- hadolint for Dockerfiles (https://github.com/hadolint/hadolint)
- The `go vet` command (https://golang.org/cmd/vet/)
- Flake8 for Python (http://flake8.pycqa.org/en/latest/)
- ShellCheck for Bash (https://www.shellcheck.net/)

Now that you have your container security under control, let's look at the next level—the Pod.

13.3 Pod security

Kubernetes allows us to define the permissions for a user in a Pod and for a Pod outside of the Linux namespace (for instance, can a Pod mount a volume on a node?). Compromising a Pod can compromise a cluster! Commands such as `nsenter` can be used to enter a root process (/proc/1), create a shell, and act the same as a root on the actual node that runs the compromised Pod. The Kubernetes API allows for defining a Pod permissions and further secures the Pod, nodes, and overall cluster.

> **NOTE** Some Kubernetes distributions, such as OpenShift, add far more security layers, and you may need to add more configurations to use API configurations such as a security context.

13.3.1 Security context

Remember how we mentioned you should not run a container using the root user? Kubernetes also allows a user to define a user ID for a Pod. In the Pod definition, you are able to specify three IDs:

- runAsUser—The user ID used to start the process
- runAsGroup—The group used for the process user
- fsGroup—A second group ID used to mount any volumes and all files created by the Pod's processes

If you have a container that runs as the root, you can force it to run as a different user ID. But, again, you should not have a container that runs as root because you can allow the user to accidentally miss the securityContext definition. The following YAML snippet contains a Pod with a security context:

```
apiVersion: v1
kind: Pod
metadata:
  name: sc-Pod
spec:
  securityContext:
    runAsUser: 3042
    runAsGroup: 4042
    fsGroup: 5042
    fsGroupChangePolicy: "OnRootMismatch"
  volumes:
  - name: sc-vol
    emptyDir: {}
  containers:
  - name: sc-container
    image: my-container
    volumeMounts:
    - name: sc-vol
      mountPath: /data/foo
```

When the Pod starts, NGINX runs with user ID 3042.

The user ID 3042 belongs to group 4042.

If the NGINX process writes any files, they are written with the group ID of 5042.

Changes the ownership of the volume before mounting the volume to the Pod

A mount point

Let's walk through this using a kind cluster. First, start your cluster:

```
$ kind create cluster
```

Next, create a NGINX deployment using the default container:

```
$ kubectl run nginx --image=nginx
```

You now have a running NGINX Pod. Next, exec into the Docker container that runs the kind cluster:

```
$ docker exec -it a62afaadc010 /bin/bash
root@kind-control-plane:/# ps a | grep nginx
2475  0:00 nginx: master process
⇒ nginx -g daemon off;
2512  22:36   0:00 nginx: worker process
```

The process for NGINX is started as root.

We can see that the NGINX process is running as root, and, yes, that is not the most secure. To prevent this, clean house and launch the other Pod. The next command removes the NGINX Pod:

```
$ kubectl delete po nginx
```

Now, create the Pod with the security context using the following command:

```
$ cat <<EOF | kubectl apply -f -
apiVersion: v1
kind: Pod
metadata:
  name: sc-Pod
spec:
  securityContext:
    runAsUser: 3042
    runAsGroup: 4042
    fsGroup: 5042
  volumes:
  - name: sc-vol
    emptyDir: {}
  containers:
  - name: sc-container
    image: nginx
    volumeMounts:
    - name: sc-vol
      mountPath: /usr/share/nginx/html/
EOF
```

And guess what happens? The Pod fails to start. Take a look at the logs:

```
$ kubectl logs sc-Pod
```

This command outputs

```
/docker-entrypoint.sh: /docker-entrypoint.d/ is not empty, will attempt to
➥ perform configuration
/docker-entrypoint.sh: Looking for shell scripts in /docker-entrypoint.d/
/docker-entrypoint.sh: Launching /docker-entrypoint.d/
➥ 10-listen-on-ipv6-by-default.sh
10-listen-on-ipv6-by-default.sh: error: can not modify /etc/nginx/conf.d/
➥ default.conf (read-only file system?)
/docker-entrypoint.sh: Launching /docker-entrypoint.d/
➥ 20-envsubst-on-templates.sh
/docker-entrypoint.sh: Configuration complete; ready for start up
2020/11/08 22:44:59 [warn] 1#1: the "user" directive makes sense only if
➥ the master process runs with super-user privileges, ignored
➥ in /etc/nginx/nginx.conf:2
nginx: [warn] the "user" directive makes sense only if the master process
➥ runs with super-user privileges, ignored in
➥ /etc/nginx/nginx.conf:2
2020/11/08 22:44:59 [emerg] 1#1: mkdir() "/var/cache/nginx/client_temp"
➥ failed (13: Permission denied)
nginx: [emerg] mkdir() "/var/cache/nginx/client_temp" failed
➥ (13: Permission denied)
```

What is the problem here? Why did this not work? The problem is that NGINX needs specific configurations in order to run as a non-root user, and many applications require configurations to run as the root. For this specific case, take a look at http://mng.bz/ra4Z or http://mng.bz/Vl4O for more information.

The take away is this: don't run your containers as root, and use a security context to ensure that they are not running as root.

> **TIP** SSL certificates are a pain, and the code that uses those certificates can be just as difficult. You can often run into a problem with code that checks that a certificate's user matches the process ID user. This creates havoc when you mount a TLS certificate as a Secret, which does not use the fsGroup. A current limitation in Kubernetes is when a mounted Secret does not match the fsGroup.

13.3.2 *Escalated permissions and capabilities*

Within the Linux security model, traditional UNIX permissions fall into two categories that describe a process—privileged and unprivileged:

- A *privileged user* is a root or one whose effective user ID is zero because we can use sudo to act as the root.
- An *unprivileged user* is a user whose ID is not zero.

When you are a privileged user, the Linux kernel bypasses all Linux permission checks. That is why you can run the dreaded command rm -rf / as root. Most distros now at least ask if you want to delete the entire filesystem. When you have unprivileged access, all security permission checking is, in effect, based on the process's ID.

When defining an unprivileged user and giving them an ID, you are able to provide the user with *capabilities*. These capabilities give an unprivileged user permission to do certain things, like making changes to file UIDs and GIDs. All of these capability names are prefixed with CAP; the capability that we just mentioned is CAP_CHOWN. That is great in Linux, but why do we care?

Remember that we said not to run as root? Say we have a Pod that says that it needs to make a node networking iptables change or manage BPF (Berkley Packet Filter), such as a CNI provider, and we do not want to run that Pod as root. Kubernetes allows you to set the Pod's security context, define the user ID, and then add specific capabilities. Here is an example of the YAML:

```
apiVersion: v1
kind: Pod
metadata:
  name: net-cap
spec:
  containers:
  - name: net-cap
    image: busybox
    securityContext:
      runAsUser: 3042
      runAsGroup: 4042
      fsGroup: 5042
      capabilities:
        add: ["NET_ADMIN", "BPF"]        ◁─── Gives the user CAP_NET_ADMIN
                                              and CAT_BPF capabilities
```

One thing you will notice is that we removed the CAP prefix. Instead of CAP_NET_ADMIN, we have NET_ADMIN. We can do a lot of fun things using CAP permissions, including allowing a Pod to reboot a node with CAP_SYS_BOOT. Also, inside of CAP permission exists a subset that is called CAP_SYS. These are very powerful permissions. For instance, CAP_SYS_ADMIN basically sets root permissions.

We have DaemonSets, Pods, and Deployments that administer our Kubernetes cluster, set iptables rules, bootstrap Kubernetes components, and so forth. There are so many use cases. Again, when you can, don't run as root, but give the process the fewest permissions as possible via a CAP privilege. Admittedly, this is not as fine-grain as we might like. For instance, there is no one permission to mount a filesystem. In that case, you should use CAP_SYS_ADMIN.

13.3.3 Pod Security Policies (PSPs)

> **NOTE** As of Kubernetes v1.21, PSPs are deprecated and are scheduled for removal in the v1.25 release, and they are being replaced by Pod Security Admission (see http://mng.bz/5QQ4). We are including this section because many people have used PSPs previously, and at the time of writing this book, Pod Security Standards are just in Beta.

In order to enforce the creation of proper Pod security contexts, you can define a Pod Security Policy (PSP) that enforces a defined security context setup. Like all other Kubernetes constructs, the PodSecurityPolicy is an API object:

```
apiVersion: policy/v1beta1
kind: PodSecurityPolicy
metadata:
  name: example
spec:
  privileged: false  # Don't allow privileged Pods!
  # The rest fills in some required fields.
  seLinux:
    rule: RunAsAny
  supplementalGroups:
    rule: RunAsAny
  runAsUser:
    rule: RunAsAny
  fsGroup:
    rule: RunAsAny
  volumes:
  - '*'
```

This code snippet sets a variety of arbitrary rules around SELinux, users, and so on. Note that you can't simply make every container secure. If you look at hyperkube, networking, storage plugins, and so on, you'll see that these are system-level administrative infrastructure tools, which perform privileged actions (for example, setting iptables rules), that cannot simply be run in an unprivileged manner. Now, as we enable PSPs, you'll find that many Pods may fail, and this can happen at unpredictable times. This is because PSPs are implemented at admission time by admission controllers. Let's take a look at the life cycle of a security audit for containers in a Kubernetes cluster:

- Day0—Pods can do anything, include running as root and making files on hosts.
- Day1—Developers build containers based on day0 functionality.
- Day2—Security auditors get a hold of this book.
- Day3—RBAC is added to clusters. Now API calls are restricted to administrative accounts.
- Day4—PSPs get added to your cluster.
- Day5—Half of your nodes go down for maintenance.
- Day6—Several Pods are not healthily restarted.

The reason that Day 6 takes a while after the PSP addition is because once a Pod dies, its PSP is going to be tested in production. Thinking back to the way containers work, a running container already has a PID, has run any commands it needs, and is associated with a host network device. Thus, changing policies when containers are running does not securely eliminate threat vectors, but rather, prevents them from being introduced in new places. Figure 9.1 shows the PSP process for Kubernetes.

This is an important concept to take with you throughout the rest of this chapter. Every policy you implement might not be undoing the sins of the past. Exposed IP

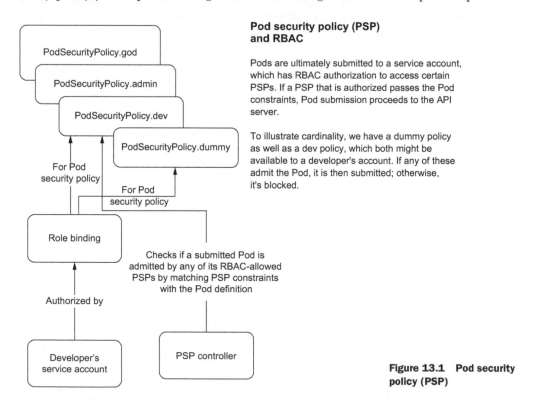

Pod security policy (PSP) and RBAC

Pods are ultimately submitted to a service account, which has RBAC authorization to access certain PSPs. If a PSP that is authorized passes the Pod constraints, Pod submission proceeds to the API server.

To illustrate cardinality, we have a dummy policy as well as a dev policy, which both might be available to a developer's account. If any of these admit the Pod, it is then submitted; otherwise, it's blocked.

Figure 13.1   Pod security policy (PSP)

addresses, compromised SSL certificates, and open NFS mounts are still just as relevant in your Kubernetes data center as they were in your vSphere data center, and the rules of security don't significantly get easier to implement because you've containerized your applications.

13.3.4 Do not automount the service account token

By default, a service account token is automounted to a Pod. That token is used to authenticate with the API server in the Pod's cluster. Yes, this is *bad!* Bad enough that one of the authors has personally used profanity to describe his disdain.

Why does this API token exist? Sometimes Pods need to access the API server; for instance, an Operator that maintains a database may need to. That is a valid use case. But in reality, 99.999% of the Pods that run custom software do not need access to the API server. Therefore, you should disable the automounting of the default service account token. It is as simple as adding one line to a Pod YAML definition:

```
apiVersion: v1
kind: Pod
metadata:
  name: no-sa
spec:
  automountServiceAccountToken: false    <——— Disables automount
```

Another way to address this is to turn off the default service account automount for all Pods. A service account (which we will talk about more later) also has the field `automountServiceAccountToken`. You can set any service account to not mount by default in that field.

13.3.5 Root-like Pods

With all the configurations that we have covered, it becomes like a balancing act between a Pod and a privileged user, an unprivileged user, or a unprivileged user with certain capabilities. But why is this? Why do we not just run all of our Pods as unprivileged users? Because many Kubernetes components need to act as a system administrator.

Many Kubernetes components act as root, and these Pods mostly fall under the category of networking. The kubelet runs as root, but rarely runs inside a Pod. In every node, we have CNI Pods that configure the networking for a cluster, and those Pods need networking capability privileges. Although we cannot get around some security exposures, you can reduce your risk with Pods that are root-like, including Operators:

- Limit access to those Pods by putting them into a `kube-system` or other namespaces.
- Give them the least root-like permissions possible.
- Monitor them.

13.3.6 *The security outskirts*

Kubernetes supports three other levels of Pod security that utilize Linux kernel functionality via modules or other built-in kernel features. These include

- *AppArmor*—Profiles that run under a Linux kernel module provide process-level control.
- *seccomp*—Using functionality contained within the Linux kernel, secures a process so that it only can make defined security calls, or the process is SIGKILLed.
- *SELinux*—Security-Enhanced Linux, another Linux kernel module, provides security policies that include mandatory access controls.

We are going to briefly mention these features, but won't go into them in detail.

If you are a RHEL shop, then running SELinux is understandable, but admittedly still hurts one author's head. If you are running a popular open source database or software component that has a maintained AppArmor profile, then it may make sense to use the profile. seccomp is incredibly powerful, but it takes a lot of work to maintain. Admittedly, both AppArmor profiles and seccomp are complex, and complexity often creates brittle security.

There are always use cases that require another level of process security, but as with most things, we try to follow a few guidelines, mainly: KISS (Keep it simple, stupid), the law of diminishing returns, and the 80/20 rule (before you start implementing one of these measures, get 80% of the security done).

Summary

- If we do not have a focus on security, we allow people to waltz in and invade our clusters. Security is a series of tradeoffs that are often fraught with hard decisions, but by utilizing simple and basic practices, we can reduce the impact of a security risk.
- You do not need to implement all of the security precautions yourself. There is a growing set of tools that track containers and determine what possible security holes exist.
- The most obvious place to start with Kubernetes security is at the container level. Container provenance allows you to trace the source of a container to a trusted point of origin.
- Don't run your containers as root, especially if your environment uses containers that are *not* built by your organization.
- To find common problems with containers that can cause security vulnerabilities, run a linter like hadolint.
- If your application does not need it, don't install extra software. The more you have installed, the greater your number of possible vulnerabilities.
- To secure individual Pods, you should disable the automounting of the default service account token. Alternatively, you can turn off the default service account automount for all Pods.

- Give a process the fewest permissions possible via a `CAP` privilege.
- DevOps is built on automation, as is Kubernetes, and security automation is key to reducing workload and improving systems.
- Update your containers and software dependencies.

14

Nodes and
Kubernetes security

> **This chapter covers**
> - Node hardening and Pod manifest
> - API server security, including RBAC
> - User authentications and authorization
> - The Open Policy Agent (OPA)
> - Multi-tenancy in Kubernetes

We just wrapped up securing the Pod in the previous chapter; now we'll cover securing the Kubernetes node. In this chapter, we'll include more information about node security as it relates to possible attacks on nodes and Pods, and we'll provide full examples with a number of configurations.

14.1 Node security

Securing a node in Kubernetes is analogous to securing any other VM or data center server. We'll cover Transport Layer Security (TLS) certificates to start. These certificates allow for securing nodes, but we'll also look at issues related to image immutability, workloads, network policies, and so on. Treat this chapter as an à la carte menu of important security topics that you should at least consider for running Kubernetes in production.

14.1.1 *TLS certificates*

All external communications in Kubernetes generally occur over TLS, although this can be configured. However, there are many flavors of TLS. For this reason, you can select a cipher suite for the Kubernetes API server to use. Most installers or self-hosted versions of Kubernetes will handle the creation of the TLS certificates for you. *Cipher suites* are collections of algorithms that, in aggregate, allow for TLS to happen securely. Defining a TLS algorithm consists of

- *Key exchanges*—Sets up an agreed upon way to exchange keys for encryption/ decryption
- *Authentication*—Confirms the identity of the sender of a message
- *Encryption*—Disguises messages so outsiders can't read them
- *Message authentication*—Confirms that messages are coming from a valid source

In Kubernetes, you might find the following cipher-suite: `TLS_ECDHE_ECDSA_WITH _AES_256_CBC_SHA384`. Let's break that down. Each underscore (_) in this string separates one algorithm from the next. For example, if we set `--tls-cipher-suites` in the API server to be something like

```
TLS_ECDHE_ECDSA_WITH_AES_128_GCM_SHA256
```

we can look this specific protocol up at http://mng.bz/nYZ8 and then determine how the communication protocol works. For example:

- *Protocol*—Transport Layer Security (TLS)
- *Key exchange*—Elliptic Curve Diffie-Hellman Ephemeral (ECDHE)
- *Authentication*—Elliptic Curve Digital Signature Algorithm (ECDSA)
- *Encryption*—Advanced Encryption Standard with 256-bit key in cipher block chaining mode (AES 256 CBC)

The specifics of these protocols are beyond the scope of this book, but it is important to note that you need to monitor your TLS security posture, especially if it is set by a larger standards body in your organization, to confirm that your security model in Kubernetes aligns with the TLS standards for your organization. For example, to update the cipher suites used by any Kubernetes service, send it the `tls-cipher-suites` argument on startup:

```
--tls-cipher-suites=TLS_ECDHE_ECDSA_WITH_AES_128_CBC_SHA,
⇨ TLS_ECDHE_ECDSA_WITH_AES_128_CBC_SHA256
```

Adding this to your API server ensures that it only connects to other services using this cipher suite. As shown, you can support multiple cipher suites by adding a comma to separate the values. A comprehensive list of suites is available in the help page for any service (for example, http://mng.bz/voZq shows the help for the Kubernetes scheduler, `kube-scheduler`). It's also important to note that

- If a TLS cipher is exposed as having a vulnerability, you'll want to update the cipher suites in the Kubernetes API server, scheduler, controller manager, and kubelet. Each of these components serves content over TLS in one way or another.
- If your organization doesn't allow certain cipher suites, you should explicitly delist these.

NOTE   If you oversimplify the cipher suites that you allow into your API server, you might risk certain types of clients not being able to connect to it. As an example of this, Amazon ELBs are known to sometimes use HTTPS health checks to ensure that an endpoint is up before forwarding traffic to it, but they don't support some common TLS ciphers used in the Kubernetes API server. Version 1 of the AWS load balancer API only supports non-elliptic cipher algorithms, such as `TLS_ECDHE_ECDSA_WITH_AES_128_GCM_SHA256`. The result here can be crippling; your entire cluster will not work at all! Because it's common to put several API servers behind a single ELB, keep in mind that a TCP health check (rather than HTTPS) might be easier to manage over time, especially if you require special security ciphers on your API servers.

14.1.2   *Immutable OSs vs. patching nodes*

Immutability is something that you cannot change. An *immutable* OS consists of components and binaries that are read-only, and ones that you cannot patch. Instead of patching and updating software, you can replace the entire OS by wiping the OS from the server or the cloud and then deleting the VM and creating a new one. Kubernetes has simplified the running of immutable OSs by allowing an administrator to more easily move workloads off a node (because it is a built-in feature).

Instead of having a system that automatically applies patches with your distribution's package manager, use an immutable OS. Having a Kubernetes cluster removes the notion of customized *snowflake servers*. These are servers that run specific applications and replace those with a node that is standardized, but running an immutable OS as the next logical step. One of the easiest ways to inject a vulnerability into a mutable system is to replace a common Linux library.

Immutable OSs are read-only, and because they are read-only, it becomes impossible to make specific changes, because you cannot write those changes to disk, and reduces our exposure. Using a distribution that is immutable removes a multitude of these opportunities. In general, a Kubernetes control plane (the API server, controller manager, and scheduler) node will have

- A kubelet binary
- The `kube-proxy` binary
- A containerd or other container runtime executable
- An image for etcd

All of these are baked in for rapid bootstrapping startup. Meanwhile, a Kubernetes worker node will have the same components, with the exception of etcd. This is an important distinction because etcd doesn't run in a supported manner on a Windows environment, but some users will want to run Windows worker nodes to run Windows Pods.

Building custom images for Windows workers is extremely important because the Windows OS is not redistributable, so end users must build Windows kubelet images if they want to use an immutable deployment model. To learn more about immutable images, you can evaluate the Tanzu Community Edition project (https://tanzu .vmware.com/tanzu/community). It aims to provide the broader community with a "batteries-included" approach to using immutable images along with the Cluster API to bring up usable, production grade clusters. Many other hosted Kubernetes services, including Googles GKE, also use immutable operating systems.

14.1.3 *Isolated container runtimes*

Containers are amazing, but they do fall short of completely isolating the process from the OS. Docker Engine (and other container engines) does not fully sandbox a running container from the Linux kernel. There is not a strong security boundary between the container and the host, so if the host's kernel has an exploit, the container can probably access the Linux kernel exploit and take advantage of that. Docker Engine utilizes Linux namespaces to separate processes from things like direct access to the Linux networking stack, but there are still holes. For instance, the hosts /sys and /proc filesystems are still read by a process running inside a container.

Projects like gVisor, IBM Nabla, Amazon Firecracker, and Kata provide a virtual Linux kernel that isolates a container's process from the host's kernel, thus providing a truer sandbox. These projects are still relatively new, at least in an open source sense, and are not yet predominantly used in a Kubernetes environment. These are just a few of the projects that are quite mature because gVisor is used as part of Google Cloud Platform, and Firecracker is used as part of the Amazon Web Services platform. Perhaps by the time you read this, more Kubernetes clusters containers will run on top of a virtual kernel! We can even think about spinning up micro VMs as Pods. These are fun times that we live in!

14.1.4 *Resource attacks*

A Kubernetes node has a finite amount of resources that include CPU, memory, and disk. We have a number of Pods, a `kube-proxy`, kubelets, and other Linux processes running on the cluster. The node typically has a CNI provider, a logging daemon, and other processes supporting the cluster. You need to ensure that the container(s) in the Pods do not overwhelm the node resource usage. If you do not provide restraints, then a container can overwhelm a node and impact all of the other systems. In essence, a *runaway container process* can perform a Denial of Service (DoS) attack on a node. Enter the resource limits. . . .

Resource limits are controlled by implementing three different API-level objects and configurations. Pod API objects can have settings that control each of the limits. For instance, the following YAML stanza provides CPU, memory, and disk space usage limits:

```
apiVersion: v1
kind: Pod
metadata:
  name: core-kube-limited
spec:
  containers:
  - name: app
    image:
      resources:          Provisions the initial amount
        requests:    ◁──┘ of CPU, memory, or storage
         memory: "42Mi"
          cpu: "42m"
          ephemeral-storage: "21Gi"   Sets the maximum amount of CPU,
        limits:    ◁───────────────── memory, and storage allowed
         memory: "128Mi"
          cpu: "84m"
          ephemeral-storage: "42Gi"
```

In terms of security, if any of these values are surpassed, the Pod is restarted. And, if the limits are passed again, then the Pod is terminated and not started again.

Another interesting thing is that resource `requests` and `limits` also impact the scheduling of a Pod on a node. The node that hosts a Pod must have the resources available for the initial requests for the scheduler to pick the node that hosts the Pod. You may notice that we are using units to represent requests and limit memory, CPU, and ephemeral storage values.

14.1.5 *CPU units*

To measure a CPU, the base unit that Kubernetes uses is 1, which equates to one hyperthread on bare metal or one core/vCPU in the cloud. You are also allowed to express a CPU unit in a decimal; for example, you can have 0.25 CPU units. Moreover, the API also allows you to convert 0.25 decimal CPU units to read as 250 m. All of these stanzas are allowed for the CPU:

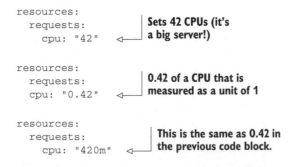

```
resources:           Sets 42 CPUs (it's
  requests:      ┌── a big server!)
    cpu: "42"  ◁──┘

resources:           0.42 of a CPU that is
  requests:      ┌── measured as a unit of 1
    cpu: "0.42"◁──┘

resources:           This is the same as 0.42 in
  requests:      ┌── the previous code block.
    cpu: "420m"◁──┘
```

14.1.6 *Memory units*

Memory is measured in bytes, in integers, and in fixed-point numbers using these suffixes: *E, P, T, G, M,* or *K.* Or you can use *Ei, Pi, Ti, Gi, Mi,* or *Ki,* which represent the power-of-two equivalents. The following stanzas are roughly all the same values:

```
resources:
  requests:
    memory: "128974848"
```
Byte plain number representations (128,974,848 bytes)

```
resources:
  requests:
    memory: "129e6"
```
129e6 is sometimes written as 129e+6 in scientific notation: 129e+6 == 129000000. This stanza represents 129,000,000 bytes.

The next stanzas deal with the typical megabits versus megabytes conversions:

```
resources:
  requests:
    memory: "129M"
```
129 megabits == 1.613e+7 bytes, which is close to the 129e+6 value.

Next, megabytes:

```
resources:
  requests:
    memory: "123Mi"
```
123 megabytes == 1.613e+7 bytes, which is close to the 129e+6 value.

14.1.7 *Storage units*

The newest API configuration is ephemeral storage requests and limits. Ephemeral storage limits apply to three storage components:

- emptyDir volumes, except tmpfs
- Directories holding node-level logs
- Writeable container layers

When a limit is surpassed, the kubelet evicts the Pod. Each node is configured with a maximum amount of ephemeral storage, which again impacts the schedule of Pods to a node. There is yet another limit where a user can specify specific node limits called *extended resources.* You can find more details about extended resources in the Kubernetes documentation.

14.1.8 *Host networks vs. Pod networks*

In section 14.4, we will cover NetworkPolicies. These give you the ability to lock down Pod communication using a CNI provider that, typically, implements these policies for you. There's a much more fundamental type of network security you should consider, however: not running a Pod on the same network as your hosts. This instantly

- Limits the access of the outside world to your Pod
- Limits the access of your Pod to the host's network ports

Having a Pod join the host network allows the Pod to have easier access to the node and, thus, increases the blast radius upon an attack. If a Pod does not have to run on the host network, do not run the Pod on the host network! Should a Pod need to run on the host network, then do not expose that Pod to the internet. The following code snippet is a partial YAML definition of a Pod that runs on the host network. You will often see Pods running on the host network if the Pod is performing administrative tasks, such as logging or networking (a CNI provider):

```
apiVersion: v1
kind: Pod
metadata:
  name: host-Pod
spec:
  hostNetwork: true
```

14.1.9 Pod example

We have covered different Pod API configurations: service account tokens, CPU, and other resource settings, security context, and so forth. Here is an example that contains all the configurations:

```
apiVersion: v1
kind: Pod
metadata:
  name: example-Pod
spec:
  automountServiceAccountToken: false       ←┘ Disables automount for the
                                               service account token
 securityContext:          ←─┐
   runAsUser: 3042            │  Sets the security context
    runAsGroup: 4042          │  and gives a capability of
    fsGroup: 5042             │  NET_ADMIN
    capabilities:
      add: ["NET_ADMIN"]
  hostNetwork: true       ←───── Runs on the host network
  volumes:
  - name: sc-vol
     emptyDir: {}
  containers:
  - name: sc-container
    image: my-container
    resources:            ←───── Sets resource limits
     requests:
        memory: "42Mi"
        cpu: "42m"
        ephemeral-storage: "1Gi"
      limits:
        memory: "128Mi"
        cpu: "84m"
        ephemeral-storage: "2Gi"
    volumeMounts:
    - name: sc-vol
      mountPath: /data/foo         ←┐ Gives the Pod a specific
  serviceAccountName: network-sa    │ service account
```

14.2　API server security

Components like binary authentication use webhooks provided by the admission controller. Various controllers are part of the Kubernetes API server and create a webhook as an entry point for events. For instance, ImagePolicyWebhook is one of the plugins that allows for the system to respond to the webhook and make admission decisions about containers. If a Pod does not pass the admission standards, it holds it in a pending state—it is not deployed to the cluster. Admission controllers can validate the API objects being created in the cluster, mutate or change those objects, or do both. From a security standpoint, this provides an immense amount of control and auditing capabilities for a cluster.

14.2.1　Role-based access control (RBAC)

First and foremost, role-based access control (RBAC) needs to be enabled on your cluster. Currently, RBAC is enabled by most installers and cloud-hosted providers. The Kubernetes API server uses the `--authorization-mode=RBAC` flag to enable RBAC. If you are using a self-hosted version of Kubernetes, such as GKE, RBAC is enabled. The authors are certain there is an edge case where running RBAC does not meet business needs. However, the other 99% of the time, you need to enable RBAC.

RBAC is a role-based security mechanism that controls user and system access to resources. It restricts access to resources to only authorized users and service accounts via roles and privileges. How does that apply to Kubernetes? One of the most critical components that you want to secure with Kubernetes is the API server. When a system user has administrator access to the cluster via the API server, that user can drain nodes, delete objects, and otherwise cause a great level of disruption. Administrators in Kubernetes are root users in the context of the cluster.

RBAC is a powerful security component that provides great flexibility in how you restrict API access within a cluster. Because it is a powerful mechanism, it also has the usual side effect of being quite complex and challenging to debug at times.

> **NOTE**　An average Pod running in Kubernetes should not have access to the API server, so you should disable the mounting of the service account token.

14.2.2　RBAC API definition

The RBAC API defines the following types:

- *Role*—Contains a set of permissions, limited to a namespace
- *ClusterRole*—Contains a set of permissions that are cluster-wide
- *RoleBinding*—Grants a role to a user or a group
- *ClusterRole*—Grants a ClusterRole to a user or a group

Within the Role and ClusterRole definitions, there are several defined components. The first that we will cover is *verbs*, which include API and HTTP verbs. Objects within the API server can have a get request; hence, the get request verb definition. We often think about this in terms of the create, read, update, and delete (CRUD) verbs defined in the creation of REST services. Verbs you can use include

- *API request verbs for resource requests*—get, list, create, update, patch, watch, proxy, redirect, delete, and deletecollection
- *HTTP request verbs for non-resource requests*—get, post, put, and delete

For instance, if you want an operator to be able to watch and update Pods, you can

1 Define the resource (in this case, a Pod)
2 Define the verbs that the Role has access to (most likely list and patch)
3 Define the API groups (using an empty string denotes the core API group)

You are already familiar with API groups because they are the `apiVersion` and `kind` that appear in Kubernetes manifests. API groups follow the REST path in the API server itself (/apis/$GROUP_NAME/$VERSION) and use `apiVersion $GROUP_NAME/$VERSION` (for instance, `batch/v1`). Let's keep it simple, though, and not deal with API groups just yet. We'll start with the core API group instead. Here is an example of a role for a specific namespace. Because roles are limited to namespaces, this provides access to perform list and patch verbs on the Pod resource:

```
# Create a custom role in the default namespace that grants access to
# list, and patch Pods
kind: Role
apiVersion: rbac.authorization.k8s.io/v1
metadata:
  name: Pod-labeler
  namespace: rbac-example
rules:
- apiGroups: [""] # "" refers to the core API group
  resources: ["Pods"] # the
  verbs: ["list", "patch"] # authorization to use list and patch verbs
```

For the previous example, we can define a service account to use the role in that snippet like so:

```
# Create a ServiceAccount that will be bound to the role above
apiVersion: v1
kind: ServiceAccount
  metadata:
    name: Pod-labeler
    namespace: rbac-example
```

The previous YAML creates a service account that can be used by a Pod. Next, we'll create a role binding to join the previous service account with the role that was also defined previously:

```
# Binds the Pod-labeler ServiceAccount to the Pod-labeler Role
# Any Pod using the Pod-labeler ServiceAccount will be granted
# API permissions based on the Pod-labeler role.
kind: RoleBinding
```

```
apiVersion: rbac.authorization.k8s.io/v1
metadata:
  name: Pod-labeler
  namespace: rbac-example
subjects:
  # List of service accounts to bind
- kind: ServiceAccount
  name: Pod-labeler
roleRef:
  # The role to bind
  kind: Role
  name: Pod-labeler
  apiGroup: rbac.authorization.k8s.io
```

Now you can launch the Pod within a deployment that has the service account assigned to that Pod:

```
# Deploys a single Pod to run the Pod-labeler code
apiVersion: apps/v1
kind: Deployment
metadata:
  name: Pod-labeler
  namespace: rbac-example
spec:
  replicas: 1

  # Control any Pod labeled with app=Pod-labeler
  selector:
    matchLabels:
      app: Pod-labeler

  template:
    # Ensure created Pods are labeled with app=Pod-labeler
    # to match the deployment selector
    metadata:
      labels:
        app: Pod-labeler

    spec:
      # define the service account the Pod uses
      serviceAccount: Pod-labeler

      # Another security improvement, set the UID and GID the Pod runs with
      # Pod-level security context to define the default UID and GIDs
      # under which to run all container processes. We use 9999 for
      # all IDs because it is unprivileged and known to be unallocated
      # on the node instances.
      securityContext:
        runAsUser: 9999
        runAsGroup: 9999
        fsGroup: 9999

      containers:
      - image: gcr.io/pso-examples/Pod-labeler:0.1.5
        name: Pod-labeler
```

Let's recap. We have created a role with the permissions to patch and list Pods. Then, we created a service account so we can create a Pod and have that Pod use the defined user. Next, we defined a role binding to add the service account to the role. Lastly, we launched a deployment that has a Pod defined, which uses the service account that was previously defined.

RBAC is nontrivial, but vital to the security of a Kubernetes cluster. The previous YAML was taken from the Helmsman RBAC demo located at http://mng.bz/ZzMa.

14.2.3 *Resources and subresources*

Most RBAC resources use a single name, like Pod or Deployment. Some resources have subresources, such as in the following code snippet:

```
GET /api/v1/namespaces/rbac-example/Pods/Pod-labeler/log
```

This API endpoint denotes the path to the subresource log in the `rbac-example` namespace for the Pod named Pod-labeler. The definition follows:

```
GET /api/v1/namespaces/{namespace}/Pods/{name}/log
```

In order to use the subresource of logs, you would define a role. The following shows an example:

```
apiVersion: rbac.authorization.k8s.io/v1
kind: Role
metadata:
  namespace: rbac-example
  name: Pod-and-Pod-logs-reader
rules:
- apiGroups: [""]
  resources: ["Pods", "Pods/log"]
  verbs: ["get", "list"]
```

You can also further restrict access to the logs of a Pod by naming the Pod. For example:

```
apiVersion: rbac.authorization.k8s.io/v1
kind: Role
metadata:
  namespace: rbac-example
  name: Pod-labeler-logs
rules:
- apiGroups: [""]
  resourceNames: ["Pod-labeler"]
  resources: ["Pods/log"]
  verbs: ["get"]
```

Notice that the `rules` element in the previous YAML is an array. The following code snippet shows how you can add multiple permissions to the YAML. The `resources`, `resourceNames`, and `verbs` can be of any combination:

```
apiVersion: rbac.authorization.k8s.io/v1
kind: Role
metadata:
  namespace: rbac-example
  name: Pod-labeler-logs
rules:
- apiGroups: [""]
  resourceNames: ["Pod-labeler"]
  resources: ["Pods/log"]
  verbs: ["get"]
- apiGroups: [""]
  resourceNames: ["another-Pod"]
  resources: ["Pods/log"]
  verbs: ["get"]
```

Resources are things like Pods and nodes, but the API server also includes elements that are not resources. These are defined by the actual URI component in the API REST endpoint; for example, giving the `Pod-labeler-logs` RBAC role access to the /healthz API endpoint, as the following snippet shows:

```
apiVersion: rbac.authorization.k8s.io/v1
kind: Role
metadata:
  namespace: rbac-example
  name: Pod-labeler-logs
rules:
- apiGroups: [""]
  resourceNames: ["Pod-labeler"]
  resources: ["Pods/log"]
  verbs: ["get"]
- apiGroups: [""]
  resourceNames: ["another-Pod"]
  resources: ["Pods/log"]
  verbs: ["get"]
- nonResourceURLs: ["/healthz", "/healthz/*"]    ⟵  The asterisk (*) in a nonresource
  verbs: ["get", "post"]                              URL is a suffix glob match.
```

14.2.4 Subjects and RBAC

Role bindings can encompass Users, ServiceAccounts, and Groups in Kubernetes. In the following example, we will create another service account called `log-reader` and add the service account to the role-binding definition in the previous section. In the example, we also have a user named `james-bond` and a group named `MI-6`:

```
kind: RoleBinding
apiVersion: rbac.authorization.k8s.io/v1
metadata:
  name: Pod-labeler
```

```
      namespace: rbac-example
subjects:
  # List of service accounts to bind
- kind: ServiceAccount
  name: Pod-labeler
- kind: SeviceAccount
  name: log-reader
- kind: User
  name: james-bond
- kind: Group
  name: MI-6
roleRef:
  # The role to bind
  kind: Role
  name: Pod-labeler
  apiGroup: rbac.authorization.k8s.io
```

NOTE Users and groups are created by the authentication strategy that is set up for the cluster.

14.2.5 *Debugging RBAC*

Granted, RBAC is complex, and it's a pain, but we always have the audit log. Kubernetes, when enabled, logs an audit trail of security events that have affected the cluster. These events include user actions, administrator actions, and/or other components inside the cluster. Basically, you get a "who," "what," "from where," and "how" if RBAC and other security components are utilized. The audit logging is configured via an audit policy file that is passed into the API server via `kube-apiserver --audit-policy-file`.

So we have a log of all events—awesome! But wait . . . you now have a cluster that has hundreds of roles, a bunch of users, and a plethora of role bindings. Now you have to join all of the data together. For that, there's a couple of tools to assist us. The common theme between these tools is the joining of the different objects used to define RBAC access. In order to introspect RBAC-based permissions in cluster roles, RoleBindings and the Subject need to be joined. The Subject can be users, groups, or service accounts:

- *ReactiveOps has created a tool that allows a user to find the current roles that a user, group, or service account is a member of.* `rbac-lookup` is available at https://github.com/reactiveops/rbac-lookup.
- *Another tool that finds which permissions a user or service account has within the cluster is* `kubectl-rbac`. This tool is located at https://github.com/octarinesec/kubectl-rbac.
- *Jordan Liggit has an open source tool called* `audit2rbac`. This tool takes audit logs and a username and creates a role and role binding that match the requested access. Calls are made to the API server, and you can capture the logs. From there, you can run `audit2rbac` to generate the needed RBAC (in other words, RBAC reverse engineered).

14.3 *Authn, Authz, and Secrets*

Authn (user authentication) and *Authz* (authorization) are the group and permissions that an authenticated user has. It may seem odd that we are talking about Secrets here as well, but some of the same tools used for authentication and authorization are used for Secrets, and you often need authentication and authorization to access Secrets.

First and foremost, do not use the default cluster administrative certificates that are generated when installing a cluster. You will need an IAM (Identity and Access Management) service provider for authenticating and authorizing users. Also, do not enable username and password authentication on the API server; use the built-in capability for user authentication utilizing TLS certificates.

14.3.1 *IAM service accounts: Securing your cloud APIs*

Kubernetes containers have identities that are *cloud native* (these identities are aware of the cloud). This is beautiful and terrifying at the same time. Without a threat model for your cloud, you cannot have a threat model for your Kubernetes cluster.

Cloud IAM service accounts comprise the basics of security, including authorization and authentication for people and systems. Within the data center, Kubernetes security configuration is limited to the Linux system, Kubernetes, the network, and the containers deployed. When running Kubernetes in the cloud, a new wrinkle emerges—the IAM roles of nodes and Pods:

- IAM is the role for a specific user or service account, and that role is then a member of a group.
- Every node in a Kubernetes cluster has an IAM role.
- Pods typically inherit that role.

The nodes in your cluster, specifically those that run on the control plane, need IAM roles to run inside the cloud. The reason for this is that a lot of cloud-native functionality in Kubernetes comes from the fact that Kubernetes itself has a notion of how to talk to its own cloud provider. As an example, let's take a cue from GKE's official documentation: Google Cloud Platform automatically creates a service account named compute engine default service account, and GKE associates it with the nodes it creates. Depending on how your project is configured, the default service account may or may not have permissions to use other cloud-platform APIs. GKE also assigns some limited access scopes to compute instances. Updating the default service account's permissions or assigning more access scopes to compute instances is not the recommended way to authenticate to other cloud-platform services from Pods running on GKE.

Your containers, therefore, have privileges in many cases that are on par with the nodes themselves. As clouds evolve to make more granular permission models for containers, this default will likely improve in the future. It remains the case, however, that you need to ensure that the IAM role or roles have the least amount of permissions applicable and that there will always be ways to change these IAM roles. For instance, when using GKE in Google Cloud Platform, you have to create a new IAM role in a project for a cluster. If you do not, the cluster usually uses the compute engine default service account, which has editor permissions.

Editor in Google Cloud allows a given account (in this case, a node in your cluster, which translates to potentially any Pod) to edit any resource within that project. For example, you could delete an entire fleet of databases, TCP load balancers, or cloud DNS entries by simply compromising a given Pod in the cluster. Moreover, you should remove the default service account for any project that you create in GCP. The same problems exist in AWS, Azure, and others. The bottom line is that each cluster is created with its own unique service account, and that service account has the least possible permissions. With tools like kops (Kubernetes Operations), we can go through every permission a Kubernetes cluster requires, and kops then creates an IAM role specific to the control plane, as well as another for the nodes.

14.3.2 *Access to cloud resources*

Assuming that you have configured your Kubernetes nodes with the lowest level of permissions needed, now that you've read this, you may feel safe. In fact, if you are running a solution like AKS (Azure Kubernetes Service), you do not have to worry about configuring the control plane and only have to be concerned with the node-level IAM, but that's not all. For example, a developer creates a service that needs to talk to a hosted cloud service—say, a file store. The Pod that is running now needs a service account with the correct roles. There are various approaches to this.

> **NOTE** AKS is probably the easiest solution, but it does create some challenges. You need to limit the Pods on the nodes to ones that only need access to the cloud resources or accept the risk that all Pods will now have file-store access.

> **TIP** Use a tool like kube2iam (https://github.com/jtblin/kube2iam) or kiam (https://github.com/uswitch/kiam) for this approach.

Some newly created operators can assign specific service accounts to specific Pods. The component on each node intercepts the calls to the cloud API. Instead of using the node's IAM role, it assigns a role to a Pod in your cluster, which is denoted via annotations. Some of the hosted cloud providers have similar solutions. Some cloud providers, like Google, have sidecars that can run and connect to a cloud SQL service. The sidecar is assigned a role and then proxies the applications that connect to the database.

Probably the most complicated but more robust solution is to use a centralized vault server. With this, you can have applications retrieve short-lived IAM tokens that allow cloud system access. Often, a sidecar is used to automatically refresh the tokens used. We can also use HashiCorp Vault to secure Secrets that are not IAM credentials. If your use case requires robust Secrets and IAM management, Vault is an excellent solution, but as with all solutions that are mission critical, you will need to maintain and support it.

> **TIP** Use HashiCorp Vault (https://www.vaultproject.io/) to store Secrets.

14.3.3 Private API servers

The last thing that we are going to cover in this section is the API server's network access. You can either make your API server inaccessible via the internet or place the API server on a private network. You will need to utilize a bastion host, VPN, or other form of connectivity to the API server if you place the API server load balancer on a private network, so this solution is not as convenient.

The API server is an extremely sensitive security point and must be guarded as such. DoS attacks or general intrusion can cripple a cluster. Moreover, when the Kubernetes community finds security problems, they occasionally exist in the API server. If you can, put your API server on a private network, or at least whitelist the IP addresses that are able to connect to the load balancer that fronts your API server.

14.4 Network security

Again, this is an area of security that is rarely addressed properly. By default, a Pod on the Pod network can access any Pod anywhere on the cluster, which also includes the API server. This capability exists to allow a Pod to access systems like DNS for service lookups. A Pod running on the host network can access just about everything: all Pods, all nodes, and the API server. A Pod on the host network can even access the kubelet API port if the port is enabled.

Network policies are objects that you can define to control network traffic between Pods. NetworkPolicy objects allow you to configure access around Pod ingress and egress. *Ingress* is traffic that is coming into a Pod, while *egress* is network traffic leaving the Pod.

14.4.1 Network policies

You can create a NetworkPolicy object on any Kubernetes cluster, but you need a running security provider such as Calico. Calico is a CNI provider that also provides a separate application to implement network policies. If you create a network policy without a provider, the policy does nothing. Network policies have the following constraints and features. They are

- Applied to Pods
- Matched to specific Pods via label selectors
- In control of both ingress and egress network traffic
- In control of network traffic defined by a CIDR range, a specific namespace, or a matched Pod or Pods
- Designed to specifically handle TCP, UDP, and SCTP traffic
- Capable of handling named ports or specific Pod numbers

Let's try this. To set up a kind cluster and install Calico on it, first run the following command to create the kind cluster, and do not start the default CNI. Calico will be installed next:

```
$ cat <<EOF | kind create cluster --config -
kind: Cluster
apiVersion: kind.x-k8s.io/v1alpha4
networking:
  # the default CNI will not be installed
  disableDefaultCNI: true
  PodSubnet: "192.168.0.0/16"
EOF
```

Next, we install the Calico Operator and its custom resources. Use the following commands to do this:

```
$ kubectl create -f \
https://docs.projectcalico.org/manifests/tigera-operator.yaml
$ kubectl create -f \
https://docs.projectcalico.org/manifests/custom-resources.yaml
```

Now we can observe the Pod startup. Use the following command:

```
$ kubectl get Pods --watch -n calico-system
```

Next, set up a couple of namespaces, an NGINX server to serve a test web page, and a BusyBox container where we can run wget. To do this, use the following commands:

```
$ kubectl create ns web
$ kubectl create ns test-bed
$ kubectl create deployment -n web nginx --image=nginx
$ kubectl expose -n web deployment nginx --port=80
$ kubectl run --namespace=test-bed testing --rm -ti --image busybox /bin/sh
```

From the command prompt on the BusyBox container, access the NGINX server installed in the web namespace. Here's the command for this:

```
$ wget -q nginx.web -O
```

Now, install a network policy that denies all inbound traffic to the NGINX Pod. Use the following command:

```
$ kubectl create -f - <<EOF
apiVersion: networking.k8s.io/v1
kind: NetworkPolicy
metadata:
  name: deny-ingress
  namespace: web
spec:
  PodSelector:
    matchLabels: {}
  policyTypes:
  - Ingress
EOF
```

This command creates a policy so that you can no longer access the NGINX web page from the testing Pod. Run the following command on the command line for the testing Pod. The command will time out and fail:

```
$ wget -q --timeout=5 nginx.web.svc.cluster.local -O -
```

Next, open the Pod ingress from the `test-bed` namespace to the `web` namespace. Use the following code snippet:

```
$ kubectl create -f - <<EOF
apiVersion: networking.k8s.io/v1
kind: NetworkPolicy
metadata:
  name: access-web
  namespace: web
spec:
  PodSelector:
    matchLabels:
      app: nginx
  policyTypes:
    - Ingress
  ingress:
    - from:
      - namespaceSelector:
          matchLabels:
            name: test-bed
EOF
```

On the command line for the testing Pod, enter

```
$ wget -q --timeout=5 nginx.web.svc.cluster.local -O -
```

You will notice that the command fails. The reason is that network policies match labels, and the `test-bed` namespace is not labeled. The following command adds the label:

```
$ kubectl label namespaces test-bed name=test-bed
```

On the command line for the testing Pod, check that the network policy now works. Here's the command:

```
$ wget -q --timeout=5 nginx.web.svc.cluster.local -O -
```

The first recommendation for all firewall configurations is to create a deny-all rule. This policy denies all traffic flow within a namespace. Run the following command and disable all ingress and egress Pods for the `test-bed` namespace:

```
$ kubectl create -f - <<EOF
kind: NetworkPolicy
apiVersion: networking.k8s.io/v1
```

```
metadata:
  name: deny-all
  namespace: test-bed
spec:
  PodSelector:
    matchLabels: {}        ◁──┐ Matches all Pods
                               │ in a namespace
  policyTypes:  ◁──┐
  - Ingress        │ Defines the two policy
  - Egress         │ types: ingress and egress
EOF
```

Now, implementing this policy causes some fun side effects. Not only can the Pods not talk to anything else (except in their namespace), but now they cannot talk to the DNS provider in the `kube-system` namespace. If the Pod does not need DNS capability, do not enable it! Let's apply the following network policy to enable egress for DNS:

```
$ kubectl label namespaces kube-system name=kube-system
$ kubectl create -f - <<EOF
kind: NetworkPolicy
apiVersion: networking.k8s.io/v1
metadata:
  name: dns-egress
  namespace: test-bed
spec:
  PodSelector:
    matchLabels: {}         ◁──┐ Matches all Pods in the core
                               │ Kubernetes namespace
  policyTypes:  ◁──┐
  - Egress         │ Only allows egress
    egress:
    - to:
      - namespaceSelector:     ◁──┐ Egress rule that matches
          matchLabels:            │ a labeled kube-system
            name: kube-system
      ports:  ◁──┐
      - protocol: UDP          │ Only allows UDP over port 53, which
        port: 53               │ is the protocol and port for DNS
EOF
```

If you run the `wget` command, you will notice that the command still fails. We have ingress on the `web` namespace allowed but do not have egress from the `test-bed` namespace to the `web` namespace enabled. Run the following command to turn on egress to the `web` namespace from the `test-bed` Pod:

```
$ kubectl label namespaces web name=web
$ kubectl create -f - <<EOF
apiVersion: networking.k8s.io/v1
kind: NetworkPolicy
metadata:
  name: test-bed-egress
  namespace: test-bed
spec:
```

```
  PodSelector:
    matchLabels: {}
  policyTypes:
    - Egress
  egress:
    - to:
      - namespaceSelector:
          matchLabels:
            name: web
EOF
```

You probably noticed that NetworkPolicy rules can get complex. If you are running a cluster where the trust model is *high trust*, implementing network policies may *not* benefit your security posture. Using the 80/20 rule, do not start with NetworkPolicies if your organization is not updating its images. Yes, network policies are complex, and that is partially why using a service mesh in your organization may assist your security.

SERVICE MESH

A *service mesh* is an application that runs on top of a Kubernetes cluster and provides various capabilities that often improve observability, monitoring, and reliability. Common service meshes include Istio, Linkerd, Consul, and others. We mention service meshes in the security chapter because they can assist your organization with two key things: mutual TLS and advanced network traffic-flow policies. We cover this topic very briefly since there are entire books on this subject.

A service mesh adds a complex layer on top of virtually every application that it runs in a cluster, but also provides many good security components. Again, use your judgement as to whether adding a service mesh is warranted, but do not start with a service mesh on day one. If you want to know whether your cluster conforms to the CNCF specification for the NetworkPolicy API, you can run the NetworkPolicy test suites using Sonobuoy (which we've covered in previous chapters):

```
$ sonobuoy run --e2e-focus=NetworkPolicy
# wait about 30 minutes
$ sonobuoy status
```

This outputs a series of table tests that show you exactly how network policies are working on your cluster. To learn more about the concepts of NetworkPolicy API conformance for CNI providers, check out http://mng.bz/XW7M. We highly recommend running the NetworkPolicy conformance tests when evaluating your CNI provider for compatibility to the Kubernetes network security specifications.

14.4.2 Load balancers

One thing to keep in mind is that Kubernetes can create external load balancers that expose your applications to the world, and it does so automatically. This may seem like common knowledge, but putting the wrong service into a production environment can expose a service (such as an administrative user interface) to a database. Use tooling during CI (continuous integration) or a tool like the Open Policy Agent (OPA) to ensure that external load balancers are not created accidentally. Also, use internal load balancers when you can.

14.4.3 *Open Policy Agent (OPA)*

We previously mentioned that operators can help an organization further secure a cluster. The OPA, a CNCF project, strives to allow declarative policies that are run via the admission controller.

> *OPA is a lightweight general-purpose policy engine that can be co-located with your service. You can integrate OPA as a sidecar, host-level daemon, or library.*
>
> *Services offload policy decisions to OPA by executing queries. OPA evaluates policies and data to produce query results (which are sent back to the client). Policies are written in a high-level declarative language and can be loaded into OPA via the filesystem or well-defined APIs.*
>
> —Open Policy Agent
> (http://mng.bz/RE6O)

There are two different components that OPA maintains: the OPA admission controller and the OPA Gatekeeper. The Gatekeeper does not use a sidecar, utilizes CRDs (custom resource definitions), is extensible, and performs audit functionality. The next section walks through installing Gatekeeper on a `kind` Kubernetes cluster.

INSTALLING OPA

First, clean up your cluster running Calico. Then, let's start another cluster:

```
$ kind delete cluster
$ kind create cluster
```

Next, install OPA Gatekeeper using the following command:

```
$ kubectl apply -f \
https://raw.githubusercontent.com/open-policy-agent/gatekeeper/v3.7.0/
➥ deploy/gatekeeper.yaml
```

The following command prints the names of the Pods installed:

```
$ kubectl -n gatekeeper-system get po
NAME                                              READY   STATUS    RESTARTS   AGE
gatekeeper-audit-7d99d9d87d-rb4qh                 1/1     Running   0          40s
gatekeeper-controller-manager-f94cc7dfc-j6zjv     1/1     Running   0          39s
gatekeeper-controller-manager-f94cc7dfc-mxz6d     1/1     Running   0          39s
gatekeeper-controller-manager-f94cc7dfc-rvqvj     1/1     Running   0          39s
```

> **NOTE** You can also use Helm to install OPA Gatekeeper.

GATEKEEPER CRDS

One of the complexities of OPA is learning a new language (called Rego) to write policies. See http://mng.bz/2jdm for more information about Rego. With Gatekeeper, you will put policies written in Rego into the supported CRDs. You need to create two different CRDs to add a policy:

- A constraint template to define the policy and its targets
- A constraint to enable a constraint template and define how the policy is enabled

An example of a constraint template and the associated constraint follows. The source block contains two CRDs defined in YAML. In this example, the `match` stanza supports

- `kinds`—Defines Kubernetes API objects
- `namespaces`—Specifies a list of namespaces
- `excludedNamespaces`—Specifies a list of excluded namespaces
- `scope`— *, cluster, or namespace
- `labelSelector`—Sets the standard Kubernetes label selector
- `namespaceSelector`—Sets the standard Kubernetes namespace selector

```yaml
apiVersion: templates.gatekeeper.sh/v1beta1
kind: ConstraintTemplate
metadata:
  name: enforcespecificcontainerregistry
spec:
  crd:
    spec:
      names:
        kind: EnforceSpecificContainerRegistry   ◁──┐
        # Schema for the `parameters` field          │
        openAPIV3Schema:                             │
          properties:                                │
            repos:                                   │
              type: array                            │
              items:                                 │
                type: string                         │
  targets:                                           │
    - target: admission.k8s.gatekeeper.sh           │
      rego: |                              ◁─────────┘
       package enforcespecificcontainerregistry

          violation[{"msg": msg}] {
            container := input.review.object.spec.containers[_]
            satisfied := [good | repo = input.parameters.repos[_] ;
➡ good = startswith(container.image, repo)]
            not any(satisfied)
            msg := sprintf("container '%v' has an invalid image repo
➡ '%v', allowed repos are %v",
➡ [container.name, container.image, input.parameters.repos])
          }

          violation[{"msg": msg}] {
            container := input.review.object.spec.initContainers[_]
```

Defines EnforceSpecific-ContainerRegistry, a CRD that's used for the constraint

```
        satisfied := [good | repo = input.parameters.repos[_] ;
➥  good = startswith(container.image, repo)]
        not any(satisfied)
        msg := sprintf("container '%v' has an invalid image repo '%v',
➥  allowed repos are %v",
➥  [container.name, container.image, input.parameters.repos])
      }
---
apiVersion: constraints.gatekeeper.sh/v1beta1
kind: EnforceSpecificContainerRegistry
metadata:
  name: enforcespecificcontainerregistrytestns
spec:
  match:
    kinds:
      - apiGroups: [""]
        kinds: ["Pod"]
    namespaces:
      - "test-ns"
  parameters:
    repos:
      - "myrepo.com"
```

Now, let's take the previous YAML file and save it to two files (one with the template and the second with the constraint). On the cluster, install the template file first and the constraint second. (For brevity, we do not provide the command.) Now we can exercise the policy by running the following commands:

```
$ kubectl create ns test-ns
$ kubectl create deployment -n test-ns nginx --image=nginx
```

You can check the status of the deployment by running the following command (we are expecting that the Pod will not start):

```
$ kubectl get -n test-ns deployments.apps
NAME    READY    UP-TO-DATE    AVAILABLE    AGE
nginx   0/1      0             0            37s
```

If you execute a `kubectl -n test-ns get Pods`, you will notice that no Pods are running. The event logs contain the message that shows Pod creation failing. You can view the logs with the following command:

```
$ kubectl -n test-ns get events
7s         Warning    FailedCreate        replicaset/nginx-6799fc88d8
➥  Error creating: admission webhook "validation.gatekeeper.sh"
➥  denied the request: [denied by
➥  enforcespecificcontainerregistrytestns] container <nginx>
➥  has an invalid image repo <nginx>, allowed repos are
➥  ["myrepo.com"]
```

14.4.4 *Multi-tenancy*

To categorize multi-tenancy, look at the level of trust that the tenants have with one another, and then develop that model. There are three basic buckets or security models to categorize as multi-tenancy:

- *High trust (same company)*—Different departments in the same company are running workloads on the same cluster.
- *Medium to low trust (different companies)*—External customers are running applications on your cluster in different namespaces.
- *Zero trust (data governed by law)*—Different applications are running data that is governed by laws, where allowing access between different data stores can cause legal action against your company.

The Kubernetes community has worked on solving these use cases for many years. Jessie Frazelle sums it up nicely in her blog post entitled "Hard Multi-Tenancy in Kubernetes":

> *The models for multi-tenancy have been discussed at length in the community's multi-tenancy working group. . . . There have also been some proposals offered to solve each model. The current model of tenancy in Kubernetes assumes the cluster is the security boundary. You can build a SaaS on top of Kubernetes but you will need to bring your own trusted API and not just use the Kubernetes API. Of course, with that comes a lot of considerations you must also think about when building your cluster securely for a SaaS even.*
> —Jessie Frazelle, http://mng.bz/1jdn

The Kubernetes API was not built with the concept of having multiple isolated customers within the same cluster. Docker Engine and other container runtimes also have problems with running malicious or untrusted workloads. Software components like gVisor have made headway in properly sandboxing containers, but at the time of writing this book, we are not at a place where you can run a completely untrusted container.

So where are we? A security person would say it depends on your trust and security model. We previously listed three security models: high trust (same company), low trust to no trust (different companies), and zero trust (data governed by law). Kubernetes can support high trust multi-tenancy and, depending on the model, can support trust models in between high and low trust models. When you have zero trust or low trust with and between tenants, you need to use separate clusters for each client. Some companies run hundreds of clusters so that each small group of applications gets its own cluster, but, admittedly, that is a lot of clusters to manage.

Even if the clients are part of the same company, it may be necessary to isolate Pods on specific nodes due to data sensitivity. Through RBAC, namespaces, network policies, and node isolation, it's possible to gain a decent level of isolation. Admittedly, there is a risk of hosting a workload that different companies run to use the same Kubernetes cluster. The support for multi-tenancy will grow over time.

> **NOTE** Multi-tenancy also applies to running other environments, like development or test in a production cluster. You can, however, introduce bad actor code into a cluster by intermingling environments.

There are two main challenges using a single Kubernetes to host multiple customers: the API server and node security. After establishing authentication, authorization, and RBAC, why is there a problem with the API server and multiple tenants? One of the problems is with the URI layout of the API server. A common pattern for having multiple tenants using the same API server is to have the user ID, project ID, or some unique ID starting the URI.

Having a URI that starts with a unique ID allows a tenant to make a call to get *all* namespaces. Because Kubernetes does not have this isolation, you need to run `kubectl get namespaces` to get all the namespaces in a cluster. You'll also need an API layer on top of the Kubernetes API to provide this form of isolation.

Another pattern for allowing multi-tenants is the capability of nesting resources, and the basic resource boundary in Kubernetes is namespaces. Kubernetes namespaces do not allow for nesting. Many resources are cross-namespace, including the default service account token. Often, tenants want to have fine-grain RBAC capability themselves, and giving a user permissions to create RBAC objects within Kubernetes can give the user capabilities beyond their shared tenancy.

Regarding node security, the challenge lies within. If you have multiple tenants on the same Kubernetes cluster, remember that they all share the following items (this is just a short list):

- The control plane and the API server
- Add-ons like the DNS server, logging, or TLS certificate generation
- Custom resource definitions (CRDs)
- Networks
- Host resources

OVERVIEW OF TRUSTED MULTI-TENANCY

Many companies want multi-tenancy to reduce costs and management overhead. There is value in not running three clusters: one each for development, test, and production environments. Simply run a single Kubernetes cluster for all three environments. Also, some companies do not want to have separate clusters for different products and/or software departments. Again, this is a business and security decision, and the organizations we work with usually have budgets and a constraint on human resources.

We are not going to give you step-by-step instructions on how to do multi-tenancy. We are simply providing guidelines on what steps you will need to implement. These steps will change over time and vary between organizations with different security models:

1 Write down and design a security model. It may seem obvious, but we have seen organizations that do not use a security model. A security model needs to include different user roles, including cluster administrators and namespace administrators, and one or more tenant roles. A standardized naming convention for all of the API objects, users, and other components your organization creates is also critical.

2 Utilize various API objects:
  – Namespaces
  – NetworkingPolicies
  – ResourceQuotas
  – ServiceAccounts and RBACRules

3 Using tools like a service mesh with features like mutual TLS and network policy management can provide another level of security. Using a service mesh does add a significant layer of complexity, so only use it when needed.

4 Consider using an OPA to assist with applying policy-based controls to the Kubernetes cluster.

TIP If you are going to combine multiple environments in a single cluster, there are not only security concerns, but also challenges with testing Kubernetes upgrades. It is best to test upgrades first on another cluster.

14.5 Kubernetes tips

Here is a short list of various configurations and setup requirements:

- Have a private API server endpoint, and if you can, do not expose your API server to the internet.
- Use RBAC.
- Use network policies.
- Do not enable username and password authorization on the API server.
- Use specific users when creating Pods, and don't use the default admin accounts.
- Rarely allow Pods to run on the host network.
- Use `serviceAccountName` if the Pod needs to access the API server; otherwise, set `automountServiceAccountToken` to false.
- Use resource quotas on namespaces and define limits in all Pods.

Summary

- Node security relies on TLS certificates to secure communication between nodes and the control plane.
- Using immutable OSs can further harden nodes.
- Resource limits can prevent resource-level attacks.
- Use the Pod network, unless you have to use the host network. The host network allows a Pod to talk to the node OS.
- RBAC is key to securing an API server. It is non-trivial, but necessary.
- The IAM service accounts allow for the proper isolation of Pod permissions.
- Network policies are key to isolating network traffic. Otherwise, everything can talk to everything else.

- An Open Policy Agent (OPA) allows a user to write security policies and enforces those policies on a Kubernetes cluster.
- Kubernetes was not built initially with zero trust multi-tenancy in mind. You'll find forms of mult-tenancy, but they come with tradeoffs.

Installing applications

This chapter covers

- Reviewing Kubernetes application management
- Installing the prototypical Guestbook application
- Building a production-friendly version of the Guestbook app

Managing applications in Kubernetes is generally a lot easier then managing applications deployed on bare servers because all the configuration for applications can be done through a unified command-line interface. That said, as you move tens or hundreds of containers into a Kubernetes environment, the volume of configuration management that needs to be automated can be difficult to approach from a unified perspective. ConfigMaps, Secrets, API server credentials, and customization of volume types are just a few of the day-to-day paper cuts that can make Kubernetes administration tedious over time.

In this chapter, we'll (finally) take a step back from the internal details of a Kubernetes implementation and spend a little bit of time looking at the higher-level aspects of application configuration and administration. We'll start by thinking about what an application is and how we can install applications on Kubernetes.

15.1 *Thinking about apps in Kubernetes*

For our purposes, we'll refer to a Kubernetes application as a collection of API resources that need to be deployed for a service. The canonical example of this might be the Guestbook application, defined at http://mng.bz/y4NE. This application includes

- A Redis master database Pod
- A Redis slave database Pod
- A frontend Pod that talks to our Redis master
- A service for all three of these Pods

Application delivery involves upgrading, downgrading, parameterizing, and customizing many different Kubernetes resources. Because this is a hotly debated subject with many different and competing technical solutions, we won't attempt to solve this entire puzzle for you here. Instead, we've included a hearty dose of application tooling in this chapter because a large part of deciding how you deploy your Pods is related to how you configure them and how you install your application to begin with. We can run our Guestbook application on any Kubernetes cluster like so:

```
$ kubectl create -f https://github.com/kubernetes/examples/blob/master/
    guestbook/all-in-one/guestbook-all-in-one.yaml
```

> ### Curling from the internet
> We've noted this before, but we'll do so again: curling YAML files from the internet can be a dangerous business. In our case, we `curl` our YAML files directly from github.com/kubernetes, which is a trusted repository maintained by thousands of well-known and vetted CNCF (Cloud Native Computing Foundation) organization members. By the end of this chapter, we'll have a much more enterprise-grade and realistic way to install the same Guestbook app, so just hang tight.

After issuing the previous command, we'll soon see all of our Pods up and running with multiple replicas of our three frontend and Redis slave Pods. At its most basic level, this is what installing a Kubernetes application looks like:

```
$ kubectl get pods -A
NAMESPACE    NAME                  READY    STATUS             RESTARTS    AGE
default      frontend-6c-7wjx8     1/1      Running            0           3m18s
default      frontend-6c-g7z8z     1/1      Running            0           3m18s
default      frontend-6c-xd5q2     0/1      ContainerCreating  0           3m18s
default      redis-master-f46-12d  1/1      Running            0           3m18s
default      redis-slave-797-nv9   1/1      Running            0           3m18s
default      redis-slave-797-9qc   1/1      Running            0           3m18s
```

15.1.1 Application scope influences what tools you should use

The minute we install Guestbook, we have to ask ourselves a few obvious questions. These questions are pertinent to scaling, upgrades, customization, security, and modularization:

- Are users going to be manually scaling the Guestbook web application Pods up and down? Or do we want to autoscale our deployment based on load?
- Do we want to upgrade our Guestbook app periodically, and if so, do we want to upgrade the other Pods with it in lockstep? If so, should we build a Kubernetes Operator?
- Do we have a discrete number of configurations that arc well-defined (for example, are there a few alternative Redis configurations we care about)? If so, should we use ytt, kustomize, or some other tool so that we don't need to copy and paste large redundant chunks of YAML every time we want to save a new flavor of our application's settings?
- Is our Redis database secure? Does it need to be? If so, should we add RBAC credentials for updating or editing the namespace in which our app resides, or should we install NetworkPolicy rules alongside it? We can peruse all of the rules at https://redis.io/topics/security and implement these using Secrets, ConfigMaps, and so on. Additionally, we may need to rotate these Secrets periodically, which would introduce the need for some kind of recurring automation. (This would hint at the need for an Operator.)
- Although we could deploy our application in a specific namespace, how would we be able to track the provenance and state of the overall application's health over time and upgrade it as an atomic unit? Deploying a massive list of Kubernetes resources as an app from a big file is clumsy for multiple reasons. One is that it's not clear what our application really is once it's lost within our cluster.

15.2 Microservice apps typically require thousands of lines of configuration code

Microservices break the individual functionality of an application into separate services, each of which has its own unique configuration. This comes with a high cost when compared to large, monolithic applications, where much of the communication and security of containers is done through the inherent use of in-memory computing. Getting back to our Guestbook app, which has three microservices and 200 lines of code, we can see that anywhere from 10 to 50 lines of code are required for each API object we create.

A typical Kubernetes app for an enterprise would involve more sophisticated configuration, anywhere from 10 to 20 containers, and each one of these would typically have at least one service, one ConfigMap object, and a few Secrets associated with it. A back-of-the-envelope estimate for the amount of code in such an application's configuration would easily be thousands of lines of YAML spread over many files. It's obviously unwieldy to copy thousands of lines of code every time we deploy a new app. Let's look, then, at a few different solutions for managing Kubernetes configuration for long-running, real-world applications.

Don't be afraid to rethink your application

Before you dive too deep into the infinitude of options for applications, we'll just ask that you heed one warning: if your installation tooling is exceedingly complex, there is a high likelihood that you are masking broken elements in your underlying application. In these scenarios, it might be wise to simplify the way your application is managed. As a primary example, often times, developers make too many microservices or build more flexibility into an application than is necessary (usually because adequate testing isn't in place to measure and set the right configuration defaults). Sometimes, the best solution to configuration management is to simply eliminate configurability entirely.

15.3   *Rethinking our Guestbook app installation for the real world*

Now that we've defined our overall problem space, managing Kubernetes application configurations, let's rethink our Guestbook application with these solutions:

- *Yaml templating*—We'll use `ytt` for this, but we could also use tools such as `kustomize` or `helm3` for this functionality.
- *Deploying and upgrading our app*—We'll use a Carvel `kapp-controller` project here, but we could also build a Kubernetes Operator to do this.

Why not `helm`?

We don't explicitly want to endorse one tool over another: `helm3`, `kustomize`, and `ytt` can all be used variably to accomplish the same end goals. We prefer `ytt` because of its modular and fully programmable nature (and it is integrated with Starlark). But at the end of the day, pick a tool. `helm3`, `kustomize`, `ytt` are all great tools, but there are many other great tools out there that solve YAML overload. There's no specific reason why these examples cannot be implemented using other technologies as well. For that matter, there's always `sed`.

The Carvel toolkit (https://carvel.dev toolkit) has several different modular tools that can be used together or separately for managing the entire problem space that we've described thus far. It is, actually, the basis for much of the functionality of the VMware Tanzu distribution.

15.4   *Installing the Carvel toolkit*

The first step to exploring how to ramp up our "guestbook-fu" is to install the Carvel toolkit. We can then execute each one of these tools from the command line. The following code snippet shows the command to install the toolkit. Moving forward, we'll use `ytt`, `kapp`, and `kapp-controller` to incrementally improve and automate our Guestbook application:

```
# on macOS, do this
$ brew tap vmware-tanzu/carvel ; brew install ytt kbld kapp imgpkg kwt vendir
# or on Linux, do this
$ curl -L https://carvel.dev/install.sh | bash
```

> **Do we really need all of Carvel?**
> Although we won't need all of the Carvel tools for this chapter, we'll install them anyway because they play well together. We suggest that you explore some of them (such as `imgpkg` or `vendir`) on your own as additional exercises. Each one of the Carvel binaries is easy to run, self-contained, and takes up negligible space on your system. Feel free to customize this installation to suit your own learning goals.

15.4.1 *Part 1: Modularizing our resources into separate files*

The first logical thing to consider when looking at our 200-line wall of YAML might be to break it into smaller, more understandable chunks. The reasons for this are pretty obvious:

- Using tools like `grep` or `sed` is a lot easier when we don't have lots of duplicate strings.
- Tracking who may have changed something specific to a particular function simplifies version control for small files.
- Adding new Kubernetes objects to our file will eventually get unwieldy, so modularizing it will be an eventual requirement anyway. We might as well get ahead of it now.

We've pushed our decomposition of Guestbook into two separate directories. We put these in http://mng.bz/M2wm for you to clone and play with. Feel free to decompose the files in a way that is intuitive for you.

Following the exact decomposition steps in this section isn't mandatory because if you ask 10 different programmers how to decompose an object, you'll get 100 different answers. However, make sure to make one important modification when decomposing it: each Kubernetes resource should have a *unique name*. The Redis master deployment, for example, must not be named the same as the Redis service object. For example, in the following, we added a -dep suffix to the name of our Redis master deployment:

```
---
apiVersion: apps/v1
kind: Deployment
metadata:
  name: redis-master-dep
---
```

We've also done the same thing for the frontend YAML file. The resulting directory structure is displayed following this code snippet showing the addition of the -dep suffix:

```
apiVersion: apps/v1
kind: Deployment
metadata:
  name: frontend-dep
spec:

-> carvel-guestbook git:(master) ? tree
.
├── v0
│   └── original.yaml
└── v1
    ├── fe-dep.yaml
    ├── fe-svc.yaml
    ├── redis-master-dep.yaml
    ├── redis-master-svc.yaml
    ├── redis-slave-dep.yaml
    └── redis-slave-svc.yaml
```

> **Renaming your Redis master and frontend resource**
>
> If you're not going to use the files on http://mng.bz/M2wm and you are splitting up the guestbook YAML on your own, make sure to rename the Redis master and frontend deployment files to redis-master-dep and frontend-dep in the `metadata.name` field (as shown in the previous code snippets). This will allow us to use `ytt` later on to easily find and substitute the values of YAML constructs.

We can now test that our decomposition is equivalent to our original app by running `kubectl create -f v1/`. We'll trust you to run this command and confirm that three frontend and two backend Redis Pods are up and happily running. Then, you can set up port forwarding to locally browse the Guestbook app at port 8080. For example:

```
$ kubectl port-forward service/frontend 8080:80
Forwarding from 127.0.0.1:8080 -> 80
Forwarding from [::1]:8080 -> 80
```

Now you can easily enter a few values in the app's Messages field and see those values stored in the backend Redis database. Notice that these are also displayed for you on the Guestbook landing page.

15.4.2 *Part 2: Patching our application files with ytt*

We've got a working application with a frontend and a backend. What happens now if we decide to start hitting it with more load? We might want to allocate more CPU to it, for instance. To do this, we'll want to modify the fe-dep.yaml file to increase the `requests.cpu` value. This means that we'll need to edit some YAML:

```
containers:
- name: php-redis
  image: gcr.io/google-samples/gb-frontend:v4
  resources:
    requests:
      cpu: 100m
      memory: 100Mi
```

One-tenth of a core isn't a lot of CPU for a production application.

In the code example, we could easily replace the `100m` with a `1`, but then we would just exchange one hardcoded constant for another. It would be better if we could parameterize this value. Additionally, we may want to also increase the CPU requirements of Redis. Luckily, we have `ytt`.

The YAML templating engine, `ytt` (https://carvel.dev/ytt/), allows different customizations to YAML files using modalities like overlaying, patching, and so on. It also supports advanced constructs by using the Starlark language for implementing logical decisions for text manipulation. Because we've already installed the Carvel toolkit, let's just dive into how we can customize our application's CPU in our first `ytt` example.

> ### YAML in, YAML out
> `ytt` is a YAML in, YAML out tool, and this is an important concept to keep in mind. Unlike other tools that have come and gone in the Kubernetes ecosystem, `ytt` (like other tools in the Carvel framework) focuses on doing one specific job, and doing that very well. It manipulates YAML! It doesn't install files for us, and it isn't in any way specific to Kubernetes.

For our second (v2) iteration of this Guestbook application, we'll now add a new file (call it ytt-cpu-overlay.yaml) in a new directory (call it v2/). Our goal is to match our cpu stanza in the php-redis frontend web application with the Redis master database Pod. Here's the code:

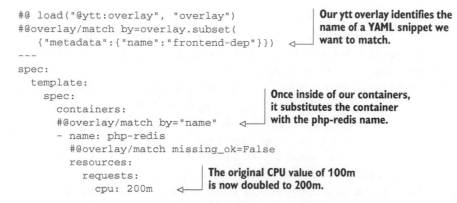

```
#@ load("@ytt:overlay", "overlay")
#@overlay/match by=overlay.subset(
   {"metadata":{"name":"frontend-dep"}})
---
spec:
  template:
    spec:
      containers:
      #@overlay/match by="name"
      - name: php-redis
        #@overlay/match missing_ok=False
        resources:
          requests:
            cpu: 200m
```

Our ytt overlay identifies the name of a YAML snippet we want to match.

Once inside of our containers, it substitutes the container with the php-redis name.

The original CPU value of 100m is now doubled to 200m.

Similarly, we can do this for our database Pod. We can make a new file, call it v2/ytt-cpu-overlay-db.yaml, that does the same thing as our previous file:

```
#@ load("@ytt:overlay", "overlay")
#@overlay/match by=overlay.subset({"metadata":{"name":"redis-master-dep"}})
---
spec:
  template:
    spec:
      containers:
      #@overlay/match by="name"
      - name: master
        resources:
          requests:
            #@overlay/match missing_ok=True
            cpu: 300m
```

> **Adds a new CPU value (this time, 300m to differentiate the two)** ← (pointing to `cpu: 300m`)

We can now invoke this transformation of our YAML. For example:

```
$ tree v2
v2
├─ ytt-cpu-overlay-db.yml
└─ ytt-cpu-overlay.yml

$ ytt -f ./v1/  -f v2/ytt-cpu-overlay.yml  -f v2/ytt-cpu-overlay-db.yml
...
            cpu: 200m
...
            cpu: 300m
```

> **Modifies the file to have higher CPU request for the master only** ← (pointing to `cpu: 300m`)

```
$ kubectl delete -f v0/original.yaml
$ ytt -f ./v1/  -f v2/ytt-cpu-overlay.yml \
   | -f v2/ytt-cpu-overlay-db.yml | kubectl create -f -
deployment.apps/frontend-dep created
service/frontend created
deployment.apps/redis-master-dep created
service/redis-master created
deployment.apps/redis-slave created
service/redis-slave created
```

Great, we've now come full circle! Originally we had a single file, which was easy to package but hard to modify. Using ytt, we took many different files and added a layer of customization on top of them, so they can then be streamed into the kubectl command like a single YAML resource.

We might imagine that our application is now ready for production because it is capable of adding and substituting our developer configurations with realistic ones. If you peruse the documentation at https://carvel.dev/ytt/, you'll see that many further customizations can also be done: adding data values, adding entirely new YAML constructs, and so on. In our case, however, we'll leave well enough alone and move up the stack to look at how our patched YAML resources can now be bundled into a single, executable application that has its state managed as a first-class citizen.

15.4.3 *Part 3: Managing and deploying Guestbook as a single application*

You might be annoyed by the number of times we've run `kubectl delete` in this book. If you've asked yourself why we've done this, it's usually because we haven't isolated our application from other applications in our cluster. One easy way to do this is by deploying an entire app in a namespace that can then be deleted or created. However, once we begin treating several resources as a single app, we have a new set of questions we want to answer:

- How many distinct applications am I running in a given namespace?
- Was an upgrade of all the resources in a given application successful?
- How many resources of each type did I associate with my application?

Each of these questions can be answered with a combination of `kubectl`, `grep`, and some clever Bash aggregations. However, this approach won't scale if you have tens or hundreds of containers, Secrets, ConfigMaps, and other resources in your app. Additionally, it won't scale across the entire spectrum of apps in your cluster, which can also easily range in the hundreds or thousands. This is where the `kapp` tool comes into focus for us.

> ### What about `helm`?
>
> `helm` was one of the earliest and most successful application management solutions for Kubernetes. Originally, it combined the aspects of stateful upgrade and resource installation with YAML templating. The Carvel project borrowed from the lessons of `helm` to separate many of these functionalities into separate tools.
>
> `helm3` is actually a much more modular attempt at managing applications that can be run in a stateless manner, similar to what we will see with the `kapp` tool. In any case, `helm3` and the Carvel ecosystem have quite a bit of overlap, and both can be used for similar cases, but they are charted by different opinions, philosophical approaches, and communities. We encourage you to explore both, especially if you feel like `kapp` is not an ideal solution for your problems. Either way, you will learn quite a lot about managing Kubernetes applications in general by following the evolution of Guestbook when using `kapp`, so keep moving forward!

Using the `kapp` tool (https://carvel.dev/kapp/) is quite easy, especially now that we have the ability to customize our applicaiton with `ytt`. To give it a shot, let's do one last cleanup of our Guestbook application in case it's still running:

```
$ ytt -f ./v1/  -f v2/ytt-cpu-overlay.yml |        Deletes the resources we made
    -f v2/ytt-cpu-overlay-db.yml |                 in the last section (in case
    kubectl delete -f -          ◄─────────────    they're still around)
```

We'll assume you've already installed the `kapp` binary. Let's now run the same `ytt` commands to generate our application, but install it using `kapp` instead of `kubectl`. Note that in this example, we're using Antrea as our CNI provider. But the CNI you run at this point doesn't really matter, as long as you have one (note that several columns in the output in this code snippet are omitted due to page restrictions):

```
$ kapp deploy -a guestbook -f <(ytt -f ./v1/        Takes the ytt statement for
➥ -f v2/ytt-cpu-overlay.yml                          generating YAML and pushes
➥ -f v2/ytt-cpu-overlay-db.yml)          ◄──────────┘ it to kapp as input

Target cluster 'https://127.0.0.1:53756' (nodes: antrea-control-plane, 2+)

Changes

Namespace  Name              Kind        ... Op      Op st.  Wait to    ...
default    frontend          Service     ... create  -       reconcile ...
^          frontend-dep      Deployment  ... create  -       reconcile ...
^          redis-master      Service     ... create  -       reconcile ...
^          redis-master-dep  Deployment  ... create  -       reconcile ...
^          redis-slave       Deployment  ... create  -       reconcile ...
^          redis-slave       Service     ... create  -       reconcile ...

Op:      6 create, 0 delete, 0 update, 0 noop
Wait to: 6 reconcile, 0 delete, 0 noop

Continue? [yN]:
```

If you type y, you'll see kapp do a lot of work, including annotating your resources so that it can later manage them for you. It will upgrade or delete the resources or give you the overall status of your app by name. In our case, we called our app Guestbook, but we could call it anything we want.

After entering "yes" (by typing y), you'll now see more information than was available from kubectl. This is because for kapp, an application is really a first-class citizen, and it wants to make sure that all of your resources come up in a healthy state. You can imagine how kapp can thus be used in a CI/CD environment to fully automate upgrading and management of an application. For example:

```
11:17:40AM: ---- applying 6 changes [0/6 done] ----
11:17:40AM: create deployment/frontend-dep (apps/v1) namespace: default
11:17:40AM: create deployment/redis-master-dep (apps/v1) namespace: default
11:17:40AM: create service/redis-master (v1) namespace: default
11:17:40AM: create service/redis-slave (v1) namespace: default
11:17:40AM: create deployment/redis-slave (apps/v1) namespace: default
11:17:40AM: create service/frontend (v1) namespace: default
11:17:40AM: ---- waiting on 6 changes [0/6 done] ----
11:17:40AM: ok: reconcile service/frontend (v1) namespace: default
11:17:40AM: ok: reconcile service/redis-slave (v1) namespace: default
11:17:40AM: ok: reconcile service/redis-master (v1) namespace: default
11:17:41AM: ongoing: reconcile deployment/frontend-dep (apps/v1)
➥ namespace: default
11:17:41AM:   ^ Waiting for generation 2 to be observed
11:17:41AM:   L ok: waiting on replicaset/frontend-dep-7bf896bf7c (apps/v1)
➥ namespace: default
```

```
11:17:41AM:  L ongoing: waiting on pod/frontend-dep-7bf896bf7c-vbn22 (v1)
➡ namespace: default
11:17:41AM:     ^ Pending: ContainerCreating
11:17:41AM:  L ongoing: waiting on pod/frontend-dep-7bf896bf7c-qph5b (v1)
➡ namespace: default
...
11:17:44AM: ---- waiting on 1 changes [5/6 done] ----
11:18:01AM: ok: reconcile deployment/redis-master-dep (apps/v1)
➡ namespace: default
11:18:01AM: ---- applying complete [6/6 done] ----
11:18:01AM: ---- waiting complete [6/6 done] ----
Succeeded
```

We can now go back and look at our application again to confirm that it's still running. Use the following command to check this:

```
$ kapp list
Target cluster 'https://127.0.0.1:53756' (nodes: antrea-control-plane, 2+)

Apps in namespace 'default'

Name       Namespaces  Lcs   Lca
guestbook  default     true  12m

Lcs: Last Change Successful
Lca: Last Change Age

1 apps

Succeeded
```

We can also use kapp to give us detailed information about a running application. For that, we use the inspect command:

```
$ kapp inspect --app=guestbook
Target cluster 'https://127.0.0.1:53756' (nodes: antrea-control-plane, 2+)

Resources in app 'guestbook'

Name                          Kind           Owner    Conds.  Age
frontend                      Endpoints      cluster  -       12m
frontend                      Service        kapp     -       12m
frontend-dep                  Deployment     kapp     2/2 t   12m
frontend-dep-7bf7c            ReplicaSet     cluster  -       12m
frontend-dep-7bf7c-g7jlt      Pod            cluster  4/4 t   12m
frontend-dep-7bf7c-qph5b      Pod            cluster  4/4 t   12m
frontend-dep-7bf7c-vbn22      Pod            cluster  4/4 t   12m
frontend-sccps                EndpointSlice  cluster  -       12m
redis-master                  Endpoints      cluster  -       12m
redis-master                  Service        kapp     -       12m
redis-master-dep              Deployment     kapp     2/2 t   12m
redis-master-dep-64fcb        ReplicaSet     cluster  -       12m
redis-master-dep-64fcb-t4hjl  Pod            cluster  4/4 t   12m
```

```
redis-master-zqdvc              EndpointSlice  cluster    -      12m
redis-slave                     Deployment     kapp     2/2 t   12m
redis-slave                     Endpoints      cluster    -      12m
redis-slave                     Service        kapp       -      12m
redis-slave-dffcf               ReplicaSet     cluster    -      12m
redis-slave-dffcf-75vfq         Pod            cluster  4/4 t   12m
redis-slave-dffcf-1wch9         Pod            cluster  4/4 t   12m
redis-slave-vlnkh               EndpointSlice  cluster    -      12m


Rs: Reconcile state
Ri: Reconcile information

21 resources

Succeeded
```

It's instructive to note that some of the objects that were created by Kubernetes under the hood, such as Endpoints and EndpointSlices, are included in this readout. EndpointSlices and their availability as load-balancing targets for Services are crucial for any app to be usable by an end consumer. kapp has captured this information for us, along with the success and failure state of all resources in our application, in a single, easy-to-read, tabular format.

Finally, we can now delete our app easily and in a complete, atomic fashion using kapp by running kapp delete --app=guestbook. This will be the inverse of our kapp deploy operation, so we won't show the output because the result of this command is mostly self-explanatory.

15.4.4   *Part 4: Constructing a kapp Operator to package and manage our application*

Now that we've bundled our entire application as a set of atomically-managed resources which have well-defined names, we've essentially built what might be thought of as a CustomResourceDefinition (CRD). The kapp-controller project allows us to take any kapp application and wrap it up with a few automation niceties. This final exploration completes our transition from "one big blob of YAML from the internet" to a stateful, automatically managed application that we can run in an enterprise situation along with hundreds of other applications. It will also introduce you, quite gently, to the concept of how one can build a Kubernetes Operator.

The first thing we'll do is install the kapp-controller tool using kapp. Here we go again, installing things from the internet, but, as always, feel free to inspect the YAML before installing it. For your convenience, here's the YAML:

```
$ kapp deploy -a kc -f https://github.com/vmware-tanzu/
      carvel-kapp-controller/releases/latest/            ┌─ Installs kapp-controller
          download/release.yml          ◄───────────────┘  using the kapp tool
$ kapp deploy -a default-ns-rbac -f
      https://raw.githubusercontent.com/vmware-tanzu/
          carvel-kapp-controller/                        ┌─ Installs a simple
            develop/examples/rbac/default-ns.yml  ◄──────┘  RBAC definition
```

You might be wondering why we needed to set up RBAC rules for `kapp-controller`. Installing the RBAC definition (default-ns.yml) allows the `kapp-controller` in the default namespace to read and write API objects as any Operator would require. Operators are administrative applications, and the `kapp-controller` Pod needs to create, edit, and update various Kubernetes resources in order to do its job as a generic Operator for our applications.

Now that `kapp-controller` is running in our cluster, we can use it to automate the `ytt` complexity from the previous section, and we can do this in a declarative way, which is entirely managed inside of Kubernetes. To do this, we need to create a `kapp` CR (CustomResource) The specification of a `kapp` application is described at http://mng.bz/PWqv. The particular fields we care about are

- `git`—Defines a cloneable Git repository for our applications source code
- `template`—Defines where the `ytt` templates to install our application live

The first thing we'll do is to create an application specification for our original Guest-book app, which will run as a `kapp`-controlled application. After that, we'll add our `ytt` templates back in:

```
apiVersion: kappctrl.k14s.io/v1alpha1
kind: App
metadata:
  name: guestbook
  namespace: default
spec:
  serviceAccountName: default-ns-sa     ◄──── Uses the service account created
  fetch:                                        previously for this app installation
  - git:                      ◄──── Specifies where our app is defined
      url: https://github.com/jayunit100/k8sprototypes
      ref: origin/master

      # We have a directory, named 'app', in the root of our repo.
      # Files describing the app (i.e. pod, service) are in that directory.
      subPath: carvel-guestbook/v1/
  template:            ◄────  Because the code for our app actually lives in carvel-
  - ytt: {}                   guestbook/v1/, we need to specify this subpath.
  deploy:
  - kapp: {}
```

At this point, the lightbulbs in your mind may be going off about continuous delivery and rightly so. This single YAML declaration lets us leave the entire management of our application to Kubernetes and to our online `kapp-controller` Operator itself. Let's give it a shot. Run the `kubectl create -f` to create the Guestbook app using the YAML snippet previously shown, and then execute this command:

```
$ kapp list
Target cluster 'https://127.0.0.1:53756' (nodes: antrea-control-plane, 2+)

Apps in namespace 'default'
```

```
Name                  Namespaces  Lcs   Lca
default-ns-rbac       default     true  14m
guestbook-ctrl        default     true  1m
...
```

We can see that our guestbook-ctrl application was made for us by the `kapp-controller` automatically. We can again use `kapp` to inspect this application:

```
$ kapp inspect --app=guestbook-ctrl
Target cluster 'https://127.0.0.1:53756'
  (nodes: antrea-control-plane, 2+)

Resources in app 'guestbook-ctrl'

Namespace   Name Kind       Owner     Conds.  Rs
default     fe   Dep        kapp      2/2 t   ok
^           fe   Endpoints  cluster   -       ok
^           fe   Service    kapp      -       ok
...
```

We actually have now integrated our application into a CI/CD system that can be managed entirely inside of Kubernetes. Great! One can now imagine building arbitrarily complicated systems for developers to submit and maintain CRDs for their applications, which are ultimately deployed and managed by the single `kapp-controller` Operator that runs in our default namespace.

If we want, we can redeploy this same application (often referred to as an "App CR") in a new namespace. To do that, we simply add or delete these by running `kubectl get apps`, because the `kapp-controller` Pod has installed a CRD for `kapp` applications in our cluster for us:

```
$ kubectl get apps
NAME        DESCRIPTION          SINCE-DEPLOY  AGE
guestbook   Reconcile succeeded  5m16s         6m8s
```

We've just implemented a full-blown Operator deployment of the Guestbook application. Now, let's try to add our `ytt` templates back in. In this example, we've pushed the `ytt` output from our previous example to a specific directory in the k8sprototypes repository (you might want to use your own GitHub repository for this exercise, but it's not necessary):

```
apiVersion: kappctrl.k14s.io/v1alpha1
kind: App
metadata:
  name: guestbook
  namespace: default
spec:
  serviceAccountName: default-ns-sa
  fetch:
  - git:
```

```
            url: https://github.com/jayunit100/k8sprototypes
            ref: origin/master
            subPath: carvel-guestbook/v2/output/
template:
- ytt: {}
deploy:
- kapp: {}
```

We can now create a new definition for our Guestbook app, which includes our `ytt` templates, by simply writing the transformed `ytt` templates to another directory. Another nicety of using an Operator to manage our applications is that we can create and delete them without any special tooling. This is because the `kubectl` client is aware of them as API resources. To delete the Guestbook app, run this command:

```
$ kubectl delete app guestbook
```

We can now just use `kubectl` to declaratively delete our Guestbook application, and the `kapp-controller` will do the rest. We can also use commands such as `kubectl describe` to see the status of our application.

We've only touched on the flexibility of the Operator model for managing and creating application definitions. As follow-up exercises, it's worth exploring

- Using the `kapp-controller` to deploy multiple copies of the same app in many namespaces
- Using the `ytt` directive inside of `kapp-controller`
- Using the `kapp-controller`'s ability to deploy and manage Helm charts as applications
- Embedding Secrets into your `kapp` applications so that you can deploy CI/CD workflows securely

This wraps up our iterative improvement of the Guestbook application. We'll conclude this chapter by looking at our old and familiar friends, the Calico and Antrea CNI providers, to see how they implement full-blown Kubernetes Operators with fine-grained CRDs for administrators.

15.5 *Revisiting the Kubernetes Operator*

The `kapp` and `kapp-controller` tools provided us with an automated, atomic way to deal with all the services in our Guestbook application in a stateful way. This, thus, introduced the concept of an Operator to us in an organic way. For many applications, using a batteries-included tool such as `kapp-controller` or, alternatively, something like `Helm` (https://helm.sh) can spare you the time and complexity of needing to build a full-blown Kubernetes CRD and Operator implementation. However, CRDs are everywhere in the modern Kubernetes ecosystem, and we would be doing you a disservice if we didn't explore them at least a little bit.

> **Operator factories**
>
> If you do decide your application is sufficiently advanced to need its own fine-grained Kubernetes API extensions, you'll want to build an Operator. The process of building an Operator usually involves autogenerating API clients for custom Kubernetes CRDs and then ensuring that these clients do the "right" thing when resources are created, destroyed, or edited. There are many tools online, such as the https://github.com/kubernetes-sigs/kubebuilder project, that make it easy to build full-blown Operators.

Let's spin up a `kind` cluster with two different CNI providers (Calico and Antrea) as a way to dive into how we use CRDs. In this case, because we'll also want to potentially add NetworkPolicy objects to our cluster, let's create a Calico-based cluster. We can use the `kind-local-up.sh` script to do this:

```
# make sure you've already installed kind and kubectl before running this...
$ git clone \
    https://github.com/jayunit100/k8sprototypes.git
$ cd kind ; ./kind-local-up.sh
```

Kubernetes-native applications often make lots of CRDs for their applications. CRDs allow any application to use the Kubernetes API server to store configuration data and to enable the creation of Operators (which we will dig into later on in this chapter). Operators are Kubernetes controllers that watch the API server for changes and then run Kubernetes administrative tasks in response. For example, if we were to look at our newly created `kind` cluster, we could see several Calico CRDs, which have specific configurations for Calico as a CNI provider:

```
$ kubectl get crd          ⟵—— Lists all CRDs in our cluster
NAME
bgpconfigurations.crd.projectcalico.org
bgppeers.crd.projectcalico.org
blockaffinities.crd.projectcalico.org
clusterinformations.crd.projectcalico.org
felixconfigurations.crd.projectcalico.org
globalnetworkpolicies.crd.projectcalico.org
globalnetworksets.crd.projectcalico.org
hostendpoints.crd.projectcalico.org
ipamblocks.crd.projectcalico.org
ipamconfigs.crd.projectcalico.org
ipamhandles.crd.projectcalico.org
ippools.crd.projectcalico.org
kubecontrollersconfigurations.crd.projectcalico.org
networkpolicies.crd.projectcalico.org
networksets.crd.projectcalico.org
$ kubectl get kubecontrollersconfigurations -o yaml
apiVersion: v1
items:
- apiVersion: crd.projectcalico.org/v1
  kind: KubeControllersConfiguration
```

```
...
spec:
  controllers:
    namespace:
      reconcilerPeriod: 5m0s
    node:
      reconcilerPeriod: 5m0s
      syncLabels: Enabled
    policy:
      reconcilerPeriod: 5m0s
    serviceAccount:
      reconcilerPeriod: 5m0s
    workloadEndpoint:
      reconcilerPeriod: 5m0s
  etcdV3CompactionPeriod: 10m0s
  healthChecks: Enabled
  logSeverityScreen: Info
  prometheusMetricsPort: 9094
status:
  environmentVars:
    DATASTORE_TYPE: kubernetes
    ENABLED_CONTROLLERS: node
  runningConfig:
    controllers:
      node:
        hostEndpoint:
          autoCreate: Disabled
        syncLabels: Disabled
    etcdV3CompactionPeriod: 10m0s
    healthChecks: Enabled
    logSeverityScreen: Info
```

We can disable healthChecks if we don't feel it's necessary.

Sets the port on which our Calico kube controller serves up its Prometheus metrics. Here's where we can change the port if needed.

Interestingly, Calico stores its configuration inside of our Kubernetes cluster as a custom object with its own types. Actually, Antrea does a similar thing. We can inspect the contents of an Antrea cluster by running the `kind-local-up.sh` script again like so:

```
$ kind delete cluster --name=kcalico      ◁─── Deletes our previous cluster
$ C=antrea CONFIG=conf.yaml ./kind-local-up.sh )
```

Creates a new cluster with Antrea as the CNI provider

After a few moments, we can look at the various configuration objects that Antrea uses, just like we did for Calico. The following code snippet shows the command to generate this output:

```
$ kubectl get crd
NAME
antreaagentinfos.clusterinformation.antrea.tanzu.vmwar
antreacontrollerinfos.clusterinformation.antrea.tanzu.
clusternetworkpolicies.security.antrea.tanzu.vmware.co
externalentities.core.antrea.tanzu.vmware.com
networkpolicies.security.antrea.tanzu.vmware.com
tiers.security.antrea.tanzu.vmware.com
traceflows.ops.antrea.tanzu.vmware.com
```

> **Custom NetworkPolicys object types: An example of why vendors really love CRDs**
>
> If we look at Calico and Antrea CRDs, we can see they have some commonalities, one being network policies. The NetworkPolicy API in Kubernetes doesn't support all possible network policies when using certain CNIs. As an example, the PortRange policy (which was only added to Kubernetes v1.21) was a vendor-specific policy in both Calico and Antrea for quite some time. Because both Calico and Antrea have their own network policy custom resources, however, users can create the newer Network-Policy objects that are understood by these specific CNIs. CRDs provide a neat way to differentiate products without having to create vendor-specific tooling for managing these. For example, you can edit a k8s.io NetworkPolicy object using the `kubectl edit` directive in the same way that you can edit any CRD.
>
> If you are interested in learning more about specific network policies that extend the network security capabilities of Kubernetes, you might be interested in http://mng.bz/aD9Y or http://mng.bz/g4mn. Of course, if you haven't learned about basic Kubernetes NetworkPolicy APIs, you may want to research those first at http://mng.bz/enBZ.
>
> Note that creating, editing, or deleting NetworkPolicy objects for Calico or Antrea results in immediate creation of firewall rules. However, editing other CRDs for these applications may not result in immediate changes to their configurations, and these changes may not be realized until you restart the corresponding Calico or Antrea Pods. Thus, although CRDs give you a way to extend the Kubernetes API server, they don't give you any guarantee of how your new API constructs will be implemented.

Our earlier installation of Calico as a CNI provider was deployed via a YAML file, which has several configuration objects associated with it. Alternatively, we could have deployed it with the Tigera `operator` tool (https://github.com/tigera/operator), which handles upgrading and creation of Calico YAML manifests for us. As a real-time configuration option, we could have installed the `calicoctl` tool, which can configure certain aspects of it for us as well.

Similarly, our installation of Antrea was done with a YAML manifest (as we discussed thoroughly in our previous chapters on CNI). Just like Calico, an Antrea cluster involves creation of several configuration components that live inside of our cluster (see http://mng.bz/J1qa).

We've now explored many aspects of Kubernetes application management. New tools in this space are released on a continuous basis, so consider this a beginning to your exploration of how to scale and manage large fleets of applications in production. For many newcomers, the addition of `ytt` to a simplistic application deployment workflow might be good enough for them to bootstrap their Kubernetes application automation.

15.6 *Tanzu Community Edition: An end-to-end example of the Carvel toolkit*

The Tanzu Community Edition (TCE) is a good way to learn about the Cluster API and the Image Builder project. TCE uses Carvel heavily for incredibly complex cluster configuration profiles and for managing fleets of microservices that need to be upgraded and modified by end users. Much of its logical core is built around the Carvel family of utilities.

If you're interested in seeing how `kapp`, `imgpkg`, `ytt`, and the rest of the tools in the Carvel stack are used in the wild, check out https://github.com/vmware-tanzu/tce and https://github.com/vmware-tanzu/tanzu-framework. These two repositories comprise the entire VMware Tanzu Kubernetes distribution's open source installation toolkit. In this distribution

- `ytt` installs and defines sophisticated cluster templates using the Kubernetes Cluster API specification.

    As an example, `ytt` substitutes Windows cluster specification files (which manually install an Antrea agent as a Windows process) for Linux cluster specifications. In time, this can be modified to use other Cluster API concepts, but at the time of this writing, you can see these examples in action at http://mng.bz/p2Z0. `ytt` applies various files in these directories one at a time to create a single, massive YAML file, which defines the blueprint for an entire cluster.

- `kapp` and `kapp-controller` reconcile everything from CNI specifications to various add-on applications used in these distributions.

- `imgpkg` and `vendir` (which we didn't dive into very deeply) are also used for various container packaging and release management tasks.

If you are interested in learning more about the Carvel utilities, you can join the #carvel channel on Kubernetes Slack (slack.k8s.io). There you'll find a bubbling community of committers that can help onboard you with specific and general questions about these utilities.

The Antrea LIVE show

As a passing note, a full introduction to various aspects of the Carvel toolkit, including how it borrowed some concepts from Antrea, is available on the Antrea LIVE show. The episodes for the stream are available at antrea.io/live. Many of the topics in this book, including Prometheus metrics, CNI providers, and so on, have been covered in other broadcasts.

Summary

- A simple way to manage apps on Kubernetes is with `kubectl` and a large YAML file, but this runs out of steam quickly. Many great tools exist to help you with YAML overload. `ytt` is one we covered in this chapter.

- The Carvel toolkit has several applications that help us orchestrate Kubernetes apps at a high level.

- You can cleanly implement customization of YAML files with `ytt` or `kustomize`.

- `ytt` can match arbitrary parts of a YAML file by adding an `overlay/match` clause to an overlay file, which is applied after the original files are read. It then builds on top of a simple, pre-existing, standard Kubernetes YAML file.

- You can treat collections of disparate YAML resources as a single application using tools such as `kapp` or `Helm`.

- If you want to package your applications in a stateful way, but don't want to build an Operator, you can use a tool like `kapp-controller`. `kapp-controller` manages collections of application resources in a stateful manner over time. This is one step below building a full-blown Operator, but it can be done in a matter of seconds with many of the same benefits.

- Operators can be used to define higher-level APIs in Kubernetes. These APIs are aware of your application's specific life cycle and involve, typically, vendoring the Kubernetes client into a container that you run in your cluster.

- Calico and Antrea both implement the Kubernetes Operator pattern for highly sophisticated Kubernetes API extensions. This allows you to manage their configuration entirely by creating and editing Kubernetes resources.

- The Carvel toolkit and many other topics from this book are covered in various episodes of the Antrea live stream on YouTube, which can be viewed at antrea.io/live.

index